THE BARBARIANS ARE COMING

Losing Control and the Consequences for Civilisation

David Nicholson

HALSGROVE

In Memory of John Hanvey, David Levy and Michael Polley

First published in Great Britain in 2025
Copyright © David Nicholson

All rights reserved. No part of this publication may be reproduced, stored in a retrieval system, or transmitted in any form or by any means without the prior permission of the copyright holder.

British Library Cataloguing-in-Publication Data
A CIP record for this title is available from the British Library

ISBN 978 0 85704 377 1

Halsgrove
Halsgrove House,
Ryelands Business Park,
Bagley Road, Wellington, Somerset TA21 9PZ
Tel: 01823 653777 Fax: 01823 216796
email: sales@halsgrove.com

 Part of the Halsgrove group of companies
Information on all Halsgrove titles is available at: www.halsgrove.com
Printed and bound in India by Nutech Print Services

Contents

Foreword and Acknowledgements 4

Introduction – Civilisation ....and its Enemies 11

Chapter One: The Fall of the Western Roman Empire 31

Chapter Two: The Resistance of the Eastern Empire 56

Chapter Three: The Exception:
The Glorious Revolution and the Ascent of Britain 92

Chapter Four: The French Revolution: Actuality 1774–1815 128

Chapter Five: 19th-Century Instability in France 164

Chapter Six: The Russian Revolution 192

Chapter Seven: Britain in Europe: From Churchill's Zurich
Speech to the fall of Thatcher 1945–90 234

Chapter Eight: Europe: The Unravelling 1990–2016 273

Epilogue: Migration and "Culture Wars" 313

Bibliography 326

Index of Names 332

Foreword and Acknowledgements

I start with a few comments, before embarking upon what is intended to be seen to be a book of objective historical analysis. Taken together, it will I hope be a guide to my political philosophy and my historical and cultural values and interests.

"The Barbarians are Coming" is the refrain in "Waiting for the Barbarians", a poem by the Alexandria-born Greek Constantine Cavafy. Perversely, in his poem, the barbarians do not arrive to conquer the civilised City. Sadly, that was not the case in most of the episodes described in this book.

The identity of the "barbarians" is clear in many of these episodes, but ambiguity might be justified in the more recent ones! I refer in passing to Putin's barbaric attack on Ukraine, but do not discuss how this might be terminated. Similarly, I do not explore the crisis generated by the barbaric Hamas terrorist attacks of 7 October 2023. The map on pages 54–55 shows that the zone between the Caspian and Red Seas has been the object of conflict for at least the last 3000 years. My earlier book describes how the Balfour Declaration, the unhappy British Palestine mandate and subsequent events contributed fuel to historic conflicts. And while the Epilogue does not specifically analyse Muslim migration into the UK, Western Europe and the USA, the frequency of pro-Palestinian demonstrations in our streets, and increasingly ugly episodes of anti-Semitism, are equally disturbing.

I give harsh descriptions of the historic acts of Mongols and Turks. Today, both peoples are peaceful, successful and friendly. I have enjoyed much travel in Turkey over the years, receiving kind hospitality. But Chapter Two describes how the people of Anatolia, steeped in Graeco-Roman civilisation and Christianity, were gradually overwhelmed and replaced from the 11th century onward, with their last cultural embers being snuffed out, after Greek aggressive folly, with the fall of Smyrna in 1922.

"A Spectre is Haunting Europe" began the 1848 Communist Manifesto. In July 2024, the spectre is not (except, perhaps, in France) Communism, but that of the populist Right. And the traditional political parties have largely brought this upon themselves. Even despite the triumph of the Centre Left in the UK, and the residual strength of the Centre Right in Germany and Spain, we are seeing a widespread revolt against the traditional liberal establishment. While the immigration factor is clear throughout Europe, including the UK, the electoral turmoil of the summer of 2024 requires further study. Meanwhile, on immigration, the challenging Right, including the UK Reform party, has the opportunity (and the duty) to hold other parties' feet to the fire.

Crucial reading underlining these events will include several articles by Matthew Syed, especially "Farage is a snake but if we were honest he would have no fangs: PMs from Blair onwards have ushered in cheap labour while vowing to stop it. That's why trust has gone." (*Sunday Times*, 9 June 2024). Similar arguments were made by Douglas Murray ("The trouble with calling everyone 'far right'", *Spectator*, 15 June), Robert Colvile ("A Tory wipeout could be the domino that topples us into European-style populism," *Sunday Times*, 16 June) and Eric Kaufmann ("No, we haven't reached 'peak woke', it's going mainstream," *The Times*, 15 June).

2024 saw UK politics in turmoil over measures to combat legal and illegal immigration. This book was first envisaged as an attack on the consequences of Brexit, alongside those of other revolutions. While, putting it charitably, the jury may still be out over Brexit, I recall Roger Knapman, some years ago, as leader of UKIP, telling me that the only way to control immigration was to leave the EU. How wrong on this he, and others, have been!

Remainers tend to be liberals on immigration and Brexiteers the opposite, so the Europe issue has inspired its own, rather bogus, "culture war". It will be clear from Chapter Eight that I have no regrets over supporting Remain and clear from the Epilogue that there are clear limits to my liberalism! I have been consistent in both these views for well over 50 years.

So I make and cite harsh judgements on recent immigration into Europe. This is not on account of prejudice; I respect and enjoy other cultures and as described in the opening of the Epilogue, I value the contribution many migrants have made to the UK. My concern is for the cultural and social consequences, including over-population, not only in the UK but elsewhere in Europe. I quote Enoch Powell's key phrase "numbers are of the essence", as distinct from his rasher claims. So the greater the proportion of alien migrants, the greater the threat to national cultures. Perhaps the "wokeist" extremists really would have the rest of us drastically dilute our British culture, history and loyalties. This point is underlined by Emma Duncan (*The Times*, 2 February 2024): to a question to teenagers as to whether they would fight for Britain, a British-born boy from an immigrant background replied negatively, adding "I'm not from here."

Some who speak out against excessive non-European immigration are themselves of recent migrant origin, not only in the UK, but, for example, in France and the Netherlands. They have perceived that if governments abdicate control over immigration, their own communities, even if apparently securely established, may not be immune from the tensions aroused.

The immigration issue will continue to create headlines and political debate, as well as swaying votes, until large-scale immigration has ceased. While many former East European migrants return to build businesses or retire in their original homelands, most non-European migration appears to be for permanent settlement. It is probably irreversible. And our taking the brightest from problematic countries round the world is highly debatable.

Reflecting on these issues, David Coleman, Emeritus Professor of Demography at Oxford, stated in a letter sent to *The Times*: "Doubling the population before the century's end and so on upwards as more and more immigrants would be needed should be rejected. Otherwise Britain would cease to be a society and become merely a geographical expression." The rest of the letter was published (25 March 2024), but this passage was removed by the newspaper.

Without doubt, failures on immigration are key factors in the shift of Conservative support to the Reform party.

There is another vital link with Europe. If we had not left, we would be in a stronger position to influence the rest of the EU in combatting trans-Mediterranean migration and in seeking to suspend adherence to European human rights requirements until these are made relevant to the present day rather than the 1950s.

In the Epilogue I quote Lionel Shriver's view that the boatloads of illegals – "a sideshow" – are dwarfed by legal immigration, described by Juliet Samuel (also quoted in the Epilogue) as "the Treasury's Ponzi-scheme fiscal modelling on legal migration, taking it up to astonishing new highs". (*The Times*, 25 January 2024). Others cite evidence, such as flatlining GDP per capita, that "blows a hole in Whitehall's assumption that we need ever more immigration to drive growth". (Iain Martin, *The Times*, 7 March 2024).

The June 2024 European Parliamentary elections witnessed a large "protest vote" by the populist Right against immigration, just as Trump's surge in the USA signifies a protest against Biden's feeble policing of the Mexican border. And the populists seem to appeal to younger voters.

David Abulafia (*Spectator*, 20 January 2024) contrasts Turin's museums, "uncontaminated by preaching about the evils of European colonialism" with the UK's Museums Association's "rants against racism and colonialism", exemplified by the extraordinary black female bronze "Sea Deity" at the National Maritime Museum, "trying to decolonise Lord Nelson." And while protesters celebrate Australia Day by demolishing a statue of Captain Cook in Melbourne, Sathnam Sangera proposes a role for the Commonwealth as "a truth and reconciliation forum for Britain's imperial past" – implying further instalments of wokeish national grovelling.

Chapters Seven and Eight show that there was plenty of scepticism in the UK about the way the EU was developing. Nor, it seems now, was this confined to the UK. But what was the alternative entity for Europe? None was never intelligently advanced, except for a plaintive wish, amounting ultimately to Brexit, to confine our European links to trade. Despite the commercial prejudices of this "nation of shopkeepers", European unity was never just about trade. Europe had a definite and welcome political, social and cultural mission. What irritated many in Britain and elsewhere, and contributed to our 2016 referendum result, was the legalistic and interventionist way in which European "law", often reflecting the views of Brussels-based liberals, flooded into the legislative and administrative inlets which legitimately belonged to the nation states.

Some Brexiteers claim that influential people, say in France, would like the EU to collapse, or at least France to leave – which would amount to the same thing. Is this a sane aspiration? Would a Europe returning to the pre-1939 crudely competing and combative states be happier, more secure, more prosperous?

We British are unlikely to welcome such chaos on our doorstep. We may be correct in assuming that our departure will not precipitate EU collapse. But we should not over-value our "friends" outside Europe as substitutes for EU membership. Like the USA, divided between Democrats beholden to "wokery" and Trump, with all the threats he carries to the strength and unity of the West? Like Raj-resenting and Russia-courting India, where Modi makes migration conditions for successful commerce? Like currently perverse South Africa, whose GDP per head has slumped compared to the world average in the past 30 years, while its average life expectancy has stagnated compared to a steady world increase?

Away from these two crucial issues, this book does not venture into current party political debate. But I will venture some observations.

Rishi Sunak's defeat was largely because loyal and decent Conservatives have been let down, partially by previous leadership mistakes, but mainly by the increasingly offensive behaviour, greed, indiscipline, disloyalty and plotting of an undistinguished parliamentary party minority. Between 2016 and 2022, with Ministers being frequently reshuffled, sacked or resigning, consistent and competent administration must have been lacking, while several individuals used their short periods of office solely to promote their future leadership ambitions. The results have been effectively described, perhaps with some exaggeration, in Rory Stewart's book, *Politics on the Edge*. How far the 2016 referendum result exacerbated all this will be debated; my view is that it is difficult to deny *post hoc, ergo propter hoc*.

Apart from the vital question, "will Starmer do better?", what will follow a Conservative defeat? One surviving fragment might be the "One Nation" group with which I have at times been associated, Remainers largely coinciding with those with "liberal" beliefs. If this group is to command respect and contribute to the future, it must produce an effective policy for controlling immigration, rather than just carping about the Rwanda policy.

It has been sadly weakened. A total of 21 Remainer MPs, of massive value to the party, were purged by Johnson in 2019, with the party whip removed; a few were graciously allowed to return and sit in the Commons or Lords. Several others, like Sarah Wollaston, joined the Liberal Democrats but were defeated in 2019. Others, also defeated then, like Dominic Grieve, former Attorney General, do not appear to have joined another mainstream party. Amber Rudd, a former Home Secretary, resigned from Parliament over the Johnson no-deal Brexit plan and campaigned for David Gauke, a former Secretary of State for Justice and Lord Chancellor (greatly praised by Stewart in his above-mentioned book), in his failed bid to be elected in 2019 as an independent in his former seat.

Even so, history might be kinder to Johnson. His lead over Ukraine merits admiration and the immediate causes of his fall are beginning to seem trivial. In weighing up what he did, and perhaps more importantly, neglected, he might be compared to an Ottoman Sultan, combining popular appeal with eccentric flaws. A successful Sultan needed an effective Grand Vizier, to help avert errors and ensure that worthwhile plans were implemented. All Boris had was Cummings, tolerated for too long and not even, unlike Vizier Kara Mustafa Pasha in 1683, finally sent the traditional Ottoman bowstring!

It will be observed that I do not, in the Epilogue, extend my attack on "wokery" to gender changing issues. I genuflect before the wise last words of Voltaire, who when asked by the priest to curse Satan and all his works, allegedly replied "Now is not the time for making new enemies."

As, *deo volente*, I pass my 80th birthday, these mundane concerns might be appropriately summed up by the splendidly ponderous words, written in the early 19th century in English, Latin and Welsh, accompanying a sarcophagus now at the church of St Mary and St Nicholas, Beaumaris, Anglesey. This was believed to have contained the body of Princess Joan, natural daughter of "bad" King John, and wife of Llywelyn the Great, Prince of Wales. Having been used for years as a horse-watering trough, it was rescued "and placed here for preservation as well as to excite serious meditation on the transitory nature of all sublunary distinctions."

Dedication and acknowledgements

Several dear friends, like John Turner and John Lee, would have contributed valuable advice and criticism, but are no longer alive to see the finished product. Richard Fox, of Wellington, who frequently asked me about "your book", died on Boxing Day, 2023.

At the start, I decided to dedicate it to three to whom my family or I owe thanks and admiration, whose expertise and interest would have attracted them to parts or the whole of this work, but were each cruelly cut off early. They are John Hanvey, died 1995 aged 52, Oxford contemporary, opinion polling expert, chairman of Harris Research Centre, my daughter's godfather; David Levy, died 2003 aged 56, Christ Church contemporary, poet, musician and counter-revolutionary philosopher, an academic sociologist who, rejecting the left-wing orthodoxies of his profession, was a strong supporter of French royalism; and Michael Polley, died 2017 aged 66, former Head of Classics at King's College, Taunton, where he taught my elder son and daughter.

Various friends have helped me by suggestions, criticism, comments or simple encouragement. They will not all necessarily agree with my conclusions or observations, but include Jenny Bacon, John Barnes (with whom I co-edited the Leo Amery Diaries), Sir Roger Carrick, David Charters, Simon Cole, Professor David Coleman, Professor David Dutton, Joe Egerton, Dermot Gleeson, Bruce Heywood, Philip Hull, Daniel Hunt, Neil Kerr, John Kirkaldy, Jackie Krendel, Tim Jones, John Ranelagh, Sir Adam Ridley, Edward Russell-Walling, and Giles Vicat. I am enormously grateful to the staff of the London Library for their help over several years. I hope I have cited, quoted and interpreted my various sources accurately and fairly. Errors are mine alone. And I have checked and sought to avoid infringements of copyright, but apologise if any have inadvertently taken place.

While I hope that my main conclusions take account of recent publications, I have only just read Robert Darnton's excellent *The Revolutionary Temper: Paris 1748–89* (Allen Lane, 2023). It sharply underlines, in considerable detail, the extent of popular hostility in Paris and other cities to the royal government in the years before the Revolution. Likewise, I have also just read the similarly detailed study by Michael Kulikowski (*Imperial Tragedy: From Constantine's Empire to the Destruction of Roman Italy, AD 363–568,* Profile Books, 2019) which is more sympathetic to the "barbarians" than other sources I have used. Even so, Kulikowski cannot deny that most of the main participants, Roman or barbarian, were fairly unpleasant characters who came to unpleasant ends: hence "the degree to which the years between 550 and 750 most often resemble not the creative transformation of an antique world but a war of all against all." (*ibid*, p313).

Finally, I thank Steven Pugsley, chairman of Halsgrove, for taking this through to publication, Lorraine Inglis for creating maps and help with illustrations, also my daughter Eleanor.

Allshire, August 2024

Louis XVI, at the guillotine.

Introduction
Civilisation ... and its Enemies

> "O patria, o divum domus Ilium et incluta bello
> moenia Dardanidum! Quater ipso in limine portae
> Substitit atque utero sonitum quater arma dedere
> instamus tamen immemores caecique furore
> et monstrum infelix sacrata sistimus arce."
>
> ("O my city, O Ilium home of gods and you Dardan battlements, famed in war. Four times at the gate's very threshold it halted and four times from its belly the armour clashed, yet we press on, heedless and blind with rage, and set the ill-omened monster on our hallowed citadel." Virgil *Aeneid* book II, lines 241–45, Fairclough translation. Aeneas describes the Trojans taking the Wooden Horse into their city.)

Many people think they know why the Roman Empire fell, or why France and Russia were overcome by revolution. Some believe they know why the Brexit vote happened. Were each of these inevitable? This book resumes a theme of my previous study.[1] Decisive historical events are not necessarily inevitable as we shall see regarding episodes during the various French and Russian Revolutions. They often occur as a result of chance, mistiming, incompetence, superstition or, as we shall also see, the decay and abdication of authority.

The other main theme will be to discuss the consequences of the collapse of authority for civilisation and human wellbeing. What happens when the barbarians arrive?

From the 15th century onwards, European states were able to enjoy security and impose power elsewhere. That has changed; "the West" no longer dominates. As Russia's war in Ukraine and the growing Chinese threat to her neighbours have brought home to us, war, possibly nuclear, with either or both threatens. Countries in the "southern hemisphere" no longer look to the West. And perhaps even more alarmingly, the United States, hitherto regarded as the citadel of democracy, is questioning its role. A recent book review points to "the prospect of a 21st-century rerun" of the 19th-century American civil war, "with the future version trailed in dire precursors like the storming of the Capitol by Trump supporters" in January 2021.[2]

The "Afterword" in Dominic Lieven's latest powerful and comprehensive study reinforces these sobering warnings: ethno-nationalism in the Subcontinent, with aggressive Hinduism "targeting the Muslim minority as the enemy within", with the risk that an act of terrorism there "could escalate into a devastating war, as happened in 1914"; and, with a glance towards the Epilogue of this present book, how does Europe respond to the combined challenges of Africa's rapidly growing population, climate change and migration.[3]

The remainder of this book discusses decisive events only in Europe and the Mediterranean world. This Introduction extends to examples beyond. Asia, in particular, experienced cycles of civilisations rising and declining. Traditional school and even university syllabuses tended to exclude such studies. As a precocious teenager in the 1950s this author could obtain insight into other civilisations only from Blackburn public library. Not only is the study of the history of China, India and the Middle East itself fascinating and illuminating, but these areas, as measured by population and wealth and the forecasts thereof, are swiftly climbing the register of the world's top economies and concentrations of power. It is not accidental that the history of these three areas should dominate the Lieven study.

The zenith and decline of civilisations

Civilisation extends beyond high living standards; it embraces flourishing arts and literature. While it is fair to point out that the high point of Renaissance Christian art coincided with the decadence of the 15th and early 16th century Papacy, much does depend on security from external assault, a stable political regime and safety from natural disasters. Remarkable cultures such as Minoan Crete are now believed to have perished from natural disasters, followed by invasion. Aztec Mexico and Inca Peru each saw civil war, culminating in destruction by better-armed invaders who also carried the germs of devastating epidemics. In Africa, in addition to the early medieval empires of Ghana and Mali and, later, Benin and Kongo, the Shona culture around Great Zimbabwe flourished between the 13th and 16th centuries. It is thought to have declined massively owing to trade route changes, exhaustion of resources including water, and finally warfare, massacre, and forced migration over Southern Africa between 1815 and 1840, involving the ravages of the Zulu King Shaka and the Matabele King Mzilikazi.

In China, India and the Middle East, high cultures existed when the inhabitants of Britain and neighbouring countries were wearing skins. And what Western Europe had built up by the mid-4th century AD experienced a serious collapse over the next centuries, in terms of material living standards, arts and culture together with individual and communal security. The Roman official and philosopher, Boethius, lamented "many things which are now known soon will not be."[4]

Recorded history gives unsatisfactory evidence about loss of human lives in collapses of civilisation. In addition to more extreme examples from Asia, did the 5th–8th centuries' replacement in England of Romano-Celtic place and personal names by Anglo-Saxon ones involve the disappearance or simply the enslavement of the former inhabitants? Even in relatively prosperous periods in Europe heavy loss of life occurred during the religious wars of the 16th and 17th centuries.

In Asia, we see repeated zeniths and declines, the latter marked by appalling losses of life from anarchy. India, for example, experienced zeniths during the period of near unity of the Subcontinent under Ashoka and the Mauryas (c300–200 BC), the Guptas (4th and 5th centuries AD), and then later under the Moghuls (c1500–1700). For example, "in the Gupta era Indian civilisation came to its mature, classical form".[5] After the collapse of Moghul supremacy in the early 18th century, strife amounting at times to anarchy followed. As the Indian-descended columnist, Matthew Syed, has acknowledged, however, "The Mauryan Empire wasn't really an empire at all since it was unable to shape almost anything outside its central region". He quotes historian Sudipta Kaviraj: "The British did not conquer an India which existed before their conquest; rather, they conquered a series of independent kingdoms … "[6]

The Subcontinent had been divided for centuries by religion. Northern India was subjected to devastating Muslim invasions, killing and enslaving Hindus and destroying their cities and especially their temples from the 10th century onward. Historian of India, John Keay, states: "Islamic jurists argued not over whether Hindus should be obliged to pay the *jizya* (the tax on non-Muslims), but whether they should be allowed to pay it. Death was the only penalty prescribed for idolaters by most Islamic schools of law." Keay adds "if we were to add together the casualties inflicted on the Hindus by the Muslims as given by our Indo-Persian chronicles, there would not have been a Hindu left alive in the Deccan."[7]

The history of China shows best a civilisation housed within, and protected by, an empire. At times, China faced similar external threats as Rome did, especially from the Mongols in the 13th century. In the century after 1840 there was dislocation from Europeans and then, in the first half of the 20th century, most bloodily, from Japan. However, the majority of China's traumas were self-generated, consisting of the rise, sometimes erratic, the zenith, decline and collapse of imperial dynasties. The six main dynasties were the Han (200 BC–AD 220), the Tang (618–907), the Song (over all China from 960, then southern Song alone 1127–1279), the Yuan or Mongol (1279–1368), the Ming (1368–1644) and the Qing, or Manchu (1644–1912).

John Keay's history describes the carnage accompanying the collapse of order: the "Warring States" period saw "the mass slaughters of the third century BC" with "slaughter on an unprecedented scale; the battles sometimes lasted for weeks … Another four years of strife and appalling bloodshed (occurred) before the Han king became the Han emperor." The Yellow Turbans' agrarian revolt at the end of the Han dynasty in AD 184 and after saw the capital Chang'an (modern Xi'an) "repeatedly sacked by avenging armies and ravaged by famine".[8] Yet the Han were the first to raise tribute from central Asia, exploiting the Silk Route, while one army may have reached the Caspian in AD 97. Under the Tang dynasty, Chang'an had nearly 2 million population in the mid-8th century: at the eastern end of the Silk Road it was then the largest city in the world.

The decline of the Tang dynasty was started by the An Lushan rebellion in 755, which produced several decades of social and economic dislocation, famine and disease, and the deaths of several million people. After division under the "five dynasties and ten kingdoms" in 907–60, the Song dynasty unified the country. "By all accounts", declares Keay, " the period of the Song was China's greatest age … it had been an era of internal tranquillity, booming trade, technological innovation and cultural sophistication", with notably some of the highest achievements of Chinese painting, especially of landscapes. Kaifeng, their capital, had a population of around a million, equivalent to that of all contemporary England under William I. A surge in industrialisation and economic activity "appears to have brought most Chinese a real rise in income in spite of continuing population growth". Even the southern Song (1127–1279), driven out of northern China by invaders, "would come to be seen as a halcyon age of imperial China". Dominic Lieven adds "the Chinese economy developed to a level seen nowhere else on earth until late eighteenth-century Britain".[9]

The Mongol conquest is estimated to have cost China 30 million lives – a quarter of the population of the year 1200. However, the temporary prestige of the rapidly Sinified Yuan (Mongol) dynasty is known to us by Marco Polo's accounts of his visits to Kublai Khan. After 1350 the Yuan dynasty succumbed to rebellion, with the Red Turbans spreading anarchy. Then the Ming, a native Chinese dynasty, gave stability and success against the Mongols. For a few decades in the early 15th century, huge Chinese fleets under Admiral Zhen He toured the Indian Ocean as far as East Africa, Arabia and the Gulf. Their purpose, however, was neither trade nor colonisation, simply the spreading of Imperial prestige and the exacting of tribute. Further voyages were abruptly forbidden by Imperial decree in the 1430s – otherwise a very powerful China might have competed with the Portuguese and other Europeans. The Ming saw the population of China climb from an estimated 65 million in 1400 to 160 million in 1600 – considerably higher than the population of contemporary Europe. Decline set in under the Wanli emperor (1573–1620), and the end came in 1644, with human and administrative failure coinciding with famines caused by the "Little Ice Age" and "massive peasant revolts".[10]

The Manchu Qing dynasty took some decades of chaos before it was established throughout China. Its most famous emperors (known by their reign titles rather than their personal names) were Kangxi (1661–1722), Yongzhen (1723–35) and Qianlong (1723–95). Great advances into central Asia were made, giving China her present borders, with vassal status imposed on Korea, Indo-China and Burma. Numerous Westerners who visited at this time "marvelled at the empire's prosperity and invariably praised its orderly government".[11] Decline saw the Taiping rebellion led by a religious maverick inspired by a debased form of Christianity, which during 1850–64 saw carnage across 16 of the 18 provinces, with estimated loss of life from war and famine at between 20 and 40 million. Humiliating defeats by Britain, France and finally Japan in various 19th century wars, and the Boxer rebellion (directed at foreign missionaries and Chinese Christians), resulted in invasion by most of the Great Powers in 1900, thus leading to the fall of the dynasty in 1912. This time, a Republic emerged. The civil wars of the 1920s, the Japanese invasions subsequently, and the Communist take-over of 1946–49, need no elaboration. After the speedy Communist victory, there followed at least three great slaughters comparable with China's worst historical experiences: the execution of a million or more landowners in the early 1950s, the famine of 1959–61 resulting from the "Great Leap Forward" (estimated death toll of between 20–50 million), and the so-called Great Proletarian Cultural Revolution (1966–76), with a death toll amounting to a few million.[12]

Recent decades have witnessed massive economic growth in China – helped, perhaps, by contentious population control (in sharp contrast to other regions of the world where rapid population growth means continuing poverty). More controversially, we see a Ming-style "Belt and Road" expansion into Africa and elsewhere, and a growing threat to south-east Asian neighbours.

India has also achieved great economic success with democracy, but the tension with Pakistan continues, and outbreaks of violence are seen with the massacre of thousands of Sikhs in 1984 after the murder of Indira Gandhi by her Sikh bodyguards, the demolition of the Babri Masjid, a 16th century mosque, by a Hindu mob in 1992, and the intercommunal Gujarat riots in 2002.

The Mongol invasions

Because the Mongol invasions took place nearly 800 years ago, they do not feature in historical recollection or teaching in the West today. Yet they involved devastation over Russia and Eastern Europe as well as most of Asia (sparing only much of India and south-east Asia). In Keay's words "their onslaught … was like nothing that history had ever known – or would again … urbanisation in much of Asia was halted in its tracks, fragile agricultural systems never recovered, and population figures are thought to have nosedived".[13]

In a recent book, Professor Peter Jackson devoted a whole chapter to Mongol devastation. Nicholas Morton's account is respectful of Mongol military and administrative skills but equally damning on the consequences to humanity.[14] The simple Mongol code provided that in rare cases (mainly immediate surrender and paying of tribute) populations were spared – but often only to supply arrow-fodder in subsequent sieges. Any sustained resistance, for example at Erzurum and Kayseri, or the killing of notable Mongols, or revolt after previous submission, as in the case of Balkh, Merv, and Hamadan, usually led to wholesale massacre. Genghis Khan's favourite grandson fell in the siege of Bamiyan (location of the famous Buddha statues), and his son-in-law in that of Nishapur – thus every living creature, even cats and dogs, were killed when these cities fell.

Sometimes skilled craftsmen and artisans were spared and deported; with women and children taken as slaves. Bizarrely, the inhabitants of one city, who had asked for quarter with the stipulation that it be guaranteed by a Muslim commander, were all slaughtered by Hulagu Khan for doubting his word.

Various historians have used phrases like "blind unreasoning fear and hatred of urban civilisation", "the providing of pasture for nomads" – the latter in place of agrarian production. Inevitably, no estimate can be made of the totals of who perished in these vast areas; especially when famine and disease followed. They included thousands of scholars – one chronicler commented that "it was necessary to seek learning in the belly of the earth, since that was where the learned were located". Estimates of tax revenues in various areas show around a eighth or a tenth raised after the conquest, compared to before. And the Mongols destroyed the irrigation and canal system of Mesopotamia, built up under the Assyrians, Sasanids and Abbasids; the surviving population was unable to restore it, so there was a rapid reduction in the size of cultivated land.[15]

It is difficult to defend Genghis Khan and his associates, though some, including Pope Francis, have attempted it. Nothing in recorded history compares with the loss of life, both absolutely and proportionately, wreaked by them – not even the excesses of Stalin, Mao or Hitler's Holocaust, although this last was unique both in its industrialised cold-bloodedness and its clear intention to destroy a whole race.

Modern times, sadly, have seen parallels with earlier cultural barbarism, with destruction of artefacts thought to conflict with ideological or religious fanaticism. The Nazis did their worst, though fortunately insubordination spared Paris from

Hitler's vengeance. Chapter Six describes the Bolshevik looting of historic Russia. The Taliban wrecked sites in Afghanistan, notably but not only the Bamiyan Buddhas, and ISIS loathsomely competed in Syria and Iraq. Russia's 2022 invasion of Ukraine saw similar acts of cultural destruction.

Hellenistics, cities, Ottoman minorities, and slavery

A civilisation, or more precisely, a civilised achievement, often overlooked, and significantly linking East and West, were the Hellenistic kingdoms, especially that of the Seleucids. These resulted from the conquest of the Persian empire by Alexander the Great in the 4th century BC. They imported the Greek language and culture across a vast area, centred on cities, often new foundations, such as Antioch in Syria and the capital Seleucia, near Babylon. Alexandria in the Ptolemaic kingdom in Egypt, was the centre of a remarkable Graeco-Egyptian synthesis. Scores of foundations, usually named after Alexander, or his successor rulers Antiochus and Seleucus, multiplied as far as present-day Turkestan and Afghanistan. By the 2nd century BC, the Seleucids were gradually forced back on a heartland of Syria and Mesopotamia, and later, along with the Ptolemies, succumbed to Roman power.

The Hellenistic kingdoms paralleled the British achievement which, by settlement or administration 2000 years later, spread European standards, traditions and culture across the four other continents.

All civilisations involved the development and growth of cities, and both chronicles and archaeology mark the devastating consequences when key cities were overthrown. The fate of Troy, illustrated at the start of this book, haunted the author at the age of seven. In Rome's wars of expansion, the deliberate and brutal destruction of Carthage and of Corinth, both in 146 BC, with the slaughter of much of the population, stand out. Both cities later regained importance, Carthage being the centre of the booming province of Africa where its 4th century population was estimated at 100,000. But most of the documentation describing its earlier achievement perished in 146.

One of the earliest recorded major city destructions was that of Nineveh, the capital of the Assyrian empire. Magnificent in its time, little remains above ground because it was built mainly of mud brick. Nineveh's maximum population was thought to be 100–150,000, but Assyria was hated by her brutally conquered and exploited subject peoples, who combined to attack it in 612 BC. Excavations suggest house to house fighting, with the city finally burnt and razed and the population massacred or deported.

In the medieval Islamic world, as noted, the ravages of Genghis Khan and his successors and later those of Tamerlane (died 1305) brought destruction and depopulation to many large cities, such as Samarkand, Bokhara, Herat, Isfahan, Damascus, Ryazan, Lahore and Delhi. But the one event that stands out, because of the city's previous importance, size and glory (its population at its greatest extent numbered a million) was the destruction of Baghdad in 1258 under the Mongol leader Hulagu. Survivors reported that the River Tigris ran black, with the ink from thousands of rare and valuable manuscripts thrown there, and red, with the blood of the inhabitants.

In modern times, the details of the Jewish Holocaust are vividly known, not only from survivors but because the Nazis obligingly kept grim detailed records. Likewise we know a certain amount from survivors about the Rwandan and Cambodian genocides, and that of the Armenians over a century ago. Hitler is supposed to have remarked, as a justification for what he was planning, "After all, who remembers the Armenians?"

Was the fall of an empire necessarily bad for civilisation? While individual Gothic/Frankish/Lombard rulers who replaced it were clever and competent, this study will show that the fall of the western Roman empire in the 5th century was particularly bad for its component parts. After 1453 Constantinople may have benefited from the Ottomans drafting in tens of thousands of migrants, but little benefit was accorded to Anatolia, Greece, and the Balkan provinces. While Ottoman rule was harsh, especially when challenged, their *millet* system ensured a degree of toleration and autonomy for the religions and cultures of subject peoples. The influence of French Revolutionary ideas challenged the *millet* system in the final years of the Ottomans, while Greek and Armenian opposition provoked a Turkish nationalist response. This led to the murderous onslaughts against the Armenians in the 1890s and after 1914.

Slavery and the slave trade existed for millennia. In most ancient and oriental societies, slavery was the alternative to slaughter after conquest, though usually restricted to women and children. In classical Greece and Rome, many could buy freedom, and many in domestic situations were treated well. As well as horrific mines, Imperial Rome developed large plantation estates, like those which later existed in the Caribbean and southern USA. Matters did not immediately change with the adoption of Christianity. While Gregory of Nyassa attacked the institution of slavery, St Augustine ducked the challenge. He saw no way of ending it and argued that slavery "was both a consequence of the fall of man and at the same time a wrong that providence prevented from being wholly harmful". However, he and others argued that mercy to prisoners of war was a fundamental principle, and bishops would sell church plate given by wealthy benefactors to redeem such prisoners.[16]

Imperial citizens were enslaved, for example, the Romano-British St Patrick taken by Irish raiders. During the Turkish invasions of Anatolia, Ephesus became a market for slaves who would predominantly be Greek Christians. There the famous Arab traveller, Ibn Batuta, "was fortunate to purchase" for forty gold dinars in 1333 a Greek virgin girl.[17]

What is most contentious to the modern mind is the 15th–19th centuries' trans-Atlantic slave trade, where those defeated in African wars and others were sold by their black captors to (usually) white traffickers. Previously, of course, black Africans had been trafficked into the Mediterranean and Levantine worlds. To set alongside "white guilt" comes this from Sean Thomas, via the *Spectator*: "Slaving has been practised with great eagerness by the nations and societies of the Islamic world … such an intrinsic part of Islam that the treatment, utility, and social status of slaves is expressly discussed in multiple verses of the Koran. Notoriously, the Koran allows slave owners sexual rights to their female chattels." He refers to estimates of "forcibly import[ing] possibly 15–20 million black Africans" to the Maghreb, Arabia and elsewhere over "perhaps 1400 years." Added to which "Barbary pirates … took white slaves" from western Europe "well into the 19th century. At least a million white slaves were seized in total."[18]

Thus, in the 16th and 17th centuries, scores of thousands of Russians and Ukrainians were trafficked as slaves into the Ottoman empire; they provided "Europe's first slave-based sugar plantations" in Ottoman Cyprus.[19] And Britain and other west European countries saw raiders take victims from our shores for the slave-markets of North Africa or Turkey; hence Charles I's Ship Money and the French expedition to Algiers as late as 1830.

The slave trade has in very recent years been thrust to the fore, by academics promoting books on the second centenary of abolition and by the American-initiated Black Lives Matter (BLM) movement. There have been calls for "apology" and some for "indemnity", though it is likely that the latter, understandably, will fall on deaf ears in the present-day cities of Liverpool and Bristol, and their Continental equivalents. It is clearly not acceptable that present generations should be made to feel guilty on account of complex occurrences centuries ago. Little of this controversy benefits race relations in the UK or the US, to put it mildly.

The record on slavery and other issues arising from colonisation has largely been corrected by Professor Nigel Biggar's recent substantial and well-researched volume, *Colonialism: A Moral Reckoning* (William Collins, 2023) though it is likely that the debate will continue, even if it is ill-informed or malignly motivated.

Anguish about slavery should be set alongside the plight of medieval serfs and their more recent successors, including children, who with minimal reward contributed to the industrial revolution. They included the hundreds of thousands who spent their working lives mining for coal or other minerals. Most of these experienced, to use the words of Thomas Hobbes, lives that were "nasty, brutish and short". And the criminal activity known as "modern slavery" obtains far too little attention or prevention.

Monarchy and sovereignty

Most states in recorded history were governed by monarchs. Exceptions were relatively few – mainly city-states: earlier Rome, Carthage, Athens, Venice, and Genoa. While in the last 300 years government in more and more states has passed to an oligarchy, an elected assembly or combination of these two, recent years have seen one person rule returning to the fore: Lenin and Stalin (and Putin), Hitler, Mussolini, and various minor European, Latin American, Asian and African dictators.

Of course, the great imperial power of the last century has been the United States of America, which took the 18th century British constitution of King, Parliament and judges, and transferred much of it into a written Constitution with divided and balanced powers of an indirectly elected President, separately elected Congress and appointed Supreme Court. The limitations of this system may be debated. Events over recent decades – even very recent years – embellish the judgement on the USA in 1945, quoted in this author's last book and attributed to Keynes: "these people could never run an empire."[20] Viet Nam, Afghanistan and Iraq were battlefields witnessing swift American decline after the zenith of 1945. As a recent *Times* letter stated "Future historians may well look back on the distraction of the Iraq and Afghan missions as the turning point when the West's decline and China's rise became well established."[21]

Monarchical government required a mechanism for the transfer of power. While it was frequently hereditary, the Roman empire, west or east, did not assume primogeniture succession. In calm times, one emperor would decide his successor, often an adopted son; this also happened in China. In times of difficulty, others from within the imperial family, or prominent persons, usually generals with powerful armies, outside it, might challenge for the purple. Thus Rome in the "Crisis of the Third Century" and later, and China, especially during the decline of a dynasty, would be plunged into a succession of civil wars. Dominic Lieven describes the destruction and instability caused to many empires by succession struggles, but makes the point that European monarchs in recent centuries could, unlike the Asiatic empires, usually count on the loyalty of an officer corps recruited from the aristocracy.[22]

Monarchical power would often suffer from weakness or tyranny. Rome's Senate had in practice ceased to wield power by the early 1st century AD. Oriental monarchies often had informal equivalents. England had the Anglo-Saxon Witan and then the medieval Parliament. This evolved: via sharing the government with the monarch as in the 17th century, to being the predominant partner – as it was by the first half of the 18th century. And until the 20th century only a tiny proportion of adult males – just over 400,000 out of a Great Britain population of 16.5 million in 1831 – was entitled to take part in elections.

Other countries were tempted to emulate the British, but did not always possess the political and social stability and maturity to enable success; hence their progress to constitutional government was frequently interrupted by episodes of dictatorship. For example, as we shall see in Chapters Four and Five, France both in 1792 and in 1848 resorted to universal male suffrage, only in each case to find this ideal exploited, then challenged and curbed by an autocrat.

The moving events of national remembrance and change in the days after the death of Queen Elizabeth II in September 2022 and the later coronation of King Charles III prompted reflections on what in the 21st century promotes power and sovereignty. Four factors can be traced. First, religion or "God", now of little obvious importance in Britain and western Europe (though still, especially as perceived in the above events, with underlying influence). It is more important in the USA and of course of massive significance in most Muslim countries.

Second, institutions – monarchy as such, Parliaments, and the law, courts and judges. In most parts of the world, outside Europe and North America, each of these, however worthy, is highly vulnerable, usually to force derived from the third factor.

So third, armed forces, whether regular or irregular. These continue to be dominant in the "Third World" and until the 1970s were potent in various European countries. England's brief experiment with republicanism, in the mid-17th century, saw Parliament and judiciary purged or overruled by the army. France saw threatened military intervention in 1958 and, more subtly, in 1968. Who can be confident that such interventions might cease? As we shall see in later chapters, while the army might be used to enforce order and authority at decisive points, it failed in this task, or was not effectively directed, in England, France and Russia in respectively, 1688, 1789–91, 1830, 1848, 1870 and 1917.

As an adjunct to the military, we see the role of "activists" – armed and somewhat undisciplined in 1790s France and 1917 Russia, and in recent years, while unarmed, having a sinister effect on British politics. The Labour party has never been able to discard its activists, even though these gave us the Corbyn leadership with its sad consequences for the EU Referendum and subsequently. As the result of a rash decision by William Hague, since 2001 the final say in the election of Conservative leaders has been with the activists, or "grassroots members", who gave us steadily increasing Euro-scepticism, the repeated by-passing of Kenneth Clarke, and the anointing of Iain Duncan Smith in 2001, Boris Johnson in 2019, and Liz Truss (briefly) in 2022.

So finally, the "popular will". How is it displayed, and can its dictates be misinterpreted or even overruled? There is no guarantee that those elected will obey the popular will. In France, especially, revolutions were made in Paris, but frequently subverted (as in the 1790s) or punished (as in 1848 and 1870–71) by the provinces. That brings us into the vexed area of referenda. The key weakness of a referendum is that it can only measure numbers; it cannot measure strength of feeling or power. Numbers of Remainers in the EU referendum suffered financially or administratively from Brexit, as well as emotionally, while apart from the hard-core fanatics, few Brexit supporters had a material or deep emotional interest in the result. Indeed, there is evidence that many of the latter now regret their vote. One day, the results of a referendum somewhere might be rejected by lawmakers, or challenged by a strongly willed minority having recourse to whatever devices might be available.

The "father" of political theory was Aristotle, and he wielded unrivalled subsequent influence both in Christendom and in Islam. His *Politics* assesses the strengths and weaknesses of various types of state – tyranny/monarchy; aristocracy, meaning rule by the most virtuous and best educated; oligarchy, meaning rule by the few, usually the wealthiest; and democracy. Representative democracy, with which we are familiar, did not exist in Aristotle's time; Athens had direct democracy, with decisions taken by all citizens qualified to vote. They formed a small proportion, estimated at between 10 and 20 per cent, of the total population of Attica of around 250–300,000, because women, slaves, ex-slaves, foreign residents and children had no vote. Thus the *Politics* seems to conclude that the best, most durable, constitution, was a polity consisting of elements of aristocracy, oligarchy and democracy, and this is what in practice governs most modern so-called democracies.

It is of course right to add, that if the establishment drastically ignores serious popular views, such as over migration and cultural challenges, as seems to be happening in Europe, the UK and, in a more complex way, in the USA, it will be challenged by what is sniffily termed populism. This argument will be developed in the Epilogue.

A clear conclusion from the events described later in this book is that, once the people intervened directly and violently, whether in France in 1789, in Russia in early 1917, the progress was downhill. The direct but non-violent popular intervention in Britain in 2016 produced economic difficulty, as well as relative international isolation and political instability.

Hence the presence in this study of Chapter Three, as a contrast. The two key features of the Glorious Revolution in England of 1688–89 were, first, the restraint of violence, and second, the exclusion of the populace from active intervention. Other contrasts, of course, were the successful and welcome revolutions against Communist rule in Eastern Europe in 1989–90, referred to further in Chapter Eight. Apart from that in Romania, they largely avoided bloodshed.

Emigrés and migration

The collapse of civilisations and the occurrence of revolutions inevitably produced refugees, sometimes called émigrés. In the 5th century we see the flight of Romans from Vandal-dominated Africa to Italy and of Romano-Britons to Brittany. The French and Russian revolutions produced large numbers, mainly of aristocrats, organised in the earlier stages of the former as a menacing army outside France. The 1688 Glorious Revolution sent British émigrés mainly to France, where they paid court to the exiled Stuarts. Pursuing a theme of the present author's *Crisis of the British Empire*, the replacement of white rule in Southern Africa by vindictive autocrats caused many whites to migrate. Thus the white population of South Africa fell from a peak of 5.2 million in 1995 to 4.6 million in 2022, while that of Rhodesia/Zimbabwe fell from a peak of 300,000 in 1975 to just under 29,000 in 2012.

Most émigré groups were unable to reverse what had driven them into exile. Forming a link between 1688 and 1792, we see the Flight of the Wild Geese, about 14,000 Irish Jacobite soldiers, with about 6000 women and children, under Patrick Sarsfield, who were permitted to sail to France by the peace treaty at the end of Irish resistance to William III. They and successive bands of Irish served the French Crown in its various wars during the next century, eventually leaving the French army in 1792 upon Louis XVI's deposition, as their oaths of loyalty had been to him rather than to the French nation. Another more tenuous link to the French crown was through one of the original Wild Geese, Daniel Murphy. His granddaughter, Marie-Louise O'Murphy, became for a while the celebrated *petite-maîtresse* of Louis XV, whose attention was apparently initially drawn by Casanova to the celebrated painting of her by Boucher. Despite everything, she lived to the age of 77. Other European states benefited more prosaically from Irish exiles: such as Field Marshal Count Peter Lacy, in the Russian army, and his son the eminent Franz Graf von Lacy, commanding Austrian armies.[23]

Eminent British opponents of Brexit have moved themselves, often with their businesses, to countries remaining in the EU; some to Ireland – the Wild Geese in reverse. And the UK's complex and contentious relationship with Ireland has certainly not been helped by Brexit.

There is another connection across the centuries, linking the fall of the Roman empire and today. Both featured a *Völkerwanderung*. a major cause of the collapse of the western Roman empire. Professor Niall Ferguson has used this word, usually describing the 5th century "barbarian invasions", to describe the trans-Mediterranean migrations from the Middle East and Sub-Saharan Africa into southern Europe, in increasing numbers since 2014, often organised by criminal gangs, and preying on the hopes of misled people expecting to exploit the EU's Schengen system of absence of internal frontier checks.

This recent influx into Europe had already caused a political backlash in most Continental European countries and, while the UK was outside the Schengen system, it must be assumed that the steady flow of film and reports of the Mediterranean and parallel crossings, and the assembly of migrants in camps around Calais, had a key influence on the outcome of the UK's June 2016 referendum on EU membership.

Christianity and paganism

This book cannot begin to discuss the effects of religion on its central themes of civilisation and authority, but the Christian churches influenced events in most of our chapters. If there was any substance in Gibbon's claim that Christianity contributed to the fall of the Roman Empire, we might have expected that the eastern empire, where Christianity was more dominant, would have succumbed first. In fact, there is no doubt that Christianity reinforced the East's resistance against Persian and later Muslim enemies.

As Peter Heather and others have estimated, Christians in circa 300 did not amount to more than one or two per cent of the population of the Roman Empire. What changed this followed the "conversion" of Constantine, described by Heather as the Emperor's gradual manifestation of new loyalties, as he perceived the unifying and motivating force of the new religion. With imperial influence the wealthy and educated classes gradually saw conversion as a necessary condition to their continuing to wield power and authority. Perhaps there is a 16th century parallel with the success of Protestantism in northern Europe: without the support of kings and princes, aided by the wish of the nobility and gentry to possess Church and monastery property, the formal Protestant "revolutions" are likely to have had limited success. Dissent towards Roman teaching and liturgies might have survived only in relative privacy, as paganism sought to survive after the 4th century.

In fact, the triumph of Christianity in the Roman empire involved increasingly fierce persecution of pagans. Theodosius, the last emperor to rule over both western and eastern empires (379–95), outlawed in 392 every form of pagan worship, even in private. He neither prevented nor punished the destruction of notable sites, such as the Temple of Apollo at Delphi and the Serapeum in Alexandria. In 415 an Alexandrian mob, aroused by Christian leaders, murdered the Neoplatonist philosopher, astronomer and mathematician, Hypatia: the 2009 film *Agora*, where she is played by Rachel Weisz, is a somewhat fictionalised account of her last days.

As Catherine Nixey has suggested, the Christians were fairly ruthless in destroying or defacing pagan art and architecture.[24] Pagan sanctuaries were "completely destroyed … especially in Asia Minor"; at Hierapolis, the temple of Apollo, the city's patron god, "was gradually torn apart stone by stone, some reused for other buildings, some sent to the lime kilns, some hacked into pieces, and the site of the temple was eventually turned into a dump for building materials".[25]

What we moderns might consider attractive deities, such as Pallas Athene, Apollo, Aphrodite and Artemis, were perceived by these early Christians as demons. Hence their traces had to be destroyed or incorporated with new names into Christian iconography. Centres of medical teaching at Smyrna, Corinth, Kos and Pergamum had healing shrines that attracted supplicants. Many were destroyed when Christianity gained the upper hand.[26] The Church's disapproval of the Grecian cult of nudity in sport might have caused the closure of the Olympic Games by Theodosius in 394. And when university teaching of classical philosophy revived in 8th-century Constantinople "it was subject to constant intolerant Church interference".[27]

Another source describes the tense exchanges between Christian secular authorities and bishops and their followers and the large rural pagan population during the 4th and 5th centuries: for the monks and others who were active, especially in Egypt, "demolition of heathen cults extirpated the memory of Julian and the legendary horrors of Diocletian".[28] The 2023 Channel Four TV series *Ancient Egypt by Train* featuring Professor Alice Roberts (anthropologist and humanist campaigner) showed evidence of Christian defacement of pagan images in Edfu.

Iconoclasm – the destruction of Christian images – in the Christian Byzantine empire had cultural consequences. Provoked by the defeats they had suffered from the seriously non-idolatrous Muslims, Iconoclasm was initiated in 726–30 by Leo III, temporarily reversed in 787, restored in 815 by another Leo (the V), and suppressed for good in 843. If it had won, "church decoration would have been limited to the depiction of gardens and swirls of vegetation as in contemporary Ummayad mosques." Even so, the loss to the Byzantine artistic heritage is massive: a "pathetically small quantity of Byzantine art ... has survived from before the middle of the 9th century".[29]

And in the 15th and 16th centuries, Roman antiquities were pillaged "on a grand scale", where the forums, the Palatine Palace and various classical temples saw their stone used to build Renaissance palaces, the Ponte Sisto and the new St Peter's.[30]

One revolution not examined in the present study is the Reformation. There is little doubt that the Papacy ensured a degree of survival of order during the so-called Dark Ages and the early medieval period. It failed to curb the barbarism which accompanied the Crusades against Muslims and, in the 13th century, against the Cathars. Not only did the Papacy become a serious secular power, only retreating from this in the last century or so, it also demanded subordination to Papal sovereignty. Insubordination was heresy. This helped to produce the Reformation in northern Europe, while in those southern European countries where Catholicism remained dominant, opposition to it after 1750 was displayed by assorted anti-clericalism, deism, secularism and Communism. In England, the political revolution – the break with Rome – opened the door to a not wholly satisfactory cultural revolution, in which most medieval religious art was destroyed.

Very significantly for modern times, whereas classical Greece and Rome had been tolerant of, even indulgent towards, male homosexuality, the Church persuaded the State to persecute it with vigour.[31] This hostility, justified by Biblical fragments, arose from the Jews in Exile reacting to Babylonian practices, and the later opposition of early Christians to Graeco-Roman practices. It lasted in Europe until very recently; however, the Orthodox and Catholic churches remain hostile, while the Anglicans are divided, with their leaders fearful of upsetting the African churches, also hostile. 35 out of 54 Commonwealth members still have criminal sanctions against homosexuality. Sathnam Sanghera cites this as a "legacy of British imperialism" – what, after 60 years of independence! And careful study would indicate that this Christian tradition was unusual: most other civilisations and cultures in history and across the world, even (despite Koranic strictures) the Islamic regimes of Caliphs, Mamelukes, Ottomans and Moghuls, have tolerated and occasionally semi-institutionalised homosexual relations. This last point is reinforced by Noel Malcolm's just-published *Forbidden Desire in Early Modern Europe: Male–Male Sexual Relations 1400–1750* (OUP, 2024).

Marxism

The theoretical inspiration for the Russian Revolution was that of Karl Marx, although his analysis had implied an outbreak of revolution in an advanced industrialised capitalist society, probably Germany. Practically all Left-wing revolutionary activity since 1917 has derived from some Marxist inspiration. The practical experience of sub-Marxism (there has never been a pure Marxist state) has been universally damning. When a biography of the eminent Communist, the late Professor Eric Hobsbawm, appeared in early 2019, readers were reminded that, when asked on television in 1994 by Michael Ignatieff, the Canadian politician and philosopher, whether Hobsbawm's commitment to Communism would have been altered if he had known of the millions forcibly starved by Stalin, he replied "probably not", adding that "the chance of a new world being born … would still have been worth backing". When asked whether "[if] the radiant tomorrow had actually been created, the loss of 15 or 20 million people might have been justified," Hobsbawm gave the "unequivocal" reply "yes".[32] Ignatieff's biography of Sir Isaiah Berlin describes Berlin writing in the thirties a short monograph on Marx: "What fascinated him (ie Berlin) was Marx's loathing for the very civilisation he himself admired".[33]

As a political alternative to mainstream private enterprise conservatism/liberalism/social democracy, Marxism is now largely discredited. Those who, in recent times, might have become its followers, refugees of rapid economic change, widening inequality, de-industrialisation, low wages, even "white flight" from cities and competition from immigrants, have instead been turning towards the populist Right. This has been pronounced in countries as disparate as France, Italy, Poland and Hungary; it is now almost universal in Europe, including the Netherlands and Scandinavia.

And Brexit …

My original plan was for this book to culminate in an indictment of the Brexit process and consequences. Brexit did not, however, come out of the blue. Reading about the Cameron government of 2010–16, I was impressed by how far by then the rot had set in, with very strong feeling in Tory grassroots and in the Parliamentary party against staying in anything resembling the EU. A new generation had arisen in the Party, with very different views to those of the wartime and immediate post-war generation dominant before 1992. And while Labour party leaders and most, though not all Labour MPs, supported remaining in the EU, it is clear that Labour voters, especially in the north and the so-called Red Wall seats (taken by Conservatives in 2017 and especially 2019) were strongly opposed to the EU. This is a prominent theme in Sebastian Payne's study.³⁴ It was simply because these voters felt neglected by the increasingly dominant metropolitan middle-class elite in Labour. After heavily voting Out in 2016, in 2019 they responded warmly to the Johnsonian slogan "Get Brexit Done". In 2024, these voters faced a dilemma.

I believe it was a mistake to contrive, through the 2016 Referendum, the crude decision of our leaving the EU against the views of a very large majority of elected MPs. Let me add, though, how I dislike that word "Union", with all the legalism and centralised autocracy that it implies; its introduction as part of the Maastricht Treaty helped to turn numbers of people against the European project. The word "Community" was far more reassuring; while "Commonwealth" is an English word which amply describes the various good things we and the other nation states sought in Europe. Britain is geographically, historically, culturally and largely politically part of Europe, but we should have set a more Euro-lite government course in and before 2016 instead of throwing the question into the street.

There is also no doubt that negotiating Brexit over five years, with continuous turbulence, saw the UK government distracted from preparing for, and coping with, such major threats as the military and commercial challenges of Russia and China and the various challenges facing our public services, including notably the Covid epidemic.

Meanwhile, Lord Tugendhat's judgement cannot be refuted: "Those advocating Leave had no plan for how to make the break. They presented no assessments about what it would mean for the British economy and for British trade" nor about the implications for Britain's "wider international relationships". Most notably, they "failed to take account of the consequences for Northern Ireland".³⁵

It is an odd coincidence that the first chapter, the fall of the western Roman empire, saw nine emperors in the last 20 years to 476 (four in the last four years), while post Brexit Britain saw four Prime Ministers in six years, with Boris Johnson and Liz Truss being removed in near-chaotic circumstances in July and October 2022.

FOOTNOTES

1 David Nicholson, *Crisis of the British Empire – Turning Points After 1880*, Halsgrove 2017.

2 Review in London Review of Books, 26 May 2022, by James Meek of Barbara F Walters, *How Civil Wars Start – And How to Stop Them*, Viking, 2022.

3 Dominic Lieven, *In the Shadow of the Gods: The Emperor in World History*, hereafter *Shadow*, Allen Lane, 2022, pp429–31.

4 Quoted by Henry Chadwick, "Envoi: On Taking Leave of Antiquity", in Boardman, Griffin and Murray, eds *The Roman World*, OUP, 1986, p405.

5 J M Roberts, *The Penguin History of the World*, Penguin, 1995 p415.

6 *Sunday Times*, 23 April 2023.

7 John Keay, *India: A History*, Harper Collins, 2000, pp206–12, 253, 276, 282.

8 John Keay, *China: A History*, hereafter *China*, Harper Collins, 2009, pp77, 79, 110–15, 186.

9 *Ibid*, pp303, 323, 341, Roberts, *op cit*, pp440–41, Lieven, *Shadow*, p150.

10 Lieven, *Shadow*, p285; also Chapter 5, pp115–51 in Geoffrey Parker, *Global Crisis: War, Climate Change and Catastrophe in the Seventeenth Century*, Yale UP, 2013.

11 Keay, *China*, *op cit*, p432 and Roberts, *op cit*, p446.

12 See Jung Chang and Jon Halliday *Mao: The Unknown Story*, Jonathan Cape, 2005.

13 Keay, *China*, p351.

14 Peter Jackson, *The Mongols and the Islamic World: From Conquest to Conversion*, Yale UP, 2017, pp153–81; Nicholas Morton, *The Mongol Storm*, Basic Books, 2023, chapters 1 to 7.

15 Last point: Thabit Abdullah, *A Short History of Iraq*, Pearson, 2003, p34; earlier quote: Jackson, *op cit*, p176.

16 Henry Chadwick, *op cit*, pp418, 420.

17 Clive Foss *Ephesus After Antiquity*, Cambridge UP, 1979, p146.

18 *Spectator Coffee House,* 13 June 2023.

19 Lieven, *Shadow*, pp208, 309.

20 Nicholson, *op cit*, p218. The quotation is used by Richard Bassett, *The Last Imperialist: A Portrait of Julian Amery*, Stone Trough Books, 2016. Bassett told the present author that a very similar comment was made by Frank Lee, on Keynes's staff, at a September 1945 meeting, but that "Paul Bareau's original note of the meeting strongly implies this was also Keynes's view."

21 Rohan Moorthy, letter, *The Times*, 22 March 2023.

22 Lieven, *Shadow*, p317.

23 Accounts of the Wild Geese are in Maurice Hennessy, *The Wild Geese: The Irish Soldier in Exile*, Sidgwick and Jackson, 1973, and Robert Shepherd *Ireland's Fate*, Aurum 1990, pp185–98.

24 Catherine Nixey, *The Darkening Age: The Christian Destruction of the Classical World*, Macmillan, 2017.

25 Brandt, Hagelberg et al, editors, *Life and Death in Asia Minor in Hellenistic, Roman and Byzantine Times*, Oxbow Books, 2017, pp1, 203.

26 Violet Moller, *The Map of Knowledge: How Classical Ideas were Lost and Found*, Picador, 2019, p25.

27 Timothy Venning, *If Rome Hadn't Fallen: What Might Have Happened if the Western Empire had Survived*, Pen and Sword, 2011, pp120, 124.

28 *The Cambridge History of Christianity,* Vol 2, *Constantine to c600*, Augustine Casiday and Frederick W Norris, editors, CUP, 2007, p186, otherwise, chapters 6 to 9.

29 Patricia Karlin-Hayter, "Iconoclasm", in *The Oxford History of Byzantium*, Cyril Mango, editor, p158 and John Julius Norwich, *Byzantium: II The Apogee*, p27, respectively.

30 Matthew Kneale, *Rome: A History in Seven Sackings*, Atlantic Books, 2017, p191.

31 Sarris, *op cit*, pp221–22.

32 Review in *Sunday Times* 27 January 2019 by Dominic Sandbrook of Richard Evans, *Eric Hobsbawm: A Life in History,* Little, Brown, 2019.

33 George Brandis, "Isaiah Berlin and the Defence of Liberty", in *Conservative History Journal* Autumn 2019.

34 Sebastian Payne, *Broken Heartlands: A Journey Through Labour's Lost England*, Macmillan, 2021.

35 Christopher Tugendhat, *The Worm in the Apple: A History of the Conservative Party and Europe from Churchill to Cameron*, Haus Publishing, 2022, p211.

Chapter One:
The Fall of the Western Roman Empire

"Who would have believed that Rome … would fall … That it would be both the mother and the tomb to all peoples." (St Jerome, quoted Peter Sarris, *Empires of Faith: The Fall of Rome to the Rise of Islam*, OUP, 2011, p36)

"A period of stark and rapid economic decline, perhaps unprecedented in recorded human history". (Sarris, *ibid*, p75)

"Any attempt to reconstruct fifth-century events brings home just how violent the process was." (Peter Heather, *The Fall of the Roman Empire*, Pan Macmillan 2005, henceforth *Fall*, p436)

More than any other ancient people, the Romans were expert at ensuring the security, comfort and health of those in their charge, hence impressive building including a remarkable system of roads, arrangements for water supply and heating, manufacture of clothes and leatherware, and usually the ensuring of security against foreign invasion. Scholarship and teaching in the Empire enabled the conveyance to posterity of much Greek literature and history, as well as that from Latin authors; similarly with Greek and Roman art. This might be counterbalanced by the cruelty of the arena and the savage reprisals against peoples revolting. We have little estimation, however, of what was lost through Roman wars of conquest and civil war, and more particularly, from the barbarian invasions and after, including Christian destruction of pagan objects. As Adrian Goldsworthy asserts, however, "there is no doubt that the areas under Roman rule experienced considerably less war and organised violence" during the Empire "than they did in the centuries before and since", with prosperity more widespread and "goods, people and ideas … able to travel further and more often than ever before".[1]

The Republican Roman virtues are well known. Once civil war and the rise of "Dictators" and "Triumvirates" changed the conventions, those virtues were weakened. So were the imperial Romans good governors? In terms of the provinces, relatively little is known to the contrary. Cicero ensured that posterity had a record of his prosecution of Verres for misgovernment, extortion and robbery as governor of Sicily. In contrast to the difficulties faced by Cicero, Goldsworthy reports that of 35 cases involving prosecutions for misbehaviour by governors or their staff between Augustus and Trajan, 28 ended in the conviction of some or all of the accused. And he adds that "no more recent empire has matched the Romans' willingness and skill in absorbing ... local elites [who] were given the prospect of success, wealth and fame" – perhaps a sideswipe at the British restrictions in India or Egypt.[2] Where government was burdensome or unreasonable, we would expect to see rebellion, as in Britain in the very early days (the Boudicca revolt) and in Judaea/Palestine, hence Jewish revolts of 66 AD and in the early 2nd century. So might we assume that provincial peace, as measured for example by St Paul's travels or Pliny's correspondence with Trajan, implied good government?

Unlike any modern empire, Rome did not fall because the provincials struggled to be free; there was "no trace of independence movements in any of the provinces", and "when provincial populations did rebel it was as Romans, supporting a claimant to the imperial purple."[3]

The central governance of the Empire seemed to move in cycles. Even Augustus, a good emperor, had as wife Livia, a ruthless schemer. Tiberius deteriorated during his reign, and Caligula and Nero were semi-insane. After the "Year of the Four Emperors" (68–69), there follows a long period of "good" emperors, from Vespasian to Marcus Aurelius (died 180). These tended to "adopt" a suitable person to succeed when he died; when this practice ceased, disputed successions resulted. The formidable Septimius Severus (193–211) is preceded and succeeded by "bad" emperors, in the persons of Commodus and Caracalla, and then we are into the "Crisis of the Third Century", where our study of "decline" really begins.

Could the Western Empire have postponed or avoided its Fall by strategic withdrawals? This would continue a theme of this author's previous book, in which doubts were expressed about "overstretch" – British imperial involvement in tropical Africa and the Middle East.[4] That book criticised the failure of Louis XIV and Napoleon to rest in the 1680s and 1810 respectively, and noted the wisdom of the Romans evacuating certain of Trajan's "jutting salient" acquisitions such as Dacia and Mesopotamia. It is hard to see, however, how the Western Empire could have withdrawn from any of its core territories without jeopardising the whole.

Timothy Venning argues the reverse, with counterfactuals based on a successful advance to the Elbe by Varus under Augustus, the retention of Dacia and Marcus Aurelius's conquest of "the Czech lands", aborted by his death.[5]

"The crisis of the third century"

A forewarning of the Empire's potential to collapse, and let in barbarian invaders,[6] occurred in the middle of the 3rd century. Undoubtedly a major cause of the collapse lay in the temporary withering away of the central power. After Severus

Alexander was murdered in 235, almost every subsequent Emperor until the accession of Diocletian in 284 died violently after an average reign of two to three years. There were 20 legitimate emperors during this time, approved by the Senate, as well as a legion of usurpers, mostly proclaimed by their troops. After the Persians defeated and captured Valerian at Edessa in 259, military and civil chiefs on the Rhine frontier set up their own regime, known as the Gallic Empire of Postumus, including much of Britain, Gaul and Spain during 259–74. Even while contesting the central power, Postumus fought the invading barbarians as a "properly Roman regime".[7] However, there were several brief civil wars during this "military anarchy", creating extensive social disorder and disruption of trade. Living standards suffered by debasement of the coinage leading to hyper-inflation.

A devastating plague ravaged the Empire after 250, with severe consequences for military recruitment and food production alike – all exacerbated by civil war and invasion. Gaul was invaded by the Goths, Vandals and Alamanni, with widespread destruction of towns. The emperor Decius was killed by Goths, who also invaded Macedonia and Greece (267), sacking Athens, Corinth and Sparta, while the seaborne Heruli raided the north and west coasts of Asia Minor. Archaeological evidence shows that the cities of northern Gaul were slow to recover from the damage done to them. A similar effect is seen in Syria and Cilicia (south-east Turkey) following the successive invasions after 253 by the Persian king Shapur, who captured and sacked several cities, notably Dura Europos, Nisibis, and Antioch. We read that the onslaught on Antioch in 256 took the citizens entirely by surprise: they were enjoying a comic theatre show when an actor realised that the archers in the citadel were not extra theatrical props but actual Persians. More tragically, the Persians transported the tens of thousands of survivors from these cities, along with those from Valerian's army, long distances to work on irrigation projects. Persian success resulted from the new and vigorous Sasanian dynasty which had replaced the decaying Parthian kingdom in 224. The Persians were resisted by Zenobia, queen of Palmyra, who was able by 271 to establish a virtually independent empire extending from northern Asia Minor through Syria and Palestine into Egypt. She was overcome by the Roman emperor Aurelian in 274.

Whether Venning's notional advance to the Elbe–Carpathian line might have averted the worst of these invasions and how far this "Crisis" permanently weakened the Empire's capacity for resistance over the following two centuries are for speculation and debate. One consequence is that it became apparent that Rome could not be the only capital of such a vast domain. We see Milan, Nicomedia and, significantly, Trier acting as capitals for the "tetrarchs" who followed, and, later, the more permanent designation of Constantinople and Ravenna as east and west capitals. After stubborn fighting by the competent Gallienus, Claudius II and Aurelian between 253 and 275, stability was eventually established by Diocletian (reigned 284–305) and by Constantine (reigned 312–337). It was assisted by an agreed delegation of powers at various times to the "tetrarchy" – Caesars who ruled parts of the Empire as subordinates to senior Emperors, the Augusti. While this did help establish more effective resistance to invaders, destructive civil wars inevitably took place between the various "tetrarchs". However, the "tetrarch" system diminished the size of armies available to non-imperial generals who might be tempted to become usurpers. Diocletian reduced the size of provinces, prescribing for each separate civil and military governors, thus further reducing the capacity for serious revolt. And as Guy Halsall argues, the 4th-century emperors, Constantine and his successors, "had managed this situation well"; they were mobile and usually resident near the frontiers; they were militarily capable and until 375 all attained the throne as adults.[8]

Until recently it was believed that entire economy of the Empire was in decline during the 3rd and 4th centuries, with falling population and land going out of use. Archaeological work in the past 60 years has refuted this: excavations show flourishing economies in the 4th and 5th centuries "with abundant and widespread rural and urban prosperity", including Syria, north Africa, Greece, Spain, southern Gaul, and Britain. The population of Britain reached a level not to be reached again until the 14th century; Peter Heather has seen "figures between 5 and 8 million bandied about" and Bryan Ward Perkins refers to estimates ranging between 2 and 6 million. A very recent publication believes that 3.5 million "is unlikely to be wildly" wrong. Some areas had seen decline or stagnation, such as central Italy and northern Gaul: a contrast of the areas of towns enclosed by walls built in the insecure days of the 3rd century and the previous occupied centres is notable: the walls of Clermont enclosed only 3 hectares of what had been an open town of 200 hectares.[9]

Weaknesses in the West

The question arises, why did the barbarians eventually triumph in the West, not the East? "In about AD 300 Persia posed an incomparably greater threat to Roman order than did Germania", and its "rise ... to superpower status had caused the massive 3rd-century crisis".[10] In 359 the Persians under Shapur II took Amida. The emperor Julian in 362–3 embarked on a very risky campaign, advancing as far as the Persian capital Ctesiphon. The Persians sprang a trap, the Romans retreated. With his army running out of supplies, Julian was killed (or assassinated) in a skirmish and his successor Jovian negotiated a humiliating peace.

The final stage of the decline of the West is usually seen as beginning with the battle of Adrianople in 378, but it was the eastern field army, including the Eastern Emperor Valens, that was wiped out on this occasion. During the 370–97 period the East needed help from the West. Geography helped the East, however: the powerful fortifications of 5th-century Constantinople proved effective until 1204, and the Roman navy kept command of the eastern seas: the barbarians (with the exception of the Vandals) lacked shipbuilding skills. Thus both the Goths and the Huns devastated the European side of the Dardanelles but did not cross into Asia Minor. By the end of the 4th and throughout the 5th centuries the Eastern Empire was at peace with Persia. Good diplomatic management exploited the fact that the Persians had their own frontier problems in Central Asia.

Evidence derived from cemeteries shows that by the 5th century the population of the German tribes had increased greatly, and their economic development and political restructuring made Germania "much more of a potential threat".[11]

It is sometimes claimed that a Roman manpower shortage caused recruitment of barbarians, but the Romans had always used barbarians in the auxiliary forces, and the accounts of Ammianus Marcellinus show no evidence of a fall in discipline. Peter Brown argues that the barbarians seemed to be substitutes for a Roman army which had weakened, but Roman elites knew how to harness barbarian military skills to their own needs. And Heather emphasises that the population of the Empire was "in excess of 70 million".[12] However, Sarris contrasts the "ruthless commitment" to Rome of the officer corps in the 3rd century with the 5th century empire dependent on outsiders whose loyalty was to warlords and chiefs.[13] And by the 5th century, the Germans outside the Empire had perceived its wealth through their growing commercial ties, and they gradually came to possess much Roman weaponry.[14]

Another often alleged cause is excessive taxation: however, it is argued that the overall tax load was usually no more than ten per cent of the agrarian surplus, within the capacities of most peasant communities: in Anatolia the tax levels reached under Diocletian continued largely unchanged until the last days of Ottoman empire. Other historians argue that widespread tax evasion had developed in both west and east.[15] In a more recent publication, Heather argues that, despite the "more demanding fiscal regime", the Empire's GDP "was at an overall maximum in the fourth century".[16]

Völkerwanderung after 375

Professor Heather's studies remain powerfully authoritative, building on important archaeological research in recent decades. His narrative makes very apparent the inadequacy of accurate details in the chronicles, once instability set in; he resorts to such phrases as "our knowledge ... is patchy," "the story takes some piecing together", "the loss of" a particular history "is a considerable handicap", "a few sparse entries in chronicles" (on Aetius's career), while "no surviving source" describes in detail Attila's great invasion of Gaul in 451.[17]

He and certain of his colleagues have been challenged by Professor Guy Halsall over whether the Germanic migrations produced the Western Empire's Fall, as Heather argues, or whether, as Halsall argues, the Fall arose more as a result of internal developments in the Empire, with the imperial authorities wilfully encouraging barbarian immigration. Thus, Halsall is inclined to believe that the barbarians were peacefully absorbed within the former imperial territories. To this sentiment Heather retorts "the determination to downplay conflict ... smells more of wishful thinking than likely reality. The written sources for west Roman collapse in the 5th century, lacunose as they certainly are, are full of implicit and explicit references to substantial conflict, both for continental Europe and north of the Channel." He adds: "Much more likely, the Anglo-Saxon takeover was a messier version of the Norman Conquest, with a new, intrusive elite taking control of the landed assets of southern Britain by ejecting and demoting the existing owners. The indigenous population must have survived in large numbers, but probably found themselves largely turned into servile peasantry."[18]

This debate has seen even stronger language used, with Halsall accusing Heather and his associates of "bizarre reasoning" and promoting a "deeply irresponsible history", even giving succour to far Right-wing extremists.[19] Research and analysis in future years will cast more light on these important matters, which reverberate today as we consider the durability of present European civilisation. The Epilogue to this present study ventures into highly turbulent waters. As we proceed to examine the events of the 4th to 6th centuries, we will find evidence which might help to reconcile the two interpretations: Halsall acknowledges that Heather and he agree on the "exposure of a critical fault-line between the imperial government and the interests of the regional elites".[20] In the light of the title of the present book, there is little doubt that the Romans in the West were almost wilfully "losing control". It is very probable, as Halsall emphasises, that as the imperial government "lost its ability to make its writ run effectively in places like Britain (and) northern Gaul", alongside the Romans' "failure to manage their 'frontier policy' ", the local elites "frequently turned to the barbarians for support". Halsall's chapter 14 gives numerous examples of local elites co-operating with the barbarian settlers. He boldly asserts – probably with an undeclared eye on present day migration, that "peaceful immigrants into the Empire needed to know where there might be a reception from previous migrants and thus a support network".[21]

As the surviving narrative of the 5th century suggests, the incidence of violence, destruction and replacement of Roman civilisation will vary according to time and place. Any "replacement" of Roman culture must take into account the cultural complexity of the Empire, with *Romanitas* forming a layer above the various ethnic and tribal cultures that existed before the Roman conquest, and with all these now having to adjust to barbarian intruders which were assuming a governing, military and often landowning role.

The migration issue and its handling explains why the West collapsed when it did. Migration intensified in the 370s when groups of "refugees", threatened by the Huns moving west from central Asia, were allowed to cross the Danube; Heather argues that this unusual concession in 376 was because Valens and his army were away on the Persian frontier. The Goths were supposed to have been disarmed: this was not fully done.[22] Intimidation by Roman officials, exacerbating food shortages, caused revolt; there was a lot of killing and devastation in roughly what is now Bulgaria. All the late Roman villas of this region that have been excavated were abandoned then, most showing a large destructive layer. It is thought that a "carefully targeted campaign of destruction aimed at members of the Roman governing class ensued."[23]

Valens called on Gratian, his western colleague, for help; Gratian was delayed by contests with other barbarian incursions. Valens was impatient, and in divided counsels the hawks won. At the battle of Adrianople in early August 378 the Goths outnumbered Valens and achieved surprise. As well as Valens himself, the Goths destroyed "the best army of the eastern Roman empire", with experienced officers and quality troops perishing. After this, Gratian held firm in the west and helped to restore the position after the new Eastern emperor Theodosius was beaten in Thessaly in 380. Peace was made in 382 but "the Empire would never get the chance to reopen the Gothic question on its own terms."[24]

A series of under-age emperors intervened: Gratian was only 23 when he was killed in 383; his co-ruler and successor, Valentinian II, died "mysteriously" aged 21 in 392; after Theodosius died in 395 he was followed in the west and east by Honorius, aged ten, and Arcadius, aged 17. Arcadius was followed in 408 by the seven-year-old Theodosius II. This produced instability, with powerful but often short-lived generals and courtiers trying to dominate, alongside frequent interventions by usurpers to the throne. Thus the reign of Honorius (395–423) is described as a "carnival of treachery, intrigue and usurpation", with the crucial negotiations with the Gothic leader Alaric in 408 handled with "phenomenal ineptitude and tactlessness". Key figures such as Stilicho and Aetius were eventually destroyed by court favourites. Halsall points to important Roman tactical mistakes affecting control of Gaul, where the capital was moved from Trier, close to the frontier, to Arles.[25]

In the years 405–08 four major invasions crossed the frontiers between the Rhine and the middle Danube: Alamanni, Burgundians and Franks across the Rhine, followed by Vandals, Alans and Suevi, and then Goths into Pannonia (modern Austria) and northern Italy, with Huns attacking what is now western Bulgaria. Heather traces "an outline trail of destruction" from Mainz through northern and then central Gallic cities. This was followed in c411 by the division and settlement of lands in Gaul and Spain, diverting the revenue of these territories from the Roman treasury.[26]

Flavius Stilicho was the first half-barbarian potential "saviour" of Rome, acting as regent for the underage Honorius. He won important victories over Alaric's Goths at Pollentia in 402 and over Radagaisus, leading Vandals and Goths, at Ticinum in 406. But he could not save Gaul, suffered other reverses, while conspiracies – several of his own making – led to his fall and execution in 408. After this, the Romans in Italy launched pogroms on the families of Goths living there; so the Gothic menfolk joined Alaric. He demanded amounts of gold and corn to pay his troops, that he and his followers should occupy the areas now covered by Austria and north-east Italy, and, finally, that Honorius should appoint him senior general. This was refused, leading to the siege of Rome, which was sacked, with the churches and people spared.

We might be permitted a degree of counterfactualism. If Valens had won at Adrianople in 378 by waiting for his western reinforcements, perhaps a firm signal would have been sent to the Goths beyond the Danube. Similarly if Stilicho in 402 had followed up his victories in northern Italy by inflicting decisive defeats on the Goths, rather than engaging in "politicking" and allowing them to retreat back into the Balkans, it would have been less likely that other German tribes in 405–06 would have taken their chances with the Western Empire.[27]

So the path of decline was not an inevitable one; there were several counterattacks by the Empire. Stilicho's successor as western commander (*magister militum*) was Flavius Constantius who defeated various usurpers and Gothic armies after 411 but died, suddenly and naturally, in 421. Sadly, after his death, "the result was more than a decade of political chaos".[28]

Probably the last major opportunity of restoration came with Flavius Aetius, from a Roman military family of Balkan origin: "the last great Roman hero of the fifth-century west … though never emperor himself, (he) was the Octavian of his time".[29] From 425 he won victories in Gaul and north Italy and became de facto ruler in the West around 433; he survived until 454. With the western army severely weakened by the civil wars and barbarian defeats of recent decades, he was obliged to use barbarians against each other, for example, Hunnic auxiliaries against Burgundians in east Gaul in 436 and Huns against Visigoths in southwest Gaul in 438–39. Simultaneously, he pushed the Franks and Alamanni east of the Rhine, while much of Spain temporarily returned to imperial control. Control was precarious, but the holding of revenue-producing territory was essential to recruitment.

However, Aetius could not prevent the Vandal advance: by 442 under Geiseric they had conquered the province of Africa (Tunisia and eastern Algeria), whose capital and port was Carthage – brutally sacked in 439 – as well as Corsica and Sardinia, thence raiding the Italian coast. This "unexpected and catastrophic" loss of Africa saw a massive threat to Italy's food supply (Africa had replaced Egypt as Rome's granary); Heather describes the Vandals as "looming directly over the jugular vein of the Western Empire". It also removed the West's last secure and productive tax base. Expeditions against the Vandals in Africa were planned in 440–1, 460 and 468, two of these three with Eastern assistance, owing to agitation by wealthy African émigrés in Constantinople. All failed completely.[30]

Unlike the Goths, Attila and his Huns had developed a siege engine capacity, enabling them to take fully defended first-rate Roman fortresses, for example, Viminacium and Naissus (Nish) – both in modern Serbia. In June 451 the Huns, having invaded Gaul via Metz and Orleans, were halted by Aetius with Roman, Visigothic (the Visigoth king was killed), Burgundian and Frankish forces near Troyes. With Tours in 732, this ranks as a "decisive battle" of western civilisation. It was the Huns' first major defeat. In 452 they invaded north Italy – capturing major cities such as Aquileia, which resisted and was completely destroyed, and others such as Verona, Pavia and Milan, which surrendered and were simply sacked. Further defeats by Aetius and disease, probably malaria, forced retreat. Attila died in 453; civil war followed between his sons, and by 469 we see survivors of the Huns seeking refuge inside the Eastern Roman Empire. We cannot imagine, or estimate, the human losses, alongside the devastation, but "the Huns' indirect role ... in having originally pushed many of the armed immigrants across the frontier, did far more harm than any damage directly inflicted by Attila."[31]

And the collapse of the Hunnic dominion enabled more Goths to move into Gaul and then Italy. Meanwhile, Emperor Valentinian III contrived Aetius' assassination in September 454. This marked the end of an era of provisional stability, with hints of recovery of both territory and status. After it, decline was swift, with a speedy turnover of emperors: several were capable but short-lived. Valentinian III was murdered in March 455 by Petronius Maximus, who was then killed in May 455 fleeing Rome from the Vandals after a reign of seventy days. Avitus followed and was deposed in 456, then dying in mysterious circumstances. Significantly, there were interregnums of several months between certain of these reigns, in 455, 461 and in 465–67.

The Vandal sacking of Rome in May 455 was far worse than Alaric's in 410: much treasure and many prisoners were taken away, including the widow of Valentinian III, her two daughters, and the surviving son of Aetius.[32] It provoked two very substantial expeditions against Vandal Africa, under two broadly supported, potentially competent emperors, who, if they had survived, might have brought recovery. Majorian (457–61) met with military successes in Gaul but his invasion armada of 300 ships, gathered in eastern Spanish ports, was raided and destroyed by Geiseric in summer 461. Majorian was deposed and then executed by Flavius Ricimer, another Romanised German, now *magister militum*. Ricimer remained dominant until 472, seeking to rule through puppet emperors, such as Libius Severus, who died in 465 and was succeeded after a seventeen-month interregnum by Anthemius in April 467. He was a general from the Eastern Empire, of "proven abilities and high pedigree", and thus obtained massive financial support from Constantinople in assembling another invasion armada for Africa, totalling 1100 ships of various sizes. In 468 after driving the Vandals out of Sardinia and occupying Sicily, this prepared to invade near Cape Bon. An attack by Vandal fireships led to complete defeat.[33]

In 467 the Empire was still functioning outside Italy: the Visigoths and Burgundians in southern Gaul accepted Anthemius' rule, and a substantial part of Spain, as well as Dalmatia and Noricum, still owed political allegiance to Rome. Halsall indicates the importance that the Vandal and Visigoth rulers attached to their links with the imperial regime.[34] "Eight years later, the bonds had dissolved." By 476 the Visigoths in Gaul had gained Arles and Marseilles, and now held all Spain except for a small Suevic enclave in the north-west. In these countries, former barbarian settlements had become kingdoms, with Roman landowners making their own compromise arrangements with the new masters. We read of *Bagaudae* in Gaul and Spain, variously seen as peasant rebels, bandits or even minor warlords.[35]

Anthemius had earlier successes in Gaul, but in 471 his son was defeated and killed there by the Visigoths. The loss of these troops "cut away the regime's last military prop" with Ricimer besieging Anthemius in Rome for several months. When the city fell in July 472, Anthemius was killed by Ricimer's nephew, Gundobad. Ricimer proclaimed Olybrius emperor; then Ricimer died of natural causes in August 472, followed by Olybrius in November. Gundobad chose Glycerius to be emperor in March 473, but Gundobad became Burgundian king and Glycerius was deposed by Julius Nepos in June 474. Nepos reigned briefly before being driven out to Dalmatia by one of his generals, Orestes. The latter proclaimed his young son Romulus Augustus emperor in October 475, intending, in tandem with his brother Paul, to rule through him. Goths had meanwhile been pouring into Italy and they demanded of Orestes one third of the land of Italy. Orestes refused: the soldiers mutinied under Odovacar who was proclaimed king on 23 August 476. Orestes fled to Piacenza, where in early September he and Paul were executed. Odovacar deposed Romulus and sent the imperial regalia and vestments to Constantinople indicating that the western imperial regime was at an end. In fact, Nepos still ruled in Dalmatia, but made no move on Italy, and was murdered in 480. Odovacar granted lands in Italy to his troops, in the absence of ready money to pay them.

The circumstances of 476 are dramatically, and despite its being fiction, probably realistically described in the opening chapters of Valerio Massimo Manfredi's *Last Legion* (Macmillan, 2003). It was less gentle than the change of government in Victorian times.

Some consequences of the Fall for western civilisation

Heather points out that most of the successor states were "effectively run by some kind of alliance between … Roman landowning elites and the emergent dynastic leaders" of barbarian forces. Whatever areas of order remained in the West, there was no single law-giving authority, no central tax structure and no centrally controlled army. The extent of disorder is indicated by slave raiding becoming "a grim feature of life on the frontiers". As he concludes: "Provincial Romanness (sic) survived in parts of the west after 476, but central Romanness was a thing of the past."[36]

This marks a turning point: while the Empire had seen numerous civil wars, usually between generals and usurpers, what came after 476 for almost fifteen hundred years was a state of frequent warfare between the various national groupings and tribes that followed the Empire. Civil society, human beings and physical infrastructure all suffered.

Several historians point out how few in number the invading barbarians were. Heather estimates that "around 110–120,000 armed outsiders played some part in bringing down the Western Empire". And, as Heather points out in the Roman context, "Any attempt to reconstruct fifth-century events brings home just how violent the process was."[37]

Impressed by the success of the Germans in the 19th century, some Victorians declared satisfaction that corrupt and degenerate rulers, and weak and decadent people, were replaced and strengthened respectively by sturdy Goths and other Germans. The Germanic rulers who followed 476 in the West were by no means free of corruption, and with some exceptions their contribution was to feud excessively with their families and neighbours, thereby ensuring relatively short lives and reigns. Halsall's narrative indicates the brutality of these contests: the losers were almost always "executed", usually along with their families and supporters. In the forty years in the first half of the 7th century, five of the six kings who ruled the East Angles died violently; a similar pattern is perceived in the Frankish kingdom.

The mixture of Germanic genes with existing Roman ones was, as indicated, on a very small scale so far as the Continent was concerned. In Britain, it is likely that many Romano-British were driven into Wales (hence the prevalence of Latinate sources for common Welsh words), as well as, until the 8th century, holding the south-west.

Did life improve under barbarian rule? The evidence available suggests not. While the new rulers were lightly scattered over places such as Italy, Gothic counts of the Goths had legal authority over Gothic inhabitants and the final say in any dispute between a Roman and a Goth. Under *Lex Salica* in Gaul the money due in compensation for the murder of a Roman was precisely half that due with respect to a Frank. The settlement of the barbarians did not, it is argued, in many areas involve great social upheaval – the Visigoths in the Garonne valley were never more than one-sixtieth of the overall population. Romans and barbarians adopted similar fashions of dress and self display – seeking mosaic floors in villas, and contriving to be buried in similar marble sarcophagi. Villas and town houses were built in Africa under Vandal rule, where Latin verse teaching and baths, theatres, and horse-racing continued. "An effective Goth wants to be like a Roman; only a poor Roman would want to be a Goth."[38]

The barbarians had become Christian: the Visigoths had converted in the days of Constantius II and Valens to what became known as Arianism, which diminished the divinity of Christ: "there was a time when He (Christ) was not." The Romans became Nicene (following the 325 Council of Nicaea which promulgated the Nicene Creed) and treated Arianism as a distinct heretical cult. Thus Roman subjects were readily identifiable as different from their adherence to Roman law and Catholic practice. Visigothic rule in Gaul was "at its most benign" but still alien. We see a sharp contrast in Italy, where after two important defeats by Justinian's armies in 552, and the support shown to these Byzantine invaders by Roman aristocracy, Goths killed Romans met during their retreat, especially Roman patricians in the cities of Campania.[39]

In the 1st and 2nd centuries Rome had a population of almost 1 million, Antioch and Alexandria around 300,000, and many other cities of the Greek East had populations of up to 100,000. Most towns in the Roman West had populations of up to 5000. By the year 600 "large areas of the hinterland of Italy, Gaul and Spain had closed in on themselves. Even in what had once been a highly urbanised region, such as Italy, city life had shrunk dramatically." In the 5th and 6th centuries the Roman cities "simply underwent a period of drastic 'abatement'". Within a century after 450, the population of Rome dropped from 500,000 to 50,000 and other western towns suffered similarly. While much of this might be attributed to the 6th century bubonic plague and Justinian's warfare, we see in contrast, Constantinople surged towards the half million "possibly the largest human settlement west of China."[40]

Even Halsall, who seems anxious to diminish the incidence of violence and destruction, sees many public buildings in towns in Africa and Italy becoming derelict and the abandonment of *fora*, as public spaces, which "must imply the decline of the towns' importance as centres of municipal government". Venning points out that buildings collapsed over decades from lack of maintenance rather than instant Germanic destruction.[41] Northern Gaul sees "much more serious decline", where the Roman social order "broke down", with some towns "abandoned". In rural Gaul "there was decay and abandonment, and the occupation of other types of site, not least caves and defended hilltop settlements." Halsall agrees with others in acknowledging that Britain "undoubtedly experienced the most drastic change".[42]

Similar in certain respects to the Afro-Asian migrants pressing into Europe in the early 21st century, "these Goths on entering the empire left their homelands for good. They were ... refugees, immigrants, allies and conquerors ... What the Goths sought was ... a share of (the empire's) wealth ... and many of their violent acts began as efforts to persuade the imperial authorities to improve the terms of agreement between them."[43] Many negotiated settlements were arranged by which the barbarians occupied land, but frequently they took what they wanted by force. While some contemporaries exaggerated the anarchy, "there is good reason to believe ... that it was those who sought to downplay violence, warfare and destruction who were the most guilty of abusing and distorting reality." Referring to Gaul and Spain in the early 5th century, Sarris adds, "The violence and destruction associated with these military events should not be underestimated." Ward-Perkins rejects what he describes as the "fashionable" idea that the Western Empire did not fall but instead experienced a mostly-benign transformation into the medieval Christian kingdoms. He asserts "the coming of the Germanic peoples was very unpleasant for the Roman population, and the long-term effects of the dissolution of the empire were dramatic."[44]

The balance of power shifted against Roman authority: after 440 we read no more of negotiated land settlements anywhere outside Italy. South of the Loire local Roman landowners made accommodations with the new rulers, who required them to give up more or less of their land: the Burgundian kingdom seems to have enforced more large-scale confiscation than the more prosperous Visigothic one. The granting to some Alans of lands in northern Gaul in 442 by Aetius was resisted in vain by the local inhabitants.[45]

In his slightly earlier Cambridge history, Ward Perkins emphasises the paucity and occasionally contradictory evidence regarding settlement, agricultural practices, landownership and population in the 5th to 7th centuries. There are even problems with archaeology: "post Roman people can easily escape surface detection." While he calls for caution before asserting post-Roman demographic collapse, he adds: "On balance, I believe that the population did drop – perhaps even drastically (ie to half or even less) of its previous Roman levels."[46]

Consequences for land ownership, religion and culture were long term: the most immediate effect on the Empire in the early 5th century was on its tax revenue, needed to maintain a large standing army for defensive purposes. The fall in revenue arose out of devastation as well as the loss of land to the barbarians. In 412 Emperor Honorius told the Praetorian Prefect of Italy to reduce to one-fifth, that is, by 80 per cent, the customary amount of taxes required from most of central and southern Italy; this rebate lasted for five years and had to be renewed in 418. This and losses elsewhere greatly reduced the income of the Western Empire. The West's army had also suffered heavy personnel losses in the early 5th century: the key document *Notitia Dignitatum* shows that between 395 and the 420s the western field army lost almost half its regiments. A later study by Heather suggests two-thirds "had been ground to dust … An army thrives on continuity, and losses on this scale would have considerably reduced the overall efficiency of the entire western military establishment."[47]

The consequences of invasions, devastation, abandonment of land, and diminution of armed forces had dramatic consequences for security, living standards and other essentials of civilisation. Levels of economic sophistication, complexity in manufacture and agriculture, and urbanism, existing under the Empire and now disappearing, would not be seen again until perhaps the 17th century. Parts of the Roman West "entered into a period of stark and rapid economic decline, perhaps unprecedented in recorded human history."[48] Large scale growing of cereal crops to feed settled populations disappeared – farmers became pastoralists, relying on the possession of sheep and cattle that could be moved to escape invaders.

Ward Perkins writes of a "startling decline" in western standards of living during the 5th to 7th centuries. He cites archaeological evidence, from tableware, amphoras and tiled roofs, for the middle and lower markets as well as the luxury market. Referring particularly to central and northern Italy, he states that after the end of the Roman world, the level of manufacturing sophistication was not seen again until at least the 14th century. While the evidence for pottery survives for the archaeologist to inspect, he believes the same "is almost certainly true of other goods," including perishable materials, such as cloth, wood, leather, basket work and metal. The evidence of pollution in the Arctic ice cap resulting from the smelting of metals, he says, was very high during the Roman period, falling back in the post Roman centuries "to levels that are much closer to those of prehistoric times". They did not recover to Roman levels until the 16th and 17th centuries. "There is no area of the post-Roman West that I know of where the range of pottery available in the sixth and seventh centuries matches that of the Roman period, and in most areas the decline in quality is startling." The same applies in respect of diversity and quantity.[49]

In Italy Roman domestic building was of stone and brick; after the 5th century, it was replaced by buildings almost entirely of wood. As for solid walls, marble and mosaic floors, under-floor heating and piped water, after the 4th century only kings and bishops lived in such luxury. Ward Perkins adds: "The ancient Romans built things on a scale and with a technical expertise that could only be dreamed of for centuries after the fall of the empire." Early medieval churches' columns, bases and capitals saw ancient marbles used without any re-carving. Referring to the new churches of post Roman Italy – "what is immediately striking about them is how small they are." In the 5th and 6th centuries, tiles, previously very commonly used, disappeared from all except buildings for the elite. Early medieval flooring, apart from that in palaces and the best churches, was beaten earth.[50]

Coinage began to disappear from daily use in the post Roman world. Apart from Britain, where new coins ceased arriving from the start of the 5th century, the decline of coinage was less sudden, but copper coinages in the West disappeared in the 6th century. During the 7th century new copper coins were minted only in areas ruled by the East Romans: Ravenna, Rome and Sicily. Local issues of copper coins occurred in areas where we suppose that a "somewhat more sophisticated economy survived" – south-west Spain, Marseilles and Rome. "Their absence elsewhere must be symptomatic of a western economy that had changed dramatically since Roman times."[51]

Archaeological surveys in western Europe have found far fewer rural sites of the 5th, 6th and 7th centuries than in the earlier Roman empire, but also evidence that urban populations had decreased dramatically. People were not fleeing from the countryside into the cities. "At first sight this evidence seems to point clearly … to a *massive* [italics in original] drop in population in the post-Roman centuries, to half or perhaps even a quarter of Roman levels." Other evidence includes the fact that stock animals in the West appeared to carry more meat in Roman times. And a critical judgement on literacy and writing is indicated by the fact that, for the first time with Justin (in the East) in 518, was the Empire ruled by someone described as not being able to read or write.[52]

While the evidence about Britain in the three centuries after the Romans left in 410 is even less satisfactory – with an absence of reliable contemporary chronicles – it is clear from archaeology that Britain suffered more than the remainder of the West. "The essential point" is that on the Continent the structure of Roman civil life remained: "in Britain it did not." A sad paradox is that the surviving Romano-British population in the western half of the island, trading in "prestigious commodities" from the Mediterranean – with Mediterranean pottery found "in high-status sites around the Irish Sea (especially around the Severn Estuary) in the fifth and sixth centuries"[53] probably suffered thereby more from the mid-6th century plague than the more isolated Saxons.

Buried treasures in East Anglia, for example at Hoxne, "speak of the sudden loss of an imperial order": 14,600 gold and silver coins were found stowed away in wooden chests, with other evidence of "the hasty departure of a *vir militaris* of the old style". Brown adds "Once the great Roman machine for taxing and circulating wealth" declined and disappeared "the economy of the entire island of Britain (and, one suspects, of other areas of western Europe) ... slipped back into conditions more brutally simplified even than the Iron Age societies which had preceded the coming of the Romans."[54]

Another estimate is that within the region that became the focus of Germanic settlement – the eastern half of England – the Romano-British population "could have been about two million at the end of the 3rd century, declining to about one million by the middle of the 5th century." The Anglo-Saxons had no use for Roman villas and towns: "the hubs of Romano-British organisation were simply left to rot." Even London was eclipsed until the 9th century.[55] Peter Heather again cites estimates of between 5 and 7 million for the population of all 4th century Roman Britain.[56] The dramatic decline to 1 million is consistent with estimates of 1.5–2.2 million for the 1086 Domesday population of England. This recent study also describes changes in farming, shifting from beef and wheat to feed the towns to mere subsistence.[57]

Heather adds that later Anglo-Saxon migrants certainly included women and children, hence the change in language as women would have ensured the teaching of their own tongue. He also argues that land drainage diminished and a smaller "scratch" plough replaced the heavier Roman plough. Furthermore, Gildas' image of violence and terror was "unlikely to have been pure imagination" and that many of the indigenous British became slaves or semi-free. Some nuancing of this, arguing against the idea that the Romano-British were wiped out or driven out, has come from a further study (*UnRoman Britain*) which points out that the pre-Roman Celtic language contained many Germanic words and that Germanic place names became frequent in Devon, despite it being held by the Romano-British until the 7th century; the Romanised aristocracy in the West continued the Latin language and adherence to Christianity.[58]

Another author concludes that "the structures of the Roman state – taxation, currency, literacy – were gone, urbanism was dead." For example, in London, the contrast between quantities of 4th century pottery and coins and "the handful" of early Anglo-Saxon finds "could not be more striking". This author adds "It seems difficult to avoid the conclusion that towns had ceased to exist by, or during, the fifth century."[59]

It is fair to mention alternative suggestions relating to Britain. New discoveries and analysis show that Roman silver and low value bronze coins continued to circulate in Britain in the 5th and 6th centuries, and that there were small scale imports of gold coins especially from Gaul; though the role of coins in commerce diminished. Continuity in the economic function of some villa estates, once believed to have been abandoned, "is also now more widely recognised". While many villa buildings fell into ruin, others were subdivided, converted into storage or other uses, or replaced by wooden aisled halls. Evidence also suggests that small-scale settlement persisted in many Roman towns into the 6th century and beyond. And recent studies emphasise that "no British town or fort of the late fourth or early fifth century has yielded any proof of having been comprehensively razed."[60]

The Anglo-Saxon conquest had an impact on the pattern of Christian life established after the conversion of Constantine. British Christianity began early, with St Alban being martyred shortly after 200. It appears to have been flourishing during the early 5th century. However, while a number of memorials recording the names of individuals "who must ... have belonged to a landed Christian elite, are found across western and northern Britain," none are earlier than the end of the Western Empire: "it seems that by the end of the 5th century an active diocesan church had ceased to function in the heartlands of the former province." While Christian congregations and "perhaps private cenobitic institutions" might have survived, "archaeologists have so far failed to track them down".[61]

During the barbarian occupation of Western Europe (as distinct from during invasions), there was some violence and intolerance, particularly from Vandals in Africa, directed at the Catholic clergy, with bishops, priests and Roman aristocrats killed. This became especially sharp under King Huneric in 484.[62] In Spain, Visigothic oppression and severe famines, which almost halved the population, facilitated the Arab conquest of the early 8th century. In Italy, Theoderic (died

526) owed his throne to Gothic followers who welcomed his supporting the Arian church and hence the use of Gothic liturgy and language. Theoderic's sensitivity to communications between members of the Roman Senate and the Eastern Emperor is shown by his suspecting plots against him by those renowned officials who were also philosophers: thus Boethius and his father-in-law Symmachus were executed in 524 and 526.

Author of *The Consolation of Philosophy* and many other works, Boethius had embarked upon an ambitious but unfinished project to translate all the Greek texts necessary for the study of the classics. Education and scholarship generally were undoubtedly victims of the barbarian conquests. The recent historian Violet Moller stated that the Lombard invasion of 568 "sounded the death knell for traditional education in Italy" (which, she acknowledges, had only ever been available to a small minority of wealthy male children). Book production "dwindled across the Mediterranean during the fourth and fifth centuries". Commercial book production continued in large cities such as Rome, but on a much smaller scale than previously. By 500, "secular book production had effectively gone underground" while the output of monasteries "grew dramatically" to meet the demand for new religious literature, such as hagiography (the stories of saints' lives). Public libraries were also a casualty: "with no-one paying for their upkeep, they fell into disuse and decayed."[63]

The records tell of some survival of the old ways – in Africa! A Roman-style town council, recording inscriptions in Latin, survived at Volubilis in western Morocco until the 650s. Some Moorish kings adopted Latin names. As late as the 11th century the inhabitants of Gafsa in Tunisia spoke what they called Latin.[64] North Africa as a whole retained and spoke Latin throughout both the Vandal and later Byzantine occupations, and only lost it after the Islamic conquest in the 7th century. "No African-Romance tongue (such as the Gallo-Romance we call French) survived."[65] And this same historian regards as "unknowable" the extent to which "the disruption of traditional loyalties and hierarchies" by the "putsch" against the Donatists – a sect regarded as schismatic by the Church – weakened the powers of resistance of African Christianity against the Muslims in the late 7th century, when "the last native Christian dominance was washed quickly away."[66]

Efforts to revive the Western Empire after 476

There was more than one attempt after 476 to create an entity resembling the Empire. Whether Theoderic, an Ostrogoth, might be considered a suitable successor to the Caesars is for erudite debate – many Roman emperors had had provincial and even barbarian blood. In fact, Theoderic did not succeed in establishing a dynasty, but he made a bold effort. Initially he had ambitions in the Eastern Empire, which did not prevent him from devastating Macedonia in 479 and Thessaly in 482. He was then persuaded to lead his people from the Balkans into Italy. He overthrew Odovacar, who was killed with his family and chief supporters. Theoderic ruled in Rome and Ravenna from 493 to 526, starting with just the Italian mainland and greater Dalmatia. By 511 he had added southern France and Spain, except the north-west corner of the latter, but he also had hegemony over the Vandal kingdom of Africa and the Mediterranean islands, the Burgundian kingdom (upper Rhone and Savoy) and the Bavarians and Thuringians in central and north Germany. By 511 he was directing the affairs of between a third and a half of the old Western Empire.

What went wrong then? We see Theoderic's good relationship with Roman landowners and the Roman church ending in the 520s. The failure of his empire to survive him lay not only in the weakness of his control of his most recent annexations but in a fierce dispute over the succession. The Eastern Empire did not recognise his choice of his grandson Athalaric as successor. When he died, in 526, Athalaric was only eight or ten, so his mother Amalasuentha assumed the regency. When Athalaric died in October 534 Amalasuentha made her cousin Theodahad co-ruler, but he obligingly murdered her in her bath tub. While the nature of her demise appears definite, the timing is less so, but she was certainly dead by the spring of 535.

Then followed the sustained campaign, under the Eastern Emperor Justinian (527–65), absorbing most of his reign and much of his resources, to regain the West. Recent historians do not see it as a concerted programme – one thing led to another. It was mainly conducted by his outstanding general, Belisarius. As an indication of the resources available, the budget of the Eastern Empire was 8.5 million gold pieces. The Emperor Anastasius, who died in 518, left 320,000 pounds of gold – 23 million gold pieces – in the treasuries. "No state west of China could mobilise such sums on a regular basis."[67]

Prompted by succession struggles and revolts among the Vandals – thus unlike the attempts in the 5th century – Belisarius' invasion of Africa in 533 was a complete success. The Vandal fleet and elite force had been sent to crush a revolt in Sardinia. One benefit was the recapture of the treasures of the Jerusalem Temple, taken by Titus to Rome in the 70s and looted by the Vandals when they sacked Rome.[68] However, fighting against Moorish tribes and occasionally mutinous Roman forces continued for 15 years, with the once prosperous province being badly ravaged.[69] After an almost bloodless occupation of Sicily in 535, and equally prompted by dissent among the Goths, in 536 Belisarius landed in southern Italy and besieged Naples. It fell, to a brutal sack. Theodahad's supporters deposed and executed him late in 536.

This Italian war proved to be of long duration, partly because Constantinople did not send enough troops: the initial force sent in 535 consisted of around 7500 men. Attempts at various points to negotiate dominion for Justinian all failed. The new Gothic king Wittigis put up a good resistance, besieging Rome. He seems to have perceived the global dimension: in 539 he sent an embassy to Ctesiphon with the message "It is clear that, if he (ie Justinian) can destroy utterly also the Goths, he will march against the Persians together with us and (the Vandals) whom he has enslaved already …"[70] So Khusro I, the Persian king, attacked. Ignoring the Roman fortresses in Mesopotamia, with Roman frontier forces diverted to the West, he took Aleppo and then in June 540 Antioch, the second city of the East, which was destroyed, and the surviving population taken captive. It was "an utter disaster, one that must be reckoned a further, if indirect, cost of Justinian's western adventurism".[71]

In 540 Belisarius, with additional forces, beats the Goths, and besieges and then imprisons Wittigis in Ravenna. Another Goth leaps forward: by the end of 541, after murdering his rivals, Totila revives the Gothic revolt and, with many Roman troops now having gone east to counter the Persians, conquers Rome, Naples and southern Italy and executes many of the Roman senatorial order.[72] Belisarius returns, again with insufficient forces, so recapturing Rome took him until April 547. He is then recalled; the token of his skill is the collapse of Byzantine power when he leaves Italy. Totila besieges Rome a second time in the summer of 549: it falls to him in early 550, with the civilian population having deserted it. The Goths raid the coasts of Dalmatia, Corfu and Epirus, and take Sicily. So Justinian makes peace with Persia in 551, and sends Narses with 35,000 extra troops; he routs the Goths and kills Totila at Busta Gallorum/Taginae near Ravenna in 552. Destroyed as a coherent mass, the Goths make an armistice; in 553–55 Narses defeats Gothic remnants and their Frankish allies. By 560 there is imperial control in Liguria and most of Venetia, and Gothic survivors are finally defeated at Brescia and Verona in 561–62.

The wars in Africa and, more particularly, Italy destroyed the Vandal-Alan and Gothic political elites around which successor states had been built. In Spain a rising against the Goths was led by Athangild from Seville; he requested aid from Justinian. A successful Byzantine invasion took place in 552, with widespread support from the Hispano-Roman aristocracy. Thus a new province, consisting of a line of ports along the south coast of Spain centred on Cartagena, with their hinterland, passed to Constantinople's control.

From 540 to 628, as narrated in the next chapter, the "running ulcer of war with Persia" absorbed the attention of the Eastern Roman Empire. Justinian never visited Italy to "deploy and redeploy patronage in a similar way to his fourth century predecessors", and there was, subsequently, no unified Roman command there.⁷³ Thus in 568 there came the swift loss of north Italy to the Lombards who had been driven out of the mid-Danube area in 568 by the Avars. The Lombards occupied, first, the Po valley and then, via their central upland duchies Spoleto and Benevento, the Apennines. Only the coasts of Ravenna, Rome, and the plains of south Italy and Sicily remained to the Empire. Could Eastern Roman rule in Italy have been consolidated without the Lombard invasion? As it was, the Byzantine-held parts were ruled directly from Constantinople until the 8th century, Carthage remained an imperial city until 698, Ravenna until 751, and the Popes remained subjects of the Eastern Roman emperors. Until 800, every papal document sent to western bishops and western kings was dated by the regnal year of the emperor in Constantinople.

In Africa, the hinterland of Carthage prospered, but the province's earlier wealth depended on its links with western Mediterranean trade under the Empire. However, having assessed the archaeological evidence, Heather concludes that "everything indicates that the North African prefecture quickly became a well-integrated contributor to the life of the empire". In the Balkans, however, the Roman population "certainly suffered greater damage because of the war in Italy" at the hands of Slavic invaders.⁷⁴

The consequences for Italy were more grave. A "generation's worth of large-scale warfare punctuated by bouts of occasionally intense violence must have led to huge losses for the population". Northern Italy "completely failed to recover", and "the admittedly incomplete settlement evidence is highly suggestive of considerable population decline". However, the pattern in those areas that remained under Byzantine control "is markedly different", with southern Italy retaining commercial pottery industries selling over wide areas. It was "probably richer than any other part of the old Roman west in the seventh and early eighth centuries"⁷⁵

Alongside all this, there had been natural disasters. In the late 530s extreme climatic instability included a period in 536–7 when the sun's rays were blocked partially by heavy particles, probably after a volcanic eruption in East Asia. Temperatures fell worldwide with consequences for crops, and possibly for rat migrations in Africa. Possibly as a result of this latter, the ravages of bubonic plague between 542–70 "emptied the coastline of the western Mediterranean". It "burned out the heart of the maritime world on which the military exploits of Justinian had depended and crippled the provisioning of the cities of his empire".⁷⁶

Apart from Charlemagne's brief success, in Dominic Lieven's view "no true empires existed in Latin Europe from the collapse of the western Roman Empire … until the reign of Charles V in the early sixteenth century". And Sultan

Suleyman the Magnificent "would never address Charles V as emperor because he considered himself to be the sole heir to the Roman imperial tradition" as ruler of Constantinople.[77]

Meanwhile, a millennium earlier, Justinian's "over-reach" led to Byzantine weakness and decline, and what we may term the "crisis of the 7th century".

FOOTNOTES

1 Adrian Goldsworthy, *Pax Romana: War, Peace and Conquest in the Roman World*, Weidenfeld and Nicolson, 2017, p411.
2 *Ibid*, pp290, 296.
3 Bryan Ward Perkins, *The Fall of Rome and the End of Civilisation*, OUP 2005, p176; Goldsworthy, *op cit*, pp11, 405.
4 Nicholson, *op cit*, pp13–5, and Chapters Two and Five.
5 Venning, *op cit*, p58.
6 "Barbarians" are fiercely described by Judith Herrin *Byzantium: The Surprising Life of a Medieval Empire*, Allen Lane, 2007, p23: "With no written language, no coinage, no law or recognisable system of government".
7 Heather, *Fall*, p66.
8 Guy Halsall. *Barbarian Migrations and the Roman West 376–568*, CUP, 2007, hereafter Halsall, *Migrations*, p111.
9 Peter Brown *The Rise of Western Christendom*, 2003, p106; Heather, *Fall*, p113 and footnote 17 for Britain; Ward Perkins, *Cambridge Ancient History, vol xiv, Later Antiquity: Empire and Successors 425–600*, CUP 2000, hereafter *"Cambridge"* pp315–19; Max Adams *The First Kingdom: Britain in the Age of Arthur*, Head of Zeus, 2021, p21.
10 Heather, *Fall*, pp48, 97.
11 *Ibid*, *Fall*, pp87, 97.
12 Brown, *op cit*, p102; Heather, *Fall*, p182.
13 Sarris, *op cit*, p 45; also Heather, *Fall*, p247.
14 Heather, *Fall*, pp456, 458.
15 Brown, *op cit*, p57. For tax evasion, see Peter Sarris, in *The Oxford History of Byzantium*, edited by Cyril Mango OUP, 2002, pp38, 40, 45. All other references to Sarris are to *Empires of Faith*.
16 Heather, *Rome Resurgent: War and Empire in the Age of Justinian*, OUP, 2018, hereafter *Resurgent*, p60.
17 Heather, *Fall*, ppxii, 239, 283, 337.
18 Heather, *Race, Migration and National Origins*, in *History, Memory and Public Life*, Routledge, 2018, pp93–94.
19 Halsall blog in 2011; Halsall "Two Worlds Become One: A Counter-Intuitive View of the Roman Empire and Germanic Migration", in *German History*, vol 32(4), OUP 2014, pp515–32.
20 Halsall, *Migrations*, p19.
21 *Ibid*, p420.
22 Heather, *Christendom: The Triumph of a Religion*, Allen Lane 2022, hereafter *Christendom*, p168; Halsall, *Migrations*, p176.
23 Heather, *Fall*, p145; Sarris *op cit*, p34.
24 Heather, *Fall*, pp180, 190.
25 Halsall, *Migrations*, pp209, 215, 224.
26 *Ibid*, pp204, 206, 436.
27 Ward Perkins, *op cit*, p57.
28 Heather, *Fall*, pp256–57.
29 *Ibid*, pp281–82.
30 Brown, *op cit*, p60; Heather, *Fall*, p272, 275, 296.
31 Heather, *Fall*, p348.
32 *Ibid*, p379.
33 *Ibid* pp392, 398–99, 403–06.
34 Halsall, *Migrations*, chapters 8 and 9.
35 Heather, *Fall*, pp394, 416–17, 433; Halsall, *Migrations*, p218.
36 Heather, *Fall* p432; Heather *Christendom*, p166.
37 Heather, *Fall* pp436, 446.
38 Sarris, *op cit*, p71, Heather, *Christendom*,

pp165–66; final quote, Brown, *op cit*, p103.
39 Ward Perkins, *op cit*, pp76–7.
40 Brown, *op cit*, pp12, 21.
41 Venning, *op cit*, p33.
42 Halsall, *Migrations*, pp322, 329, 347, 348, 354, 357.
43 Ward Perkins, *op cit*, p52.
44 Sarris, *op cit*, pp37, 48; Ward Perkins, *op cit*, p10.
45 Ward Perkins, *op cit*, p55.
46 Ward Perkins, *Cambridge*, pp324–27.
47 Heather *Fall* pp247–8, 298; Heather *Christendom*, p170.
48 Sarris, *op cit*, p75.
49 Ward Perkins, *op cit*, pp87, 94–5, 106.
50 *Ibid*, pp3, 109, 148–9.
51 *Ibid* pp112, 117.
52 *Ibid*, pp139, 169.
53 Halsall, *Migrations*, pp363, 378.
54 Brown, *op cit*, p126.
55 Population estimate by Heinriche Harke quoted by Jean Manco *The Origins of the Anglo-Saxons*, Thames and Hudson, 2018, p124; other reference, Manco, p126.
56 Heather, *Empires and Barbarians: Migration, Development and the Birth of Europe*, Macmillan, 2009, hereafter *Barbarians*, p269.
57 Stephen Rippon, Chris Smart and Ben Pears, *The Fields of Britannia: Continuity and Change in the Late Roman and Early Medieval Landscape*, OUP, 2015, pp324, 337.
58 Heather, *Barbarians*, pp293, 296, 301, 304; Miles Russell and Stuart Laycock, *UnRoman Britain: Exposing the Great Myth of Britannia*, The History Press, 2010, pp199–200, 219–225.
59 James Gerrard, *The Ruin of Roman Britain*, CUP, 2013, pp73, 78–9, p163.
60 Susan Oosthuizen, *The Emergence of the English*, Arc Humanities Press, 2019, pp32–3, 35–6, 42–3, 77, and figure on p45; Adams, *op cit*, p55.
61 Adams, *op cit*, p334.
62 Heather, *The Restoration of Rome*, Macmillan, 2013, hereafter *Restoration* p138; Sarris, *op cit*, p91.
63 Moller, *op cit*, pp21, 24.
64 Brown, *op cit*, pp157, 138, 232.
65 James O'Donnell, *Augustine, Sinner and Saint* Profile Books, 2005, pp115, 117.
66 *Ibid* p224.
67 Brown, *op cit*, p177.
68 Heather, *Resurgent*, p147.
69 Halsall, *Migrations*, pp500–01; Heather, *Resurgent*, pp237–51.
70 Quoted in Heather, *Restoration*, p159.
71 Heather, *Resurgent*, p220.
72 Halsall, *Migrations*, p504.
73 *Ibid*, p515.
74 Heather, *Resurgent*, p276, 283.
75 *Ibid*, pp296–97.
76 Brown, *op cit*, pp155, 181.
77 Lieven, *Shadow*, pp180, 215.

The Eastern Frontier.

Chapter Two:
The Resistance of the Eastern Empire

"Persia is (only a matter of) one or two thrusts and no Persia will be after that. But the Rum (East Romans) … are people of sea and rock … Alas, they are your enemies to the end of time." (The Prophet Muhammed, *hadith* or saying, quoted Brown, *op cit*, p297)

"Were it not for that great oriental bastion of Christendom, what chance would Europe have had against the armies of the King of Persia in the 7th century, or those of the Caliph of Baghdad in the 8th? What language would we be speaking today, and what god would we worship?" (John Julius Norwich, *Byzantium:I The Early Centuries*, p27)

"Now the spider is chamberlain in Caesar's palace/And the owl hoots the watch on the towers of Afrasiab." (Sa'adi, Persian poet c1210–1291; lines recited by Sultan Mehmet II as he occupied the deserted imperial palace on 30 May 1453, the day after the fall of Constantinople.[1])

Overview

Perhaps the most important contrast between the history of the Eastern Empire, in this chapter, and the fall of the Western Empire, in the previous one, would come under the heading of "consequences". Today we assume – and evidence was given to support this – that life under the Roman Empire in the West, at least before its last few decades, was better than in its successor states. In the case of the East, the main enemies were very advanced civilisations – Sasanid Persia and the Umayyad and then the Abbasid caliphates. It is almost certainly the case, however, that the Byzantine Empire was, as John Julius Norwich states in the quotation at the head of this chapter, a barrier to the Persians or the caliphate overrunning post-Roman western Europe. And from the 7th century almost to the end, the Byzantines played a key role in denying to various Muslims dominion and occupation over what we now know as Turkey – the expanses of Asia Minor then featuring Graeco-Roman culture and Christianity, alongside a mixed population supporting that culture and religion, which St Paul's "missionary journeys" had traversed and which might have remained within European Christendom.

Would the Persians or the caliphate have found it easy to secure control of western Europe? As we shall see in this chapter, the military power of each was formidable. In addition to large armies, both had formidable navies and large numbers of war engines – facilities not, it seems, available to the barbarians of the West. As Judith Herrin suggests, "the broad swathe of the early Muslim conquests would have been replicated throughout the Balkans and further west, where the Slavonic and Germanic peoples would not have been able to resist."[2]

Such an overrunning would not, as clearly seen in the case of Spain, have diminished the quality of life or civilisation in the West: it might well have enhanced it. But as implied in the Norwich quotation, it would have dramatically changed the religion and culture of the West. Assuming that such changes became permanent – although the example of Spain indicates no permanence – they could have had quite dramatic effects on the history of Europe and the wider world. These effects would have been strongly marked in the centuries after 1300, preventing or delaying what Bernard Lewis describes as "a Western upsurge": external maritime exploration and trade, internal economic development leading to the technological and industrial revolutions, scientific developments, all cultural aspects of the Renaissance, and political and institutional development. It is significant that, after 1300, the West advanced by leaps and bounds in all these respects, whereas the Islamic world stood still.

The crisis over recent centuries in the Islamic world has been examined by various scholars, notably by Bernard Lewis. He asks why the discoveries, the scientific breakthrough and the rest, did not occur "in the richer, more advanced, and in most respects more enlightened world of Islam". He does not find a convincing answer, but points out that Islam, centred on the Middle East and using the Silk Road to China, had no use for seaborne discoveries which would work much to the detriment of Middle Eastern prosperity. He criticises closed minds in Islam: the failure to translate, especially in the 16th to 18th centuries, classical Greek poetry, drama, philosophy, even non-Muslim or pre-Muslim history, and adds "in the course of the twentieth century it became abundantly clear that … compared with … Christendom, the world of Islam had become poor, weak and ignorant". Modernising attempts had been "disappointing"; updated armies were defeated; "impoverished and corrupt economies" needed external aid or "an unhealthy dependence on … fossil fuels". Phrases such as "a string of shabby tyrannies" leap up.[3s]

After listing the modern bogeys cited by Islamic apologists (Western imperialism, including US power, the Jews and Palestine), Lewis might be nearer the truth in targeting the Mongol invasions for their "destruction of Muslim power and Islamic civilisation". He explains that the Mongols overthrew an empire that was already fatally weakened. The political power of the Abbasid caliphate was seriously declining by the 11th century when, divided between warlord families and tribes, it was overcome by the Mongols' barbaric precursors, the Seljuk Turks. The Great Seljuk Empire reached its zenith under Malik Shah (1072–92), extending from Anatolia and Syria to Samarkand and Afghanistan.

While, as we shall see, Seljuk techniques of invasion and conquest were barbaric, under Persian influence they became patrons of literature and learning, and museums display their artistic achievements. A modern comprehensive study is in A C S Peacock's *The Great Seljuq Empire.* (Edinburgh University Press, 2015)

The caliphate was remarkable in its earlier centuries, embracing the lands from "the Indus to Spain" under one religion, one ruler, a common currency (*dinar* and *dirhams*), and greatly developed trade. It had few internal frontiers and usually tolerated the "People of the Book" (ie Christians and Jews), who had to pay the *jizya*.

The Byzantine Empire retained Roman multi-nationalism. Even after the loss of the Levant, in the 7th century, Constantinople governed Italians, many still Greek-speaking, various Balkan Slav nationalities, Greeks, the various peoples of Anatolia, Armenians and at times parts of Mesopotamia and Syria. After recognising the achievements of the caliphate at its zenith, this study has not examined in detail the effect of the invasion by the Seljuks and other Turks on Asia Minor as they gradually occupied it. Only in the 20th century, it seems, did the area regain the relative prosperity and stability of the first centuries AD.

While acknowledging the brilliance of Byzantine art and culture (subject to the removal of most artistic evidence before the mid-9th century by iconoclasm), the bravery and skill of Byzantine military and naval forces, and the devotion of most of the population to Orthodox Christianity, it must be admitted that the ruling elite were for much of the time exceedingly unpleasant. Treachery and rebellion, often for spurious reasons, were endemic, and as a result, a large number of emperors were murdered, sometimes without clear proof owing to the administration of poison. Of the 39 emperors ruling between 780 and 1204, 19 were forcibly deposed, six through outright murder with another two dying through blinding, plus foul play suspected in three other deaths.[4] Many emperors, pretenders and suspected claimants who survived, were maimed by being blinded; to rule, an emperor had to be physically whole. Male children of deposed emperors and claimants usually suffered one or other of these fates. And even a "hero" emperor who served the Empire well in the military field, such as John Tzimisces in 969, came to the throne by a coup in which he himself murdered his equally "heroic" predecessor, Nicephorus Phocas.

We modernists, used to the more civilised processes of succession in Western Europe over the last 700 years or so, might ask "why were these people so horrible?" They are similar to many rulers of the Roman Empire and the caliphates (the Abbasids were anxious to exterminate every last one of the Umayyad dynasty). The same is true of the barbarians. And the Ottoman Turks only ensured an orderly succession by decreeing (until quite late on) that each succeeding Sultan should immediately have all his brothers strangled. So perhaps the conclusion is that, in the circumstances, it all seemed normal and necessary.

The East was fortunate in the 5th century, diverting the Germanic tribes and Huns which assailed the West. The 6th century saw the East regaining large parts of the Western Empire: Italy, the Africa province and south-east Spain. Subsequently, the East had to fight off Avars, then Slavs, mainly Bulgars but sometimes "Rus" or Russians, as well as Lombards or Normans in Italy. Slav invasions of the Balkans, and the loss of key fortresses such as Sirmium and Singidunum (the site of the *kalemegdan* in Belgrade), in 582–84 deprived the Empire of "this invaluable centre of troops, supplies and tax revenue".[5] All the time they faced a hugely powerful enemy further east – Persia until the 620s, the caliphate until the 11th century, Seljuk Turks from the 11th to the 13th century, other Turkish tribes and finally the Ottomans, who having surrounded the small area ruled by Constantinople, brought this relic of Empire to an end in 1453.

We see a pattern emerge: the dominion of the Eastern Empire reaches a peak, and then faces a crisis which threatens its existence. Almost miraculously, it surmounts the crisis, builds up to another peak, and then comes another crisis. The various descents into crisis usually coincide with poor leadership by weak emperors, one often swiftly succeeding another. The surmounting and recovery are usually, though not always, handled by able emperors or better still, able dynasties.

The crises were: the Persian threat in 600–20, the Arab invasions starting almost immediately after, continuing to be a major threat until steady recovery in the 9th and 10th centuries; the invasions by the Seljuks and the aftermath of the disastrous defeat at Manzikert in 1071, handled, with some territorial recovery, by the Comnenus dynasty; the treacherous Fourth Crusade of 1204 and the near extinction of Byzantine rule, followed by a frail recovery and the final mainly cultural blossoming until the end.

And, inevitably, the territory and actual strength of the Empire after each recovery is less than at the time of the previous recovery.

"The last Great war of antiquity"

Howard-Johnston's description rings true: not since the Carthaginian wars had such a titanic international contest taken place, with so much at stake. How did the two powers compare?

Like the Romans, the Persians were also vulnerable to attack from the north. So in the late 4th century the Persians repaired relations with Rome in order to repulse the Hunnic challenge. Meanwhile emperor Theodosius II (408–50) devoted vast sums to the defence of Constantinople, building and repairing the land walls.

Persia became more powerful during the 6th century. The King taxed more – Persia experienced a similarly rapid fiscal, monetary and bureaucratic expansion as Rome had under Diocletian and Constantine. After 550 the power of the Huns collapsed, so the Persians were able to concentrate on the Roman frontier. Thus the Eastern Empire suffered the deportation of the entire population of Antioch in 540 and that of Apamea in 573. Thousands of Christian slaves were settled in new towns and villages in Mesopotamia which saw large state-sponsored schemes of development and irrigation (including trunk canals which doubled as commercial waterways); the area became an economic powerhouse. Not only slaves came from the West: after Justinian closed the Athens Academy, the pagan philosophers fled to Persia.[6] And dissident Christians from the West, such as the Nestorians, often found a refuge there.

Syria and the Levant were in the front line. During the 6th century they suffered from excessive taxation to finance Justinian's wars, savage Persian raids and disastrous earthquakes, as well as loss of markets in the impoverished West. A major source of Byzantine weakness was religious strife, arising from the refusal of large sections of the Church in Egypt and Syria to accept the Christological definition laid down at the Council of Chalcedon in 451. The emperors of the latter half of the 5th century tried by persecution, persuasion and compromise to resolve this, without success. Egypt was a "monolithically Monophysite province";[7] Syria was more equally divided.

Further war with Rome saw the revived Persians taking Theodosiopolis (modern Erzurum) and the heavily fortified (but only lightly garrisoned) Amida (modern Diarbekir). The Romans had successes in Armenia. Peace was made in 506 and these two cities returned to the Empire, which refortified them, alongside Edessa, Batnae, Melitene and Sergiopolis, thus preventing Edessa from falling to Persian king Khusro I in 543. In later wars, the Byzantines failed to capture Nisibis (571), while the Persians attacked the great fortress of Dara. After a six month siege, this fell, with many killed and the remainder enslaved. In 576 the Byzantines and Armenians defeated the Persians west of Melitene, but in 588 the Byzantine garrison in Martyropolis handed it over to the Persians.

Then Persia faced revolt and civil war; for complex but honourable reasons the Byzantines supported Khusro II against his rival Vahram. After the success of Khusro peace was made: the terms agreed in 591 saw gains, with Khusro ceding Martyropolis and Dara, and making concessions in the Caucasus. The new emperor, Maurice, faced a severe diminution of tax revenues because of plague. Difficulties in paying the Balkan field army led to its revolt in 602 under Phocas. Not only were Maurice and his family killed, but Phocas very savagely purged the Byzantine elite.

Purporting to be avenging Maurice, who had restored him to his throne, Khusro launched attacks in 603 – "a massive war of attrition ... (with) layer by layer of Roman forward defences stripped away".[8] Dara fell after a long siege in 605, and by 610 all the Byzantine cities east of the Euphrates had fallen. By 608 the Persians had overrun Armenia, Cappadocia, Paphlagonia and Galatia and camped on the Asian shore of the Bosphorus. In 608 the two Heracliuses, father and son, revolted against Phocas who was killed in October 610; the younger Heraclius became emperor.

The real Byzantine collapse came in the early years of Heraclius. He tries to negotiate; Khusro simply executes his ambassadors. He tries to defend Anatolia, but is badly defeated near Antioch in 613. The Persians conquer Syria and Damascus in 613 and capture Caesarea in Cappadocia. There is evidence of Jews in Jerusalem helping the Persians; together they massacre much of the Christian population of Jerusalem and enslave the rest when the city falls in 614. The Persians systematically destroy churches, except for the Church of the Nativity at Bethlehem, on account of its mosaic showing the Magi in Persian costume.

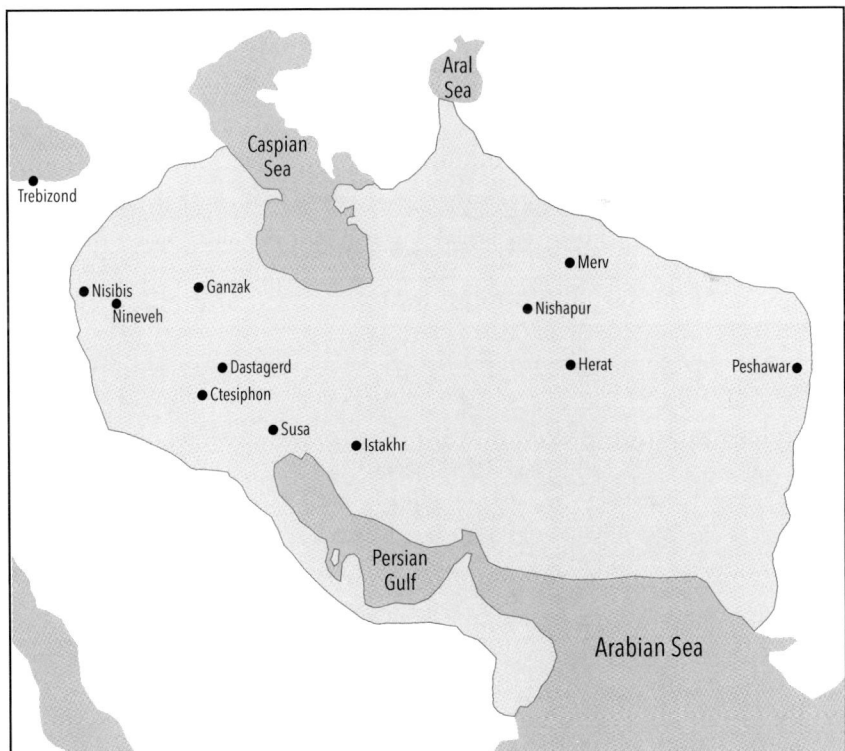

Borders of the Sasanian Empire.

The Persian fleet attacks Cyprus, and in 618 they invade Egypt, with Alexandria falling in 619 and the province fully occupied by the end of 621. In 623 Ancyra (Ankara) is captured, while Persian fleets capture Rhodes and other islands and devastate Asia Minor's coastlines. In the view of a key historian of this period, "Khusro had taken the decision to liquidate the Roman empire some time before – probably as early as the winter of 615–6 ... Khusro was on the point of eliminating Persia's old rival ... at the western end of Eurasia."[9]

The Byzantines were galvanised rather than depressed by all this. Heraclius started the "thematic" military organisation of Byzantine-held Asia Minor. Each "theme" was placed under a *strategos* and soldier-farmers received inalienable grants of land in return for hereditary military service. He brought in crisis measures to raise money: official and military pay was halved, churches were stripped of their gold and silver ornaments.[10]

He developed his massive, extensive and most impressive counter-offensive which carried his armies into the heart of Persia. Simultaneously, the Persians were besieging Constantinople, in alliance with the Avars, but Heraclius, justifiably, retained faith in the land walls. In 624 he struck at Theodosiopolis and then at Dvin, the capital of Persarmenia. He invaded the "holy land" of Sasanian religion in Atropatene, devastating much of the country. In 625 his army marched past Mount Ararat, capturing Martyropolis and Amida but only narrowly avoiding defeat north of Adana. Then, based on Trebizond, he invaded Persia. He defeated Khusro in person and destroyed the premier Zoroastrian fire temple at modern Takht-i-Sulaiman near Ganzak. From winter quarters in the Caucasian principality of Albania (modern Azerbaijan), he appealed not only to the Christian leaders in the area, but also to the *khagan* of the Turks.

In 626 he took a risk, deciding to stay in the east, while the Avars and a Persian army continued to threaten Constantinople. The land walls held firm and an Avar attempt to ferry Persian troops across the Bosphorus by canoe was defeated. Meanwhile, in 626–27 Heraclius and his Turkish allies captured Tbilisi, later capital of Georgia. In December 627 a decisive battle saw the Persians defeated near the ruins of Nineveh. Heraclius advanced on the Persian capital Ctesiphon, ravaging and plundering the country north of it, including several royal palaces, while Khusro fled from his palace at Dastagerd. Panic set in among the Persians, Khusro was deposed in favour of his son Kavad/Shiroe (end February 628) and then murdered (yet it was "a virtually bloodless coup".)[11] The coup leaders released political opponents and Byzantine prisoners of war. Peace was made, and with Persian rulers dying or being murdered in rapid succession, the Persians evacuated all the territory they had conquered, and the frontier eventually returned to that established in 591. The fragments of the True Cross, captured by the invaders, were restored to Jerusalem in 630.

Khusro's "rule was harsh and inflexible", with a massive weight of taxation building up. Howard-Johnston cites a well-informed 9th century treatise showing a 43 per cent increase of Persian tax revenue between 607–08 and the fall of Khusro; some, of course, of this would come from the occupied areas.[12]

Consequences of the Persian war

Throughout almost the whole of the Eastern Empire from central Greece to Egypt, the 5th and early 6th centuries were a period of remarkable expansion. This is shown by increased settlement, with a mass of newly built rural houses, often in stone, churches and monasteries, together with new coins and new potteries. On the Aegean coast this came to a sudden halt.[13] As a result of the Persian invasions – and the ravages of plague – cities such as Corinth, Athens, Ephesus and Aphrodisias shrank to a fraction of their former size; recent evacuations at Aphrodisias indicate that much of it had become an abandoned ghost town in the early 7th century.

Enormous and lasting damage was done to the infrastructure and quality of life in Asia Minor. Sardis had been a great city until very late in the 6th century. After the Persian sack in 610 it became a fortress on a hill-top, made almost entirely out of blocks re-used from the old city. At Ephesus the continuity on the old site was broken, and it became "a shadow of its former self in size , wealth and grandeur". The temple of Artemis, a wonder of the ancient world, saw its stones used to fortify the hill and build the basilica of St John; some of the marble was burned into lime for mortar. The picture indicated by archaeology from all the late Roman cities of western Asia Minor is very similar: "severe reduction in city size … abandonment or destruction of formerly inhabited areas, is one of the most striking phenomena …" Ephesus "came to consist of two separate centres a mile apart."[14] Even Constantinople shrank in wealth and population from her peak in about 500. Building activity there practically stopped in about 600, being limited to strengthening fortifications and repair of aqueducts: "Dark Age Constantinople was a ruin – its urban space invaded by orchards and cemeteries, its old public buildings abandoned or converted to artisanal activity." [15]

The ground was being prepared for a shift of communal loyalty: "it seems that many of the Greek-speaking elite in Syria emigrated to the security of North Africa or Rome." As a result of the Persian occupation, many younger generation Syrians had no memory of imperial rule. As Byzantine control was re-established, religious differences arose again. In contrast, if the Muslims/Arabs had attempted to invade in the 580s they would have been "seen off very quickly", discovering firm defences and resistance well organised.[16]

The religious issue was more pronounced in Egypt: in the towns and villages and monasteries along the Nile and in the desert the imperial Church of Alexandria was regarded as "alien, oppressive and above all, heretical". Heraclius had determined to enforce religious conformity, so after the Persian evacuation a new persecution, possibly lasting for ten years, took place. It involved executions and torture, for example of Menas, the brother of Benjamin, the Coptic patriarch.[17]

While the new tax revenues from Africa and Sicily were coming on stream by the end of Justinian's reign, expenditure was massively increased by wars with Persia. Could Heraclius have held on to his success after forcing peace from Persia after 628? Peter Heather compares this with the 3rd century crisis when the whole Empire "bounced back" under Aurelian and his successors. He grimly answers his own question. "It was the rise of Islam which fundamentally changed the course of East Roman history": the Byzantine claim to be "a uniquely divinely guided state", designed to bring Christian civilisation to the globe, lost much of its force after two thirds of the empire had been conquered by the leaders of a different but monotheistic religion.[18]

Timothy Venning has a contrasting counterfactual. If there had been no war in 602–29, or an earlier Byzantine victory, this would have left "fewer towns and fortresses damaged, more troops garrisoning the area, a less ravaged countryside, less mutual antagonism of Jews and Christians in Palestine, and a greater will to resist" the Arab challenge.[19]

The Arab conquests to 780

"These years (641–780) can rightly be called the Dark Age of Byzantine history: a time of military reverses, political instability, economic regression, and declining education, which has left but a scanty record for modern historians." The Eastern Empire, which had lost two of its three largest cities (Antioch and Alexandria), and almost all its speakers of Syriac and Coptic, to the Muslim invaders, was considerably less prosperous, populous and secure than in the 6th century.[20]

The Arab war began badly for the Byzantines, and got worse. The Arab/Muslim technique was to terrorise the rural population, with unfortunately limited Byzantine military response. Areopolis near Kerak was the first city to be captured by the Muslims in the winter of 633–34. Then in February 634, they defeated the Byzantines at Dathin near Gaza and even more decisively at Ajnadayn on 30 July 634. The latter was a real battle in the open and made the Byzantines less eager for such combat. There was a further Muslim victory at Scythopolis, and in 635 the Muslims captured Damascus and Homs. In early 636 they temporarily evacuated these in face of a Byzantine counterattack. This led to the Yarmuk.

The lengthy battle of the River Yarmuk in August 636 was the decisive battle, not only for the possession of Syria and Palestine but for prospective control in Egypt and later north Africa.[21] Many Byzantines were killed, including troops falling down steep slopes into wadis; the Muslims suffered heavily too. The combination of the irregular terrain, the heat and dust storms, makes this comparable to those other decisive Christian defeats at Manzikert in 1071 and Hattin in 1187. As with these, the Byzantines saw division and mistrust between the various leaders, also between Greeks, Armenians and Christian Arabs. The contest was not won by weight of numbers; it is possible that the Byzantines outnumbered the Muslims.

After this, Damascus and Caesarea were exceptional in the duration of their resistance; at Caesarea in 640 the garrison and civilians were killed when it fell. Beirut and Laodicea/Lattakieh then fell. More often, citizens put up only a token resistance in order to obtain reasonable terms. "There can be no doubt that the Byzantines lost Syria because the townspeople failed to resist the invaders."[22] In some places the inhabitants greeted the approaching Muslims with drums and cymbals.

After Damascus, the Muslims captured Baalbek, Homs, and in 637 Jerusalem, then Gaza. In 638 they occupied northern Syria and in 639 Byzantine Mesopotamia, with invasions of Armenia and Cilicia in 640. Byzantine counterattacks were abortive. Muslim treatment of the opposition varied: in Mesopotamia, Edessa and Harran/Carrhae surrendered quickly, the former on the condition that the Christians could keep their cathedral,[23] but Dara was stormed and every Byzantine there was killed. So Amida, with its massive walls, and other places then surrendered.

This might be contrasted with the Muslim treatment of the Zoroastrian Persian ruling class, who were not "People of the Book". When the Muslims took Susa they killed all the Persian nobles and after the conquest of Istakr there was a large massacre especially of noble Persian families who had taken refuge there; the Muslims singled out symbols of the old religion for destruction. Likewise, in India, fighting men and priests were killed.[24]

The Byzantine losses in the Muslim conquest of Egypt were severe, and the death of emperor Heraclius in 641 and the resulting succession crisis demoralised defenders. So on Easter Monday 641 the Byzantines surrendered the fortress of Babylon (later within Old Cairo). Alexandria fell in December 641: it was retaken by a Byzantine counter attack from the sea in late 645 – but was besieged and again fell in the summer 646, with much slaughter. There was evidence that the Copts (Monophysite Christians) sometimes helped the Muslims against the Byzantines.[25]

The Arabs/Muslims had certain advantages. They travelled light and thus were able to cover vast distances. They had good leadership and high morale from their religious motivation. The local people, including elite groups, were not expecting trouble with Arabs; local officials had not prepared civilians to resist. Heraclius knew the area well, better than any recent emperor, but he failed to make preparations with friendly Christian Arabs. Imperial officials had stopped the tribute traditionally paid to these frontier tribes, the Ghassanid Arabs, who had previously acted as an early warning system.

Except for Caesarea, the civilian population was rarely engaged in fighting. There was no evidence of a mass flight of the Syrian population. As Kaegi states, there was "more to be lost than gained in defending Antioch to the last man".[26] Non-Muslims who wished to leave conquered regions were allowed to go to Byzantine territory, their lands being redistributed among the invaders.

The Muslims made most progress up to around 700, but their efforts were interrupted by three civil wars in the caliphate in 656–61, 680–92, and 747–51. Under Mu'awiya as governor of Syria and then Caliph between 643 and 680, yearly raids into Asia Minor began, with in 664 the Arab army wintering there. These obtained loot, while the Byzantines saw their homes and lands devastated, and people killed or enslaved. The Muslims became powerful at sea. In 649 a large fleet landed on Cyprus, looting and ravaging; in 650 they occupied the island. After a major sea battle and a decisive victory in 654, they seized the islands of Crete, Rhodes and Kos. In 670 Muslim fleets raided Chios and Smyrna and in 672 they fortified the Cyzicus peninsula to act as a base for an assault on Constantinople. The latter was besieged in 673–78 but failing to breach the walls, the Muslims made peace in 679, evacuating the Aegean islands.

Meanwhile the Byzantines had gradually lost their hold on north Africa. From the middle of the 7th century Carthage suffered from what has been described as "monumental melt-down". The "results of archaeological surveys and some excavation suggests … [that the] once vast and impressive cities had mostly been ruined or reduced to the size and appearance of fortified villages."[27] The Byzantines suffered a major defeat in 647 near Sufetula/Sbeitla in south Tunisia, and by 678 their rule was confined to Carthage and its environs. Muslim feuds enabled Carthage to survive until caliph Abd al-Malik attacked in 694: Carthage fell. The Muslim centre moved to Qairawan.

Muslim weakness over the next few decades coincided with the decline of the Umayyad dynasty, which was overcome by the Abbasids in 750. We see the start of Byzantine counter-offensives. The emperor Justinian II (685–95, 705–11) invaded the Caucasus, occupying Armenia, Iberia, and Caucasian Albania. In 688–90 he organised the transport across the Aegean of scores of thousands of

Slavs from Thrace to Bithynia (now organised as the Opsikion theme). He even invaded Syria in 700 and defeated an Arab invasion of Cilicia.

Leo III "the Isaurian", emperor in 717, faced a massive Arab attack on Constantinople in 717–18, but this onslaught was the last under the caliphate. The use of Greek fire, an inflammable and virtually inextinguishable substance, brought to Constantinople by Syrian refugees from the oil rich areas of northern Iraq, ensured a decisive defeat of the Arab fleet, while their land army suffered terribly during the fierce winter. Greek fire was of vital assistance to the Byzantines in the following centuries: we have an account of how some Bulgarians captured a supply of the substance and the tubes used to project it, but were unable to make them work.[28]

This temporary revival by the Byzantines culminated in a further invasion of North Syria in 746 and a large victory at sea in 747. Simultaneously, in the West, Ravenna was finally captured by the Lombards in 751. With Rome now abandoned, the only territory there held by the Byzantines was in southern Italy.

Byzantine–Arab/Muslim frontier warfare

By 700 the Eastern Roman Empire had lost three quarters of its former revenues. Until the mid-9th century it faced potential annual attacks from the caliphate, the latter possessing a budget 15 times greater. Byzantine armies were usually outnumbered by five to one.[29]

Before the 730s, the Byzantine response was very localised. From the 660s to the end of the second siege of Constantinople in 718, Byzantine forces were "stretched to the point of collapse".[30] Especially during the 660s and 670s Arab armies faced little opposition to their forays through the Taurus and into northern Asia Minor. As their field armies were unable to defeat the attacks, the Byzantines resorted to the fortification of towns and cities, for example, Miletus, Pergamum, and Sardis near the Aegean coast, Seleucia and Mopsuestia (Mamistra) in Cilicia, and Ancyra, Kotyaion (modern Kutahya) and Akroinon (modern Afyon Karahisar) inland. Akroinon saw a major Byzantine victory over the Arabs in 740, the first one in a fully pitched battle – both the Arab commanders fell as did the major part of their army. Normally, however, troops were scattered to warn people of an invasion so they could flee with livestock and other possessions to strong points or hilly terrain. For example, the remnants of the population of Tyana moved to better fortified Magida/Nigde. Few real cities remained in central Asia Minor; the Muslim geographer Ibn Hawqal complained "rich cities are few ... most of it consists of mountains, castles, fortresses, cave dwellings and villages dug out of the rock or buried under the earth".[31] This clearly describes the troglodyte villages in Cappadocia.

After 693 the Arabs ceased long-distance raids, concentrating now on the border regions, with the aim either to wear down Byzantine resistance or else to incorporate as much of the devastated area into the caliphate. Byzantine tactics along the border were to form a buffer zone on an almost uninhabited no man's land, destroying captured strong-points rather than garrisoning them. Population was transferred to Thrace.

The Cilician plain formed the border zone, originally rich and fertile, with several places, cities in antiquity, which had been devastated by the earlier Persian and Arab invasions. The Muslims tried to occupy and develop three large centres: Mopsuestia and the better known Adana and Tarsus. The first named was colonised and the walls refortified in 703, while a garrison of Khurasanis, from north-east Iran, was settled in Adana in around 758. Although it was the last to be resettled, Tarsus became the most important; from 787 it became the base for subsequent Arab raids.

The population of Tarsus in the 10th century showed two thirds being single men – that is, fighters. Similarly, Melitene/Malatyah was colonised in late Umayyad times: when the Umayyads weakened the Byzantines retook and destroyed the city. It was rebuilt by the Muslims in 757.

Before 717 Muslim defeats were a rarity; these now became more frequent, with six defeats between 720 and 740. Unlike the Umayyads, whose capital was Damascus, the Abbasids, who developed Baghdad and tended to look east, made no attempt to capture Constantinople. However, "raids, great and small, remained an almost annual feature of frontier life", taking place except when impeded by disturbances in the Muslim world. Hence there were none between 743 and 754, or between 809 and 830.

Consequences of the Muslim invasions

Walter Kaegi estimated the population of the Greek East in the 2nd century – the "age of the Antonines" – at 28 to 34 million. By 630, he states, it had "probably declined by 20 per cent to 40 per cent, if not more, to between approximately 17 million and 27 million." He suggests that by the late 7th century, after the territorial losses to the Muslims, the total population may have fallen to 7 million or less in the areas still under imperial control. While much of this decline resulted from plague, it contributed to the weakness of the East.[32]

Unlike the consequences from the Roman retreat in the West, which were materially, as well as culturally, disastrous in the succeeding centuries, the East benefited for a considerable time from the Muslim conquests. The local Arab elites had a keener interest in commerce and trade than either the late Roman or Persian aristocracy had possessed. "The opportunities resulting from the creation of a vast unified currency zone stretching from the Atlantic to the Indus, and a major expansion in the volume of coinage in circulation, were seized upon by members of this elite, whose enterprise ... would turn the Muslim Near East into the economic powerhouse of the West Eurasian world."[33]

How do we square this economic prosperity with the decline in the size of various cities? The impact of plague and earthquakes was undoubted a factor, but another is that the Muslims developed different centres of population: Baghdad (after 750), Damascus, Cairo, Qairawan, Kufa, Basra and Mosul. During the 6th century terrible earthquakes destroyed the coastal towns between Tripoli and Tyre. Little rebuilding took place, and urban life and prosperity there had been greatly reduced by the end of the 6th century. Concentrated urban populations would have suffered from plague more than rural or nomadic peoples, and this tallies with urban decline and a relative resilience of rural communities.[34]

Ward Perkins also argues that the influence of the Arabs was initially good. The Levant and Egypt in 700 were prospering, with sophisticated potteries at cities such as Jerash and new copper coins coming into circulation. This he contrasts to the Aegean, where copper coins and good quality pottery had virtually disappeared. He also asserts, however, that parts of the Levant did not regain the levels and density of population of late Roman and early Arab times until well into the 19th or even 20th centuries.[35] Other sources refer to dramatic falls in coins in circulation in cities such as Ephesus, Pergamum, Athens and Corinth between 668 and 811, after which the number rose considerably. Judith Herrin admits that this problem "continues to puzzle historians" and speculates either that fewer coins were minted or that more coins might be excavated at castles and fortified sites on the eastern borders. "The gap," she states, "seems to mark the low point in Byzantine economic power."[36]

Thus, similar to the West, in the remaining territory of the East Roman Empire the cities "increasingly took on the appearance of shrunken fortified compounds" with underground citadels in Anatolia for refuge.[37] Some destruction dates as far back as the Gothic invasions of the 3rd century – such as with Athens and Ephesus, where the whole harbour district of the latter had been devastated in 262 and many buildings lay in ruins for a century or more. Other cities had shrunk to a fraction of their original size as a result of the Persian invasions. Archaeology shows that the inhabited area of most Byzantine cities fell by more than a half between the 6th century and the 8th, though most continued to exist.[38] Except for those few cities which already had strong fortifications, inhabitants built walls round the most defensible areas, using ancient spolia for this purpose, and in some cases moving the sites from the plains to more easily defensible hills. The fact that these would be places of refuge during raids is clear from their often being called forts (*kastra*).

An example might be seen in Antioch and its hinterland, as an indication of what was happening in northern Syria. With a population exceeding 300,000 in Roman times, Antioch flourished in the 4th and 5th centuries, but suffered severe earthquakes in 526, 528 and later. In 540 it was captured and depopulated by the Persians, and in 542 suffered from the first outbreak of bubonic plague. Of its condition during the Persian occupation and the Heraclian reconquest, virtually nothing is known.

The villages in its hinterland prospered based on olive production, enjoying trade across the Mediterranean from ports such as Seleucia and Laodicea/Lattikieh. From the evidence of inscriptions these communities were booming between the late 4th and early 6th centuries, with an expanding population colonising new, marginal lands on the edge of the desert. Under the Arabs, Antioch was much smaller than the classical city; it had lost many of public buildings, including theatres and hippodromes. The 9th and especially the 10th centuries represented the nadir of its fortunes. When the Byzantines reconquered it in the late 10th century, there was renewed church building, but the population was too small to garrison the circuit of its walls. Similarly, other coastal cities declined well before the Muslim conquest and remained dormant thereafter. In contrast to Damascus, Aleppo and Antioch, none of these coastal cities retained its classical street plan. A third group of inland towns survived as urban centres for the first 150 years of Muslim rule but decayed to "vanishing point" in the 9th and 10th centuries; these included Gerasa/Jerash, Philadephia/Amman, Chalcis/Qinnasrin and Apamea.[39]

In Asia Minor, there was a distinct shift away from arable agriculture towards pastoralism and mixed farming. Around Constantinople and in those parts relatively shielded from Arab raids, such as Bithynia and the Aegean coast, much more of the late Roman infrastructure survived. In contrast, the other Antioch, in Pisidia, never recovered from an Arab onslaught in 713.

In the European part of the Empire, decline was powerfully apparent. In the decades after 690, according to a treatise attributed to emperor Constantine VII Porphyrogenitus in the 10th century, all of Greece would be "slavonised and turned barbarian".[40] Slav settlement was mostly in highland, forest and marginal zones, as denoted by place names; the Greek-speaking Christian population survived in the lowland and coastal areas. Initially through trading contacts, the Slavs began to speak Greek, and gradually became absorbed in the Empire – joining the army, adopting Christianity and paying taxes to Constantinople.

"Since the time of Alexander, power and influence in the lands of the eastern Mediterranean had been in the hands of Greek-speaking city dwellers with loyalties and contacts all over the Mediterranean world. Suddenly, within a generation of the Prophet's death in 632, all this had vanished and nine centuries of history and culture seem to have virtually disappeared ..."[41] For the first half century after the Arab conquest, bureaucracy in Syria and Egypt continued to use Greek and was staffed by local Christians.[42] By the early 8th century Arabic, hitherto the language of the desert tribes, became the language of government and administration, supplanting Greek, Coptic, Syriac and Pahlavi. During the 9th and 10th centuries the use of Greek virtually died out in the caliphate.[43]

While it is true that, in provinces distant from the centres of Muslim power, such as upper Egypt, local Christian elites remained firmly in control for centuries (in Jerash one small mosque co-existed alongside fifteen fully functioning Christian churches), more generally "within a century after the death of Justinian, the populations of Syria and Egypt, having fallen under Muslim rule, would even forget that they had once lived under a Christian empire". Brown explains this: it was a " ... firm vote on the part of the silent majority of the settled populations of the Near East for the stability of empire – of any empire – over potential anarchy".[44]

The Church became the dominant force in Byzantine cultural and intellectual life; "what classical Greek authors' works we possess today have primarily come down to us because Byzantine monks chose to copy them." However, literature tended to be limited to that used for religion, with very little record retained of documents valuable for history.[45]

The Byzantines regain the initiative 800–1071

In addition to fighting the eastern frontier war, the Empire faced threats from the north: a large Russian raid on Constantinople in 941 was only defeated by the use of Greek fire by the Byzantine fleet. The main European threat came from the Bulgars. In 811 the Byzantines suffered a great defeat by the Bulgars; the emperor Nicephorus was killed. After further successes in 812 the Bulgars besieged Constantinople, where they failed, but in 813 they took Adrianople and carried off its inhabitants. While the Bulgar king was baptised in September 865, the Bulgar *boyars* remained attracted to the old pagan ways and welcomed breaches with Constantinople. King Symeon inflicted serious defeats in 892, 893, 896 and in 913–4 and 919–23, with Adrianople again taken. After this period, for around 50 years Bulgaria ceased to be a threat, and when the threat returned under King, now Tsar, Samuel, the Empire was led by highly competent emperors: Nicephorus Phocas (963–69), John Tzimisces (969–76) and Basil II Bulgaroctonus – the Bulgar-Slayer (976–1025).

And there was a constant threat to Byzantine territories in Italy, which after 751 were confined to Sicily and the toe and heel.

The caliph Harun al-Rashid early in his reign reformed the administration in the frontier provinces to provide more resources for *jihad*. From 776 to the end of Harun's reign in 809 there were large scale incursions; that in 776 reached Ancyra, then Dorylaeum and the sea of Marmara; 797 saw expeditions to Ancyra, 798 to Ephesus.

After a long lull, owing to civil war between Harun's sons after his death in 809, another large invasion took place in 838 under Caliph Mutasim, "the most fully reported of all the Muslim expeditions ... no doubt because the caliph was personally in charge ..."[46] The Muslims suffered greatly from lack of water and fodder on the march, as the local people had fled with their flocks and stores. The invaders captured a deserted Ancyra and then besieged Amorium, a powerful fortress in a strategic position. It only fell through treachery, and this was followed by a mass slaughter of the inhabitants, the remainder being taken into slavery. These included the 42 "martyrs" of Amorium, who having survived captivity after seven years refused to turn Muslim and were killed. After this great raid, the Muslims reverted to the defensive. During the 9th century generally, it seems that the Byzantines were taking as many Muslim captives as vice versa.

The Empire suffered blows from surprising sources: exiles from Muslim Spain successfully invaded Crete in the 820s and Muslim Aghlabids from Tunisia invaded Sicily, finally capturing Syracuse in 878. Both posed a great threat to the security of the Empire's coasts, so frequent attempts were made to win back Crete, succeeding temporarily around 840.

Byzantine naval successes built up. There was a daring naval raid on Damietta in Egypt in 853 which set fire to the city and scores of Muslim vessels. Other naval successes off the Syrian coast were followed by another successful raid on Damietta in 859 and victories on land in 863, one at Mayyafariqin/Martyropolis. The tide was clearly turning, and the emperor Michael who died in 829 was the first emperor for half a century to die in his bed.

Basil I (867–86), founder of the Macedonian dynasty, which was to last for nearly two hundred years, took Zapetra and Samosata and other strongholds in the Euphrates valley, but suffered defeats at Melitene and Tarsus. The Muslims in Sicily took Taormina, the last imperial stronghold, in 902. Other Muslims threatened Cilicia and in 904 took Thessalonica with great bloodshed. In 905 the Muslim fleet was badly defeated, while the Byzantines captured Tarsus. In 908 the Byzantine fleet captured Laodicea/Lattikieh, ravaging it and its hinterland. In 912 they again failed to reconquer Crete and suffered a great naval defeat off Chios. In 909–13 a Muslim army ravaged Armenia but was repulsed in 914.

By 946 the Caliphs of Baghdad had lost all real control of the frontier region, with power in Baghdad passing to Persian military adventurers, the Buyids. The

Islamic Middle East was breaking up into rival states. No member of the Abbasid family led *jihad* against the Byzantines after Caliph Mutasim (833–42). Mutasim's successor, Wathiq (842–47) "did not share his father's enthusiasm for the holy war" – though there was a major raid which reached the Bosphorus in 844. He then authorised a "large-scale exchange of prisoners" on the Byzantine frontier in 845.[47] Wathiq is sufficiently obscure that William Beckford in 1786 published a sensational Gothic fantasy novel about him, *Vathek*. Prisoner exchanges on frontiers during the 9th and 10th centuries helped to normalise relations, as shown in the verse epic by Digenes Akrites about marriage alliances and raiding parties: the hero's father was an Arab emir who carried off a Byzantine bride and later converted to Christianity.[48]

We now see the invasion of Muslim territory behind the frontier, starting under John Curcuas, an Armenian general. In 932 he captured Manzikert and other towns on the north shore of Lake Van and in 934 Melitene fell, the first important Arab emirate to be reconquered. Aleppo was threatened and in 942–44 Curcuas marched by way of Amida, Nisibis, Edessa and Dara. In 958–9 another brilliant general, John Tzimisces, captured Samosata. After yet another failure to recapture Crete in 949, a big attack was launched under emperor Nicephorus Phocas in 960. Herakleion was besieged for eight months and fell in March 961 and with it control of the island. 962 saw great successes in Cilicia, with the capture of Tarsus in 965, the main Arab base for raids. The Christian East "saw deliverance at hand" and the Patriarch John of Jerusalem urged the emperor to invade Palestine (the local Muslim population burnt him at the stake for this).[49] In 969 the emperor invaded the heart of Syria, sacking Shaizar, Hama, Homs, Tortosa, and Laodicea/Lattakieh, capturing Antioch in October and Aleppo in December. Thanks to Nicephorus, who was deposed and murdered after a court intrigue that year, the Byzantine army was now first class, with very fine generals.

John Tzimisces, his successor, had to face the Fatimids who in 969 established a caliphate in Egypt and Palestine. They attacked Antioch in 971 and in 973 inflicted a sharp defeat on a Byzantine army near Amida. John launched a large offensive in 974, in conjunction with the Armenians. Amida and Martyropolis paid ransoms; he captured Nisibis. The question is put, why did he not advance to Baghdad? Runciman believes, with justice, that he saw the Fatimids, rather than the Abbasids, as more dangerous.[50] In 975 he took Emesa/Homs, then Baalbek, Damascus, Tiberias, Nazareth, Caesarea, and then Sidon, Beirut, and Byblos; all these, however, were briefly held and at Tripoli he was defeated. He captured and garrisoned castles south of Antioch, but did not attack Jerusalem and was mortally ill by the end of the year, dying in January 976.

Basil II's long reign (976–1025) saw the decisive defeat of Bulgaria. In 996, with Basil in the east, the Bulgarians killed the governor of Thessalonica and invaded Greece as far as Corinth, while they took control of the hinterland of Bosnia, with only the Greek-speaking cities of the Dalmatian coast holding out. Their decisive defeat came in 1014 at the defile of Cimbalongus/Clidion near Seres; about 15,000 Bulgarians were captured and, it is said, 99 out of every 100 was blinded. Guided by the few unblinded, the wreck of the Bulgarian host returned home; Tsar Samuel died when he saw the survivors: Judith Herrin states "there are many reasons to doubt the story." Bulgaria was now subjected until the 1180s. Without the Bulgarian distraction, Basil – or his predecessors – might have recaptured Jerusalem or advanced on Baghdad.[51]

In the east, the Byzantines suffered a major defeat by the Fatimids near Antioch in 994; in 995 Basil relieved Aleppo from a Fatimid siege, and went on to sack Emesa (Homs), raiding as far as Tripoli. Clearly, not all of John's successes had been retained. Basil died in December 1025 as he was planning an invasion of Sicily.

A comparison of the relative power of the Byzantine empire in 1000 shows it stretching from Crete to the Crimea, from the Adriatic to the eastern Caucasus. From 992 until late in the 12th century, it had close contacts with Venice, with several doges sending their sons to be educated in Constantinople. By 1050, it had taken Edessa and Ani the old Armenian capital. John Julius Norwich believed that if Isaac I Comnenus, who came to the throne in 1057 and started to rebuild the strength of the army, had survived 20 years, the army would have proved a match for the challenges of the 1070s. Sadly, Isaac died of a fever caught campaigning in 1059.[52]

The Empire's two neighbours and rivals, the Abbasid caliphate and the Carolingian empire, had both fractured into smaller units. And it now had (largely) religious unity, lacking in the Muslim domains divided between Sunni and Shia; the Fatimid rulers were Shia. Constantinople headed a powerful bureaucracy, a strong standing army, and a comprehensive taxation system – each largely absent in the Carolingian realm.[53] The Empire was also a society in which literacy was highly appreciated and it "took for granted a developed level of record-keeping that was almost unparalleled in the early Middle Ages".[54]

It faced more challenges from northern barbarians, the Pechenegs, making devastating raids in the Balkans (1048–53) as far as the outskirts of Thessalonica and, in 1091, towards Constantinople. The emperor Alexius was badly defeated by them in 1087, before another barbarian tribe, the Cumans, turned on the Pechenegs and virtually wiped them out.

Italy turned out to be a disaster area. In 1038 the Byzantines had invaded

Sicily and captured Messina and then Syracuse in 1040. Then the Arabs regained control except for Messina. By the end of the reign of Constantine IX Monomachus in 1055 the Normans under Robert Guiscard were invading Byzantine territory in Apulia, Calabria and Sicily. In 1059 Robert was invested by the Pope with the Dukedoms of these three territories. By 1072 he controlled most of Sicily, in 1071 he captured Bari, the capital of Apulia, and by 1081 he was invading the Balkans aiming for Constantinople. He died in 1085; as Norwich says "had he lived another few months … Alexius Comnenus might have proved one of the more transitory – possibly even the last – of the Greek emperors of Byzantium".[55]

In the East, from 1045 much of Armenia was Byzantine but later emperors foolishly persecuted the Monophysite Armenians, imposed heavy taxes and compelled the disbanding of the Armenian national militia; simultaneously alienating the Armenians and rendering them defenceless. And the Armenians first bore the brunt of a new force from Central Asia, the "ferocious and destructive" Seljuk Turkish nomads in search of plunder and permanent new pastureland. Fuller dramatically asserts that "throughout this period of degeneracy there [was] … not the slightest realisation that the empire was approaching a precipice" and that the army "was a highly organised vacuum – the shell of a blown egg".[56]

Fuller quotes another formidable historian on the Seljuk techniques of warfare and annexation, which is vital to the "civilisation" theme of this book. The Seljuks "exterminate the cultivators of the soil in the extensive plains, in order to leave the country in a fit state to be occupied by their own nomadic tribes. The villages, farmhouses, and plantations were everywhere burned down, and the wells were often filled, in order that all cultivation might be confined to the immediate vicinity of fortified towns." Thus "whole provinces were left vacant for their occupation before the Seljouk (sic) power was able to conquer the cities".[57]

The Seljuks devastated the country round Lake Van in 1054, ravaged Kars in 1052 and Armenia in 1056 and 1057. They raided deep into imperial territory, reaching Sebastea/Sivas in 1059, when they also sacked the Armenian city of Ardzen and massacred or enslaved most of its inhabitants (the survivors fled to Theodosiopolis which they renamed Ardzen-i-rum, hence Erzurum). In 1064 Ani, the Armenian capital, suffered sack and massacre: the guide book describes its site today (visited by the present author in 2015) as "a melancholy, almost vacant, triangular plateau … little more than an expanse of rubble". By 1067 the Seljuks were invading as far as Caesarea in Cappadocia "which was subjected to another merciless sack".[58] Without much effective resistance, they got within 100 miles of Ancyra.

The emperor who had to face this threat was Romanus IV Diogenes (1068–71), described as "able", "hard working" and "brave". In 1068–9 he defeated the Turks at Neocaesarea/Niksar, then invaded Syria capturing Hierapolis, the modern Manbij. The Turks attacked Amorium and Iconium, but hitherto Romanus's "successes … had more than cancelled out his defeats".[59] In 1071 he assembled a very large army, but few were professional soldiers or well equipped. Seljuk sultan Alp Arslan was keen on a truce as he was unsure of victory, but the emperor felt obliged to fight to avert the hostile plotting of the Ducas family, rivals for the throne. The Manzikert campaign proved a complete disaster for the Byzantines. Before the battle more than half their army had deserted, either through treason or as a result of a defeat near Khelat, now Ahlat, by Lake Van. While the Turks knew of Romanus's movements, he was ignorant of theirs. During the battle Andronicus Ducas spread the word that the emperor had been defeated; this was false, but the flight of a large part of the army resulted. The best troops were killed, and Romanus was captured, being released after making a treaty with the Seljuks.

"The real tragedy … lay not in the battle itself but in its appalling epilogue."[60] If Romanus had been permitted by his own side to retain his throne he would have observed the terms of the treaty he made with the Turks; Alp Arslan did not want to conquer the empire as his objective remained Shia Fatimid Egypt. And if Romanus had been succeeded by a competent emperor, Byzantine defences might have held. The Seljuks did not begin any systematic invasion of Asia Minor until the summer of 1073. By then there was military chaos, with the population of Armenia moving south-west into the Taurus mountains. Tens of thousands of nomadic Turkoman tribesmen swarmed into central Asia Minor, with the Christians "abandoning their villages to be burnt and their flocks and herds to be rounded up by the invaders".[61] Fuller quotes a French historian, Laurent, "It is difficult even to imagine the complete ruin the Turks left behind them … On their departure all that was left were devastated fields, trees cut down, mutilated corpses … In a few years, Cappadocia, Phrygia, Bithynia and Paphlagonia lost the greater part of their Greek population." Laurent waxes furious: while in 1050 Byzantine Asia Minor was important in population and wealth, thirty years later "it was merely a desert", with places from Caesarea and Sebaste to Nicaea and Sardis "remaining almost empty".[62]

The surviving Greeks did their best to escape to the coasts of the Black Sea and the Aegean; some survived in mountain districts, but large numbers adopted Islam and "were gradually merged into the Turkish race".[63] Significant Greek and Christian populations remained in these coastal areas until the "catastrophe" of 1922 and ensuing population exchanges. The trauma of the latter is illustrated in

Louis de Bernières's 2004 novel, *Birds Without Wings*.

It is possible that the French account, written during the First World War, was influenced by French support for Greeks, hostility to Turks allied with the Germans, and French ambitions of post-war expansion in the area. However, a modern account of the Seljuks indicates that they destroyed fortifications and cities without intending to occupy these permanently; "apparently seeing them as a potential threat to the nomads' control of the pastureland".[64]

As we saw with the fall of the western empire, the sources are sometimes absent, confusing or misleading. One source is the impressive *Alexiad* by Anna Comnena. Her father, a young general named Alexius Comnenus came to the throne in 1081. One of his early key services was to unite two competing families – the Comneni and the (tiresome) Ducas – by marriage alliances. However, she did not write this semi-hagiography of her father until several decades later, possibly around 1148. Following her, many historians have assumed that the Turks overwhelmed Asia Minor speedily after Manzikert. In his recent study of Alexius and the First Crusade, Professor Peter Frankopan argues against this. Despite disputes over the Byzantine throne during the 1070s, the Byzantine hold over Asia Minor was "fairly robust" in the early 1080s, though he acknowledges Turkish raiders attacking Cyzicus opposite Constantinople, while the Turkish allies of a Byzantine pretender occupied Nicaea probably as early as 1081. Antioch and the Cilician cities had also fallen to the Turks, initially in 1085, finally by 1094–95. Yet, as Frankopan argues, there was "no need for a crusade" in the 1080s; Alexius was helped by alliances with key Turkish rulers, Suleyman and the senior Seljuk sultan, Malik Shah. The latter seems, however, even then to have controlled the central part of Asia Minor from the 1080s, which he called the Sultanate of Rum – as a claim to succeeding the Roman realm. Various factors produced deterioration, notably the deaths of these key allies in 1085 and 1092 respectively.

Other Turks now took Nicomedia, even closer to the capital, in 1091. The emir Chaka occupied Smyrna and invaded the islands from Lesbos to Rhodes, while the Danishmend Turks swept through Cappadocia. "News of the devastating collapse" spread through western Europe, conveyed by travellers: the "failure" was "rapid and spectacular" and "universal", with much of the coast and the route to Antioch now in Turkish hands. So when, after Alexius's desperate pleas, Pope Urban II at Clermont in 1095 called for a crusade to fight the Turks, people knew what he was talking about.[65]

The 12th century recovery (1081–1204)

One of Alexius's greatest services to the Empire was his careful handling and supplying of the various waves of western forces passing through Constantinople, making up the First Crusade. Its leaders did not keep the promises made to him of accepting his suzerainty over the lands they conquered, but they helped him recapture Nicaea in 1097. While the Crusade progressed across Asia Minor, he regained the west and south coasts and valleys, with Byzantine rule being restored in Chios, Rhodes, Smyrna, Ephesus, Sardis, and Philadelphia in 1097–1099. In 1099, a Byzantine fleet assisted the Crusaders in capturing Laodicea/Lattakieh and other coastal towns as far as Tripoli; these were retained by the Crusaders. Alexius also recaptured various vital fortresses, including the trio of Adana, Tarsus and Mopsuestia. He failed to recover the central core of Anatolia, where the population had previously been an important recruitment source for the Empire. His 37 years on the throne (1081–1118) to a considerable extent counterbalanced the misgovernment of the 13 monarchs over the preceding 56 years, 1025–81.

Towards the end of Alexius's reign, Turcoman nomads infiltrated the valleys of western Anatolia, where the climate was more attractive and the pasture for their flocks much richer than on the arid plateau of central Anatolia. Thus they effectively cut off Attaleia/Antayla.

Meanwhile the Danishmend Turks, taking land from the Sultanate of Iconium, had during the 1120s captured Caesarea, Ancyra, and Kastamon. From 1130–35 emperor John Comnenus campaigned against them, recapturing Kastamon and advancing beyond the Halys river. The death of the emir Ghazi in 1134 produced civil war amongst the Danishmends. In Cilicia, in 1137 John recaptured Adana, Tarsus, Seleucia/Selifke and Anazarbus/Anavarza from Armenians and Crusaders. He finally captured Antioch-in-Pisidia and strongpoints in the High Taurus. In 1142 he marched through Cilicia to Turbessel, the second capital of the county of Edessa. Planning an attack in 1143 on the huge Templar fortress of Baghras, he received a wound in a hunting accident which turned septic and killed him in April 1143. If, as Norwich suggests, he had enjoyed a few more years of life, "he would almost certainly have extended Byzantine power deep into Syria – perhaps even into Palestine …"[66]

In 1144 came the conquest of Crusader-held Edessa by Zengi, Atabeg of Mosul. He was the father of Nur ed-Din, predecessor of Saladin. Nur forged a powerful empire in Syria and Egypt which Saladin used to defeat the Crusaders in 1187 and capture Jerusalem. The fall of Edessa stimulated the Second Crusade which crossed Asia Minor in 1147. The emperor Manuel (1143–80) warned the Crusaders not to take the water-less and more dangerous direct route through Anatolia but to keep to the safer coast; they ignored this advice. The German army was nearly annihilated at Dorylaeum. Joined by German survivors the French contingent was fiercely attacked round Ephesus, and further defeated at Laodicea/Denizli. King Louis, his household and as much of his cavalry as could be carried then sailed from Attaleia towards Antioch. Eventually, the Crusade wasted its energy attacking Damascus, driving it into Nur ed-Din's confederation. Failing before Damascus, the army suffered huge losses on its retreat in Syria at the height of summer.

Manuel's skilful diplomacy, and some campaigning, ensured that the route to the Holy Land through Anatolia remained open to pilgrims. In alliance with Nur ed-Din and the Danishmends, he defeated the Seljuks and obliged them in 1162 to return all the Greek cities occupied in recent years. On account of his Balkan preoccupations, where he was successful, and Italian aspirations, where he was not, Manuel neglected Asia Minor for ten years. The situation there deteriorated. In 1176 Manuel took a large army via the Meander valley in an advance on Iconium. The Sultan offered him peace on generous terms but the younger nobles in his army pressed for battle. This took place: the army was ambushed in a pass at Myriocephalum; half of it was lost. Peace was agreed, on condition that Manuel destroyed certain fortifications, but greatly demoralised, he fell ill and died in 1180.

The battle was decisive in that it saved the Seljuk Sultanate and prevented the Byzantines extending their domains into central Anatolia, though the military balance between the two belligerents was not greatly affected.[67] The Byzantines inflicted a sharp defeat on the Turks near the River Meander in 1177, and Byzantine Asia Minor was retained but weakly held for more than another century.

After Manuel's death the Empire fell into a period of chaos. With three emperors in 19 years; as Norwich declares "each was in his own way disastrous."[68]

A gross example of misgovernment was a massacre of Latins in Constantinople by disorderly Greeks in 1182; retaliation involved a Norman sacking of Thessalonica in 1185. Then, provoked by dynastic rivalries, and impelled by the greed of the Venetians in particular, the Fourth Crusade in 1203 was misdirected to attack Constantinople. The city was stormed twice by the Crusaders, and the second, very brutal, sack destroyed or removed everything of beauty or value. Norwich explains that the Venetians, unlike the French and Flemings, understood the significance of what they were looting and removed it to adorn Venice.[69]

The final 250 years (1204–1453)

From the disaster of 1204 to the final conquest by the Ottoman Turks the Empire lasted almost 250 years, not counting for much in area or strength, but preserving nuggets of civilisation to pass on to the Western Renaissance, well under way by 1453.

Fracturing had begun before 1204 – Bulgaria and Serbia had seceded in the mid-1180s, and various independent lordships arose around this time in Greece,

Cyprus and western Anatolia, while the "Empire of Trebizond", which became the international centre for Black Sea and Silk Route commerce, was established in 1204; it survived until 1461. The partition of the Byzantine empire in 1204 resulted in the so-called "Latin Empire of Constantinople", ruled by a series of Frankish emperors until 1261 but reduced to little more than the capital after 1225; the "Kingdom of Thessalonica", which returned to Greek control in 1224; the "Principality of Achaia" in the north-west Peloponnese, which saw its remnants absorbed by the Greeks of Mistra in 1430; and the longer-lived multi-national "Duchy of Athens and Thebes", which passed from Boniface of Montferrat to a Burgundian knight, then to Catalan mercenaries and finally to Florentine control until conquered by the Ottomans in 1450. Venice obtained and kept, mainly until the 17th century, the Ionian islands, many of the Aegean islands, Crete, and key fortresses and harbours such as Methone and Coroni in the south-western tip of the Peloponnesus.[70]

Greek-controlled successor-states included the Empire of Nicaea (which recaptured Constantinople in 1261), and the Despotate of Epirus, which through its capital at Arta, and trading with Venice and Ragusa/Dubrovnik, became a centre for preserving Byzantine religion and culture. The most successful emperor of Nicaea was John III Ducas Vatatzes (reigned 1222–54), who defeated the Franks in Anatolia, gained Thessalonica and Bulgarian Thrace, drove the Seljuk Turks from the Meander valley and reconquered Samos, Chios, Lesbos, Cos and Rhodes. He reasserted suzerainty over Epirus and prepared for the Byzantine recapture of Constantinople, which took place almost without fighting in 1261. The old times were scarcely restored: as Norwich remarks of Constantinople, "Everywhere was desolation: churches in ruins, palaces razed, once-prosperous residential areas now reduced to piles of blackened timber." Since 1204, many houses had "been demolished and used for firewood … there had been no attempt at rebuilding …"[71]

While the Western Church had not endeared itself by exiling Orthodox bishops in favour of Latins in the areas controlled by the Franks, this did not prevent a newly attempted compact in 1274. At the Council of Lyons, the first emperor of the Palaeologan dynasty, Michael VIII (1261–82) accepted papal primacy and Catholic doctrines on purgatory and the *filioque* clause. As with subsequent compacts, it brought little military benefit and destroyed Michael's credibility with his people – despite his assurances that the length of the sea journey meant that the Patriarchs would lose virtually nothing of their effective independence.[72]

The fate of Constantinople was, predictably, influenced by the rise and fall of other neighbouring states – as rivals, enemies, or when they fell, as bases for the developing Turkish stranglehold. The most immediate enemy was Charles of Anjou, king of Sicily, who also ruled south Italy and parts of France. He was routed by the Byzantines at Berat in Albania in March 1281, and his attempt to assemble a new armada provoked the Sicilian Vespers at Easter 1282 – the massacre of all the French on the island of Sicily, which now fell to King Peter of Aragon who had no interest in restoring the Latin Empire at Constantinople.

In Anatolia, before 1261, the Byzantines still controlled Lydia and most of Caria, including the richest parts of the Meander valley, the Aphrodisias plateau and the Cnidus peninsula – all protected by powerful frontier fortresses. The reconquest of Constantinople, however, turned attention to the west; the Anatolian border guards were no longer paid, and so revolted or defected. So in the 1260s much of Caria and Cnidus was lost to advancing Turks and the population abandoned the Meander valley. After 1274 Aphrodisias and Antioch-in-Pisidia fell and the Turks ravaged round Miletus and the Cayster valley. The whole area round Ephesus fell to the emir of Aydin in 1304.[73]

The Seljuk Sultanate had been shattered by the Mongols in 1243. Other Turkish tribes and thousands of Turcoman nomads from Persia and Iraq fled westward into Byzantine territory. By the start of the 14th century only a few major strongholds, Nicaea, Nicomedia, Sardis, Brusa, Philadelphia and Magnesia on Meander, and ports such as Ania/Kusadasi were still in Byzantine hands. The island of Prinkipo/Buyukada in the sea of Marmara had become a vast refugee camp for Greeks from Anatolia. In 1302 a local emir, Othman, the founder of the Ottoman dynasty, laid waste to virtually all Bithynia.[74]

While Catalan mercenaries, ostensibly in the service of the emperor between 1303 and 1311, ravaged Byzantine lands in Thrace, Macedonia and north-west Anatolia, in 1307 Othman destroyed the communications between Nicaea and Nicomedia. In 1326 the Turks took Brusa/Bursa after a long siege and made it their capital until grander sites became available. After the emperor Andronicus III had been defeated in 1329 on the shores of the sea of Marmara, Nicaea fell in March 1331, and Nicomedia in 1337. All that remained of the Empire in Asia was the isolated town of Philadelphia which the Byzantines held until 1391.

Agriculture and commerce were in crisis and the population diminished and impoverished. A bioarchaeological study of the health and diseases of infants and children in Byzantine Anatolia between 600 and 1350 revealed very poor living conditions in the 13th and 14th centuries, in contrast to those of children during the 7th to 10th centuries.[75]

The Empire was greatly weakened by civil wars. Although it sometimes found the right men to lead it – such as John Cantacuzenus (1347–54) – it was bankrupt, demoralised, under attack from every side and limited to Thessalonica,

Adrianople, Thrace, and a few islands in the northern Aegean. By contrast, the Serb Stephen Dushan, the self-styled emperor of the Serbs and Greeks, had conquered Macedonia, Albania, Epirus, Aetolia and finally Thessaly by the time of his death in 1355. He spoke fluent Greek, and absorbed Greek officials into his administration, with Greek titles, clearly but vainly aiming at taking Constantinople.

In 1354 the Ottomans occupied the fortress of Kallipolis (Gallipoli), as a spearhead for their invasion of Thrace, which fell easily to them. In the 1360s they captured Philippopolis/Plovdiv from the Bulgarians and then Adrianople which became their next capital. In every city and village occupied, a large part of the native population was transported to slavery in Asia Minor, with Turkish colonists settling in their place. In 1371 the two most powerful Serb rulers and their army – with Dushan's empire now divided – were annihilated by the Ottomans near the Maritsa river, west of Adrianople. Several of the surviving Serb lords submitted as tributaries to Sultan Murad, and emperor John V in 1372 made a treaty with Murad agreeing to convey regular tribute and troops to the Ottoman army on demand; this arrangement lasted for 25 years. Murad started the *devshirme*, the compulsory recruitment of boys from Christian families, converted to Islam, then educated and trained into an elite Ottoman corps known as Janissaries. These played a key role in the Ottomans' subsequent victories, while some ran the administration.

So the Ottomans advanced. Murad captured Ochrid in 1380, Serres in 1383, Sofia in 1385, Nish in 1386, and Thessalonica in 1387. He was assassinated at the moment of decisive victory over another Serb army at Kosovo Polje in 1389. His talented and aggressive son, Bayezit, annexed the core of Bulgaria in 1393. Manuel II was obliged by treaty to help the Ottomans enforce the surrender of the last surviving Byzantine stronghold in central Asia Minor, Philadelphia, and to assist in a campaign on the Black Sea coast in 1391. He wrote to a friend about the devastation of the country through which they passed, "There are many cities in these regions but they … have no people, and when I ask the names of the cities, the answer is always 'we have destroyed these places and time has destroyed their names'".[76]

Manuel renounced the treaty with the Sultan in 1394, and as a result Constantinople faced eight years of Ottoman threats, including a lengthy siege in 1394–95 and an assault in 1397. Despite privation – in which the only areas available for cultivation were the plots and gardens within the walls – the city survived. In 1396 what has been described as "the last of the great international Crusades", consisting of substantial forces from France, and contributions from other European states, marched down the Danube and joined large forces of

Hungarians and Wallachians. Because of the blockade, the Byzantines were unable to send land or sea forces to help. Through incompetence – as so often happened in previous crusades – this vast force was annihilated by Bayezit at Nicopolis, south-west of present-day Bucharest, in September 1396.

Manuel spent three years travelling in Italy, France and England seeking aid (1400–03). All had now good reasons not to get involved. Constantinople was saved this time by Tamerlane's massive Mongol invasion, which defeated and captured Bayezit at the Battle of Ankara in July 1402, going on to capture Bursa and Smyrna before turning back east. If Tamerlane had stayed in Anatolia, Ottoman power might have ended; as it was, it faced collapse following civil war among Bayezit's four sons. A peace treaty favourable to Byzantium (no more tributary obligations, recovery of Thessalonica and other coastal lands) was signed early in 1403. By 1413 Mehmet I had triumphed in these civil wars, but Manuel's diplomacy kept the peace until Mehmet died in 1421.

Confrontation followed between Murad II and Manuel's eldest son John VIII who "stupidly resolved to incite an internal rebellion against the new sultan".[77] Murad attacked both Constantinople and Thessalonica, and ravaged the Peloponnese. With a massive effort, and much death and destruction, Murad conquered Thessalonica in 1430. At the time, its inhabitants numbered 2000 people.

Yet another surrender to Rome took place, with John agreeing at the Council of Ferrara-Florence in 1438–39 to accept papal primacy, conceding that the *filioque* dispute "was based on a semantic confusion" and under protest agreeing to the Latin ban on the marriage of clergy. And "as in the past, the benefits of union turned out to be negligible for Byzantium".[78] The Council was universally condemned in the East.

There was a Balkan Christian military revival during the 1440s, with leaders in Transylvania, Hungary, Serbia and Albania defeating the Ottomans at Nish in 1443, occupying Sofia and fighting Murad at Varna (10 November 1444). There the Christians, greatly outnumbered, were once again annihilated. To teach the Greeks a lesson, Murad broke through a great wall where the Corinth canal now is, with the aid of his new cannons, and devastated the coast and the route towards Mistra, killing and taking thousands of captives (1446–47).

Cometh the time, cometh the man, or in this case, two men. In 1451 Murad died and was succeeded by the 19-year-old Mehmet, Fatih Mehmet or Mehmet the Conqueror. He was determined to capture Constantinople and began his assault on 6 April 1453. Such was the strategic significance of Constantinople's position, he persuaded his ministers that, with the possibility of the Byzantines entrusting their capital to Italians or Franks, "his own Empire ... could never be safe while the city remained in Christian hands."[79]

The efficient Turkish preparations for the siege and assault, including the use of their magnificent cannon, and the desperate efforts of the Byzantines and their very few European allies – mainly Genoese (just under 5000 Greeks and just under 2000 foreigners) to defend 14 miles of walls, are well known.

The Byzantines were led by the emperor Constantine XI, who had acceded to the throne four years earlier. He fell in battle defending his city on 29 May – a day henceforward regarded by Orthodox Greeks as especially ill-omened. After the inevitable sack and massacre (the latter less than in 1204), Mehmet sought to rebuild and repopulate, including organising 5000 Muslim families to move in.[80]

The Despotate of the Morea, based on Mistra, was conquered in 1460, and in August 1461, David Comnenus, the last emperor of Trebizond, surrendered. Two years later, he, his three sons and his nephew were executed in Constantinople. And in 1472, Sophia, Constantine XI's niece, married Ivan III ("the Great"), the Grand Prince of Muscovy. Their grandson, Ivan the Terrible, is made to say in his coronation scene in Sergei Eisenstein's 1943 film: "Two Romes have fallen; a third Rome, Muscovy, stands. There will not be a fourth Rome." Tsarist Russia was to become the scourge of the Ottoman Empire from the 17th century onwards.

Envoi: the Byzantine legacy

It is an inevitable paradox that Byzantium was able to spread her civilising power through her communications with those European nations she most frequently fought. She was able to recruit Bulgaria and Serbia to Orthodox Christianity. A greater achievement was the conversion of Kievan Rus – with the baptism of Prince Vladimir in around 988. The prince had been making inquiries of the various monotheistic religions, including Islam and Judaism, and "his choice of Byzantine-style Christianity was not inevitable".[81] Other missions went to peoples who in the end joined Rome rather than Constantinople – Saints Cyril and Methodius went to the Moravian "empire" (incorporating Czechs, Slovaks and some Poles).

The role of the foundations on Mount Athos (the Great Lavra was founded in 962–63) was significant. The seed sown proved durable, as Orthodox Christianity survived pagan Mongol rule in Rus and an even longer period of Turkish rule in the Balkans. The Byzantines wisely translated the Greek Bible into a written language – Cyrillic – invented by its scholars in order to facilitate the conversion of the Slavs, in contrast to their rivals insisting on everything sacred being in Arabic or Latin.

The Byzantine cultural revival in the 8th and 9th centuries contributed to the preservation of a sizable portion of the ancient Greek classics and early Christian writings, including Plato, Aristotle, Herodotus, Thucydides and the great dramatists. "From the point of view of western culture it may even be said that this act of salvage constitutes our greatest debt to Byzantium ... The Greek classics as we know them have come down to us in Byzantine manuscripts ... All the literature in question survived because it was recopied at the time ... What was not recopied has been lost."[82]

Emperor Constantine VII Porphyrogenitus (912–59) played an important role. He concentrated on compiling, employing teams of collaborators, a treatise of the Empire's foreign relations, a survey of its provinces, a collection of older treatises on agriculture and veterinary science and, "by far the biggest of his projects", an anthology of excerpts from a wide range of historians. Only six printed volumes have survived of this last-named, out of probably over 200. "Old texts were not copied at random; they were copied because they were considered useful ..." Without much of what was copied, "we would know much less than we do about Byzantium."[83]

The book edited by Mango has a full chapter (by Ihor Sevcenko) on *Palaiologan Learning* during the period 1261–1453. In this period about 150 laymen and ecclesiastics were active mostly at Constantinople but also at Nicaea, Arta, Thessalonica, Trebizond and Mistra. Their learning included the tables and treatises compiled by Arab and Persian astronomers which reached the Greek world (via Tabriz and Trebizond) about 1300. By a "lucky coincidence", Byzantine knowledge of Greek, ancient texts and access to manuscripts was increasingly valued in Italy. Meanwhile, the emperor Manuel II (1391–1425) was a "brilliant figure in the fourteenth-century revival of letters".[84]

However, the Patriarch Photios (858–67), known as "the inventor of the book review", preserved notes on plays of Aeschylus that are now lost. This in itself, in Judith Herrin's view, indicates "how much literature has been lost".[85]

Liveliness of cultural life was also noted in the two other centres of late Byzantine civilisation – Mistra and Trebizond. Mistra was the eventual home of "the most original of all Byzantine thinkers", George Gemistos Plethon. Manuel II was his friend and admirer and might well have saved him from being prosecuted for heresy. Having studied – in Turkish-held Adrianople – Aristotle, Zoroastrianism and Jewish cabbalistic philosophy, he saw Byzantium as the inheritor of the civilisation and literature of classical Greece. His "heresy" consisted of "highly subversive" lectures on Platonism." As a good Platonist he shared his master's frequently-expressed disapproval of Athenian democracy, infinitely preferring the discipline of Sparta" – hence Mistra, five miles from the ruins of Sparta, suited him. He proposed radical political and social reforms in memoranda addressed between 1415–18 to Manuel and his son, Theodore, the Despot of Mistra, as well as a new and idiosyncratic religion derived from ancient Persia and classical Greece. He died aged 90 in 1452.[86]

Cultural Byzantinism survived the Ottoman conquest. As Elizabeth Jeffreys and Cyril Mango declare, "The subject Orthodox population, both Greek and Slav, remained for the most part segregated from its Muslim neighbours … constituted into a single 'nation' (*millet*), placed under the authority of the patriarch of Constantinople."[87] After the Ottomans conquered Syria, Palestine and Egypt in 1516–17, the patriarchates of Alexandria, Jerusalem and Antioch and the pilgrimage sites of Palestine and Sinai were brought "into the Greek network", subject to the one proviso, "which the patriarchs had no trouble in observing … that the Church should remain loyal to the Sultan". That helps to explain why Patriarch Gregory V anathematised and excommunicated the Rumanian-based Alexander Ypsilantis for heading the Greek revolt of early 1821; it did not save the Patriarch who was hanged on Easter Sunday, 22 April 1821, on the Sultan's orders, to Greek and international outrage.

There was successful competition to the Byzantine route into western Europe. Constantinople was, inevitably, a major repository of ancient texts, but it was "not somewhere that science was studied with any degree of originality or rigour" – nor did translation and thus transmission take place there on a large scale.[88] Hence Violet Moller selects Toledo, Salerno and Palermo as the places where Arabic culture came into closest contact with Christian Europe – as well as the Levant during the Crusades and, of course, Venice.

She also draws attention to Christian censorship, pointing out that the Muslim raiding into Anatolia was not exclusively in search of treasure: it "was a major focus of the Abbasids' search for ancient Greek texts in the 9th century". A 10th century Arabic source, cited by her, describes an ancient temple in western Anatolia "locked since the time the Byzantines became Christians" which was full of ancient books. When the Arabs under Harun sacked Ancyra, the search for such books was a key aspect. And while the Christians in Syria and Egypt preserved Galen's medical works, enabling Arab scholars to use them in the 9th century, his philosophical works, which were distasteful to Christians, fell into obscurity.[89] 7th century Ravenna is criticised over the state of medical learning. "By this point, the medical corpus was a shadow, both in quality and quantity, of the enormous wealth of theory and debate that had prevailed in the ancient world." The Church frowned on the study of anatomy, hence this was left out of the curriculum. In 1417 a copy of *De Rerum Natura* by Lucretius was discovered, having been suppressed by the Church for its heretical ideas for over a millennium.[90]

In the centuries before the Renaissance, Palermo was one key link between the Byzantines and the West. The court of Roger II (count of Sicily from 1105, king 1130–54) was trilingual, using Greek, Latin and Arabic. His chief minister from 1126 was George of Antioch, a Greek who began his career with the Byzantine administration in Syria. The architecture, particularly of Palermo – the Concathedral, the Capella Palatina and the Norman palace, as well as the nearby cathedral of Monreale, shows a massive Byzantine influence as well as an Arabic one. Roger's grandson, the Holy Roman emperor Frederick II Hohenstaufen, known as "*Stupor Mundi*" – the "wonder of the world" – king of Sicily from 1198, Holy Roman emperor ruling largely from Sicily 1220–50, also patronised scholarship and encouraged translation.[91]

Before 1453, Greeks were coming in large numbers from areas threatened by invasion, bringing vast numbers of texts from Constantinople. This increased after 1453. A chair of Greek was established at Padua university in 1463. One of the great scholars was Basilios Bessarion (1403–72) from Trebizond, who had studied Neo-platonism in the Peloponnese with Plethon. Described as "a conduit for the movement of people, ideas and books from Byzantium to Italy … he saved huge swathes of Greek culture that would otherwise have been destroyed by the invading Ottoman Turks." He was made a cardinal, most unusually, and set up a library –the "most richly-endowed of all the libraries formed during the Renaissance". This was presented by him in 1468 to the Senate of the Venetian Republic, forming the nucleus of the library of St Mark's – the *Biblioteca Marciana*. His bequest is estimated " at nine hundred excellent volumes in Greek and Latin". Bessarion wrote to the Doge about Greeks "arriving … from their homelands, they debark first at Venice … and there they seem to enter another Byzantium".[92]

In sum, the Eastern Empire was distinguished for three major contributions to civilisation. First, its commitment to the Orthodox Church, as displayed in grand basilicas, with mosaics, frescoes and carvings in ivory, as well as the surviving personal icons. Much religious art perished under the earlier Iconoclastic emperors as well as under Seljuks and Ottomans, but the early 14th century interior decoration of the church of St Saviour in Chora (Kariye Camii), in Istanbul, is a surviving gem (if the present-day Turks will allow it). Byzantine religious art contributed, directly or indirectly, to what survives today in Russia, Ukraine, Armenia, Georgia, Syria and the Levant, as well as Ravenna, Venice, Sicily and elsewhere in southern Italy.

Second, it ensured continuation of Roman organisation and law, especially through Justinian's Code of classical jurisprudence without which the study of Roman legal theory would have become impossible. This included the Byzantine coronation ritual, with regalia, crown, orb and sceptre, which were all imitated in Western Europe.

Third, its enduring Greek inheritance and secular education which "preserved much of classical, pagan, learning", including "the ancient Greek romance, various forms of metric verse, hymns and epics [which] all flourished," as well as knowledge and study, though not the enactment, of the great Greek dramas. Judith Herrin states that the combination of all these made the Byzantine legacy unique.[93]

Among the great names of Byzantine historiography, theology and literature are Zosimus, a 5th century pagan, Procopius, secretary to Belisarius, John Malalas, and Jordanes, all 6th century chroniclers; the theologians St John Chrysostom, and the two St Gregories of Nazianzen and Nyssa, all 4th century. Later came chroniclers Leo Diaconus in the late 10th century, Psellus, John Zonaras, John Skylitzes and Anna Comnena, all 11th century, and the author of the *Strategicon* of Cecaumenus on the art of war, also in the 11th century. Some poetry or epigrams survive, from Paul the Silentiary in the 6th century, Constantine Cephalas (10th century), Theodore Prodromus and Nicetas Eugenianus in the 11th and 12th centuries, and Maximus Planudes (13th century). Most notable there is the 12th century epic poem by an anonymous author about the hero Digenes Akritos in the Byzantine–Arab frontier wars. There was a late flowering of historians: Laonicus Chalcocondyles, George Phrantzes and Michael Cristobulos of Imbros, all in the 15th century.

The Eastern Empire fostered a rich musical tradition, but few manuscript sources survive, and relatively few studies exist. Dr Nicolas Bell, former Curator of Music MSS at the British Library, states: "The music used in church services is exceptionally well preserved in hundreds of manuscripts, while virtually nothing survives of music in secular contexts." Our written sources contain reports of court ceremonies, as well as dancing, and some illustrations exist of the instruments used. Dr Bell continues: "All that is known today therefore concerns the chants sung in church, without instruments, according to traditions extending back to the origins of the Byzantine rite in 4th-century Constantinople and continuing in modified form in the Orthodox churches of today."

Those seeking architectural survivals of Byzantine glory east of Istanbul and Greece might find the search frustrating. In relatively recent travels, William Dalrymple gave examples of modern Turks trying to abolish history, though it seems that the main objects of their attention were Armenian rather than Byzantine. In 1986 in Sivas he saw a graveyard where Greek and Armenian tombstones jostled alongside others inscribed in Turkish. Returning the following year, he saw that the Armenian stones ("perhaps fifteen heavy slabs and memorials") had all gone; the custodian "denied that any such stones had ever existed", and he encountered other evidence that Armenian antiquities had been "smashed up", and the rubble "carefully removed".[94] Later, working as a journalist on the *Independent*, he was able to amass "a body of evidence which showed the alarming speed at which the beautiful, ancient and architecturally important Armenian churches of Anatolia were simply vanishing from the face of the earth".

Elsewhere, Dalrymple found unexpected Byzantine survivals. Climbing over a small wall in Syria separating two farms, he noticed that it was composed of "discarded doorjambs, carved tympana and inscribed lintels, an almost ridiculous richness of fine Byzantine sculpture", adding that such material was so "debased in value by the embarrassment of its profusion" that it was used for walling. "Wandering through a Byzantine villa" in northern Syria "through a succession of cool, high-ceilinged rooms, the stone still fitted perfectly … I felt sure that more of the ancient world had survived for longer in the Byzantine East than any of the surviving sources … now indicate."[95]

Another recent (re)publication gives impressive photographic evidence of glories now lost. 1909 saw the publication of *The Thousand and One Churches* by Sir William Ramsay and Gertrude Bell, with photographs taken by the latter of what the republication's editors describe as "remarkable architecture dating between the 5th and 11th centuries" in Lycaonia, south-east of Konya in southern Turkey. They add that the authors "witnessed the disappearance of the monuments almost as they were examining them"; by now, over a century later, many at this and related sites have long since gone.[96]

"A detail much moves me.

At the coronation at Vlachernae of John Cantacuzene …

As they had only a few precious stones

(The poverty of our poor empire was great)

They wore artificial ones. A lot of little bits of glass,

Red, green or blue." [97]

FOOTNOTES

1 Afrasiab was the mythical king of the Central Asian barbarians, enemies of Persia and seen by the latter as an agent of Ahriman, the Evil Principle.

2 Herrin, *op cit*, p87.

3 Bernard Lewis *What Went Wrong: The Clash between Islam and Modernity in the Middle East*, Weidenfeld and Nicolson, 2002, pp139–40, 151–57 for this and the following paragraph. While Lewis (1916–2018) was a polymath of the Middle East and Islam, he had become controversial in various ways in recent decades, including support of US neocons over Iraq and Iran.

4 Magdalino, "The Medieval Empire", from *The Oxford History of Byzantium*, edited by Cyril Mango, OUP, 2002, p201.

5 Venning, *op cit*, p139.

6 Moller, *op cit*, p20.
7 Brown, *op cit* (1996 edition), p127.
8 James Howard-Johnston, "Al-Tabari on the last great war of Antiquity", in *East Rome, Sasanian Persia and the End of Antiquity*, Ashgate Variorum 2006 p5.
9 James Howard-Johnston "Heraclius' Persian Campaigns and the revival of the Eastern Roman Empire 622–630", article VIII in *East Rome, Sasanian Persia and the End of Antiquity*, pp3, 4; subsequently *Campaigns*.
10 Peter Sarris, "The Eastern Empire from Constantine to Heraclius (306–641)", in Mango, ed, *The Oxford History of Byzantium*, p55. All other Sarris references are to *Empires of Faith*.
11 Howard-Johnson, *Campaigns*, p6.
12 Howard-Johnston, "Pride and Fall: Khusro II and His Regime", Article IX in *East Rome, Sasanian Persia and the End of Antiquity*, pp102–03.
13 Ward Perkins, *op cit*, pp124, 126–7.
14 Heather, *Restoration*, p189. Foss, "The Persians in Asia Minor", EHR 1975 pp721–47; also Foss, *Ephesus After Antiquity*, CUP, 1979, p87; Herrin, *op cit*, p148.
15 Cyril Mango "Constantinople", in Mango, *op cit*, pp69–70.
16 Hugh Kennedy *The Great Arab Conquests* Weidenfeld and Nicolson, 2007, hereafter *Conquests* p70.
17 *Ibid*, pp143, 145–6.
18 Heather, *Restoration*, p200.
19 Venning, *op cit*, p146.
20 Warren Treadgold, "The Struggle for Survival (641–780)", in Mango, *op cit*, pp129, 142.
21 Walter E Kaegi, *Byzantium and the Early Islamic Conquests*, CUP 1992, has a description and analysis of the campaign and battle in pp112–146.
22 Hugh Kennedy, "The Last Century of Byzantine Syria; A Reinterpretation", in *The Byzantine and Early Islamic Near East* Ashgate Variorum 2006, p147.
23 Kennedy, *Conquests*, p95.
24 *Ibid*, pp123, 129, 184, 306.
25 Kaegi, *op cit*, p24.
26 Kaegi, *op cit*, p149.
27 Kennedy, *Conquests* p203–4, quoting C J Wickham *Framing the Early Middle Ages*, Oxford 2005, p641.
28 Herrin, *op cit*, p147.
29 Brown, *op cit*, p383.
30 Kennedy "The Arab–Byzantine frontier in the eighth and ninth centuries: military organisation and society in the borderlands", in *The Byzantine and Early Islamic Near East*, Ashgate Variorum 2006, subsequently *Frontier*, p82. Much of the next few paragraphs is derived from this article.
31 Quoted Kennedy, *Frontier*, p97.
32 Kaegi, *op cit*, pp27, 30.
33 Sarris, *op cit*, p298.
34 Kennedy, *The Last Century of Byzantine Syria* in *The Byzantine and Early Islamic Near East*, Ashgate Variorum 2006, pp168–69, 183.
35 Ward Perkins, *op cit*, pp127, 145.
36 Warren Treadgold, "The Struggle for Survival 641–780", in Mango, *op cit*, p147; Herrin, *op cit*, pp153–4.
37 Sarris, *op cit*, pp302–03.
38 Clive Foss, "Life in City and Country", in Mango, *op cit*, pp78, 84; also illustrations of cities' areas in *ibid*, p143.
39 Kennedy, "Antioch: from Byzantium to Islam and back again", in *The Byzantine and Early Islamic Near East*, Ashgate Variorum 2006, p196.
40 Quoted Sarris, *op cit* p309.
41 Kennedy, *The Last Century of Byzantine Syria; A Reinterpretation* in *The Byzantine and Early Islamic Near East*, Ashgate Variorum 2006, p142.
42 Kennedy *Conquests* pp97, 160.
43 Cyril Mango, "The Revival of Learning", in Mango, *op cit*, p214.
44 Brown, *op cit*, p189.
45 Sarris, *op cit*, p303; Treadgold, *op cit*, p149.

46 Kennedy, *Conquests*, pp220–24.
47 Hugh Kennedy, *The Court of the Caliphs*, Phoenix 2005, p231.
48 Herrin, *op cit*, p145.
49 Steven Runciman, *The First Crusade*, CUP 1951, p30.
50 *Ibid*, p31.
51 Herrin, *op cit*, p218; Venning, *op cit*, p151.
52 Norwich, *Byzantium II, The Apogee*, Viking, 1993, p337.
53 Paul Magdalino, "The Medieval Empire 780–1204" in Mango, *op cit*, pp179–80.
54 Herrin, *op cit*, p121.
55 Norwich, *Byzantium, III, The Decline and Fall*, Viking, 1995, p25.
56 This and previous sentence quotes from Fuller, Maj.Gen. J F C, *Decisive Battles of the Western World*, Volume I, BCA by arrangement with Cassell, 2003, first published 1954, pp391–2, 397.
57 Fuller, *op cit*, p393–4, quoting George Finlay's *History of Greece* III, pp19–20.
58 Norwich, *op cit*, II p 343.
59 Description of Romanus, Norwich II p345; his campaign Fuller, *op cit*, pp398–99.
60 Norwich, *op cit*, p357.
61 Runciman, *op cit*, p66.
62 Fuller, *op cit*, p404, quoting J Laurent, *Byzance et les Turcs Seljoucides*, Berger-Levrault, 1914–19, pp106–09; the present author has quoted and translated more.
63 Runciman, *op cit*, p72.
64 A C S Peacock, *The Great Seljuq Empire*. Edinburgh University Press, 2015, p239.
65 Peter Frankopan, *The First Crusade: The Call from the East*, The Bodley Head, 2011, chapters 3 to 6, quotes on pp60, 63, 65.
66 Norwich, III, pp84–5.
67 Magdalino, *The Empire of Manuel I Komnenos 1143–80*, CUP 1993, p99.
68 Norwich, *op cit*, III p156.
69 *Ibid*, p179.
70 Stephen Reinert. "Fragmentation 1204–1453", in Mango, *op cit*, pp250–53.
71 Norwich, *op cit*, III p215.
72 Reinert, *op cit*, p257–58.
73 Foss, *Ephesus* pp141–43.
74 Herrin, *op cit*, p283.
75 Brandt and Hagelberg *et al*, editors, *op cit*, chapter 18, pp286–305.
76 Quoted Norwich, *op cit*, III p350.
77 Reinert, *op cit*, p276.
78 *Ibid*, p279.
79 Norwich, *op cit*, III p417
80 Reinert, *op cit*, p283; Herrin, *op cit*, p319.
81 Jonathan Shephard, "Spreading the Word: Byzantine Missions", in Mango, *op cit*, p236.
82 Cyril Mango, "The Revival of Learning", in Mango, *op cit*, p217.
83 *Ibid*, pp221–23.
84 Sevcenko, in Mango, *op cit*, p293; last quote Reinert, in Mango, *op cit*, p249.
85 Herrin, *op cit*, pp128–29.
86 Norwich, *op cit* III pp392–93.
87 Mango, *op cit*, p294.
88 Moller, *op cit*, p9.
89 *Ibid*, pp27–28, 53.
90 *Ibid*, pp176, 187, 245.
91 *Ibid*, pp211–12, 228.
92 *Ibid*, pp247–49, 253–54.
93 Herrin, *op cit*, pp142, 321–22, 329.
94 William Dalrymple, *From the Holy Mountain*, Harper Perennial 2005, pp82–83.
95 *Ibid*, pp179, 181–82.
96 Ramsay and Bell, *The Thousand and One Churches*, with a new foreword by Robert G Ousterhout and Mark Jackson, University of Pennsylvania Museum of Archaeology and Anthropology, Philadelphia, 2008, pp*ix*–*x*.
97 Poem by Cavafy *Of coloured glass;* Robert Liddell, *Cavafy A Critical Biography*, Duckworth, 2000, p199.

Chapter Three:
The Exception: The Glorious Revolution and the Ascent of Britain

"My brother will lose his kingdom by his bigotry and his soul for a lot of ugly trollops."
(Charles II, quoted Tim Harris, *Revolution – The Great Crisis of the British Monarchy 1685–1720*, Allen Lane, 2006, p9.)

"If the Queen had made an ape her general, and this ape had won so many victories, I should be on the side of the ape." (Sophia, Electress of Hanover, quoted W S Churchill, *Marlborough, His Life and Times,* Vol IV, George C Harrap, 1938, p487.)

Until 1752, all dates used in Britain were according to the Julian Calendar, thus Old Style. These were in the 17th century ten days, in the 18th century 11 days, behind the Gregorian Calendar or New Style used in most Continental countries. As this chapter mainly relates to English/British affairs, dates are normally given in Old Style, with the occasional New Style date being described NS.

As Margaret Thatcher stated on the tri-centenary of the "Glorious Revolution", it "established the tradition that political change should be sought and achieved through Parliament. It was this that saved us from the violent revolutions which shook our continental neighbours …"[1] While by 1695 this had ensured that power decisively passed from the Crown to Parliament, it did not enlarge the electorate. The other main effect was in the field of foreign policy.

By the middle of the 17th century, France had replaced Spain as the most powerful European state. Despite this, in the late 1650s, Cromwell decided to support France against Spain in a short war. Then Charles II became Louis XIV's pensioner. French subsidies kept him from dependence on Parliament. He went to war with the Dutch in 1672 by agreement with Louis. Under parliamentary pressure, he made peace in 1674 and after that Louis "does not seem to have taken him seriously as a possible ally".[2]

The Glorious Revolution in 1688–89 brought the three British kingdoms into war in Europe, with the objective in effect of protecting the balance of power by opposing Louis's aggressive policies.

This important development would not have happened without the Roman Catholic factor. Mary I's persecution of Protestants, including the burning of Cranmer, Archbishop of Canterbury, and Hooper, Ridley and Latimer, senior bishops, and nearly 300 others, shocked what existed as public opinion. With the accession in 1558 of Elizabeth, it was not until February 1570 that the Papacy declared war on her. Pius V's bull *Regnans in Excelsis* claimed that "Elizabeth, the pretended Queen of England and the servant of crime" was a heretic and released all her subjects from any allegiance to her, excommunicating any that obeyed her orders. This coincided with the Revolt of the Northern Lords in 1569–70, which had posed a serious threat to her but was suppressed with several hundred executions. The Massacre of St Bartholomew in France in August 1572 alarmed Protestants in England. Concern was sustained by the Ridolfi Plot, which aimed to assassinate Elizabeth in favour of the nearest Catholic claimant, Mary Queen of Scots. It failed, and the later, failed, Babington Plot in 1586 led to the execution of Mary.

The notorious Spanish Armada of 1588 was designed to invade, conquer and convert England, as was a feebler attempt in 1596. Spanish agents and forces poured into Ireland to support an Irish Catholic rebellion which engaged the English until 1603. Catholic conspirators produced the Gunpowder Plot of 1605, directed against James I, now king of Great Britain, and members of the Lords and Commons. All this made the mainstream of opinion hostile to Rome.

It did not, however, prevent the employment of important and loyal Catholics in high office under James I, Charles I and Charles II. And Protestant squires tended to be on good terms with their Catholic neighbours, recognising their loyalty. There was a residual concern over a possible Catholic threat to take back the abbey lands; but speaking in 1679 in the City, James, Duke of York, by then a recognised Catholic, made clear that it was in his own interest to defend all rights of property, and this issue was not reopened.

Neither the revolution of 1688–89 or the Hanoverian succession of 1714 was inevitable – there was an element of chance in both. The first arose as a result of incompetence almost amounting to misgovernment. The outcome was threefold. First, a new dynasty took power, which survived various revolts and firmly established itself in the nation's goodwill. Second, a constitutional settlement evolved, diminishing the power of the monarchy, increasing that of Parliament and increasing cross-party strife. And third, an increasingly wealthy and powerful United Kingdom now more frequently and successfully put its strength into European wars to preserve the balance of power, and by the extension of these on a transcontinental scale, acquired the foundations of an Empire in all five continents.

James II's misgovernment

The Popish Plot of 1679, a fraudulent concoction allied to the scheming of the Whig leaders, facilitated an (almost) unique attempt (for Britain) to change by legislation the line of royal succession. The aim was to exclude King Charles II's brother, James, Duke of York, from the succession on account of his being a Roman Catholic. There was bloodshed: the innocent victims of the revolutionary plotters, all executed or died in prison, totalled 35 throughout the country during 1679–81. They included the two Catholic archbishops in Ireland (Plunkett of Armagh, the primate of Ireland, was executed, Talbot of Dublin died in prison) and nine Jesuits executed, while another 12 died in prison.

Three separate Parliaments, between 1679 and 1682, tried to pass an Exclusion Bill; they were frustrated by defeat in the Lords and by dissolution. The third Parliament, meeting in Oxford, was summoned to Christ Church Hall and dissolved so suddenly that only the King, and none of the Lords, was in his robes.[3]

The royalists' return match came after the Rye House Plot of 1683, intended to assassinate the King and the Duke of York. This proved abortive, owing to the intended victims not making their proposed journey. One of the conspirators sold the secret to the government, and several notable persons were implicated in the confessions and revelations which followed. A total of 12 were executed, including two MPs, the Sheriff of the City of London and the former Warden of the Cinque Ports; ten were imprisoned, including three peers and three MPs, and another ten, including the Earl of Shaftesbury, a Whig leader, fled or were exiled. The Earl of Essex cut his throat in the Tower.

Charles II ensured the passage of the Succession Act in Scotland in August 1681, providing that on the death of the king the Scottish crown passed to the next in line, regardless of his religion. If Exclusion had triumphed in England, that might have meant war with Scotland, with English legitimists backing the Scots.

The Duke of Monmouth, a natural son of Charles, was the Exclusionists' candidate for the throne. After the Rye House plot he had fled to the Netherlands. Shortly after James came to the throne, in May 1685, Monmouth landed at Lyme Regis with about 150 followers. Up to 5000 mainly west-country men rallied to him, but with an absence of sympathetic risings in the north or in London, they were annihilated by the King's troops at Sedgemoor. Both Monmouth and the Duke of Argyll, who had attempted a rising in Scotland, were captured and executed in London and Edinburgh respectively, while under Judge Jeffreys, about 250 persons suffered death and 850 were transported to servitude in the West Indies.

Despite all this, James received an enthusiastic reception when he became King, and he could count on very loyal Parliaments in England and Scotland, elected in the spring of 1685. In his opening speech to Parliament, James repeated the promise made on his accession – to "defend and support" the Church of England and to "preserve this Government, both in Church and State, as it is now by Law Established".[4] However, as Tim Harris states, "James came undone because he failed to realise the extent to which the strength of the monarchy was based on this alliance between the crown and the Tory-Anglican interest."[5]

In 1685 James told Barillon, the French ambassador, that he intended to grant Catholics "entire liberty of conscience and free exercise of their religion; this is a work of time and it can be brought about only step by step". He later added that Monmouth's rebellion and the consequent expansion of royal forces gave him the opportunity for arming and employing Catholics who should not be subject to Test Acts which required all office holders under the Crown to take the Anglican sacrament. "I make no doubt if once liberty of conscience be well fixed, many conversions will ensue."[6] This was a brave aspiration, as the Catholic population of England was estimated at between one and five per cent of the total of 5.5 million; although one fifth of the peerage and a tenth of the gentry were Catholic, so Catholics appeared more powerful than they were.[7]

James's commitment is borne out by what Lauderdale, Charles II's powerful Scottish secretary, told his chaplain, one Dr George Hickes: James "has all that weakness of his father without his strength … he is as very Papist as the Pope himself, which will be his ruin". Hickes asked "will he venture the loss of three kingdoms for his religion?" Lauderdale replied "Yes, if he had the empire of the whole world he would venture the loss of it, for his ambition is to shine in a red letter after he is dead." In May 1686 the earl of Sunderland, Lord President of the Council, claimed to d'Adda (originally a Papal unofficial envoy who in July 1687 became Papal nuncio) that if the Test Acts of 1673 were repealed, there would be no Protestants left in England after two years.[8]

The King tried to persuade his personal friends at court to become Catholics: Rochester, former Lord President, refused and was dismissed as Lord Treasurer. The King tried to get a commitment from those in his service who sat in Parliament to repeal the Test and penal laws; he failed. He tried to persuade William of Orange (his son-in-law) to approve repeal in return for a voice in all civil and military appointments. In "a remarkable letter" to William, Lady Sunderland described this as a trap, as James could evade his promises.[9] James also tried, in vain, to convert princess Mary, having failed with his other daughter, Anne. And because of the religious and social dominance of the place, various inept episodes in Oxford seem to have rankled. In 1686 an Anglican who had turned Catholic was allowed to remain as master of University College; he set up an oratory in the college. John Massey, a known Catholic, was appointed by dispensation to be Dean of Christ Church (the head of the college). The King ordered the fellows of Magdalen to elect another Catholic as president; after a long dispute the resisting fellows were expelled and replaced by Catholics.

He increased the standing army from just over 8500 inherited from Charles to nearly 20,000 by the end of 1685. Neither the Tudors nor his father and brother had had such a peace-time force. He gave numbers of commissions to Catholics, in violation of the Test Act. Lord Halifax, who had spoken most forcefully against the Exclusion Bill, challenged this in council; James sacked him as Lord President. Following protests from the Commons asking that no more Catholics should be appointed to the army, which got a "stinging public rebuke" from the King, he prorogued Parliament in November 1685; it was never to meet under him again. He dismissed from his council all who had voted against his interest, including Bishop Compton of London. "It revealed a deeply ingrained arbitrary streak to his personality, an inability to tolerate anyone who would not support what he wanted to get done."[10]

Lauderdale, as Scottish secretary, had built up the strength of the Crown in Scotland until he retired in 1680; thus James was "able to rule Scotland almost as an absolute monarch and to show how he would wish to rule in England".[11] In Ireland, Tyrconnell, Lord Lieutenant, persuaded James that most Protestants in Ireland were Cromwellians and republican sympathisers, so the King authorised him to purge the army of them. Thus, while in 1685 all the officers and most of the rank and file had been Protestants, by September 1686 67 per cent of privates and 40 per cent of officers were Catholics, with Protestant chaplains replaced by Catholic priests. By the autumn of 1688 90 per cent of the army in Ireland was Catholic.[12]

In addition, in Ireland Jesuits were allowed to set up Catholic schools and in June 1688 James ordered vacancies in government sponsored schools to be filled by Jesuits. He reversed outlawries against eleven Irish lords to increase Catholic representation in the Irish upper house. While probably no more than 5 per cent of the Protestant population left Ireland during James's reign, Dublin lost 25 per cent of its Protestants.[13]

Argyll's rebellion gave James the excuse to appoint a Catholic (the Earl of Dumbarton) to the command of all forces in Scotland. In 1686 the Scottish Lord Chancellor Lord Perth converted to Catholicism, then Perth's brother, the Earl of Melfort, Secretary of State for Scotland in London, also converted. To cement his power, James removed 11 Protestant Scottish privy counsellors and put Catholics in their place. Expressions of concern by clergy saw the archbishop of Glasgow and the bishop of Dunkeld deprived of their sees.

In February 1687 James issued a Declaration of Indulgence for Scotland, with moderate Presbyterians being allowed to meet in private houses. The biggest gain was for Catholics who were offered not only toleration but also access to office with the repeal of the Test oath. The Presbyterians refused the benefit because it was restricted. This Declaration was used as the model for the one in England. James's toleration was carefully targeted: it was mainly directed at, and welcomed by, those such as Quakers and Baptists who tended not to be involved in public life. These were small but significant groups in England but infinitesimal in Scotland.

It would be wrong to see James as subservient to Louis XIV, simply in view of his taking money from France and post-1688 French support for him. He tried to keep England out of the threatening war in Europe, and was far from approving of Louis's aggression which was partly directed at Catholic powers: Spain and the Austrian Habsburgs. He stood up to Louis over North American disputes and renewed existing treaties with the Dutch. He did not approve of the revocation of the Edict of Nantes in 1685, especially the cruelty involved, but he was suspicious of Huguenots, believing them to be Republicans, and thus had no desire to welcome many of them into England.

In England, meanwhile, an Ecclesiastical Commission was set up to discipline Protestant clergymen; it suspended Compton from his duties as Bishop of London. The purge developed: by March 1688 19 new Lord Lieutenants had been appointed, 13 of whom were Catholics; one third of Deputy Lieutenants and one fifth of JPs were by the end of 1687 Catholics. These all had, in the circumstances of the time, very great electoral influence: the aim was to secure the election of MPs who would repeal the Test Acts.

James issued the English Declaration of Indulgence on 4 April 1687. Many Dissenters were suspicious; Halifax put his finger on the issue in his *Letter to a Dissenter* in August 1687; as the principles of the Church of Rome were hostile to liberty of conscience, dissenters were "to be hugged now, only that you may be the better squeezed at another time".[14]

The Declaration was republished on 3 May, with a royal order that it should be read in churches on two successive Sundays. It was read in just seven churches in the Metropolitan area, and in three of these, including Westminster Abbey, the congregation walked out. Across the country no more than 200 churches out of over 9000 saw the Declaration read.[15] This led to the petition of the Seven Bishops, including Archbishop Sancroft, asking to be excused from distributing and reading out the Declaration, not for religious reasons but "because that declaration is founded upon such a dispensing power as hath often been declared illegal in parliament". They met the King, who called the petition a "standard of rebellion".[16] The dissenters' leaders later visited the Bishops in prison in the Tower, where the latter also received supportive letters from Scottish Presbyterians. Even Sunderland was opposed to any attempt to punish the bishops, who were not arrested until 8 June. James intended to exercise clemency after their conviction for seditious libel. Crowds attended the trial and welcomed their acquittal on 30 June; significantly, soldiers on Hounslow Heath drank the bishops' health.

Coincidentally with this came the birth of a son to the Queen on 10 June, causing general surprise as James and the Queen had had no children. Many had up to this time awaited James's own demise, knowing that his nearest heir was his daughter Mary, married to William of Orange. This birth meant that the Catholic succession was assured. Protestants were sceptical that the baby was James's – there was "general suspicion of a fraud".[17]

The revolution

It seemed that the country would welcome change, not violent revolution or loss of control, but an orderly transfer if that could be done. So William of Orange had made it clear that he would only bring a force into Britain if he received a written invitation from a number of leading men. This document was agreed on the day the bishops were acquitted and in July it was brought to him by Arthur Herbert, lately vice-Admiral. It promised that "we, who subscribe this, will not fail to attend your Highness upon your landing." The names attached were in cipher: the Earl of Danby, longstanding chief minister of Charles II, Edward Russell, cousin of the Lord Russell who had been executed after the Rye House Plot, Henry Sidney, brother of Algernon Sidney who had also been executed; the suspended bishop of London, Henry Compton; and three peers, Viscount Lumley, and the earls of Shrewsbury and Devonshire. Danby and Compton were considered Tories, the other five Whigs. There were omissions: Halifax was "too circumspect", while others, such as Lord Churchill (later Marlborough), the army commander, were known to be sympathetic to the plotters.

Both William and Mary shared the general suspicions over the parentage of the royal baby. Mary "became convinced that her father had been guilty of a crime so horrible that only his dethroning by her husband could save both church and state. There is no more poignant illustration of the Protestant inability to trust Catholics, however well known and loved."[18]

In 1686 the Dutch fleet was weak and William had no money. The Dutch States General, however, were persuaded to vote for 490 ships to use against the pirates of Algiers, and 4 million guilders were voted for fortifications on the southern frontier; he was able to borrow the whole amount at once. The "Great Elector" of Brandenburg died in May 1688; he had been unwilling to act against France. His son, William's first cousin, was prepared to help, as was the Duke of Hanover. These represented Protestant Germany, key to the Grand Alliance of the next twenty-five years. On 8 October (NS) William told the foreign affairs committee of the States General that the Kings of France and England desired to subvert both the protestant religion and the Dutch republic. He did not intend to dethrone James but would secure the meeting of a free parliament. Literature produced for European consumption stressed the need for Dutch intervention to check Louis's aggression: England would join the anti-French alliance.

James began to compromise; on 24 August he announced Parliament was to meet on 27 November; writs were sent out on 18 September, and recalled days later as he decided a general election would cause confusion. He made promises over the Church of England and indicated a wish to restore DLs and JPs recently removed. He removed the suspension of the Bishop of London and restored the dismissed fellows of Magdalen. On 5 October he abolished his Ecclesiastical Commission. A general pardon, with very few exceptions, was issued and some of the Catholic Lord Lieutenants were removed.

The invasion was a huge gamble by William. His English associates expected that the English navy, with its tradition of fighting the Dutch, and its recollection of James as Lord High Admiral from 1660 to 1673, would support James. So they urged William, who was not confident that either army or people would desert James, to bring as many ships as possible. Both the English army and fleet had informal associations of Protestant officers. An observer thought that if the fleet had been ordered to fight the Dutch, most captains would not have done so.

James was reluctant to believe he was in danger, At the end of August Bonrepos, Louis XIV's special envoy, told James that if he did not believe the Prince of Orange was going to attack him, "he was the only person in Europe of that opinion";[19] though James did ask Louis to keep French ships ready at Brest. If Louis had complied – he did not – this would probably have doomed William's venture. In the mid-1680s both the Dutch and the French were each equal if not superior to England at sea. A report in 1686 found 142 out of 179 English ships unfit for service but plans were undertaken to repair them all by 1689. The French ambassador warned the Dutch that Louis would treat any attack on England as one directed at himself. The Dutch were reassured when, crucially, Louis marched against Philippsburg on the upper Rhine.

Even without the French, William might never have succeeded in making a landing. The sea journey was likely to be rough: it was a "huge risk launching a military campaign so late in the season".[20] At least 200 transports were required to carry his army, and "transporting an army by sea in the face of an un-subdued enemy fleet is one of the most hazardous operations conceivable".[21]

The English fleet was under the supreme command of Lord Dartmouth, a Protestant but a close adherent of James. In the circumstances, especially given the weather, it would have been too dangerous for it to attempt a close blockade of the Dutch coast. It seems both Dartmouth and James believed that the Dutch would not attempt to land without fighting at sea first.

William's first attempt to sail was on 19 October (NS), but adverse westerly winds prevented this until 11 November (NS). His initial aim was to head northerly for James's opponents in north England, headed by Devonshire and Danby, but the east wind on the 12th drove his ships in a south-westerly direction. An organised rebellion was being prepared in the north, with plentiful supplies and good roads; whereas the potential rebels in the south-west were thought to be cowed by the savagery with which Monmouth's rebellion had been suppressed. However, Herbert, who commanded William's fleet, favoured the west from a naval angle.

On the morning of the 13th (NS) the Dutch were sighted by the English fleet, which was lying between Clacton and Foulness. The English were "just too late to catch the Dutch" – the flood tide and the east wind made it impossible for them to get round the sandbanks on the south side of the Thames estuary.[22] The Dutch reached the Straits of Dover by noon on the 13th and their transports in convoy extended to within a league of the shore on either side.

Alarmingly missing Torbay, its target, and facing the prospect of landing at Plymouth – "hopelessly remote … even if the commander proved friendly" – William's fleet was saved by the same "Protestant wind", which again changed and blew them back to Torbay. There the landing began on 5/15 November. Dartmouth's captains unanimously advised him not to engage if the possibility of hindering a landing had passed; as their opinions were taken separately "it would seem that professional opinion coincided with the politics of the disaffected".[23] Only on the 26th (OS) did Dartmouth sail for Torbay; storms prevented contact and caused him to return to Portsmouth.

William's *Declaration … Of the Reasons Inducing him to Appear in Armes in … England* was published in the Hague. It was largely drafted by Danby, with William rejecting extreme Whiggish proposals to rehearse grievances not only against James but against Charles II and Tory Anglicans. It blamed the King's counsellors, accusing them of overturning "the Religion, Laws and Liberties" of the three kingdoms, promoting "Arbitrary Government", and endeavouring to introduce "a Religion which is contrary to Law". These evil counsellors had invented the King's suspending power, purged judges, procured the appointment to public office of Catholics who were rendered by law "Incapable of all such Employments", promoted Catholic worship, set up Jesuit schools, and purged the lieutenancy, magistracy and town corporations of those who refused to agree to the repeal of the Tests and penal laws. Finally, it was William's design to "have a free and lawful Parliament assembled as soon as possible" to address grievances.[24]

William appeared outnumbered on land. He had over 10,000 regular infantry and 3000 regular cavalry, together with Huguenot, Swedish, Brandenburger and Dutch volunteers, many of whom were professional soldiers. But James sent nearly 30,000 troops to camp on Salisbury Plain. Perversely, James brought the whole Scots army to help, thus facilitating the revolution in Scotland, where William was popular, and James had four Irish regiments with him; the rumoured terror aroused by these made them counter-productive.[25] A royal proclamation ordering all subjects to arm to defend the country provided a pretext for many conspirators to arm themselves. And the one attempt to arrest a conspirator, Lord Lumley, was a fiasco as the agent sent was himself a conspirator![26]

William occupied Exeter on 9 November, where much support rallied to him from Devon, Dorset and Somerset: the Duke of Beaufort was the only Lord Lieutenant to "make any concerted effort to stop supporters joining the Prince".[27] The campaign was not bloodless; there were some skirmishes with 30 fatalities at Wincanton on 21 November and at Reading (between 30 and 50) on 9 December.

With James reaching Salisbury by 19 November, William passed through Chard and Yeovil on the 21st. By then the momentum of desertion from James was building: on 12 November, Viscount Cornbury, commander of the royal dragoons, and Thomas Langston, with the Duke of St Alban's regiment of horse, deserted and crossed into William's lines (taking however few of their troops with them). Others came over in the following week. James was already planning to send his queen and baby son to France and "this was calculated to speed his own demoralisation"; he was "personally half-beaten by the time he put himself at the head of his army". He was suffering from severe nose bleeds, rumoured to have been symptoms of a minor stroke.[28] A council of war took place on the 22nd; Feversham, the army commander, wanted to retreat to London, Churchill wanted to stand firm. James decided on retreat to a new defensive line on the Thames by Marlow. That night Churchill absconded – a most significant blow – followed by other aristocrats, including Prince George of Denmark (the husband of Princess Anne). All this greatly demoralised the remaining troops.

James had no intention of negotiating with William or meeting Parliament until the invasion had been repelled. He forbade anyone to have contact with the invaders "upon pain of high treason". Sunderland, Lord President, was losing his nerve – at the end of November he was dismissed. As the King was failing to reassure even his leading subjects, it is not surprising that there was "no resurgence of loyalty in face of the invaders".[29] On 30 November, the *Gazette* announced that Halifax, Nottingham and Godolphin were to negotiate with William on James's behalf. William delayed seeing them until he got to Hungerford on 7 December. He then replied that both armies should remain 30 miles outside

London; both men would preside over the opening of a new Parliament, either unarmed or accompanied by the same number of guards.[30]

The passivity of James's supporters in the west had encouraged rebellion in the north. A rising in Cheshire was headed by Lord Delamere, a Whig, in alliance with the Tory Earl of Derby. Consistent with British confusion of territorial titles, the Earl of Devonshire marched his tenants into Derby on 17 November, proceeding to Nottingham by the 20th. Delamere joined them there on the 21st and then headed by way of Birmingham and Worcester to join Williamite supporters in Bristol. Devonshire remained in Nottingham, joined by forces from Northamptonshire and Buckinghamshire, and then on 2 December by princess Anne and Bishop Compton. They then marched to Oxford, a small army of 1500, with many having joined it to protect the princess, not necessarily to support William.

On 22 November Danby seized York and by the beginning of December had obtained the surrender of the important garrison at Hull. He was not resisted by the Duke of Newcastle, who played an ambiguous role, while Danby's Tories concerted plans with Devonshire and his Whigs. In East Anglia, the Duke of Norfolk raised the militia for William, taking Norwich and King's Lynn. On the Welsh borders Lord Herbert of Chirbury, with the gentry of Worcestershire and Herefordshire, seized Worcester and Ludlow. Everywhere measures were taken to disarm the local Catholics.

Plotters in the fleet decided the time was ripe to give the commander, Lord Dartmouth, the prince's letter (written on 12 November). Dartmouth replied to William, putting the fleet at his disposal, promising to remove all Catholics from command and to do his best to resist any French forces that appeared. On the 14th William reached Windsor, with Churchill and Grafton trying to bring the disintegrating royal army under control.

James arrived back in London on the 26th. He was panicking and fearful and told Barillon that if he placed himself at the mercy of a free Parliament "I should be forced to undo all that I have done for the Catholics and to break with the King of France." He told a meeting of various Lords on 27 November: "he had read the story of King Richard II". On 22 December, before his second and final flight, he told Lord Ailesbury "if I do not retire, I shall certainly be sent to the Tower, and no king ever went out of that place but to his grave." [31]

So he decided to flee the country, sending his wife and baby son to France on 10 December. He tried to follow on the 11th but was stopped in Faversham. He returned to London on 16 December, and sent Feversham, his army commander, to William to invite the latter to the capital. William, now in a position of strength, arrested Feversham for having disbanded his army without paying it.

William met a group of peers in Windsor and asked advice about what to do about James. Delamere, Macclesfield and Stamford – all firm Whigs – wanted him put in the Tower. William rejected this: Mary would not have tolerated it. James, having ordered his Coldstream Guards to give way without fighting in London, spent one night (17–18 December) in Whitehall palace guarded by the Dutch guards! He then left by barge for Rochester, accompanied by two boatloads of Dutch guards, and set off for France on the 23rd. "In this the motive of uncle and nephew was to allow a second flight by James."[32] William entered London on the 18th.

James left behind a manifesto, which referred to his stay in his palace in London, surrounded by the Dutch guards, and to the arrest of Feversham. What protection, James asked, could he expect from a man guilty of "the greatest aspersion upon me that malice could invent" that is, denying the parentage of the baby Prince of Wales. William Lloyd, Bishop of St Asaph, described this as a "Jesuitical masterpiece."[33] James certainly had reason to fear. After he fled the first time, on 11 December, crowds of several thousands in London attacked all houses where they suspected mass was being said or priests lodged, including the Spanish and other Catholic ambassadors' residences; that of Barillon, the French ambassador, was guarded by troops. Underlying this disorder were rumours over threats from Irish troops from places as disparate as Dartford, Norfolk, Surrey, the Midlands and Doncaster.[34]

William called a meeting for 26 December of the surviving MPs from Charles II's reign, plus the Lord Mayor, aldermen and 50 representatives of the common council of London, with MPs from James's 1685 parliament ignored. He assumed responsible government on the 28th. In the elections to the subsequent Convention Parliament, there were only 50 contests, with some constituencies deciding to have one Whig and one Tory. Thus the parties were matched, with 174 known Whigs, 156 known Tories and 183 new members.

William was very wisely totally unattracted by any plan to claim the crown by right of conquest ratified afterwards by Parliament. But by running away, James effectively forced him and the Tory leaders to accommodate themselves to Whig views. Most of the Tories and the bishops were against a break in the succession. They favoured either the restoration of James on specific terms, or a regency under Mary with James keeping the title of king. Failing either of these, they preferred to settle the throne on Mary alone. The main body of the Tories favoured the idea that James might return and William would be Regent – surely an exceedingly messy outcome. They argued, however, that if it was once conceded that the lawful ruler might be removed, any subsequent monarch would be vulnerable.[35]

William urged both haste and the need for unity because of "the dangerous condition of the Protestant Interest in Ireland" and the state of foreign affairs. France had declared war on the Dutch on 26 November (NS), and before the Convention met on 23 January 1689 William ordered Barillon, the only foreign diplomat to accompany James to Salisbury, to leave the country in 24 hours.[36] The debate in the Convention's Commons on 28 January was opened by Gilbert Dolben, a Tory, who argued that "the king is demised" – he said the law meant "deserted the Government" – *demisio* meaning "laying down." While some Whigs made the case for abdication, there was concern for the consequences if the Scots went a different way. And recognition had to be given to the existence of the Prince of Wales. Popular feeling was strongly against James and for William.

The Commons resolution accused James of endeavouring "to subvert the Constitution of the Kingdom by breaking the original contract between king and people, and by the advice of Jesuits and other wicked persons having violated the fundamental Laws and having withdrawn himself from the kingdom, has abdicated the government and that the Throne is thereby become vacant". On 29 January, the Commons passed a further resolution "that it hath been found, by Experience, to be inconsistent with the Safety and Welfare of this Protestant kingdom to be governed by a Popish Prince". The Lords unanimously agreed with this, but the proposal for a regency, as the King being a Catholic "was incapable of Administering the Government", attracted powerful support in the Lords and was only defeated by 51 to 48. William then made it clear at a meeting with Danby, Halifax and other peers on 3 February that he would return to Holland, with his army, if the Convention decided for a regency or to make Mary queen alone. The politicians would thus have no protection if James returned with French troops. Furthermore, Mary had written to Danby stating that she had no wish to reign alone.

A "truculent letter" from James was discovered, showe he was preparing to invade Ireland. On 6 February the Lords agreed with the Commons that the throne was vacant; on the 12th the Declaration of Rights was approved by the Convention and on the 13th William and Mary were proclaimed king and queen of England (as agreed without a division in the Convention on the 6th).

The Declaration of Rights stipulated that after the deaths of William and Mary the crown should pass to the heirs of Mary or if she was childless to Anne and her heirs. It also laid down two new oaths to be taken by all those previously required to take such oaths, one of allegiance to King William and Queen Mary and the other, the oath of supremacy. This latter stated "[I] from my heart abhor, detest and abjure as impious and heretical this damnable doctrine and position, that Princes excommunicated or deprived by the Pope or any Authority of the see of Rome may be deposed or murdered by their subjects or any other whatsoever."[37] The Bill of Rights eventually laid down that no one could come to the throne who was *or ever had been or had married a papist*.[38]

The monarch still had the right to determine all questions of policy, foreign or domestic, choose ministers, veto parliamentary legislation, and determine when and for how long Parliament should sit. The monarch's need for a regular income, however, meant that Parliament would have to meet every year. After resisting it in 1689 and 1693, in 1694 William accepted a Triennial Bill to limit the duration of each parliament; elections would happen every three years or sooner.

The vast majority of English people are believed to have accepted the dynastic shift. By the end of 1690 most prominent laymen and clergy had sworn allegiance to the new monarchs. Some others felt a bond of loyalty to James – his closest political advisers, personal servants, some colleagues from the armed forces and, of course, many Catholics and some Anglicans who "could not accept the legitimacy of the new regime and persisted as Jacobites or non-jurors". About 400 clergy (about 3.5 per cent of all clergy) refused the oaths and became non-jurors, as did ten peers, 61 former or present MPs and nearly half the bishops, including Archbishop Sancroft. Dryden lost his post as poet laureate for refusing allegiance; up until his death in 1700 he published plays and poems defending James. The majority of non-jurors were not Jacobites in any meaningful sense – they simply felt bound by their oaths to James. It is thought that they would not have welcomed his return nor were willing to seek it. In this respect, Jacobitism was "not a significant force in England in the immediate aftermath" of 1688–9.[39] Various assassination plots against William gave the Whigs an excuse to press office holders and members of the two Houses to declare that he was the "rightful and lawful" king, with penalties for those who refused.

Scotland and Ireland

The other two kingdoms witnessed serious fighting. In Scotland the out-turn was similar to that in England; in Ireland it was less happy.

The low level to which James's support in Scotland had sunk is shown by the difficulty the Scottish council had in encouraging public celebrations for the birth of the Prince of Wales.[40] The Earl of Perth resigned in the second week of December after anti-Catholic rioting in Edinburgh. He fled to the Highlands, but was arrested and imprisoned until 1693.

On 10 January 1689 a Scottish assembly meeting with William in London unanimously agreed to invite him to assume the running of all civil and military affairs. On 16 March the Scottish Convention heard two letters from William and James, the former moderate, while James was uncompromising. This made the assembly more determined to settle the Government on William; the *Claim of Right* stated "no Papist can be King or Queen of this realme." James had "forfaulted" the Scottish throne by altering it "from a legal limited monarchy to an arbitrary despotic power".[41]

June 1689 saw rebellion headed by Viscount Dundee in the Highlands, with James hoping to join these forces in Scotland with an army from Ireland. The Government's army was beaten at Killiecrankie on 27 July. "Bonnie" Dundee, however, was killed; the rebels lost momentum, were beaten at Dunkeld on 21 August and finally put down at Cromdale on 1 May 1690.

As before in the 1590s and the 1640s, Ireland proved a much harder nut to crush. By early February 1689 Tyrconnell had raised an army of around 45,000. These forces were short of arms and clothing and had no siege train. In the countryside they pillaged cattle and grain and the houses of Protestants. During that winter large numbers of Protestants fled to western England and Wales.

James landed at Kinsale on 12 March 1689, receiving a great reception. He summoned a Parliament for 7 May and as some Ulster counties refused to make returns, the House that met was overwhelmingly Catholic. To James's dismay, it passed an Act of Attainder, listing nearly 2500 individuals, mainly Protestant landowners, who would suffer the penalties of treason , viz both death and confiscation of estates, unless they returned to allegiance by a certain date.

Ireland suffered a "bloody and long" war.[42] James regained control over most of the north except Derry and Enniskillen. The former was blockaded; after facing starvation, it was relieved in July 1689. With reluctance, William sent over a well-armed force of 20,000, largely Dutch, Danish and Huguenot; he decided that he would have to command in person. In the Battle of the Boyne on 1 July 1690 William's well-manoeuvred 36,000 soundly defeated James's 25,000. William's success was celebrated by *Te Deum*s in St Peter's Rome and the Catholic capitals of Vienna and Madrid – all allied against Louis XIV. Again panicking – his Irish supporters were very critical of him for this – James fled to France. William took Dublin on 5 July. The war dragged on for another year, but the French did not provide muskets and powder for the large but ill-trained Irish army that was raised. 5000 or so French troops arrived but were under restricting orders, as Louis's main aim was to divert William from his Continental operations. William tried and failed to storm Limerick on 27 August 1690; he lost over 2300, a "major loss of trained manpower" and raised the siege on the 29th.

The French then withdrew most of their troops, and the Jacobites were eventually defeated at the hard fought but decisive battle of Aughrim on 12 July 1691, where they lost around 7000 killed and 450 taken prisoners, against Dutch Ginkel's loss of just under 2000 killed. Galway and Sligo surrendered and 23,000 demoralised and badly equipped Irish were besieged in Limerick by land and sea. The war ended when Limerick surrendered on 3 October. The Treaty of Limerick, very wisely, allowed recalcitrant Irish troops to go to France, and it is thought that around 12,000 did so.

The Irish war was being waged against the background of a serious naval threat from France. Even after the indecisive battle of Bantry Bay on 11 May 1689, the English were not able to interrupt French communications with Ireland; the French fleet had been landing troops and stores in Bantry Bay.

During the 1690s and the early 18th century, a series of measures "dramatically curtailing the rights and religious freedoms of Catholics" in Ireland were enacted.[43] Membership of the Irish Parliament was confined to Protestants by English parliamentary legislation of 1691 requiring all office holders in Ireland and members of the parliament to take the oaths of allegiance and supremacy stipulated by the English Declaration of Rights, and to subscribe a declaration against transubstantiation – actions no Catholic could undertake. They were prohibited from voting, sitting on juries, serving as constables or in the armed forces, or acting as schoolmasters or private tutors.

The Irish Parliament's Banishment Act of 1697 deported all Catholic bishops, Jesuits and regular clergy. In 1698 Catholics were prohibited from practising law; hence the only profession open to them was medicine. Thus between 1703 and 1789 some 5500 Catholics registered themselves as converts to the Church of Ireland, and other measures over inheritance meant that the proportion of land held by Catholics fell from 22 per cent in 1688, to 14 per cent in 1703 and to around five per cent by 1779. And contemporaries estimated that between 50,000 and 80,000 Scottish (Protestant) families settled in Ulster during the reigns of William and Anne.[44]

"It is ... true of these laws as of the previous penal laws, that they were not rigidly and consistently enforced ... laxity increased as time went on. No one suffered death for his religion." But "there could henceforth be no doubt of Ireland's subordinate status".[45] A realistic conclusion is that the religious divide – and religion was important until the late 20th century if not beyond – probably would have doomed any Irish contentment within the wider British alignment.

A turning point

Most Protestants in the three kingdoms believed they had been saved from a genuine Popish Plot. There is, however, no evidence that James was planning a sudden and violent take-over in the interests of his Church, or that he was envisaging persecution of the 16th century Marian variety. While his apologists might argue that he had a modern view of toleration, it is extremely unlikely that this was realistic. The Catholic Church of the time was not noted for policies of toleration. In France, the one country where a Catholic state had by treaty tolerated a Protestant minority, this toleration had three years previously been brutally removed. James himself hoped that the removal of bars on Catholics holding civil and military office would tilt (he had hoped more speedily than proved to be the case) towards gradual Catholic supremacy. Whether such a Catholic regime would eventually tolerate any kind of Protestant dissent is extremely doubtful.

With the death of Queen Anne's sole surviving child in 1700, the government in 1701 passed the Act of Settlement, designating the succession after Anne to the Electress Sophia of Hanover, and her descendants. There remained doubts whether English Tories would, in the event, support the Hanoverian succession.

An important constitutional question occurs: if James had remained on the throne, with his policies undiminished, would the Union with Scotland have taken place? There can be no doubt that the Union, when it came in 1707, proved to be in the long-term interest of both kingdoms, with freedom of trade with England and her colonies, increasingly settled by Scots, and unification of the currency. Would it have appealed to James, as a measure essentially stimulated by the two Parliaments? Union was described as an "Act for securing the protestant religion and presbyterian church government" as a "fundamental condition" – and would undoubtedly in practice have weakened James's "absolutist" hold on Scotland.

The most significant change was in foreign affairs. If James had remained on the throne, it is unlikely that he would have actively backed France in her great war, beginning in 1688, against most of Europe, including Catholic Austria, Spain, Bavaria and Savoy. He would, however, have simply remained neutral, and it is unlikely that Britain's neutrality would have been enough to protect the European balance. Would James have helped to save the Netherlands, much of Germany, and parts of Italy from absorption into a French empire of the extent that Napoleon was to create a century later? Both before and since this period, Britain had been opposed to having a hostile power dominating the Netherlands. The wars of 1689–97, 1702–13 and 1742–48 saw most British land fighting in the southern Netherlands with the intent of protecting this area from absorption in France.

Once James and his baby son and heir were ousted from England, both became dependent on French armies, fleets, and dynastic and diplomatic recognition and support. If either had regained the throne, it is likely that this active alliance with France would have continued, to the detriment of the European balance, as well as to Britain's ability to make the colonial gains she made over the next 70 years.

Two great continental wars
a) The Nine Years' War 1689–97

The growth of French power during the 1670s had already stimulated anti-French feeling in England. French economic growth under Colbert's high tariffs made City merchants hostile. England was also alarmed at the growth of the French navy. In April 1689 the Commons condemned French schemes "for the subversion of the liberties of Europe", and argued that England should help to maintain a balance of power. England perceived the military and commercial dangers if France obtained the southern (the then Spanish) Netherlands.

An invasion scare in 1696, with James moving to Calais, was to coincide with "the most dangerous of all the plots against William". He was to be murdered on his return from his weekly hunting in Richmond Park. The plotters talked, and nine conspirators were executed.

The Whigs set up an association to defend the King's person and the Junto, a group of Whig leaders, demanded that members of both Houses should subscribe to this to defend "their rightful and lawful monarch". It is significant that 100 Tories in the Commons and about 20 in the Lords refused.[46]

The European war of 1688–97 took place between France, without allies, and the Grand Alliance established in May 1689 by a treaty between William on behalf of the Dutch and (later) England with the Emperor, Bavaria and Denmark; Spain and Savoy joined it in 1690. Its objective was to resist Louis's actions of aggrandisement since the last major peace treaty, that of Nijmegen in 1678. By 1688–89 Louis was encroaching on the archdiocese of Cologne and the electorate of the Palatinate. In addition to the Dutch and Denmark, several Protestant German states were now sufficiently alarmed to join the alliance, notably Brandenburg, Saxony and Hanover.

The French aroused what Clark terms "a nearer approach to German national resistance than Louis XIV had ever encountered before",[47] this especially caused by their evacuation and devastation of the Palatinate and Baden in early 1689, when Heidelberg, Mannheim and another 20 towns, plus countless villages, were burnt. However, the French performed strongly in the war. Their fleet, of 90 ships of the line, was only slightly outnumbered by the combined English and (declining) Dutch fleets at just over 100. France launched more warships than England in the early 1690s, while England increased her sea power relatively during the late 1690s and by 1700 had overtaken France.[48]

Invasion might have followed a naval reverse off Beachy Head in July 1690, but the French did not have an invasion force ready because Louis was concentrating on the Netherlands. Invasion forces were prepared in the summer of 1692, but secrecy was lost.[49] In early June 1692, the French were seriously defeated, losing

15 ships of the line and transports, by a far larger Anglo-Dutch fleet in the bay of La Hogue. After this, their main effort was in commerce raiding: the ravages of Jean Bart and the capture or destruction of over 80 of the 200-strong Anglo-Dutch Smyrna convoy off Lagos in Portugal in June 1693. The City of London ranked this last as the worst financial disaster since the Great Fire.

On land, the French had superior numbers in the earlier years but, by their choice, it was more a war of trenches and sieges. William's forces reached their highest number in 1694, at 90,000, (about a third of the foot and half the cavalry were foreign mercenaries).

In the years 1689–93, the French defeated the Allies at Fleurus, Steenkirk, and Neerwinden, capturing Mons, then Namur, then Charleroi, routing the Duke of Savoy at Staffarda and Marsaglia, and invading Spain. The tide began to turn in 1694, when the Allies for the first time outnumbered the French in the Netherlands and while France was suffering from an economic crisis, with harvest failures and a severe famine. (Two million died in France in the winter famines of 1693 and 1709.)[50] Namur was retaken in 1695, but in the final months of the war the French took Ath and Alost, Cartagena in the Caribbean, and Barcelona. Peace was made at Ryswick in late 1697. To gain favour at Madrid over the vexed issue of the Spanish succession, Louis gave back some of his conquests, including Catalonia, Luxembourg and other places in the southern Netherlands, where the Dutch were allowed to strengthen their defences by placing garrisons in various fortresses (the "Barrier Fortresses").

This and the next great continental war proved very expensive for England. The Crown's total annual income under James never exceeded £3 million, whereas in the last full year of the 1688–97 war annual military spending alone had reached £8.1 million. It peaked at £10.2 million per annum in the following decade, during the War of the Spanish Succession.[51] While Charles II's army had cost £283,000 in 1684, and James II's £620,000 per annum, between 1692 and 1697 the army and navy *each* cost an annual average of £2.5 million. During the War of the Spanish Succession, Parliament voted funds in 1706 for 50,000 troops recruited from the British Isles, rising to 75,000 such troops by 1711; Britain also paid for large numbers of foreign troops – so by 1709 the total pay bill was for around 150,000.[52]

To assist all this, the National Debt was started in 1692, and the Bank of England was created in 1694. This raised substantial sums at a lower rate of interest than that paid by France and others. As well as considerable levies on foreign trade, in 1693 England introduced her first high yield direct tax – the Land Tax. It was to finance all the wars of the 18th century, and its burdens upset the country gentry, who were the backbone of Toryism.

Prohibitions and tariffs enabled a group of industries newly established by Huguenot refugees, such as silk weaving, papermaking, cutlery and plate glass manufacture, to take root. Despite a run of bad harvests, England was becoming an increasingly prosperous capitalist country.

b) The War of the Spanish Succession 170213

The sickly King of Spain, Charles II "The Bewitched", was childless. By the time he died, in 1700, there were two surviving claimants, one a Bourbon, Louis's grandson, Philip, and the other the Austrian Emperor's second son, the archduke Charles. Various partition treaties had been made to ensure that the vast Spanish dominions, in Europe and America, should not pass wholly to one of the claimants. In his will, the dying Charles bequeathed all his possessions to Philip, and Louis accepted this.

Events swiftly moved against a peaceful outcome. The French set about occupying the Spanish Netherlands while the Elector of Cologne allowed the French to occupy towns in his territory threatening the Dutch. The French also entered Lombardy, so on 7 September 1701 (NS) England, Holland and the Emperor formed another alliance. And Louis caused massive offence in England, first, by prohibiting all imports into Spanish America from England, Scotland and Ireland, and second, when James II died (17 September, NS), by recognising his son James "the Old Pretender" as King of England. "England's performance in the previous war had not disabused Louis of the idea that she was a lightweight power", hence "a general offensive was in prospect against England's whole commercial and colonial position".[53]

War broke out weeks after William's death in a riding accident on 19 March 1702 (NS). France was less isolated than in the previous war, with Bavaria as an ally, to threaten the Austrian homeland, and the support of most in Spain and the Spanish dominions, who welcomed Philip, now the Vth of Spain. That France found this war much more difficult is evidence, first, of her economic exhaustion, and second, a tribute to the skill of the Allies' two key commanders, Marlborough, who commanded English, Dutch and German troops in the Netherlands and nearby, and Prince Eugene of Savoy, who commanded Imperial troops, initially in Italy, and later in conjunction with Marlborough.

At times, especially in the early years, Marlborough was hampered by the caution of the Dutch government, whose forces he commanded. Thus, while he captured Liege in 1702, the Allies lost ground in Germany; in 1703 he captured Bonn and Limburg. Meanwhile the steady advance down the Danube of French and Bavarians, under Marshal Tallard, produced the crisis of the war, with the Austrians also facing a Hungarian rebellion. Marlborough persuaded the Dutch to let him take his army from the Netherlands to Bavaria, where he joined with Eugene. Defeating the Franco-Bavarians at the Schellenberg, near Donauwörth, at the end of July, on 13 August 1704 (NS) Marlborough obtained a decisive victory at Blenheim. Tallard was captured, half his men were casualties and nearly all his guns were taken: "the first great French defeat in battle since Louis XIV became king, the first resounding victory of an English general since the Middle Ages".[54] The Emperor obtained control of Bavaria and the support of more German princes.

Another decisive victory by Marlborough at Ramillies, near Namur, in May 1706 shattered another large French army; Marlborough then captured Brussels, Antwerp and fortresses in the southern Netherlands. In 1708 came the third of Marlborough's great quartet of victories, at Oudenarde; this led to the surrender first of the town and then, in December, the citadel, of Lille in France. Ghent and Bruges swiftly went to the Allies, who began to think of an advance on Paris. In the autumn of 1708 the French made tentative overtures for peace, but were abruptly told that the Spanish monarchy must go to Charles, and if Philip refused to abdicate France should help to remove him from Spain; in the English slogan, "no peace without Spain." This proved the high point for the Allies.

Black describes how the British army "reached a peak of success that it was not to repeat in Europe for another century"; skilled in fire discipline, more effectively so than the French, and in massed cavalry charges, which were decisive in three out of four of Marlborough's great victories.[55]

There was fighting in Spain where initially the Allies made progress: in 1704 Barcelona fell, and, most importantly for Britain, Gibraltar. In 1706 Aragon rose against the French, and Charles was crowned in Madrid. Castile, however, rallied against him and in April 1707, at Almanza, the Allies under Galway were routed by the reinforced French. In the same year the British took Sardinia, Majorca and then Minorca, which latter they retained for the next 48 years. In 1707 a British attack on Toulon made the French destroy most of their warships there.

September 1709 saw Marlborough's Pyrrhic victory at Malplaquet, where the field went to the Allies but they suffered double the casualties of the French. The Allies gained Tournai and then Mons. In Spain Stanhope twice defeated the French, but then was forced to surrender at Brihuega (December 1710), and Charles was thrust back into Catalonia. The French now decided to try and entice the strongest of their enemies, Great Britain, to peace.

Peace and the Hanoverian succession

The Tory opposition held that England should concentrate on naval warfare and gaining colonies, while avoiding hugely expensive land wars with unreliable continental allies. By the end of this war, largely due to French reverses, the Royal Navy was twice the size of the French fleet. Before this policy could bear fruit there was increased party strife and two elections.

The start of the war in 1702 saw it supported by the bulk of the nation: it was a matter of defending the Queen from the devices of the Pretender and the French. Many leading politicians, nevertheless, exchanged civilities with the Pretender, their motive being "insurance". This was not confined to arch-Tories – Marlborough corresponded regularly, and so did such a Whig as Somers.

The Pretender planned a descent on Scotland in March 1708 when discontent with the Act of Union was high. He was to sail, with about 4000 troops, under a French naval escort, from Dunkirk. Alerted by British intelligence services, James's expedition was pursued to the Firth of Forth. In stormy weather, the French admiral refused to land him or the troops. The episode contributed to the Tory defeat in the election taking place over the following weeks: 45 seats changed hands, giving the Whigs a majority.

Taxation, conscription, poor harvests and high prices prompted a majority of the opposition Tories to press for an early peace. The Queen shared their exhaustion with the war and objected to the Whig ministers forced upon her "some of them irreverent about religion and some half republican".[56] Importantly, she also became estranged from Sarah, Duchess of Marlborough, whose husband welcomed Whig support for carrying on the continental war.

The Queen removed her Whig ministers in the summer of 1710. Robert Harley now headed an almost wholly Tory ministry, and that autumn's election gave them a majority of three to one. As early as July 1710 the ministry was secretly in touch with the French minister Torcy. Tory priorities were displayed. There were unsuccessful expeditions against Port Royal in Acadia (Nova Scotia) in 1704 and 1707, and another attack on Canada failed in 1708. In 1710 Port Royal was captured, and the other Tory leader, Henry St John, planned a descent on Quebec. A fleet and 5000 men failed to effect a landing. Eight transports were wrecked in the St Lawrence estuary in August 1711, with the loss of nearly 900 soldiers and sailors.[57]

The new government weakened the support going to Marlborough in the Netherlands. Even so, in 1711 he broke through Marshal Villars's *ne plus ultra* lines, still hoping to march on Paris. The young Emperor, Joseph, suddenly died of smallpox, and his successor, speedily elected in October 1711, was archduke Charles himself. There was no wish in England to see him also King of Spain, so peace preliminaries were pursued with vigour. The Franco-Spanish side conceded Nova Scotia and Newfoundland, as well as Gibraltar and Minorca; the fortifications of Dunkirk, a nest of privateers, were to be demolished; and Spain would give England equal trading rights with France. Queen Anne's title to the throne, denied at the start of the war, was to be acknowledged, as was the Hanoverian succession.

The Whigs joined with the Dutch, the Empire and the German princes, to resist this agreement. In December 1711 the Earl of Nottingham moved an amendment to the Address that "no peace could be safe or honourable to Great Britain, or Europe, if Spain and the West Indies [sic] were allotted to any branch of the House of Bourbon".

The amendment was carried by eight votes in the Lords, but defeated 232–106 in the Commons. Secure now with the support of the Queen, who added twelve Tory peers by creations and "calling up" eldest sons, the government counter-attacked; Marlborough was dismissed from all his offices on trumped up charges of peculation. He withdrew to the Continent in 1712, not to return until the day of Queen Anne's death. His descendant and biographer, Winston Churchill, acknowledged, "[in] ten campaigns, … he had won four great battles and many secondary actions … and had taken by siege thirty fortresses … broken the military power of France … [and] had never sustained a defeat or even a serious check … The annals of war contain no similar record."[58]

Churchill, although *parti pris*, is also scathing about the Tory leaders' betrayal of Britain's Allies, adding that "to describe Bolingbroke (St John) as a good liar would be a misstatement: he scattered his lies with such profusion that he wasted them."[59] His chapter xxxiii is entitled "The British Desertion". George, Elector of Hanover since 1708 and soon to be King of Great Britain (he became heir to the British throne when his mother Sophia died in May 1714), vehemently opposed the peace talks, arguing "the fruits of this war will be lost if Spain and the Indies remain in the hands of the Duke of Anjou (ie Philip V), for this will soon render France once more in a state *to give the law to Europe.*"[60]

Marlborough's successor in the Netherlands was the Duke of Ormonde, who was told by St John not to hazard a battle or a siege; the letter was copied to the French! Ormonde had a chequered subsequent career. On his accession, George I stripped him of his military posts. Accused of plotting with the Jacobites, he was impeached for high treason, with his estate forfeited. He subsequently moved to Spain whence he took part in a Spanish and Jacobite plan to invade England in 1719.

The remaining allied forces, under Eugene, were badly defeated at Denain in July 1712 and then, between August and October, lost Douai, Le Quesnoy and Bouchain.

The personalities and philosophies of these two, Harley and St John, were key to Tory fortunes over the years 1710–14, both over peace-making and the

Hanoverian succession. St John believed that England should keep clear of expensive Continental wars, as she was "a bystander in European affairs except where her security was threatened".[61] He did not question the necessity of fighting France but wanted more action against French colonies and trade. The Queen disapproved of his licentious life style: Swift's *Journal* records: "Lord Radnor and I were walking the Mall this evening; and Mr secretary (St John) met us and took a turn or two, and then stole away, and we both believed it was to pick up some wench; and tomorrow he will be at the cabinet with the queen; so goes the world."[62] He was also reputed to be a Deist, that is, not a Christian.

Many of the large Tory majority were suspicious of Harley. During the winter of 1710–11 they formed the October Club, numbering 150 and tightly organised, to press the government for places and the impeachment of various opponents. After Harley had been made Earl of Oxford in 1711, in 1712 the Queen refused St John the earldom of Bolingbroke, giving him just the viscountcy thereof. He was angry at this: Churchill describes Bolingbroke's "chagrin and latent malice of one who instead of thirty pieces had received only twenty-five".[63]

Their main tension came over the succession. "It is generally agreed … that, while both Oxford and Bolingbroke were in touch with the Pretender and for a time at least prepared to contemplate his restoration on the death of the Queen, Oxford at bottom was for Hanover, while Bolingbroke was more sympathetic to the Stuart cause." Bolingbroke courted Jacobite supporters in Parliament, leading some of the Jacobite leaders to believe "he really design'd the King's restauration [sic]" but that Oxford stood in the way.[64] He made a brief mission to France in August 1712, being seen in public with the Pretender.

Most Tory ministers agreed that a Stuart restoration was dependent on James changing his religion. In early 1714 (his letter was dated 26 February 1714 NS) he promised "reasonable security" for Protestantism, whatever that meant, but refused to abandon his Catholicism, and this "seems to have ruled out the possibility of his succession for Oxford, and probably for Bolingbroke as well." James, it seems, had given "secret assurances to the Pope that, once restored to the throne, he would do his utmost to restore the true religion also."[65]

Peace negotiations proceeded, with Britain recognising Philip V in return for a pledge that the crowns of France and Spain should never be united. Charles left Spain in March 1713, and Philip captured his last stronghold, Barcelona, in 1714. Britain and the Dutch, along with Prussia, Savoy and Portugal, signed the Treaty of Utrecht with France on 11 April 1713 (NS). The Empire did not sign the Treaty of Baden until September 1714.

The Queen was turning against Oxford in 1713; he began drinking heavily in the autumn. "Hanover Tories" emerged, either those who supported the national interest as provided for in the Act of Settlement, or simply those who feared impeachment for high treason when George came to the throne. The Whigs tried to exaggerate the threat to the Protestant Succession and alleged Tory Jacobite tendencies. They forced the ministry to accept a Lords motion for an address calling for the Pretender's removal from Lorraine, where the French, obeying the Utrecht requirement that he should leave France itself, had sent him. They contrived two debates on "the succession in danger", together with a Lords motion calling for the Pretender's capture "dead or alive" and a later vote in the Commons promising a reward for this out of public funds of £100,000.

While the Tories were divided, the Whigs, fearing a possible coup, were preparing for the worst. They perceived Bolingbroke working to ensure Tory command of all institutions including the armed forces. While the army was reduced to a peace-footing, the regiments disbanded were not those most recently raised: "there was no doubt that the regiments being kept were selected for their fidelity" to the Tories.[66] All the commands in the fleet, army and fortresses were in the hands of trusted Tories or even Jacobites: a Jacobite governed Edinburgh, Ormonde himself was Warden of the Cinque Ports and "in close touch with Berwick". Coincidentally, the Duke of Berwick, a marshal of France from 1706, was the Old Pretender's illegitimate brother, and his mother, Arabella Churchill, was Marlborough's sister.

When it was thought the Queen was about to die, in December 1713, the Whigs, including Marlborough, and the Hanoverians had "hurried meetings" and made "strenuous appeals".[67] The Whigs are alleged to have formed an association, collected arms, and enrolled troops; Marlborough, Cadogan, Stanhope and Argyll, acting together, made agreements with the Dutch and Hanover for ships and troops. Argyll and Stair took similar measures in Scotland.[68] Clark expresses doubt as to how far these preparations went, as no leading Whig subsequently claimed credit for them. The (Tory) Government would have had excellent ground for arresting the Whig leaders, but although its intelligence service was good, it "arrested no one and accused no one".[69]

It is not now thought that Bolingbroke was actively scheming for the Pretender's return; he wanted to build up his political position so as to be indispensable. As this was impossible under Oxford; he asked the Queen to dismiss Oxford. She demurred, so Bolingbroke, putting himself at the head of the high church grouping – as opposed to Oxford, who was of Presbyterian origin and was supported by Presbyterian electors – promoted a Schism Bill, to suppress dissenting schools and academies. It passed the Commons by more than 100. With Oxford hesitating, Bolingbroke moved it in the Lords, where it passed by 77 to 72.

Churchill believes that civil war might have resulted from Bolingbroke's "caprice and ambition ... the wickedness and inherent degeneracy of this richly gifted man", but adds "he gained the power, but time was denied him".[70] Now Oxford, with Lords support, called for an inquiry into the contentious and possibly corrupt role played by Bolingbroke and others over the Spanish Trade Treaty. On 27 July 1714, after a long and acrimonious debate in Cabinet Council, the Queen dismissed Oxford.

This whole episode exacerbated Anne's illness. During the night of the 30 July and the following day, the Privy Council – not only Whigs but Bolingbroke and his Tory colleagues – made preparations for the Hanoverian succession, recalling troops from Flanders, mobilising the fleet under the Whig Earl of Berkeley, ordering it to patrol the Channel, and alerting the Dutch in case they were needed.

On 1 August, Anne died. The Privy Council set up a Council of Regency as provided for by the 1706 Act. George was peacefully proclaimed King. The most prominent Tory leaders met: Ormonde, Bolingbroke, Wyndham and Francis Atterbury, Dean of Christ Church 1711–13 and now bishop of Rochester. One source has Atterbury saying aid must be sought from Louis XIV and James III's accession proclaimed: "he would at the Royal Exchange read, in his lawn sleeves, the Proclamation. Upon this Lord Bolingbroke said that all our throats would be cut. To which the Bishop reply'd, that if a speedy resolution be not taken, by God all will be lost. Lord Bolingbroke harangued ... and the Bishop ... in a great passion, said that this pusillanimous fellow will ruin our country; so he quitted them." In Professor Basil Williams's view, Bolingbroke's refusal to accompany Atterbury was not out of cowardice but out of "a sense of [the] futility" of the action. It is a good anecdote, however another historian records: "Even Dr Stratford, who would let nothing go by that was to Atterbury's detriment, dismissed [this] whole tale as a palpable and malicious fabrication." While Atterbury was a member of the Lords committee that drew up an address of congratulations to George I, "contemporary gossip, and worse still, opinion at the Hanoverian court, thought otherwise" about his loyalties.[71]

Atterbury was eventually arrested in 1721 on the discovery of a plot for the capture of the royal family and the proclamation of "King James III"; he was put in the Tower. He had carried on his correspondence with the Stuarts so cautiously that the evidence was not sufficient to justify conviction. However, a bill of pains and penalties passed Parliament in 1723 depriving him of his spiritual dignities and banishing him for life.

The Hanoverians: stability and the Augustan age

Apart from their Protestantism, and their acceptance of the 1688–89 Settlement, the first two Georges were a dismal pair, the first not speaking English at all, the second only with a pronounced accent. Not surprisingly, George I turned against the Tories; Whig leaders obtained Cabinet posts. The real business was handled by a trio of Townshend, Stanhope, and Walpole, this last to be the first "prime minister" from 1721–42. Early 1715 saw an election in which the Whigs obtained a majority of about 150.

In August 1714 Bolingbroke was dismissed and the papers he had not destroyed were sealed up. Facing the threat of impeachment, he fled to France in March 1715, in effect, admitting guilt. He became secretary of state to the Pretender and was his key adviser for the 1715 rebellion. At home, he was attainted of high treason, condemned to death, with his property and titles forfeit. As a result of his leaking secret business to his mistresses and his sharp criticisms of the handling of the 1715 Revolt, the Pretender dismissed him in February 1716 and he was subsequently pardoned in England, with the death penalty revoked. He remained deprived of estates and titles and was unable to sit in the Lords.

Impeachment was prepared against Oxford for making the Treaty of Utrecht: he spent two years in the Tower and was acquitted by his peers in 1717.

Ormonde, also facing impeachment, remained in England until August 1715, preparing the ground for revolt, especially in the west country. There were anti-Hanoverian riots in London, Oxford (frequently) and Staffordshire. These alerted the Government. From his knowledge of English conditions, Bolingbroke was convinced that England, not Scotland, was crucial to success. Thus he deplored the dislocation[72] caused by Ormonde's sudden flight to France in August and the precipitate raising of the standard of revolt in Scotland on 6 September by the Earl of Mar, who had been secretary of state for Scotland until 1714. James was not an impressive or skilled leader, communications between Bolingbroke in Paris and James in Lorraine were monitored and hampered by the British ambassador, Lord Stair, money for arms and equipment was scarce, and the death on 1 September of Louis XIV was a massive blow to the Jacobites. The Duke of Orléans, Regent during the minority of Louis XV, was anxious to keep on good terms with London.

Stanhope and Townshend, the two secretaries of state, showed great energy and skill in obtaining information of Jacobite preparations, despatching ships to keep watch, adding reinforcements to the army and putting troops into Jacobite-influenced areas such as Bristol, Bath and Oxford. The rising in the south-west, suffering from poor leadership, indecision, government intelligence, and the arrests of Lord Lansdowne, Sir William Wyndham, five other MPs and two peers, was nipped in the bud. Ormonde attempted landings but failed to raise support. A rising in the north-east was reinforced from Scotland where many Lowlanders rallied to the Jacobites, who marched to Preston where, numbering 4–5000, they were surrounded and surrendered on 13 November.

The same day Mar, having delayed his march on Edinburgh, fought the indecisive battle of Sheriffmuir, north of Stirling, and retired on Perth, where he was joined by James, who landed on 22 December. James made state entries into Dundee and Perth in early January 1716, but his forces were outnumbered by the assembling Hanoverian forces, including 6000 Dutch troops. These marched on Perth, and with Mar's forces disbanding, James returned to France on 4 February (his intention being to give his followers more chance of making favourable terms).[73] By April the rising had been suppressed in both kingdoms, and the government was clement in its punishments, with only 26 captured officers suffering death. Seven peers were condemned to death, of whom four had their sentences commuted, and Lord Nithsdale was rescued by his wife (by exchanging clothes with her maid) the day before his execution.

The immediate consequence was a measure to avoid a general election in 1718 – the Septennial Act, which extended the life of each Parliament from three to seven years, thus helping to entrench the Whig Supremacy.

In 1719, during a brief war with Spain, while Ormonde's plan to land in south-west England proved abortive, a small Spanish force landed in north-west Scotland. It and some Jacobites were defeated at Glenshiel in June; the Scots returning to their homes and the Spaniards surrendering.

The stabilisation of politics in Britain after 1714 was largely due to peace. But the truth was that people in Britain became much better off during this period. Agricultural prices remained low. England was a grain exporter from the 1670s and a heavy exporter after 1715. She faced no danger of the famines that struck Scotland in the 1690s or France in 1693 and 1709, thus food riots were very infrequent. Refined sugar and tobacco had ceased to be luxuries by 1700, tea by 1730.[74]

The 1715 rebellion might have succeeded had the "political desperation felt by many Tory gentlemen been matched by desperation of a more material kind". This was not so, and we read of the "surprising frailty of the Jacobite conspiratorial base in England between 1716 and 1727, … the total inertia of the English Jacobites … at moments of opportunity such as the Atterbury plot or the sudden death abroad of George I" in 1727.[75]

Foreign trade grew massively in the 1670s and 80s and afterwards. Opportunities not only in the City but in the provinces helped younger sons, while the families of the gentry were getting smaller. Careers were increasing in medicine, law, the armed services, the civil service, and teaching/tutoring. Agrarian improvements brought opportunities for estate stewards or land agents. And, unlike in France, there was a good social mix.

In 1702, the National Debt had been reduced from the £14 million of 1697 to £12 million; by 1713 it had trebled. In the most recent, and in the coming mid-century wars, public finance was so organised that it could fund large armies and fleets, including subsidising allies.

And the new stability, prosperity and confidence was good for civilisation. The period 1680–1760 was hailed as Britain's Augustan age, alongside the Scottish Enlightenment, while high cultural achievement continued during the reign of George III and the Regency. The arts flourished, even music (in which the British tended to have periods, such as most of the 19th century, of relative neglect): we owe Handel to the Hanoverian kings' encouragement, and before him, Purcell reigned with distinction, as did Thomas Arne and William Boyce.

The names of most of those who made this an Augustan age are familiar to every educated household today. Perhaps at its summit we can perceive Sir Isaac Newton (1642–1727). Voltaire, attending his funeral in Westminster Abbey, contrasted the honour done to Newton in England, with the persecution he would then have suffered (for his religious views) in France.[76] Newton gave an impetus to the astronomical work at the Greenwich Royal Observatory, constructed in 1675–76, and to the Royal Society, which originated in 1660. The second Astronomer Royal was Edmund Halley, holding this post from 1720–42; he accurately forecast the return in 1758 of "Halley's Comet". Others in the field of science, where advances took place in the fields of electricity, chemistry, medicine and botany, included Robert Boyle (died 1691), Robert Hooke (died 1703) and John Harrison (1693–1776), inventor of the marine chronometer essential to calculating longitude.

It was a time for fine poetry, literature and philosophy: Alexander Pope, Jonathan Swift, Daniel Defoe, Henry Fielding, Dr Samuel Johnson, Joseph Addison, Adam Smith, David Hume, Oliver Goldsmith, John Gay, William Congreve, Lawrence Sterne, Tobias Smollett, Thomas Gray, Horace Walpole, Colley Cibber, George Berkeley and Lady Mary Wortley Montagu all flourished in this period. John Dryden died in 1700, Samuel Pepys in 1703, John Locke in 1704 and John Evelyn in 1706; David Garrick lived 1717-79, Edmund Burke published his first treatises in the late 1750s, while Edward Gibbon's main work was after 1760. Many of these were polymaths – Lady Mary, for example, was a traveller in the Levant as well as a letter writer and poet, and she pressed for the administration of smallpox inoculation.

Another polymath was Sir Hans Sloane – physician, naturalist and collector, who on his death in 1753 bequeathed to the nation his collection of over 70,000 items. This provided for the foundation of the British Museum and the Natural History Museum.

Painting, particularly portrait painting, flourished: Joshua Reynolds, Thomas Gainsborough, William Hogarth, Godfrey Kneller, Jonathan Richardson, and, after 1760, George Stubbs and George Romney. Other noted names include Grinling Gibbons, sculptor and wood carver, Louis Roubiliac, sculptor, Thomas Chippendale, for furniture, Lancelot "Capability" Brown, for formal gardens, and Josiah Wedgwood (1730–95), for his great pottery business.

And it was appropriate that an "Augustan age" should produce magnificent buildings. In contrast to France, where great palaces and chateaux mostly belonged to, and were originated by, monarchs, Britain's great houses were built for aristocrats, often of the Whig/*Duke of Omnium* variety. The most prominent Whig was the 1st Duke of Devonshire who between 1687 and 1707 created much of Chatsworth House. One seat, the only non-royal stately home termed a "palace", and built on virgin ground in one leap, was of course Blenheim – the gift from a grateful Queen and the nation to another 1st Duke (Marlborough); the architects were Sir John Vanbrugh and Nicholas Hawksmoor.

Vanbrugh and Hawksmoor had already worked together on Castle Howard, another magnificent pile. Before architecture, Vanbrugh had been writing ribald post-Restoration comedies.

Another polymath, as he was also an anatomist, astronomer and mathematician, Sir Christopher Wren, is normally associated with Charles II's reign and St Paul's, but he lived until 1723, and St Paul's was not finished until 1711. As well as numerous London churches after the Great Fire, he designed college chapels at Cambridge, the Sheldonian Theatre at Oxford (1668), Kensington Palace (1689–96), the Royal Naval College, Greenwich, and the Wren Library at Trinity College, Cambridge (1676–84). Wren also designed Tom Tower at Christ Church, Oxford, in 1681–82. There Henry Aldrich, Dean of Christ Church (1689–1710) designed the magnificent Palladian Peckwater Quad, built by John Townesend as master mason between 1706 and 1711. The adjacent Christ Church Library was built by John and his son William Townesend, but not started until 1717 or completed until 1772.

Another noted architect of this period was James Gibbs, whose works included St Martin-in-the-Fields (1720–27), the Radcliffe Camera at Oxford (1736–49), and the Senate House at Cambridge (1721–30). Robert Adam (1728–92) flourished as a Scottish neo-classical architect and furniture designer, the son of William Adam (1689–1748), Scotland's foremost architect. Robert was involved in the magnificent development of the Edinburgh New Town, initiated by a design competition in 1766 (won by the 26-year-old James Craig), with work beginning in the 1770s.

Finally, despite the wars, the British continued and advanced the Grand Tour, serving various purposes, whereby the wealthy examined and purchased (to furnish and illuminate these great houses) artistic objects from classical times, the Middle Ages, and the Renaissance and Baroque periods.[77]

Naval prowess and colonial conquests 1742–63

The two mid-century wars – Britain's war against France from 1742 to 1748 as part of the War of the Austrian Succession, and then the Seven Years' War (1756–63) show the development of factors governing British policy. A consequence of the Hanoverian Succession was the demand from the first two Georges for help from Britain to defend their electorate's territory – from Prussia and France, allied in the first war, and then from France in the second. It was also in Britain's interest to defend the southern, now Austrian, Netherlands against France; this territory could otherwise act as a French base for invasion, for commerce raiding, and as a threat to Britain's Dutch ally. France had made deep inroads there in the 1688–97 war and started the 1702 war in occupation of the whole. Underlying both these objectives was the earlier theme of supporting the balance of power against French aggression.

Neither George I or II visited northern England , the midlands or the west country, let alone Scotland or Wales, whereas the latter visited Hanover eleven times between 1729 and 1755, usually accompanied by a British minister, with each trip lasting several months.[78]

1745 saw a more menacing Jacobite invasion than that of 1715. The dynasty was more firmly established but it is estimated that a third of Tory MPs showed Jacobite sympathies in the period 1715–54,[79] as well as a substantial number of London business magnates, including six Lord Mayors between 1740 and 1753. The key was French support. A serious French invasion, under the redoubtable Marshal de Saxe, had been in preparation in February 1744. This had caused panic in London, with the Admiralty removing all buoys in the Thames, troops in Bristol, Chester and elsewhere ordered to march to London, the dockyard workforce told to prepare to defend Sheerness, and troops from Ireland diverted from heading for Flanders to land at Bristol. A great storm had dispersed the French, with many transports sunk, and they were reluctant to try again.

However, the Young Pretender was more vigorous than his father or the Earl of Mar in 1715. He landed on 23 July 1745, captured Perth and then Edinburgh on 17 September. At the battle of Prestonpans on the 21st, Sir John Cope's artillery and cavalry did not prevent his army being speedily destroyed by a Highland charge. Carlisle fell after a short siege on 17 November and the Pretender marched through Preston, Manchester and Macclesfield and entered Derby unopposed on 4 December. But he had received few new recruits or funds and suffered a number of desertions, and he and his chiefs received false information (from a Whig agent) that 9000 Government troops were waiting on the road south. They believed this and did not hear any news from the French, who were assembling troops in Calais and Boulogne. So Charles started retreating, with great reluctance, as his officers would go no further. It had been a narrow escape for the Hanoverians; French intervention would have made all the difference as Charles had large numbers of secret sympathisers in England and Ireland.[80] He defeated another English army at Falkirk on 17 January 1746, but privateers with reinforcements and money for him were captured by the Royal Navy. The Duke of Cumberland concentrated his forces; at Culloden he had 9000 to the Pretender's starving and exhausted 5000. All went wrong for the latter, and Cumberland's competent artillery and bayonet work finished the job.

France, meanwhile, was suffering financial, economic (more poor harvests) and trade stresses and in 1747 came some key British naval victories. The first battle of Cape Finisterre in May 1747 saw Anson capturing four warships and several merchantmen. In October Hawke won the second battle of Cape Finisterre, forcing six out of eight French ships of the line to surrender. After this, France was not able to escort major convoys bound for the French colonies. Her commerce suffered, while British sea power dominated the North Atlantic, the Caribbean and the Mediterranean.

At the peace of Aix-la-Chapelle, perhaps reflecting the consequences of maritime defeats, the French returned their substantial southern Netherlands gains (and Madras which Britain had lost in 1746 because of an inadequate garrison), in return for the British returning Louisbourg and Cape Breton in Canada.

The Seven Years' War, which started on the Continent in 1756, after previous exchanges in North America and India, saw early signs of a change of strategy by Britain. It involved a major "Diplomatic Revolution" in Europe, with France deciding to ally with her enemy in the previous war, Austria, against the aggressor in that war, Prussia, which thus sought British support. This meant there was no French threat to the Netherlands, Austrian territory. Even at the start the British government refused to send troops to Germany. It was at the head of a force of Hessians and Hanoverians that the Duke of Cumberland, defeated at Hastenbeck on 26 July 1757, then capitulated after an energetic French pursuit. The government, however, could not abandon Hanover, and in April 1758 agreed to pay for an army of 55,000 there to protect Frederick's western flank from the French. Some of these troops were British. Under Prince Ferdinand of Brunswick, much more capable than Cumberland, this denied Hanover to the French. At Minden, on 1 August 1759, the Anglo-German army under Ferdinand soundly defeated the French. Further successes at Warburg, on 31 July 1760, and in July 1761 and June 1762 followed.

Outside Europe, by this time, the British enjoyed more resources and better co-operation between army and navy commanders than in previous conflicts. 1759 saw a serious French invasion threat, planned by Choiseul, then the leading French minister. This was frustrated by two great British naval victories, first off Lagos in Portugal in August 1759, where the French lost three ships captured and two destroyed, with the rest blockaded in the Tagus, and then in November, at Quiberon Bay. Superior British gunnery and seamanship there cost France five ships of the line, including their two flagships, while another four went ashore with their backs broken. All possibilities of a pro-Jacobite invasion were dissipated by these two defeats. The accession in 1760 of the young George III, "glory[ing] in the name of Briton", in contrast to the elderly and alcoholic Charles, cemented this. And under Hanoverian pressure, Pope Clement VII refused to recognise Charles as king when the "Old Pretender" died in 1766, and the Catholic sovereigns of Europe followed this negative lead.

By 1762 the Royal Navy had about 300 ships and 84,000 men. This strength resulted from political support, strong public finances, and a large shipbuilding programme since 1756. It was well led, with Lord Anson, as First Lord 1751–62, and admirals like Boscawen, Hawke and Rodney.[81] This naval strength enabled Britain to pursue her ambitions outside Europe. Fighting in India had started in 1752, during European peace. After various French defeats, the treaty of Allahabad in 1765 recognised British supremacy in Bengal and Bihar.

In America, fighting had also started in 1752 in the Ohio valley, with French attacks on pro-British Indian tribes. There was an early reverse: at Monongahela in July 1755 Braddock's regulars were disastrously defeated, losing nearly 1000 casualties out of 1500.

With war formally declared in 1756, the French were outnumbered: their colonial population was 70,000, contrasted with over a million in the British North American colonies. The French commander, Montcalm, was to show skill and bravery, but Britain gave priority to this campaign. In 1758 William Pitt "the Elder", as Secretary of State and Leader of the House, "took a leading role in planning a massive three-pronged offensive on New France."[82]

A string of French forts gradually fell. For the 1759 attack on Quebec, unlike those in 1690 and 1711, Britain had reliable pilots and harbour facilities, with a military force of 8600, 49 warships, 119 transports and over 13,000 sailors – and the genius of Wolfe. Montcalm had 13,000 in the area but was outmanoeuvred. Wolfe's force was equal in numbers, superior in training and morale, and British volley fire and then a bayonet charge won the battle. Quebec surrendered on 18 September 1759. A substantial French force remained in Canada, inflicting a defeat on the British in the battle of Sainte-Foy (28 April 1760), and besieging Quebec. British reinforcements arrived after the ice cleared in mid-May. They advanced on Montreal and on 8 September, the French, with only 3500 troops, surrendered.

In the West Indies, Guadeloupe was captured in 1759, Martinique in 1762, Dominica in 1761, and Grenada, St Lucia and St Vincent all in 1762. Spain finally joined her fellow Bourbon state in 1761. Havana surrendered in August 1762. Manila, with weaker defences, was taken by surprise in October. Both were returned at the Peace of Paris in 1763, but Manila encouraged British interest in the Pacific, which led to the voyages of Captain Cook.

By the early 1760s the balance of power had ceased to play a prominent role in ministerial or public discussion of British policy; "instead, now the crucial struggle was for maritime mastery … central to both the competing interests in North America, the West Indies and the Indian Ocean, and transoceanic trade."[83]

The policy change was cemented when George III succeeded in 1760. He had told Bute, his first minister, in 1759 about reverses in North Germany: "I fear this is entirely owing to the partiality (George II) has for that horrid Electorate which has always lived upon the very vitals of this poor country."[84]

The Seven Years' War and especially the victories in 1759, made Britain the global superpower of the 18th century, as well as laying the foundations for the international dominance of the English language today. So long as the Royal Navy was larger than, or defeated, hostile navies, Britain controlled the main trade routes. But it does not follow that Britain was more powerful *on land* than each of France, Prussia, even Austria, or the rising strength of Russia. If the Royal Navy lost control of the Channel, Britain might succumb to a hostile invading force, as might have happened, but manifestly did not, in the 1740s, or in 1759, or during the Revolutionary and Napoleonic Wars.

From this pinnacle of success there was a decline, both in the War of American Independence (1776–83) and then the French Revolutionary Wars (1792–1801). Naval victories at the end of the former, especially the Saints (1782), followed by Camperdown (1797), the Nile (1798) and Trafalgar (1805), gave Britain an unmatched command of the sea, only interrupted in 1941–2.

FOOTNOTES

1 House of Commons, 7 July 1988, col 1233.
2 J R Western, *Monarchy and Revolution: The English State in the 1680s*, Blandford Press, 1972, p103.
3 Edward Vallance, *The Glorious Revolution*, Little, Brown, 2006, p41.
4 Quoted Harris, *op cit*, p71.
5 *Ibid*, p29.
6 Quoted, Western, *op cit*, p191.
7 Desmond Seward, *The King over the Water: A Complete History of the Jacobites,* Birlinn, 2019, p4.
8 Quoted, Western, *op cit*, pp192–3, 204.
9 *Ibid*, p205.
10 *Ibid*, p196; Harris, *op cit*, p100.
11 Western, *op cit*, p148.
12 Harris, *op cit*, p127.
13 *Ibid*, pp130, 134, 138.
14 Quoted Western, *op cit*, p227.
15 Harris, *op cit*, p261.
16 Western, *op cit*, p232.
17 *Ibid*, p235.
18 Western, *op cit*, p253.
19 Western's words, *op cit*, p256.
20 Harris, *op cit*, p4.
21 Western, *op cit*, p261. Vallance, *op cit*, p113, refers to 400 "flyboats".
22 Western, *op cit*, p263.
23 *Ibid*, p263, footnote.
24 Harris, *op cit*, p280.
25 Western, *op cit*, p138.
26 Vallance *op cit*, p117.
27 Harris, *op cit*, p283.
28 Harris, *op cit*, p279; Seward, *op cit*, p16.
29 Harris, *op cit*, p272.
30 Vallance, *op cit*, p143.
31 Barillon quote, Vallance *op cit*, p141; the two later ones from Western, *op cit*, p287.
32 Western, *op cit*, p296.
33 *Ibid*, p299.
34 Vallance, *op cit*, pp149–50.
35 Western, *op cit*, p300.
36 Sir George Clark, *Oxford History of England: The Later Stuarts 1660–1714*, Oxford UP, Second Edition, 1956, p148.
37 Quoted, Western, *op cit*, p316.
38 Present author's italics.
39 Harris, *op cit*, p362.
40 *Ibid*, p367.
41 Quoted, *ibid* p395 and Vallance, *op cit*, p204.
42 Harris, *op cit*, p445.
43 Harris, *op cit*, p502.
44 *Ibid* pp504–5, 508.
45 Clark *op cit*, p311, Harris *op cit*, p512 for these two consecutive quotes.
46 Geoffrey Holmes *Politics, Religion and Society in England 1679–1742*, Hambledon Press, 1986, p205.
47 Clark, *op cit*, p161.
48 Jeremy Black, *Britain as a Military Power 1688–1815*, Routledge, 2002, p79.
49 *Ibid*, p80.
50 Stephen Clarke *The French Revolution and What Went Wrong*, Cornerstone, 2019, p48.
51 Harris, *op cit*, p491.
52 Black, *op cit*, pp47–8.
53 Western, *op cit*, pp393–94.
54 Clark, *op cit* p209.
55 Black, *op cit*, p55.
56 Clark, *op cit*, p225.
57 Black, *op cit*, p122.
58 Churchill, *op cit*, Vol IV, p457.
59 *Ibid*, p574.
60 Quoted *ibid*, p487; italics in original.
61 Sheila Biddle, *Bolingbroke and Harley*, George Allen and Unwin, 1975, pp112–14.
62 Quoted, Biddle, *op cit* p69.
63 Churchill, *op cit*, p565.
64 Biddle, *op cit*, p262.
65 Biddle, p262. The assurance to the Pope point in Basil Williams, revised by CH Stuart, *Oxford History of England: The Whig Supremacy 1714–60* Oxford UP, 1961, p158.
66 Clark, *op cit*, p245.
67 Churchill, *op cit*, pp601–2 for these quotes.
68 *Ibid*, p606.
69 Clark, *op cit*, p244.
70 Churchill, *op cit*, pp617, 619

71 Williams, *op cit* pp150–1; Gareth Bennett *The Tory Crisis in Church and State: The Career of Francis Atterbury, Bishop of Rochester*, Clarendon Press, 1975, p182; final point, DNB entry on Atterbury, Vol II, pp233–38.
72 Williams, *op cit* p159, cites Sir Charles Petrie's article in *Transactions of the R.Hist.S.* IV, xviii, pp85–106, showing the "widespread preparations for a Jacobite rising in the west of England and the sudden collapse of these plans on the flight of Ormonde."
73 Black, *op cit*, pp21–24.
74 Holmes, *op cit*, p254.
75 *Ibid*, pp263–64.
76 Williams, *op cit*, p378.
77 See Jeremy Black *The British Abroad: The Grand Tour in the Eighteenth Century*, Sutton 1992.
78 Jeremy Black *America or Europe? British Foreign Policy 1739–63*, UCL Press, 1998, subsequently referred to as Black, *America*, p93.
79 Eveline Cruickshanks *Political Untouchables – The Tories and the '45*, pp18–9, quoted Seward, *op cit*, p201.
80 Seward, *op cit*, pp250–2.
81 Black, *op cit*, pp107–8.
82 *Ibid*, p140.
83 Black, *America*, p181.
84 *Ibid*, p101.

Chapter Four:
The French Revolution: Actuality 1774–1815

"That, Sire, is how the people treats its kings," said a revolutionary officer to Louis XVI as they passed the toppled statue of Louis XIV in Place Vendôme *en route* for the Temple prison on 13 August 1792, to which Louis replied: "It is fortunate that it confines its attention to inanimate objects." (John Hardman, *Life of Louis XVI,* Yale UP, 1993, p222)

"Those who did not live during the years before 1789 do not know the sweetness of life." (*"Celui qui n'a pas vécu au dix-huitième siècle avant la Révolution ne connaît pas la douceur de vivre."*) (*La Confession de Talleyrand,* Paris, 1891, p57.)

Prelude

As de Tocqueville observed, revolutions tended to happen not when things were at their worst but when they were starting to improve. This was the case during the reign of Louis XVI, with the economy "showing signs of movement toward 'take-off' into an industrial revolution,"[1] and the abolition of judicial torture, toleration returned to Protestants, the end of official censorship, and better ways of averting famine after bad harvests. Perhaps these improvements whetted the appetite for change.

France certainly suffered from the fairly rigid class hierarchy of the *ancien regime*, displayed, for example, by the failure of the émigrés after 1790 to mount a threat to the revolutionary regime. That is not to belittle the serious attempts that were made at reform before 1789. The failure to carry these efforts through, caused by the weakness and indecision of the monarch, and the failure of his key ministers to co-operate with him and with each other, tragically paralleled in Russia before 1917, produced the nihilism of Revolution.

Another possible myth was that the Revolution might have been averted even after it had started. Even after the abortive Flight to Varennes we see various forces or powerful individuals who believed that the Revolution had gone far enough; these, in conjunction with the King and Queen might have created a constitutional monarchy on English lines. Success would have involved risk, skill, cohesion, and probably some bloodshed: we shall trace these key turning points.

"*Après nous, le deluge*" [2]

As well as being the most populous country in Europe (after Russia), and the most prosperous (after Britain), 18th-century France might claim to be the intellectual power-house of Europe. Yet clearly France was deeply in crisis and its monarchy considerably undermined by the time that Louis XVI came to the throne.

The reign of Louis XIV, who died in 1715, saw France rise to a summit of power and glory by the early 1680s, and then, by engaging in two long and vastly expensive wars with virtually the whole of Europe, suffer ruinous defeats, as well as large death-tolls. In addition to war casualties, two devastating famines caused 2.8 million deaths in 1692–94 and a further million in 170910. Coming to the throne at the age of five, Louis XV benefited from a peaceful policy under the Regency of the Duc d'Orléans, who died in 1723, and under his successor as chief minister, Cardinal Fleury, who died in 1743. However, Louis's reign was then dominated by two further enormously expensive wars, that of the Austrian Succession (1741–48) and then the Seven Years' War (1756–63).

Between the advent of Fleury and the aftermath of the 1741–48 war, peace-time state spending increased by over a third. The Austrian war cost France 1000 million livres (equivalent to approximately 7 billion US dollars at current rates), causing the annual cost of servicing the debt to rise to 72 million livres.

These vast amounts were not, in the event, well spent. As was seen in Chapter Three, France's international position in 1750 was a strong one, with a powerful navy and great opportunities of empire building under Dupleix in India and also in the Ohio valley and the Mississippi basin in America. Conflict, however, was imminent in both arenas, as was disaster. Outstanding commanders like Saxe and Löwendal in the Austrian Succession War contrasted with Vaudreuil, Soubise, Contades and Conflans in the Seven Years' War. In addition, as Frank McLynn states: "The besetting sin of France during the Seven Years' War [was] dissipation of resources and inability to concentrate on a single clear objective." She persisted in the war in Germany when her colonies were under dire threat. The then Foreign Secretary, Cardinal de Bernis, raised this question in 1758, to which Louis XV sharply rejoined "You are, like all the rest, an enemy of the Queen of Hungary."[3] So the French alliance with Maria Theresa, contrived by the King's mistress, Madame de Pompadour, and thus the reason for the campaigning in Germany, held firm while the colonies were being lost.

Determined to bring victory, Bernis' successor, Choiseul, planned an invasion of Britain. As an example of useless extravagance, throughout 1759 France built 300 flat-bottomed vessels (100 feet long, 24 feet broad and 10 feet deep) in the ports between Le Havre and Nantes. By the end of the year, 30 million livres had been spent on these alone – enough to build 30 ships of the line. Preparations for invasion, bizarrely, were made in the closing months of the year, when the seas round the British Isles were noted for storms: flat-bottomed vessels could only operate in a calm. "Nothing had really been thought through and everything left to chance," and the short campaign which led to the decisive defeat in Quiberon Bay (14–20 November 1759) took place during a rising storm.[4] The consequences were two-fold: the massive diminution of the prestige of the monarchy, in a country where victory counted almost whatever the cost; and, second, the cost itself – the main cause of the crisis in the French monarchy which led directly to the events in 1789 and after.

The situation was not irretrievable. In the 1770s the French public debt was no larger than Britain's, but it required an additional two per cent in interest payments to service, given a perceived risk of defaulting. France's problem was in raising revenue and the political and social tensions this created. The nobles, clergy and the *pays d'états* – Brittany, Languedoc, Provence, and Burgundy – were mostly protected from regular taxation. The system of self-assessment was vastly inefficient: the personal fortunes of the Princes of the Blood were such that in theory they should have paid about 2.4 million livres in *vingtièmes* (a five per cent tax); in fact, they paid less than 200,000 livres. The Duc d'Orléans (*Premier Prince du Sang*), who voted for the execution of Louis XVI and then was himself later guillotined, claimed "I pay more or less what I like."[5] However, France's *general* taxation system was less regressive than the British system, because the latter relied far more on indirect taxes which affected the cost of living. The French system, relying as it did on tax farmers and the hierarchy of parish collectors and district and regional receivers, was far more inefficient and "inherently corrupt", as so much revenue ended with the collectors.[6]

Discrimination against the bourgeoisie in the state's most important professions was thought to be the Revolution's main driving force. This discontent is described by a prominent French historian: "Money and merit were coming up against 'birth'; in their path they found the state, guaranteeing privileges." However, "it is now generally recognised that the boundary between nobles and wealthy commoners was hugely porous ... nothing was easier or more common for a wealthy man than to buy a title."[7] Estimates of noble numbers range from 110,000 to 400,000, the majority being small-scale landowners.

As well as being liable for taxes from which the nobles might well be immune, the peasants resented the nobles' hunting rights and other burdensome feudal dues, which were demanded with "ever increasing severity."[8] In 1789 the peasants owned possibly as much as a third of the land, but this greatly varied. In the North, 60–70 per cent held less than one hectare and 20–25 per cent less than five.[9] Except at harvest time or grape picking, there was no readily available work; a few beaters were taken on in the winter. This labour force was fiercely exploited; pay in the spinning, weaving and knitting industries in the villages was pathetically low. French rural wages were about 75 per cent lower than those in England, while food prices were the same. While good harvests in each of 1783, 1784, 1785 and 1787 helped preserve peace, in 1788 a freak hail storm destroyed most of the harvest in northern France.

Most of the clergy were poor, the aristocracy dominating the higher echelons of the Church: about 30 elite families held the most prestigious and wealthy positions.

Another myth is that the government of France was an absolute monarchy with no limits to royal power. This was not the case. Quite apart from the sheer inefficiency of the central government, the principal limits consisted of the parlements, dating back to the Middle Ages. The most significant of these was the Parlement of Paris, whose jurisdiction covered half of France, alongside another 12 provincial parlements. They were courts of appeal, but they also had considerable administrative powers, including endorsing tax measures or royal loans, as well as regulating the grain trade, the control of public meetings and press censorship. In 1715, the Regent Orléans restored the parlements' right of remonstrating with the Crown over complaints about royal legislation, a right which had been removed in 1673. The Parlement of Paris grew bolder during the 18th century: the "dumb obedience" of magistrates under Louis XIV now turned into a "dangerous truculence". [10] By mid-century they were challenging *lits de justice*, which the king convoked to proclaim his decisions. An example of this increasing power occurred in 1764: the Parlement, inflamed by the Jansenists (a dissident religious group within the Church) pressurised Louis XV so that, very reluctantly, he expelled the Jesuits from France.

The main issues between the parlements and the Crown related to taxation: the Crown wished to meet its debt and expenditure without increasing the burdens on the poorest. That meant taxing the nobles and clergy. Back in 1749 Louis XV instituted the *vingtième*, payable by all landowners. He regarded it as a permanent tax, but the parlements claimed it was temporary. The provincial parlements, controlled by the nobility, encouraged riots and Louis gave way on the permanence issue. A general assembly of the clergy negotiated a *don gratuit*, but its yield was "measly": one to three per cent of the Church's total income.[11] Wartime losses in India, the Indies and America deprived France of colonial earnings. A second *vingtième* was levied at the beginning of the Seven Years' War in 1756, and a third one in 1760. At the conclusion of that war both *vingtièmes* were expected to be removed, but the finance minister attempted to introduce a land survey for a better assessment of this tax: the nobility habitually overawed royal tax assessors so this tax yielded only half its potential. [12] Aware that this would greatly increase payments, the parlements resisted. Louis forced the legislation through the Paris Parlement with a *lit de justice*, but continued opposition in the provinces led him to give way and dismiss the finance minister; his successor ensured that the second *vingtième*, while extended, would be on the old property assessments. Thus it would not increase over time with the national income and hence these taxes remained inefficient.

Choiseul promoted reforms after 1763 until he fell in 1770, and these made possible the successes of France's involvement (1778–83) in the American War of Independence. The army saw reform, with Prussian-style discipline and better pay scales, also in matters of organisation, staff planning, artillery and battle tactics.[13] By 1763 the fleet was virtually non-existent, but Louis XVI took a considerable interest in its recovery. Paradoxically, the real benefits of this would only be seen after 1792. 1763–78 also saw an economic revival and a trade boom.

The early 1770s saw the "Maupeou revolution": Maupeou was chief minister in 1770, and his "triumvirate" also included Controller-General Terray and, from 1771, d'Aiguillon as Foreign Minister. They witnessed "the last chance for absolute monarchy to reassert itself in the face of the parlements", restructuring the state's administration and finances "in ways which would pre-empt the Revolution of 1789."[14] It started with a royal Edict of Discipline which the Parlement (of Paris) sought to obstruct. So, in December 1770, the Parlement was suspended. After five summonses to return to their duties, the magistrates were surprised individually on the night of 19 January 1771 by musketeers, who required them to sign yes or no to a further request to return. Thirty-eight magistrates gave an affirmative answer, but on the exile of their former colleagues by *lettres de cachet* (arbitrary incarceration) they retracted and were also exiled. With the Parlement dismantled, the triumvirate installed the council of state to administer justice pending the establishment of six superior courts in the provinces and of a new Parlement in Paris, in which magistracy would no longer be a hereditary prerogative but be administered by salaried officials appointed by the Crown.

Voltaire praised this, applauding the suppression of the old hereditary magistracy: "I would prefer to obey a good lion, born stronger than myself, than two hundred rats of my own kind." However, the *noblesse de robe* hoped Maupeou would "crack under pressure".[15] By the end of 1771, the new system was established. Certain Princes of the Blood who had become allied to the *parlementaires* were exiled from Court. A renewed attempt was made to tax the privileged and exempted groups, with the royal intendants revising tax assessments to ensure that the landed elite paid more. In 1772, the budget came close to balancing: "a remarkable achievement less than a decade after the Treaty of Paris" which ended the Seven Years' War.[16]

While the reforming efforts seemed irresistible, so long as the King supported them, Louis XV was mortal and his death on 10 May 1774 signalled the end of the Maupeou revolution. Maupeou and Terray were replaced on 24 August 1774 by Miromesnil (as Keeper of the Seals) and later by the economist Turgot, promoted to Controller-General. Maupeou is said to have remarked of Louis XVI, "I had won for the king a case that has lasted three hundred years. He wishes to lose it again …" The Paris Parlement was reinstated in its pre-1771 form in November 1775 and the provincial parlements were also recalled.[17]

This was Louis XVI's problem: as Lieven describes "he was well-educated, kind and well-meaning", but his "wavering, uncertainty and delay … became a fatal weakness in a time of crisis and revolution". He was "the least military of all the Bourbons", failed in 1789 to "take the lead of the reform agenda" and then wavered between reformist and aristocratic advisers.[18]

In the latter part of his reign, public hostility to Louis XV had increased, partly on account of his immoral private life; the stricter morality of his successor did not, in the event, help him. The intellectual ferment of the time produced hostility to the regime. Voltaire, in particular, saw the contrast with England, where secular attitudes enabled science to flourish, and citizens enjoyed personal and religious freedom. In France, science and learning were hindered by the Church and *lettres de cachet* flourished. Mirabeau and Diderot were also prominent in this anti-Establishment movement, with the latter's claim: "No quarter for the superstitious, for the fanatical, for the ignorant or for fools, malefactors and tyrants." As late as 1766 the Paris Parlement upheld a lower court sentence on the chevalier de la Barre, ensuring his mutilation and execution "for silly juvenile pranks involving blasphemy". In the other scale the *Encyclopaedia* edited by Diderot and D'Alembert contained, after a learned article on cannibalism, the note "see also: Holy Communion".[19]

Montesquieu encouraged admiration of post-1688 England. Later came the episode of Beaumarchais' anti-feudal play *Figaro*: the King tried to prohibit it, but the Comte d'Artois (later Charles X) had it performed privately. With textual changes – it was set in Spain rather than France – it eventually opened in Paris in April 1784 with huge success. "Louis's detestation was the play's best advertisement." [20]

Louis XVI's good intentions: Turgot, Necker and Calonne

Louis XVI's new adviser, the Count of Maurepas, put forward the case for a central authority, a prime minister; Louis XV had prospered when Cardinal Fleury held that position. As a sign of things to come, Louis declined this advice.

The regime faced an early crisis involving popular disorder. In September

1774 Turgot, then finance chief, abolished the regulations governing the grain trade. Free trade in grain was only workable when the harvest was good, as it had been in the 1760s. That of 1774 was poor, with the price of bread almost doubling, so there were riots in the spring of 1775. This Flour War involved attacks on bakers, profiteer millers, rich farmers and grain convoys, with the government losing control of the Ile de France and four adjacent provinces. The revolt was put down with some brutality; 25,000 troops were concentrated and some fired on the crowds. These excesses influenced the reluctance to order troop interventions in 1789.

Turgot may have been contemplating an attack on feudal dues, while developing plans for provincial assemblies. Lamoignon-Malesherbes, with his "customary insight" recommended to the King the establishment of these bodies, which would have "the advantages, without the disadvantages, of Provincial Estates". They "would rid the King of the pressure which is beginning to be brought to bear upon him ... for Estates, be they Provincial or General".[21] Malesherbes, with liberal reforming ideas, was briefly a minister; he was later the King's defence counsel in his trial before the Convention in 1792, and was himself guillotined, along with many of his family of both sexes, in 1794. Like other ministers, Turgot needed continued support from the King, but "Louis was not to prove good at steadfastness". On 12 May 1776 Turgot was dismissed: he had lost the support of public opinion and he was assuming the airs of a prime minister, with Louis saying: "Monsieur Turgot wants to be me, and I do not want him to be me."[22]

Jacques Necker became *de facto* finance minister. Facing opposition from the parlements to increases in taxation, Necker paid for the American war by borrowing at generous rates of interest. This war's total costs to France were 2000 million livres, adding 1000 million livres to the state's debts, with annual interest payments of 100–130 million. By the late 1780s France's national debt may have been almost the same as Britain's – around £215 million – but the interest payments each year were nearly double, at £14 million.[23] Brooding during the Revolution over these financial consequences, Louis was to regret the decision to enter the war. He was, however, fully informed of all the steps which led to it – supplying the rebel colonists with money, arms and volunteers and in 1778 formally recognising their independence.

There was cautious progress under Necker; a pilot administration – similar to a Provincial Assembly – was set up in Berri in 1778. Whereas Turgot's Assemblies would have been elected, under Necker the King appointed a third of the members, who co-opted the rest. The assembly allocated the taxes owed by the province, and supervised public works, with the aim of weakening the power of the parlements and facilitating the raising of loans and taxes. Another assembly was set up in Montauban in 1779, while two more were planned elsewhere.

Things began to go wrong in 1780, with a clash between Necker and Sartine, the Minister of Marine, who spent heavily during the war; Sartine was dismissed. With rates of interest rising to ten per cent in the early 1780s, in 1781 Necker published his *Compte Rendu au Roi* – a statement of royal revenue and expenditure. It "was a fraud" with "half of current revenue needed to service the debt";[24] it contained figures for a typical rather than an actual (wartime) year. So expenditure was put at 254 million livres whereas in 1780 it had been 677 million. However, courtiers resented his parsimony and insistence on accountability, as well as the *Compte Rendu* showing details of pensions paid to them. The Comte de Provence (later Louis XVIII) leaked in April 1781 a memo which Necker had earlier written to the King supporting provincial assemblies and criticising the parlements and intendants: a pamphlet war ensued. In May 1781 Necker asked Louis for entry into the State Council and control over army and navy spending. This would have placed him above Vergennes, the foreign minister, and others, so Louis refused and Necker resigned. Subsequent esteem was shown by people of all classes making pilgrimages to his estate, while Catherine the Great invited him to Russia.

Royal financial problems were not insuperable in 1781. Debt had been higher at the time of the Treaty of Utrecht in 1713 and was similar when the Peace of Paris was signed in 1763. Matters greatly worsened in the following years; in 1781–83 as much was borrowed as Necker had borrowed in the five years 1776–81. Vergennes, who became *Chef de Conseil* restored most of the venal posts suppressed by Necker and even some which Turgot had abolished. Necker's reliance on loans meant that "the very idea of new taxation had to be re-won".[25] Castries, now Minister of Marine, quarrelled violently with Vergennes over France's modest gains at the peace in 1783. He would have liked to continue the war but this could not possibly be afforded, especially after defeats at sea. In the Battle of the Saintes (9–12 April 1782), a French invasion force aimed at Jamaica was dispersed, with five French ships of the line destroyed or taken, 3000 soldiers and sailors killed or wounded and 5000, including the admiral, the Comte de Grasse, taken prisoner. British losses were minimal.

With the appointment of Charles-Alexandre de Calonne as finance minister, "perhaps the most decisive of the reign", the *ancien regime* was given its last chance. His position was somewhat insecure from the start. Consisting of himself, Breteuil and Vergennes, the ministry represented "three ambitious ministers with conflicting philosophies and power bases".[26] Indeed, the vulnerability of finance ministers is marked by there being no fewer than ten in the 15 years 1774–89.

Calonne had ideas in advance of his time: state spending should promote the circulation of money and by creating purchasing power should increase tax revenue. He believed that Necker's royal household spending cuts had deterred potential lenders to the state. With France adopting the new technology developed in England and rapidly industrialising, Calonne promoted investment in infrastructure projects, especially roads and canals (such as the Canal du Midi linking the Mediterranean via the Garonne to the Atlantic), in heavy industry (Le Creusot, the most advanced iron foundry complex), in projects in large cities and a huge naval fortress at Cherbourg. In the 1780s, new industries such as cotton, coal, iron, glass and chemicals saw great progress, even by comparison to England, as well as sugar and tobacco production linked to the colonies. And between 1765 and the 1780s, the time taken to travel from Paris to certain distant cities was halved.

Many of the younger officers who trained in the military academies set up at this time would stay in the army after the Revolution, taking the opportunity of speedy promotion after the royalists had fled: "the officers who would later … conquer most of Europe were mostly products of Louis XVI's centres of military excellence."[27]

These measures produced good growth rates but there was no time to benefit public revenues, and by 1786–87 signs of a speculative boom were apparent. Loans were called in, and early 1787 saw five major bankruptcies in large state financiers.[28] A downturn in agricultural prices also left many peasants with few resources when bad harvests occurred in 1788.

At this point the Queen's reputation was – quite unjustly – damaged by the lurid and complex saga of the Diamond Necklace. This object, worth at least £10 million in today's money, was to have been made for Mme du Barry, mistress of Louis XV, who never received it as it was unfinished and she fell from favour when he died. A major church figure, the Cardinal de Rohan, wishing to regain Marie Antoinette's favour, was exploited by his own mistress, Jeanne de la Motte, a confidence trickster, to offer the necklace to the Queen. The Queen in fact played no part in the saga; in pursuit of his reconciliation scheme, Rohan met a woman in darkness thinking it to be the Queen. In fact it was a prostitute hired by la Motte, and the latter used Rohan's money, guaranteed by forged letters ostensibly from the Queen, to buy the necklace, which la Motte and her accomplices broke up and sold on the black market. On the Feast of the Assumption, 15 August 1785, with mass at the palace of Versailles about to be celebrated by Rohan, he was arrested and interrogated in the King's presence. Conveyed to the Bastille, he was there supported by "a veritable Who's Who of the French aristocracy, headed by two Princes of the Blood;" his supporters wore the colours of red and yellow to symbolise the red-robed cardinal lying on a bed of yellow straw. Public opinion ignored the royal family's account of the episode. As Furet remarked "the kingdom thought like the cardinal. When majesty ceases to be majestic, there can no longer be such a thing as *lèse-majesté*."[29]

Louis and the Queen were attacked by pamphlets. Rohan and others arrested were to be tried by the Parlement, Breteuil having assured the King that Rohan would be found guilty. In fact, in May 1786, the Parlement found la Motte guilty (she was branded and given life imprisonment, but swiftly escaped), while Rohan was acquitted by 26 votes to 23. "Some of the mud must have stuck and a popular stereotype of Marie-Antoinette arose that was the opposite of the truth: she was regarded as extravagant and lascivious, whereas she was parsimonious and … chaste."[30] Hardman's latest study shows various senior ministers and advisers behaving like traditional "snakes in the grass" during this tawdry and, for the Queen, eventually tragic episode.

Breteuil exaggerated Calonne's failures, leaking to the press, and intriguing with court circles and magistrates in the Parlement. The rift between the two made it impossible for the government to sustain control of the Parlement. When Calonne realised he would not get his full programme passed in 1786, he planned to detach two proposals – the extension of stamp duty and the alienation of Crown lands – and persuade the Parlement to agree them in December 1786. Miromesnil, the Keeper of the Seals, advised the King ("and Louis was never to forgive him for this advice"[31]) that there was no hope of getting these through the Parlement, so the attempt was not made.

Calonne's "last gamble" was to summon an Assembly of Notables. This was a body of assorted nobles, ecclesiastics and others who met in extraordinary times; only twice in the 16 century, and twice in the 17th. This step "did not create the crisis; it was the King's response to an already existing one". Perhaps under Miromesnil's influence, Louis decided not to "pack" the Assembly: so only a handful of members were commoners. The total included all Louis's brothers and male cousins; 12 dukes, 33 noble *parlementaires,* 12 bishops and archbishops. All the key people of the Parlements were included and they must have known what was planned; a cartoon appeared of them as turkeys, captioned "with what sauce would you like to be eaten?"[32]

Calonne's plan was to replace the *vingtièmes* by a unitary land tax, payable in kind by all landowners irrespective of rank. It would be permanent and graduated according to property values, but because it was open-ended, the Notables claimed that this raised constitutional issues. He also planned to abolish the *corvée, gabelle* and *taille* (respectively forced unpaid labour, the unpopular salt tax, and a cruder land tax from which nobles and clergy were exempt), each of which greatly aggrieved the peasants; Calonne intended to replace them by this new tax. He also promoted provincial assemblies: by the end of 1787 20 of these were operating, with half the members appointed by the King from each of the three social orders and the remainder co-opted. The King "became enthused by the ethos of fairness about the reforms ... designed to alleviate the lot of the common people". In the view of an expert on the reign, "The French Revolution [began] ... as a programme of reform submitted to the King by one of the most devoted and orthodox servants the monarchy ever possessed ... Calonne."[33]

Calonne was assisted in developing this programme by the young Abbé de Talleyrand-Périgord and the Comte de Mirabeau, who would play a long and a short role respectively in subsequent French history. In the Third Estate, which included many non-noble landowners, merchants, lawyers and other professionals, Calonne "saw a vast untapped source of support for royal authority". With clergy having to pay the new land tax at the same rate as everyone else, we should not be surprised that "it also seems likely that Calonne envisaged some kind of dissolution of the monasteries". As a further example of the disarray among his key advisers, Louis was anxious that Miromesnil, the Keeper of the Seals, endorsed this programme, as he saw a danger of Miromesnil enabling the Notables to become an instrument of aristocratic revolt. As Hardman sadly concludes, if all the ministers and the interests they represented had earlier supported Calonne's programme, Louis would not have needed to turn to the Notables in the first place.[34]

Vergennes died in February 1787; he had shielded Calonne from the hostility of other ministers, notably Breteuil. The Notables opened on 22 February, with Calonne showing himself weak at political management, as well as shocking them by indicating the size of the deficit. The deputies thought the figures were exaggerated to persuade them to accept radical measures. The King explained that these "great and important" plans aimed to improve revenue, assure a stable surplus and free commerce from impediments, hence "alleviating the poorest section of my subjects".[35] There was hostility from the start to Calonne, however, from the clergy, the *parlementaires* and Necker's supporters, with a threat to reject the Land Tax and "mangle the Provincial Assemblies beyond recognition". Calonne referred to "the perfidy of my main collaborator", Miromesnil, who was alleged to have held secret meetings with members of the Assembly to concert opposition. The Queen's protégé, Loménie de Brienne, the Archbishop of Toulouse, headed the attack "acting almost as a leader of the Opposition". Brienne had previously been denied further preferment by the King because "an Archbishop of Paris must at least believe in God".[36] Information to the other parlements about decisions taken was efficiently co-ordinated so opposition would be uniform when edicts came to be registered.

Calonne wrote to the King on 26 or 27 February "I can now no longer doubt that the clergy and all the disaffected deputies think that the Land Tax is sure to be rejected unanimously": the Assembly of the Notables almost entirely consisted of those who would be adversely affected. He wanted the King to make his own views known. "The Princes … want the instructions in writing and approved by Your Majesty in person."[37] Drawn up by Calonne, such an instruction was read out by each Prince to his committee on 28 February, laying down various principles over the tax which the King did not regard as being "open to discussion". In early April when the strength of the opposition had become clear, the King tried to appeal to the Third Estate through a document, the *Avertissement*, or warning, read in pulpits and given wider publicity. This claimed that the opposition was selfish and sectional. It was too little, too late and, anyway, unconvincing as the King himself had picked the Assembly members.

With the American revolutionary theme of "no taxation without representation" beginning to sound, it was La Fayette who put forward a proposal for an Estates-General, which had a better claim to represent the nation than either the Notables or the parlements. The second *vingtième* was due to expire in 1791, so he suggested asking the King for a truly national assembly for that time. The Comte d'Artois "asked whether it was the convocation of the Estates-General he was requesting. He [La Fayette] replied that this was precisely the object of his request."[38] This proposal, which was to trigger the Revolution, gathered support.

Although the Queen's circle – Artois and the Polignacs – had supported Calonne through the Notables episode, she herself had never liked him. The King was isolated and lacked the counsel of Vergennes. Brienne persuaded the Queen to forward a memorandum hinting that the only way to get the Notables to endorse the reforms was by dismissing Calonne. The King wanted to dismiss various people including Breteuil – which the Queen prevented – and Miromesnil, and while they were discussing sackings the Comte de Provence entered: "Sire, whilst you are at it why not dismiss them both?" Louis did so: a resentful Calonne fell on 8 April 1787.

Besenval, commander of the Swiss Guards, compared the fall of Calonne to that of Strafford in England in 1641, and Louis had perceived this himself, because of "his almost obsessive interest in the life of Charles I".[39]

The Austrian ambassador Mercy wrote to Joseph II on 19 May "The King's authority is all the more grievously compromised by the abandonment" of Calonne, in that his plans "had been so openly approved by the King …" In his later study, Hardman notes the various signs which showed Louis was depressed:

he hunted more frequently and ate immoderately, becoming stouter. In his 1993 study Hardman had concluded that in the history of Louis XVI "the *Ancien Regime* ended with his decision to convoke the Notables and the Revolution began when he was forced to sacrifice Calonne".[40]

Calonne's sharpest critic, Brienne, became principal minister. "There is something very sad in [Louis] having to employ a man whose meagre talents he had exposed in their exchange of memoranda." Having realised how bad the financial situation was, Brienne got backing for a loan of 80 million livres and then tried to persuade the Notables to accept a modified version of Calonne's programme. In the words of the Marquis de Castries, Navy secretary, the Notables "enveloped their half-acceptance in so many words that those who refused and those who accepted are indistinguishable …"[41] So the Assembly of the Notables was dismissed on 25 May 1787.

At a meeting of the State Council on 19 July, the King asked why the public mood was so bad. Castries, who had become his major critic, said that the public was surprised that he planned new taxation but "makes no personal sacrifice"; there were complaints over the building of stables for the newly acquired palaces at Rambouillet and Saint-Cloud. Castries added "whereas he has made a bad choice (Calonne) which has led to the ruin of his finances, he seems disposed to make his subjects pay the price". As well as his indecisiveness and his failure to support loyal and capable ministers, these criticisms are further evidence that, for all his good intentions, Louis in part merited criticism. When he later resigned, Castries told the Queen, "As a Frenchman, I want the Estates-General, as a minister, I feel bound to tell you that they could destroy your authority."[42]

Brienne put measures separately to the Parlement, starting with the least controversial, so free trade in grain, commutation of the *corvée* and the establishment of provincial assemblies, were accepted. On 6 July the edict extending stamp duty was rejected; the Parlement declared that only the Estates-General was competent to grant a permanent tax. After it had objected to the *lit de justice* to enforce the tax measures on 6 August its members were exiled to Troyes until 20 September; then Brienne agreed to withdraw the two taxes and the Parlement accepted two *vingtièmes* over the next five years. In a further compromise, the King abandoned the new taxes in return for a loan of 500 million livres over five years at the end of which the Estates-General would meet. It was expected that would pass on 19 November but a dispute erupted over constitutional procedure in which the Duc d'Orléans queried the legality of registering this edict. Understandably impatient, Louis retorted petulantly "*C'est légal parce que je le veux*" ("it is legal because I wish it"), an episode described by Jones as a "pure, unadulterated and politically insensitive … distillation of absolutist doctrine". Orléans was then exiled to his estates by a *lettre de cachet*. This alarmed people: if it could happen to him, who could be safe? "The whole episode shows the royal government at its worst: indecisive, capricious, bad-tempered." [43]

In early May 1788 the government announced a radical programme to bypass the Parlement, by removing the judiciary from politics by conferring their powers on a new body, the *Cour plenière*. The King would be able to make uniform laws for France rather than allow modification by the parlements. As evidence of feeble counsels at the centre, the *Cour* only met once and Brienne did not bother to appoint all its members. Simultaneously, the parlements enunciated the *Fundamental Laws of the Kingdom*, of which the most significant was that no new taxation could be agreed without the consent of the Estates-General. The *parlementaires* were summoned to Versailles for the 8th, when the King registered the edicts and then ordered them to go on vacation. With a substantial deployment of troops, all remained calm in Paris, but insubordination towards royal authority spread through the provinces during the summer and early autumn of 1788, with popular risings in places as disparate as Pau, Rennes and Grenoble. Much of this was led by the nobility.

The unrest affected royal finances. Despite the gravity of the financial situation, the Assembly of Clergy met that summer, complained about the granting of civil status to Protestants the previous year, and offered a "pitiful" 1.8 million livres over two years instead of the 8 million which Brienne requested. Brienne now tended to see the Estates-General as a way of mobilising the Third Estate: "Since the nobility and clergy abandon the king, who is their natural protector … he must throw himself into the arms of the commons and use them to crush the other two."[44] How this was to be achieved, without damage to the monarchy or the social fabric of the nation, is completely unclear, but the very sentiment was a sign of how desperate things were.

Brienne was also trying to mobilise opinion against the parlements, while the provincial assemblies, which had started well, were put on hold because of the disorders. The convocation of the Estates-General was announced in August 1788; it was to meet on 1 May 1789. Meanwhile, the Queen, urged on by Artois, transferred her favour from Brienne to Necker. Brienne was dismissed on 26 August 1788 and Necker recalled as director general of finances. On departing Brienne advised the King not to recall the parlements "or your monarchy will be destroyed and the state with it". [45] Feebly, Louis ignored this, and on 23 September the parlements were recalled, without conditions, and to public rejoicing.

Lamoignon, who had become Keeper of the Seals, resigned in mid-September 1788 and shot himself in May 1789. Not to be confused with Lamoignon-

Malesherbes, who was guillotined in 1794, he was "the last true servant of the old monarchy" and had a dire vision of the future: "The Parlements, the Nobility and the Clergy have dared to resist the King; before two years are out there will no longer be any parlements, nobility or clergy."[46]

From the return of Necker to the fall of the Bastille

On his reappointment, Necker is said to have lamented "Had I but had the fifteen months of the Archbishop of Toulouse"; implying that royal authority had declined so far over this period that he had limited opportunity for decisive action. This was, in 1789, to be "the central tragedy of the reign: the misunderstanding between the King and the Third Estate which led to a collapse of royal authority and a damaging and widespread belief in the King's duplicity".[47] The King was seen to have sided with the nobility, whereas the truth was more complex. In his *Travels in France during the years of 1787–9*, published in 1792, Arthur Young reported that there was nothing to check the outpouring of publications against the clergy and nobility, the latter being "most disgustingly tenacious of all old rights." Young liked the King – "personally the honestest man in the world", adding that he was indecisive and not helped by his brothers.[48]

13 July 1788 saw a great storm, with hail across most of northern France, destroying much of the harvest. Necker bought grain abroad to prevent famine, but bread prices rose, and large numbers of unemployed rural paupers and vagrants caused rioting in the main centres during March and April 1789, for example at Orléans on 24–25 April and in the Paris faubourg Saint-Antoine on 27–28 April, with the French Guards killing or wounding about 50 rioters.[49] This persuaded the King to hold the Estates in Versailles rather than in Paris.

With these misfortunes dominating the lives of the great majority, the process of election of the Estates-General went ahead. The fear of its being dominated by nobles and clergy was countered by a concession for the doubling of the numbers of the Third Estate. Yet that delegation of 604 contained not a single peasant or working man: instead, there were around 90 merchants and manufacturers, 40 landowners, about 170 lawyers and the remainder were office holders "of one sort or another". Two thirds of the First Estate were parish priests, outnumbering the 51 bishops; this would become significant in the summer of 1789.[50]

Otherwise, the government displayed an "evident lack of clarity over its objectives" for the gathering.[51] Popular caricatures during the spring and summer of 1789 showed a nobleman and a cleric in fright at the sudden wakening of a sleeping lion – the People. The nobility was unable to control the election campaign, while the scale of consultation for the Third Estate was extraordinarily wide, involving a lengthy process of indirect election.

The elections saw *cahiers des doléances* (ledgers of grievances) formed, and some thought this was more important than the actual election. Necker refused to interfere and chastised royal officials who did so. Three quarters of peasant *cahiers* demanded relief from royal, seigneurial or ecclesiastical exactions, emphasising the underlying theme of unfairness. Their demands matched "almost exactly" what Necker, Calonne and Brienne had been proposing to the Parlement.[52] But they also displayed general distrust at the King's role in managing the finances, were critical of royal absolutism and almost unanimous over the need for taxes and new legislation to be agreed through the Estates-General. Many among the nobles as well as in the Third Estate looked enviously at the Church's wealth.

Various trivial issues implying hierarchy combined to increase the tensions between the orders – for example the required sober dress of the Third Estate compared to the extravagant garb of the *noblesse*. There was no code of procedure, hence a degree of chaos. Significantly, the Third Estate allowed the public in to witness proceedings whereas the other two orders met behind closed doors. There was great interest in Paris and elsewhere in these; Mirabeau tried to start a newspaper to report all proceedings, and when the government closed it, he published under the guise of a letter to his constituents. And the Duc d'Orléans' Palais-Royal was the centre of subversive activity via clubs, pamphlets, newspapers and café debate.

Matters moved rapidly during June and July, supporting the view that the meeting of the Estates fuelled the Revolution. The Third Estate encountered delays in meeting the King directly in June, simply because the Dauphin had died, a loss which shattered Louis. He did see these deputies a few days later, when their impatience produced from him the words: "There are no fathers then among the Third Estate." As a further example of how brittle things were, on 20 June the accident of doors to their chamber being locked caused the Third Estate to go *en masse* to a hall which had been a tennis court – hence the Tennis Court Oath not to disperse. They thought the King had planned violence; this was not so. Louis thought they would all be reasonable; he "had no inkling" that the Third Estate would try to take power.[53] After he had put forward his reform programme on the 23rd, accompanied by a large military presence, the master of ceremonies wanted each order to retire, to which Mirabeau declared that it would require bayonets to make them budge.

The Third Estate decided to assume the name National Assembly on 17 June, with the King typically failing to appreciate its significance: "it's only a phrase". The other orders began to join this body, which declared it would take over taxation decisions. On the 19th the clergy voted by 149 to 137 to join the Third

Estate and on the 21st the King insisted the Assembly should meet and vote in separate orders. On the 24th, 47 nobles, led by the Duc d'Orléans, joined the Assembly, and on the 26th the King gave way and ordered the rumps of the first and second estates to join the Assembly.

Various events hastened the first explosion. The hostility of the King's brothers, Artois and Provence, to Necker was displayed at meetings of the State Council on 20, 21 and 22 June. A careful plan was drawn-up by Breteuil, the Duchesse de Polignac, and Artois, with the support of the Queen. Artois rushed ahead prematurely: Necker was dismissed on 11 July, along with other reformers, weeks before Breteuil planned he should be. Thus the dismissal occurred before most of the regiments summoned to Paris had arrived.[54]

These troops, amounting to 30,000, mainly German and Swiss, were commanded by Broglie, who became war secretary. When the Third Estate proclaimed itself the National Assembly, no one believed the privileged orders would give in. Rumours included the Comte d'Artois going to Spain, returning with a foreign army, and the Prince de Condé being prepared to massacre thousands. Gold in France was being taken abroad by émigrés, allegedly to pay mercenaries, while British premier William Pitt was believed to have agents acting with aristocrats for the destruction of ships and the capture of ports.[55]

There was a widespread assumption that the King planned to dissolve the Assembly and subdue Paris by force; as Hardman remarks, "There is not a shred of evidence for this assumption."[56]

Paris now rose up, with the mob first attacking the Invalides for arms and gunpowder then, finding inadequate supplies, the Bastille. The French Guards, it seems by now on the side of the mob, organised effective artillery fire on the Bastille. The Governor and several defenders were killed and their heads paraded around the city. One deputy, Pierre Victor Malouet, said after the fall of the Bastille, "if the Court had been at Paris instead of Versailles, it would have been the ministers [and] the Princes who would have been slaughtered." Hardman adds that: "the most recent study of the Royal Army suggests that it could and should have been used with good hopes of success and that the failure to do so destroyed its morale."[57]

From the Bastille to Varennes

The Venetian ambassador reported on the events of 14 July: "There no longer exists either executive power, laws, magistrates or police. A horrible anarchy prevails."[58] At an emergency meeting of the Council on the night of 15 July, Breteuil advocated a royal flight to Metz where there were reliable troops – this was to be Louis's objective two years later. The idea was supported by Artois and the Queen, but Provence begged him not to flee, and Broglie remarked "we can certainly go to Metz but what do we do when we get there?" Louis rejected it, "obsessed as he was by the fear of civil war or of his cousin of Orléans seizing a vacant throne". He was fascinated by the fate of Charles I; here, he thought of that of James II. This fear was not an illusion: Barentin, Keeper of the Seals under Louis XVI and Chancellor under Louis XVIII, told the royal historiographer Moreau on the 16th, "I believe we must have recourse to another dynasty."[59] Thus Louis temporised, withdrawing the troops from round Paris and recalling Necker.

Breteuil then fled the country, as did the Comte d'Artois, his mistress, and his friend Vaudreuil, leaving the King isolated and downcast. They were followed by waves of emigration; it is estimated that, eventually, 150–160,000 fled, including women and children. Perhaps half came from the Third Estate, a quarter from the clergy, perhaps only 25,000 from the nobles but these included big names, big money and were the main source of a threatening army formed at Koblenz.

Municipal revolution took place in Paris; the royal provost of the merchants, an ancient post, had been ousted by an elected mayor, Bailly. Saint-Priest, who became minister for Paris, wrote, "royal authority had already ceased to exist in Paris." During that summer the King "proved remarkably unwilling – maybe even unable – to communicate". In face of the serious rumours about military intervention by reactionaries, "his silence was his undoing … he was hoist by the petard of his own taciturnity".[60]

After the news of the fall of the Bastille emerged, there were riots in other cities: Strasbourg, Marseilles, Rouen and Nantes. By 20 July in Bordeaux, Lyons, Nancy, Limoges and Amiens the royal administration was being challenged. The King was told that he could not count on most of his troops. In parts of the countryside, what was known as the Great Fear broke out. This included the destruction of the Abbeys of Jumièges and of Savigny, where valuable medieval art was lost.[61]

The Great Fear in the countryside had as its background soaring food prices and unemployed workers flocking into the towns, to beg for charity or work. Householders who refused shelter or food were threatened. Firewood and grain were stripped from forests and fields. This coincided with a political crisis, a belief that the Court and the aristocracy were planning to disperse the Third Estate and overawe Paris by force of arms and – rather oddly – simultaneously despatch brigands into the provinces.

Lefebvre showed that the Fear had precise boundaries of time and place: it began on 20 July in the west and ended on 6 August on the Spanish border. It was limited to around six regions and bypassed some of the main centres of peasant discontent. Brittany, Alsace, Lorraine and the Landes were hardly affected. Requests for the abolition of tithes had been included in *cahiers*: "such an abolition has now come into effect", with peasants saying "quite openly that there will be no collection without bloodshed". Lefebvre adds "Well before 14 July, the privileged classes were faced with a strong community of resistance from the lower orders", with some people making it clear to their *seigneur* "that they considered themselves well and truly freed by the Estates-General from all the dues they had hitherto paid".[62]

After the news of Necker's dismissal circulated, a number of towns took measures to resist a *coup d'état* and reinforce the National Assembly. In Nantes and elsewhere all public funds were seized, elsewhere the people took control of powder magazines and arsenals. Château-Gontier organised a militia, in Dijon crowds seized the château and armouries, imprisoned the military commander, and confined all nobles and priests to their homes. In Colmar on 24 July it was claimed that "The Queen had a plot, nearly on the point of execution, to blow up the National Assembly by a mine, and to march the army instantly to massacre all Paris"; the originator of this rumour said he had seen a deputy's letter stating this.[63]

The Great Fear in the east was stimulated in the Château de Quincey in Franche-Comté on 19 July by the explosion of a powder barrel (probably an accident, but alleged as a counter-revolutionary plot). Orders by the King in Council (forged, of course) directed the people to burn châteaux. Normandy witnessed an apology for an attack on "so kind a master, but they had received information that His Majesty wished it so". The parish priest of Péronne said he had seen a paper stating that "in the King's name all people in the country are allowed to enter all the châteaux of the Mâconnais to demand their title deeds and if they are refused, they can loot, burn and plunder; they will not be punished."[64]

Lefebvre describes in detail armed revolts in the Normandy *bocage*, Franche-Comté, part of Alsace, and Hainault. Most of the Châteaux between the Orne, Flers and La Ferté-Macé were attacked on 23–25 July, but not burnt. Burning happened in the east in Franche-Comté, where the feudal system had been particularly strong. There the Châteaux du Saulcy, de Charmoille, Vauvillers, Sainte-Marie, Scey-sur-Saône, Mailleroncourt and Mamirolle, along with various abbeys and priories were sacked and usually burnt. Destruction in the Mâconnais included Senozan, de Mercey, Malfontaine, des Ecuyers and Ozenay châteaux burnt, as well as an attack on the abbey of Cluny.[65] But overall only three landlords are known to have been killed.

The Great Fear went away as suddenly as it came – helped by the Assembly's decision on 6 August to sweep away all feudal privileges. And, in fact, the Court faction most tempted towards violence had dissolved, with its various leaders leaving the country.

It is curious how the violence in Paris and elsewhere in France (which was, of course, to worsen greatly over the next four years) became celebrated in the national anthem of republican France: the *Marseillaise,* with such lines as "Do you hear the roar of fierce soldiers in our countryside? ... They have come to cut the throats of your sons and your women." Composed in 1792, it was disused under Napoleon and the Restoration Monarchy, was briefly resurrected in 1830, but only officially re-adopted in 1879 when it was clear that the Republic had come to stay. Giscard d'Estaing, former President, remarked that it was ridiculous to sing about drenching fields with impure Prussian blood as a German Chancellor paid a friendly visit to Paris, while an (unsuccessful) 1992 campaign to change the words attracted over 100 prominent French citizens, including Danielle Mitterrand, wife of the then President.

While France experienced a calmer period over the next 20 months or so, with one major exception, the Assembly became enveloped by an atmosphere of idealistic fantasy. The proposal by noble leaders to abolish seigneurial dues was agreed at a stroke. On 26 August came the *Declaration of the Rights of Man,* which "invested the nation rather than the ruler with political sovereignty".[66] The deputies refused to consider any amendments of detail from the King, who was kept isolated from the legislative process. This extended to the fact that a loose grouping, known as the *monarchiens,* and linked to Mirabeau, saw their own proposals, especially that for a bicameral legislature (as in Britain and the US), rejected by a large majority on 10 September. December 1789 saw the abolition of intendants, the extremely powerful royal-appointed heads of provinces. In February 1790 these ancient provinces were divided into 83 usually smaller *départements.* A year later came the final abolition of parlements, cementing the institutional revolution. The new constitution provided that of around 7 million adult males, 4 million were given voting rights. And on 4 February 1790 the King swore to uphold the Constitution. While this was well received, the Assembly ignored his request that they attend to the deficit and when asked to confirm the King as head of the army and administration, it refused to vote on the proposal. [67]

The exception to calm – in fact, a key development in the Revolution – occurred in the autumn of 1789. Louis had refused on 18 September to ratify the overthrow of feudalism or the *Declaration of the Rights of Man.* Increasing food shortages in Paris added to rumours that the King was concealing large stores. Louis summoned a French regiment to guard Versailles, and on arrival this Regiment de Flandres was greeted by a lavish banquet, with provocative toasts and the tricolour cockade replaced by white royalist rosettes. By 3 October all this was reported, with exaggeration, in Paris, where the Palais-Royal continued its role in fanning agitation.

This was the pretext for "the long-expected march on Versailles", by the women of Paris. Moderate deputies had asked the King to withdraw to Compiègne and transfer the Assembly to Soissons, both considerable distances from Paris; Louis himself had proposed this on 12 July. Hardman argues "At this point – probably at this point alone – the king could and should have made a stand." He had demonstrated his willingness to compromise and shown his opponents to be intransigent; thus "people would have flocked to Compiègne". [68] But now he refused the idea. Saint-Priest and three others, all ex-soldiers, proposed withdrawal to Rambouillet, but four civilians, including Necker opposed on financial grounds. Any of these moves would have taken the Court and the Assembly away from proximity to the Paris mob. October saw the women reach Versailles, in search of bread and in dreadful weather. Matters went wrong; the usually indecisive King delayed his response to the mob's demands. Extremists threatened the Queen's person and two of her bodyguards were killed and decapitated. Then La Fayette, as commander of the National Guard, gained control, and on the morning of the 6th the royal family was escorted by the mob to Paris. "Fatally" the King agreed to La Fayette's request; this was "a turning point", with the King and the National Assembly now effectively prisoners in Paris.[69]

It was this event – not the Queen's later execution – that provoked Edmund Burke's famous polemic ("I thought 10,000 swords must have leaped from their scabbards to avenge even a look that threatened her with insult") in his 1790 *Reflections on the Revolution in France*.

Two powerful figures might at this point have saved the King and firmly established a constitutional monarchy: the orator and deputy Mirabeau and La Fayette himself. Sadly, they failed to work together: they were not allies, and the latter's motives were at times questionable. The Queen had come to distrust La Fayette, blaming him for the failure to prevent the attack on Versailles. Although he approved of the annexation of church estates, Mirabeau was concerned to contain the revolution: "when you undertake to run a revolution, the difficulty is not to make it go; it is to hold it in check."[70] He was not wholly trusted either by the Assembly or by the Court, but was now acting as a paid royal spy, keeping the King informed, and wanting Louis to accept a British-style constitutional monarchy. He established contact with key moderates, notably Antoine Barnave, who later said "it is time to stop the Revolution" before it degenerated into an attack on property or even civilisation.[71] Mirabeau's sudden death, on 2 April 1791, was terminal to a civilised outcome.

The King eventually changed his mind over flight from Paris after the end of 1790 when the ecclesiastical policy of the Assembly became apparent. The idea of nationalising Church property was being openly discussed; the land alone was estimated at between six and ten per cent of France's total cultivable surface. The Assembly voted to do it in principle on 2nd November 1789 and the Civil Constitution of the Clergy in July 1790 made the Church a sector of government administration, with salaries to be paid by the state and popular election of bishops and curés, while the number of bishops would fall from 135 to 83. All this would require papal permission; Pius VI was hostile to the Revolution in general and the Civil Constitution in particular. His formal opposition was not displayed until the spring of 1791, but he warned Louis of it in July 1790.

In November 1790, the Assembly decreed that all clerics must swear an oath of allegiance to the Civil Constitution. Louis eventually accepted this on 26 December. While half the priesthood took the oath, only seven out of 83 bishops did so. Talleyrand called it "perhaps the biggest political blunder of the Assembly". It was a "serious political miscalculation", in Davidson's view, as "the clergy were in effect being asked to renounce their long-standing commitment to the hierarchy, the principles and therefore the legitimacy of the Church".[72] Riots and threats to life accompanied the expulsion of non-jurors and their replacement by "constitutional" clergy.

Louis's two great aunts, Adélaïde and Victoire, daughters of Louis XV, had left for Rome in February 1791. He decided that the remaining royal family should spend Easter 1791 at the Queen's palace of Saint-Cloud (celebrated by a non-juror). While they had stayed there from 4 June to the end of October 1790, on 18 April 1791 a crowd and National Guards turned back the carriage with the royal family in it at the Tuileries, preventing departure for Saint-Cloud.

This intensified the King's plans for flight, prepared over several weeks. Starting at night on 20 June, it fell foul of a succession of delays, mistakes and misfortunes: for example, the time wasted in making detours out of Paris and the slowness of the specially constructed carriage, described by one writer as "the hearse of the Monarchy". Delay led the Duc de Choiseul with 40 hussars to withdraw, thinking the escape had been postponed. At Sainte-Menehould the assembly of dragoons aroused so much suspicion in this ultra-revolutionary town that their captain felt unable to use them. At Clermont, the town would not let the troops leave with the carriage and they, who had been fraternising with the inhabitants, refused to obey an order to force their way out. Then one Drouet recognised the King from his image on a banknote and assembled a posse in Varennes. "The use of force by the two bodyguards would quite possibly have enabled the carriage to cross the river" there, but this was not done.

Intervention by the loyal and disciplined troops of Marshal Bouillé (in contrast to much of the rest of the army), even if they had caught up, would have involved widespread bloodshed. Louis subsequently wrote to him: "Civil war horrified me and I did not want to shed the blood of my subjects … I do not want to rule by violence." [73]

What would have happened if the flight had succeeded? By this stage most of France was committed to at least moderate revolutionary principles. What would the King have done and who would he – or could he – have worked with? Or was it by then too late? The popular assumption that the King planned to leave France and return at the head of foreign troops and émigrés is shown by an analysis of escape plans and his manifesto to be false. He was irritated by the nobles, especially the émigrés, and planned to set up a headquarters at Montmédy – in France but close to its northern border. He had left behind a *Declaration du Roi addressée à tous les Français* in which he declared how he was "revolted to see the anarchy and the despotism of the clubs which dominated the Assembly".[74] He criticised the Assembly for the continued financial mess, the destruction of France's diplomatic hegemony and the introduction of religious schism. He failed to market it, perhaps by placarding it on the walls of Paris. At 16 pages it was too long and included a lengthy "regurgitation of events" since the meeting of the Estates-General. It was suppressed by the Assembly, yet "one can derive from [it] a programme for a constitutional monarchy with a strong Executive".[75]

The Assembly chose to pretend that the King had been kidnapped by a conspiracy of aristocrats led by Bouillé. After this, his sanction was no longer required for bills to become law, the Ministry of Justice applying the seal on instructions from the Assembly. By the end of 1791 some 6000 officers – about half the entire officer corps – had left the country, many joining the émigrés; over 3000 did so since a new oath now omitted the King's name.

By chance and in contrast, Louis's brother and eventual successor (as Louis XVIII), the Comte de Provence, had about the same time a "relatively easy and rapid journey" to Mons in the Austrian Netherlands, interrupted only by stops at inns while the horses were changed. Provence was not allowed to descend from the carriage "for fear that his distinctive Bourbon waddle – the gait for slowly proceeding through a crowded palace – would betray him".[76]

The descent to terror

On 16 May 1791 Maximilien Robespierre had persuaded the current Constituent Assembly's deputies to exclude themselves from standing for election that autumn to the new Legislative Assembly, thus depriving it of the status and confidence that experience would give. It is not surprising that the new deputies were to preside over the descent to the Reign of Terror. These elections in June to September 1791 showed very low turnout – lower in the towns than in the country: in Paris it was only ten per cent. Enthusiasm for the Revolution was apparently diminishing. The deputies who had served in the Constituent Assembly paid a price for their comparative moderation: by 1799 nearly one in ten of them had been executed or murdered, one in five spent time in prison, and about a quarter sought to emigrate.[77]

Initially 264 – eventually 334, nearly half – of all newly elected deputies signed up with the *Club des Feuillants* – or *Girondins* – who were moderate but suffered from divided leadership. 136 deputies signed up to the *Club des Jacobins* which became a fiercely extreme and eventually dominant minority. Around 300 occupied the undeclared centre: *La Plaine*. Debates were dominated by the moderates for some time, and they might have maintained that supremacy if they had taken care to cultivate the *Plaine*; they failed to do so.

So 1791–92 saw an ebb and flow between the extremists and the moderates. The King worked with the Assembly on the new constitution during the summer of 1791. A demonstration for a republic on 17 July in the Champ de Mars was fired on by the National Guard under La Fayette and the *maire* of Paris, Bailly, with about 50 killed. While this harmed the popularity of La Fayette and Bailly, and the latter was later guillotined, the moderate revolutionaries now had the upper hand and various Jacobins went into hiding. The King vetoed two vindictive measures, one to deprive non-juring priests of their pensions and the other sentencing as traitors, with confiscation of property, all émigrés who did not return by the end of the year.

The extremist Marat attacked all moderates including the Assembly "in order to ensure public tranquillity, two hundred thousand heads must be cut off". After the 17 July shooting, he declared "I would have led them to stab the general [La Fayette] … burn the despot [the King] in his palace and impale our atrocious representatives [the Assembly] in their seats." Other Jacobins accused the Girondins of being in the pay of the Court, and Marat urged soldiers to massacre their officers.[78] A few months later, the Girondins persuaded the Assembly to impeach Marat on grounds of sedition (14 April 1792), but he was acquitted. That and a failed attempt to relocate to Bourges showed the Girondins' weakness.

But they played their part in the move to extremism. From the outset they sought confrontation with the King by "introducing savage legislation against the émigrés and the refractory priests and by seeking war with the Queen's brother the Emperor Leopold II". Without the Girondins' "wrecking tactics", even at this late stage a "strong constitutional monarchy at peace with Europe" might have emerged.[79] The Girondins' plan was to render the King unpopular by making him exercise his veto. What tilted the balance against the moderates was the outbreak of war. France, with the reluctant assent of the King, but with an overwhelming vote of deputies, declared war on Austria and Prussia on 20 April 1792. The downhill run was rapid. In the words of the Girondin Reinhard (who served briefly as foreign minister in 1799), the war "revolutionised the Revolution".[80] The Queen was accused in the Assembly on 15 May of betraying French war plans to the enemy. Between 27 May and 8 June the Assembly, still under Girondin control, abolished the King's constitutional bodyguard, only set up in March. In early July a campaign began for Louis's dethronement and the Assembly was flooded with petitions from the clubs. A plan was made for the King to go to the palace at Compiègne with La Fayette's support; the latter intended the King to issue a proclamation forbidding his brothers or foreign troops from advancing further. This might have calmed matters, but Louis was persuaded by the Queen, who distrusted La Fayette, to reject the proposal.

Even now, the fall of the monarchy was not inevitable. "Paris was equally divided", the Assembly discredited, "a majority of the *départements* favoured the King", but his supporters were "timid and paralyzed by his own timidity and above all his fatalism." Meanwhile Robespierre's Jacobins, with offers of free hospitality, persuaded the volunteers coming from the provinces not to depart for the Front but to "stay on to lend a hand in bringing down the monarchy".[81]

A large demonstration tried to take over the Tuileries on 20 June, but was evicted. The Brunswick Manifesto, named after the Allied commander, issued on 25 July 1792, threatened carnage to the people and destruction to Paris if the royal family were harmed. This was totally counter-productive, as was the Declaration of Pillnitz, procured by the Comte d'Artois on 27 August from the Emperor and the King of Prussia, to restore Louis to his rightful position. An angry Louis criticised Artois for going "to that conference at Pillnitz without my consent", adding that "the courage of the nobility … would be better understood if it returned to France to augment the forces of the men of goodwill."[82]

These declarations and defeats in the face of the Allied advance aroused revolutionary panic. The mob, this time successfully, stormed the Tuileries on 10 August; the King and Queen took refuge with the National Assembly, which declared he was "suspended from his functions". Meanwhile, 500 of the Swiss Guard, which had fired on the mob in defence of the palace, were massacred there, with another 60 killed after being taken to the Hôtel de Ville. About 100 aristocrats who had also tried to protect the Tuileries were killed. Three days later, the royal family was taken to the Temple prison.

News in early September of the capitulation of Toulon to Britain (on which France had also declared war) and the fall of Verdun and Longwy to the Austro-

Prussians made the newly elected Convention declare Terror "the order of the day". The September massacres followed, with around 1200 prisoners killed: 37 were women, a third were clergy (including 115 priests, one Archbishop and two bishops at the Convent des Carmes), nobles or political prisoners, the remainder ordinary criminals or vagrants, including children. The heads of the Comte de Montmorin, formerly foreign minister, and of the Princesse de Lamballe, friend and companion of the Queen, were impaled. A circular was sent to all *départements*, concluding "we are marching against the foe, but we will not leave these brigands behind us to cut the throats of our children and our wives."[83] This letter led to similar massacres in provincial prisons. It also claimed that a large number of deputies were involved in a plot to massacre French patriots, so "a large number of ferocious conspirators held in the prisons have been put to death by the people, acts of justice which seemed indispensable … The nation … will no doubt adopt this useful and necessary method at once."[84] It was countersigned by Marat and Danton, among others. On 9 September, a group of 50 prisoners travelling from Orléans to Paris was ambushed by a mob at Versailles; 43 were hacked to death, including a former Minister of War, a former Minister of Foreign Affairs, the former royal governor of Paris and another bishop.[85]

Recovery in the war – halting the Allies at Valmy on 20 September and defeating the Austrians at Jemappes on November – did not delay the descent to Terror. Robespierre increasingly took the lead, demanding punishment of those who had defended the Tuileries on 10 August. The Assembly appointed 12 of its members to go to the armies to reassert its authority (forerunners of the political commissars of the Soviet Union), forbade religious processions and confiscated gold and silver vessels used in Mass and church bells. Robespierre claimed there was no need to try Louis – "he is already condemned" – adding "Louis must die so that the nation can live".[86] The Girondins tried unsuccessfully to avoid a judicial trial of the King and would have chosen to spare him. Danton was sympathetic to this but added "If I have to give up all hope for him, I warn you that, since I don't want my head to fall with his, I shall join those who condemn him,"[87] which is what he did.

On 20 November, Roland, the Minister of the Interior, announced the discovery of the *armoire de fer* (in effect, a strongroom) which contained papers showing Louis's dealings with Mirabeau, La Fayette and Dumouriez. While none of this was sensational it contributed to the hysteria which accompanied the trial of the King on 26 December. Danton is said to have guaranteed to save the King's life if William Pitt paid him 2 million francs (a substantial inflation on 30 pieces of silver); Pitt refused.[88] Having judged him guilty by 707 to nought, the question whether the verdict be subject to popular ratification was put: 287 said yes and 424 no. The Assembly voted on motions for punishment between 14 and 20 January. Out of 721 voting only 361 voted unconditionally for death. On the morning of 20 January, 310 voted for reprieve, 380 against. The King was guillotined the next day.

After his execution, there was no closure: accusations and executions built up into the real Reign of Terror, with a purge of the non-extremists. Marat declared "all the disloyal members who neglected their duty by opposing the death of the tyrant … are traitors, royalists and incompetents."[89] Complete estimates of the totals are lacking, as many records were destroyed during the 1871 Paris Commune. Excluding the vast numbers which perished in the civil war in the west (the Vendée), it is thought that more than 40,000 died, mainly between 1793 and 1795, about half after a form of trial. Of the 2747 executed in Paris, 20 per cent were former members of the nobility, nine per cent clergy and 71 per cent from the Third Estate; 39 were previous members of the National Assembly, 45 members of the Convention and 73 members of the Commune (city council) of Paris.[90]

Robespierre led the way in lurid declarations: "Terror is nothing but … an emanation of virtue;" "Whoever trembles at this moment is also guilty;" "At the point where we are now, if we stop too soon we will die;" and "We must organise the despotism of liberty to crush the despotism of kings." Regarding the need for virtue and terror, he declaimed: "Virtue, without which Terror is fatal; Terror, without which virtue is impotent." Marat claimed, "Sacrifice 200,000 heads, and you will save a million." And General Westermann in the Vendée reported: "Following the orders that you gave me I have crushed children under the feet of horses, massacred women who at least … will engender no more brigands. I have no prisoners with which to reproach myself."

St-Just declared, "We must rule by iron those who cannot be ruled by justice … You must punish not merely traitors but the indifferent as well." He condemned Danton: "A man is guilty of a crime against the Republic when he takes pity on prisoners. He is guilty because he has no desire for virtue. He is guilty because he is opposed to the Terror." The President of the Convention admitted: "For a citizen to become suspect it is sufficient that rumour accuses him."[91]

By 1794 Robespierre's ally Barère was calling for the "extermination" of the entire British people, and the Convention ordered that no British prisoners should be taken alive. This latter does not appear to have been implemented.[92]

The whole country witnessed the closure of churches or their transformation into temples of Reason, the forced marriage of thousands of priests, the forced retirement of thousands more. Not surprisingly, in face of this and hostility to army conscription, and after the execution of the King, civil wars enveloped much of Normandy and Brittany, Bordeaux and Bayonne, Marseilles and Toulon and above all, Lyons. In Toulouse and Nîmes royalists were released from prison and Jacobins imprisoned. By mid-June 1793 some 60 *départements* out of 83 were "nominally in rebellion against the regime in Paris". In Normandy and Bordeaux the revolt was soon over and the repression was slight. Elsewhere the Republicans exceeded themselves by reprisals: "in many cases extreme, sometimes barbaric and by definition counterproductive".[93]

Lyons was besieged by a Republican army from early August, and the city surrendered on 9 October. Everywhere the rich lived was threatened with destruction (in fact, of 600 houses so threatened, only 50 were destroyed). Punishment of people, however, was "massive, wholesale and horrific".[94] 106 were executed by firing squads, 79 by guillotine, but, aided by the wholesale firing of cannons into crowds of people, the total approached 1900. The Vendée was far worse; shootings and *noyades* (drownings) accounted for about 10,000 during the winter of 1793–4. Another estimate is that in four months the revolutionary *colonnes infernales,* carrying out a decree by the Convention ordering the "destruction of the Vendée", killed some 50,000 men, women and children, with massive destruction of crops, farms and villages. In total, it was estimated that half the population of the Vendée *département* perished in some way. Many suspects, the total estimated at between 300,000 and 500,000, were held in prison until after the fall of Robespierre.

De Tocqueville pointed to the paradox: "The Revolution had been prepared by the most civilised classes of the nation and carried out by the most uncivilised and the roughest of people." In words which forecast a comparison with both Communism and Islamic extremism, he added: "It is to religious revolutions that we must compare the French Revolution if we want to understand it … It became itself a sort of new religion … without God, without forms of worship and without an afterlife, but which nevertheless, like Islam, has inundated the whole world with its soldiers, its apostles and its martyrs."[95]

Robespierre had become the leader of the Terror, having in June 1793 ousted the moderate Girondins from the Convention and executed more than twenty of them. Inevitably, the Queen was guillotined on 16 October; less inevitably, Louis's sister Elisabeth was guillotined on 10 May 1794. By then, Danton had perished (5 April); Robespierre had become increasingly suspicious of him, as he was not only turning against Terror but was well known for personal corruption. A drunken Danton shocked fellow guests by declaring that the Revolution was like a battle in which the victors shared the loot, enjoying splendid houses, fine food, "handsome clothes and the women of their dreams"; he had started spending large sums and buying land.[96] But the spring of 1794 saw growing criticism of Robespierre. Moderates saw Terror no longer justified by the threat of foreign conquest. Robespierre was mocked over his Cult of the Supreme Being; in one observation "it's not enough to be master, he wants to be God as well".[97] His Law of 22 Prairial in the revolutionary calendar (10 June) reduced defendants' rights and speeded up trial proceedings. This led to a coup on 27 July; he and St-Just were speedily arrested and guillotined; in the following week about 100 alleged associates followed them.

Immediate consequences of the revolution

The fall of the leaders of Terror produced a reaction. After some *sans-culottes* had attacked the Convention in April 1795, 20,000 troops entered the faubourg Saint-Antoine where the leaderless dissidents surrendered; retribution followed. Further arrests took place and the National Guard was purged of anyone thought to be politically unreliable.

In September 1795 Royalists and associates attempted a coup, with a force of 20,000. One of the new Directory, Barras, called on an artillery officer, Napoleon Bonaparte, for help. He seized the necessary guns and the dissidents were dispersed by his "whiff of grapeshot". It was a close-run affair; otherwise aspects of the Revolution might have been reversed. The spring of 1796 saw the end of serious fighting in the Vendée. In the elections of April 1797 to renew one third of the Convention, very few former members were returned. The majority of new members were constitutional monarchists. Had these been united and well led, and able to co-operate with the émigrés, they might have overthrown the Directory, and made peace with France's enemies. Sadly, they were disunited, badly led and were rebuffed by the die-hard émigrés, while there was at this point strong feeling in France against the return of the Bourbons.

Between 1789 and 1797, the number of sea-going vessels in French ports fell from around 2000 to 200. Foreign trade fell from 25 per cent of national wealth to nine per cent. By 1799, despite a slight recovery, French exports were only a half of 1789 levels.[98]

The Revolution was directed at the nobility. Before 1789, it was estimated that the nobility owned between a fifth and a quarter of the land. It is believed they lost half their property during the Revolution.[99] They re-emerged into national politics, especially after 1815, but retained local influence only in the west of France.

The extension of rights as a result of the Revolution was curiously unbalanced. Large proportions of the male population were given voting rights, as were Protestants. Jews were given limited rights. Yet the revolutionary government never considered giving women the vote. Briefly, it tolerated the formation of women's political societies, then in 1793 closed them down.[100] The later *Code Napoléon* was also restrictive on women's rights but forward-looking on homosexuality; in E M Forster's *Maurice,* originally written in 1913, the homosexual Maurice is advised by his therapist "I'm afraid I can only advise you to live in some country that has adopted the *Code Napoléon.*" Extraordinarily, despite a variety of constitutions, it was not until that of the new Fourth Republic in 1944 that women were given the vote. And while in September 1791 slavery was abolished in France, it was retained in the colonies.

Another historian sums up compellingly the negative consequences of the Revolution for constitutional and political stability in France. "From a practical, operational perspective, one must conclude that the French Revolution was, for at least the next hundred years, a deep and damaging failure." It produced no durable alternative to the *ancien regime,* instead "a tsunami of internecine political and social conflict which took at least a hundred years to calm down, and arguably much, much longer".[101]

Ever-expanding conquest?

These consequences were not confined to France. As the same author has cogently declared, from 1792, "France now had to fight an ever-expanding war of conquest, in order to pay for an ever-expanding war of conquest". [102]

In 1792–93, resembling later successful revolutionary regimes in Russia and China, the French Convention declared its determination to accord "fraternity and aid to all peoples who want to recover their liberty". This was reflected in its instructions to revolutionary generals. Between 1793 and 1799, alongside the "liberation" (that is, occupation and annexation) of the left bank of the Rhine, "sister republics" were established in the Netherlands, Switzerland and all mainland Italy. Sadly, wherever French armies passed, pillaging, billeting and requisitions followed, provoking peasant resistance in all these territories. Some Marshals like Masséna and Augereau "were legendary for their systematic pillaging".[103]

On this subject, the Nazi "culture vulture" Hermann Goering had a good precedent in the Directory in 1796, which authorised the pillaging of Italian museums. Under Bonaparte, the ministry of the interior proposed transferring from Italian, Dutch, Belgian, German and other subjected countries all documentation about their earlier political history to the new national archives in Paris. His "widespread and efficient plundering of art wherever his conquests took him and his armies" is acknowledged.[104]

Even before the emergence of Bonaparte, the Convention in 1794 insisted that plundered sculptures and paintings from France, Germany, Belgium and the

Netherlands (this was before the invasion of Italy) should be convoyed to Paris, as "… the proper place for them, in the interests and for the honour of art, is in the home of free men". The Directory declared in October 1796: "The French Republic, by its strength and superiority of its enlightenment and its artists, is the only country in the world which can give a home to these masterpieces. All other nations must come to borrow from our art …" And the Treaty of Tolentino in February 1797 with the Papal States required that all manuscripts in the Vatican Library written before AD 900 should be taken. Bonaparte wanted to carry off Trajan's column but was persuaded to desist when told that movement would destroy it. In Venice, the Doge's ornate ceremonial barge was destroyed. The four horses in front of St Mark's, dating from the second or third century AD, and earlier looted by the Venetians from Constantinople, were taken in 1797 and put on the Arc du Carrousel. They were returned to Venice in 1815 by order of the Austrian Emperor.[105]

In her evocative biography of Madame de Pompadour, Nancy Mitford declared that her houses and her objects of art, "would have been a good investment for France had not nearly everything she created been destroyed or dispersed during the Revolution". Four houses were "utterly destroyed", others were "altered beyond recognition", with her belongings "scattered to the four winds, sometimes to be seen in a museum or a private collection. The revolutionary government "sold them all to speculators who disposed of them piecemeal", many going to "rich English collectors".[106]

A recent study, where the title is aptly descriptive – *Books on Fire*[107] – discussed also in the Introduction to the present work, manifests the role of the French Revolution. Libraries linked to the monarchy, the nobility and particularly to the Church, as well as to political opponents (like the *Feuillants'* library in Dijon) went to scrapheaps and often to bonfires, such as on the Place Vendôme in Paris on 19 June 1792. In November 1789 ecclesiastic possessions, especially jewellery, precious metals and, of course, buildings and land, including libraries, were transferred "into the hands of the nation". An estimated total of 12 million books were "moved, re-sorted and damaged so that whatever was not destroyed was in large part lost". Cartloads of printed books and manuscripts crossed the paths of their legitimate owners in tumbrils on their way to the guillotine.

Some, indeed, went eventually to public libraries, and some were rescued by the secretary of the Russian embassy for Catherine the Great, but many others had quainter destinations. With churches deemed appropriate for the manufacture of saltpetre in 1794, the Abbey of Saint-Germain saw nearly 60,000 volumes and manuscripts from its library used as fuel, and the term "sending books to the arsenal" did not mean meeting the educational desires of the soldiery, but ripping out pages to make cartridge bags.[108]

During the 1790s, in the Low Countries, the Rhineland and northern Italy, far from acting as liberators, the French troops "retained sufficient vestiges of Jacobin propaganda to despise Catholic religiosity".[109] Belgium saw a "massive revolt" of the peasantry in 1798, partly against French religious policies, as well as conscription.

Peasant revolts were especially marked during the French retreat in 1799 in Italy, following the Battle of the Nile and Suvorov's Russian victories in Switzerland and Northern Italy. There were peasant risings against conscription in south-west France as well as in Anjou, Normandy and Brittany.[110]

After the Vendée war of 1793, what became known as the *Chouannerie* spluttered on in north-western France for several years, marked by assassination of government officials, informers and constitutional priests as well as ambushes of military columns, with the latter exacting corresponding reprisals.

The Royalist plotters, however, were doomed by incompetence as well as by betrayal through the operation of "double agents" or others who turned to help the Republic in order to save their lives. Several of their leaders and followers were very brave men and women, notably the Breton Georges Cadoudal. Reverses during these years included the capture in November 1795 of 500 items of correspondence giving the names of Royalist conspirators in Provence and Lyons and elsewhere.[111]

Bonaparte established the Consulate, with himself as First Consul. His personal position, initially open to challenge from rivals, was cemented by his decisive victory over the Austrians at Marengo on 14 June 1800. This led to the Treaty of Lunéville and the Treaty of Amiens with Britain; both recognised the French achievement of her "natural frontiers" – especially annexing Belgium and the left bank of the Rhine, as well as establishing puppet republics in the Netherlands, Switzerland and northern Italy (the Batavian, Helvetic, Ligurian and Cisalpine republics).

In true Roman style, Bonaparte planned an ambitious building project at Marengo. A column was constructed and the battlefield was to become the site of a "city of Victories" whose boulevards, named after Italian battles, would converge to a pyramid. In the event, the project was abandoned in 1815, with the column removed and the stones recovered by the local peasants.[112]

The Napoleonic opportunity

To ensure that this volume does not expand excessively , a decision was reluctantly taken to edit severely an earlier draft on the reign of Napoleon I. The events are well known and frequently described, so what follows is a summary of Napoleon's opportunity, achievements, and ultimate decisive failure.

Napoleon terminated the instability in France which the Revolution had aroused and, for a while, gave her that order to which, as hitherto an essentially monarchical nation, she was accustomed. However, like Louis XIV and Louis XV, he relied too much on warfare, in which for much of the time he was remarkably successful but which produced his final nemesis. He was ahead of his time in seeking to promote a civil code both to France and to non-French peoples with strong religious loyalties. In tune with a major theme of 19th-century history, he also gave many of the German and Italian people a sense of national unity. These must be set alongside the massive cost to human life and limb, described below. In practice, this was France's last opportunity to form and govern a European commonwealth, similar to the Roman Empire though not as extensive or, in the event, durable.

Expenditure on warfare was huge – rising from 462 million francs in 1807 to 817 million francs in 1813. In addition to unpopular direct and indirect taxes in France, "to a large but incalculable degree, Napoleonic imperialism was paid for by plunder". This included confiscations of crown and feudal properties in conquered countries, spoils taken directly from opponents' museums and treasuries, quartering French troops on them and requiring contingents from them. War indemnities in money or in kind were essential, such as the 311 million francs exacted from Prussia after Jena and the large sums paid by Austria after each defeat. The franc in the 1800s was worth about 12 modern US dollars – hence expenditure rose from about $5.5 billion to $9.8 billion and the Prussian indemnity brought about just over $3.7 billion. In Italy between 1805 and 1812 about half the taxes raised went to the French. All these "in some ways foreshadow Nazi Germany's plunder of its satellites and conquered foes".[113]

Italy proved a major problem, with the religious factor being prominent. As Broers declares: there was a "radical, almost anti-clerical spirit at work within the imperial civil service" with an "unswerving belief in the cultural superiority of the French Enlightenment [and] the strongly felt need to impose that culture on the common people of western Europe".[114]

Resistance existed in upland Piedmont, the Apennines, most of Liguria and the duchies of Parma and Piacenza, where "banditry" was only defeated by around 1807. Ten years of continuous French rule, however, failed to eradicate large scale banditry in the kingdom of Naples. A revolt in Emilia-Romagna was directed against the growing burdens of conscription and taxation. The rebels besieged Bologna in July 1809. They were repulsed but rural banditry continued until May 1810. Furthermore, "the Kingdom of Naples had never been absorbed properly into the inner empire, now it would be almost lost to it." By 1811 King Joachim Murat's effective control was confined to the larger towns and was increasingly dependent on French troops. Broers concludes: "Spain has sometimes been described as the Vietnam of the Napoleonic wars. If so, then Calabria was their Cambodia."[115]

Spain was never as key to Napoleon's security as central Italy or the north German coast. While historian Robert Harvey admits Prussia and Naples (the latter especially if helped by Britain) could act as threats to France, "there was no such excuse for the invasion of Spain. It was imperial aggrandisement [and] a terrible misreading of the country."[116]

Between 1808 and 1813 a million Spaniards are estimated to have died. The savagery of the war in both Spain and Portugal "was to mark it out from conflict in most of the rest of Europe at this time".[117] The French invasion of Spain in the winter of 1808 saw massive destruction, massacre and rape in cities such as Burgos and Toledo.

The three "Hanseatic" departments, along the north German coast, created in December 1810, have been described as the least durable of the Napoleonic system. Between 1811–13 the marshlands along this coast saw large numbers of escapees from conscription, many of whom turned to banditry. Broers grimly sums up "Almost every sector of society felt its most vital interests damaged by annexation. The flourishing urban civilisation of the North Sea coast had been ruined economically, and its sophisticated culture brutalised."[118] After the French defeat at Leipzig in 1813 there were anti-French risings in all the north German ports and in Westphalia.

Peace and consolidation might have cemented Napoleonic rule: neither was present after 1807. There were probably at least one million military deaths of Frenchmen in 23 years of war, excluding civilians.[119] Decades of warfare reduced Europe's population "by anything up to a tenth"; estimates are 5–7 million dead including civilians.[120]

In a notable meeting with Metternich in Dresden in the summer of 1813, Napoleon seems to have lost his temper with the Austrian foreign minister's demands for concessions if Austria was to remain neutral. This might explain these unfortunate remarks: "A man like me cares little for the lives of a million men," adding "I may lose my throne, but I shall bury the whole world in its ruins."[121]

France's wider industrial revolution was delayed and she did not easily return to the rapid growth of the years before 1789. Indeed, one historian has France actually de-industrialising: "The Revolution, far from being 'capitalist' or 'bourgeois', had delayed France's industrial development by fifty years."[122]

FOOTNOTES

1 Paul Kennedy *The Rise and Fall of the Great Powers*, Vintage Books, 1989, p79.
2 Remark believed to have been made by Madame de Pompadour in 1757.
3 Frank McLynn, *1759: The Year Britain Became Master of the World*, BCA, 2004, pp245, 390 for the two quotes.
4 *Ibid*, pp231–2, 356-57, 362.
5 Colin Jones *The Great Nation: France from Louis XIV to Napoleon*, Penguin, 2003, p332.
6 Kennedy, *op cit*, pp79, 82.
7 First quote, François Furet, *Revolutionary France 1770–1880*, Blackwell Publishing, 1992, p10; second quote David Bell, *Shadows of Revolution: Reflections on France, Past and Present* OUP, 2016, p118.
8 Christopher Hibbert, *The French Revolution* 1980, p32.
9 Georges Lefebvre, *The Great Fear of 1789: Rural Panic in Revolutionary France*, Pantheon Books, 1973, p8.
10 Jones, *op cit*, p44.
11 Stephen Clarke, *The French Revolution and What Went Wrong*, Century, 2018, p65; Jones, *op cit*, p97.
12 John Hardman *Marie Antoinette*, Yale UP, 2019, subsequently *Antoinette*, p127.
13 Kennedy, *op cit*, p122.
14 Jones, *op cit*, p280.
15 Voltaire quote, *ibid*, p288, also p282.
16 *Ibid*, p289.
17 An account of this complex business, perhaps the last occasion on which the *ancien régime* showed it had teeth and used them, is in Jones, *op cit*, pp279–94.
18 Lieven, *Shadow*, pp369–71.
19 *Ibid*, pp198, 271; Bell, *op cit*, p102.
20 Jones, *op cit*, p324.
21 Quoted in Hardman, *op cit*, p47.
22 Quoted in Jones, *op cit*, p 300; also p299.
23 Kennedy, *op cit*, p84.
24 Hardman, *Antoinette*, p76.
25 Hardman, *op cit*, p71.
26 Quotes from Hardman, *op cit*, p78 and Jones, *op cit*, p341.
27 Clarke, *op cit*, p238.
28 Jones, *op cit*, pp345–47.
29 Hardman, *Antoinette*, p106; Jones, *op cit*, p338; Furet, *op cit*, p32.
30 Hardman, *op cit*, pp84–85.
31 *Ibid*, p111.
32 Jones, *op cit*, p380; Hardman, *op cit*, pp87, 111–12.
33 Quotes respectively Jones, *op cit*, p381 and Hardman, *op cit*, p103.
34 Hardman, *op cit*, p106.
35 *Ibid*, p113.
36 *Ibid*, pp114, 125.
37 Quoted, *ibid*, p117.
38 *Ibid*, p116.
39 *Ibid*, p120.
40 First quote, Hardman, *Antoinette*, p138–39, second quote Hardman *op cit*, p122.
41 Hardman, *op cit*, pp125–26.
42 Quotes *ibid*, pp129–30.
43 Jones, *op cit*, p387; Hardman, *op cit*, p132.
44 Quoted, Jones, *op cit*, p391.
45 Quoted *ibid*, p393.
46 Hardman, *op cit*, pp136, 138.
47 *Ibid*, p145.
48 Quoted Clarke, *op cit*, p262.
49 Lefebvre, *op cit*, p25.
50 Jones, *op cit*, p408–09.
51 *Ibid*, p399.
52 Clarke, *op cit*, p272.
53 *Ibid*, pp292–93.
54 Lieven, *Shadow*, p371.
55 Lefebvre, *op cit*, pp61–63.
56 Hardman, *op cit*, p155, Clarke, *op cit*, p306.
57 Hardman, *op cit*, pp158, 161; SF Scott *The Response of the Royal Army to the French Revolution 1787–93*, OUP 1973, pp59, 80.
58 Quoted, Hibbert, *op cit*, p93.
59 Hardman, *op cit*, p158. Compare pp102-104 of the present work.
60 *Ibid*, p160, Jones, *op cit*, pp410, 417.
61 Clarke, *op cit*, p374.
62 Lefebvre, *op cit*, p42.
63 *Ibid*, pp81-2, 85–86.

64 *Ibid*, pp95,97, 139.
65 *Ibid*, pp105–7, 114–15.
66 Jones, *op cit*, p420.
67 Hardman, *op cit*, p178.
68 Hardman, *Antoinette*, p188.
69 Ian Davidson, *The French Revolution: From Enlightenment to Tyranny*, 2016, pp47–50.
70 Quoted, Hibbert, *op cit*, p110.
71 Hardman, *Antoinette*, p212.
72 Talleyrand quote, Hardman, *op cit*, p181; Davidson, *op cit*, p63.
73 Hardman, *op cit*, pp194–96.
74 Davidson, *op cit*, p68.
75 Clarke, *op cit*, p406, Hardman, *op cit*, p190.
76 Philip Mansel, *Louis XVIII*, Blond and Briggs 1981, p54.
77 Jones, *op cit*, p448.
78 Quoted Hibbert, *op cit*, pp140, 146; Clarke, *op cit*, p419.
79 Hardman, *Antoinette*, pp247, 310.
80 Quoted, Hardman, *op cit*, p215.
81 Hardman, *Antoinette*, pp274, 276.
82 Quoted, *ibid*, pp204, 206.
83 Hibbert, *op cit*, p178.
84 Quoted, Clarke, *op cit*, p428.
85 *Ibid*, p429.
86 *Ibid*, p445.
87 Hibbert, *op cit*, p181.
88 Hardman, *op cit*, p229.
89 Quoted, Clarke, *op cit*, p457.
90 *Ibid*, pp463, 533–34.
91 Quotes in these two paragraphs from Hibbert, *op cit*, pp225, 236, 239, 246, 248; Davidson, *op cit*, pp188, 214; Bell, *op cit*, pp157–58.
92 Quoted, Bell, *op cit*, p193.
93 Davidson, *op cit*, p171.
94 *Ibid*, p173.
95 Quoted, *ibid*, p192.
96 Hibbert, *op cit*, p167.
97 Quoted, Jones, *op cit*, p496.
98 *Ibid*, p538.
99 Munro Price, *The Perilous Crown – France between Revolutions 1814-48*, Macmillan 2007, pp51–52.
100 Bell, *op cit*, p48.
101 Davidson, *op cit*, p245.
102 *Ibid*, p135.
103 Stuart Woolf, *Napoleon's Integration of Europe*, Routledge 1991, p47.
104 *Ibid*, p10.
105 Arthur Tompkins, *Plundering Beauty-a history of art crime during war*, Lund Humphries, 2018, pp12, 63–68.
106 Nancy Mitford, *Madame de Pompadour*, Sphere Books, 1968, pp74, 134.
107 Lucien X Polastron, *Books on Fire: The Destruction of Libraries Throughout History*, English translation, Inner Traditions International, Rochester, Vermont, USA, 2007.
108 Polastron, *op cit*, pp152–61.
109 Michael Broers, *Europe Under Napoleon*, I B Tauris, 2015, p14. This is a new edition; Broers was first published in 1996 by Arnold, part of Hodder Headline.
110 *Ibid*, pp100, 106–7, 112.
111 Carlos de la Huerta, *The Great Conspiracy: Britain's Secret War Against Revolutionary France 1794-1805*, Amberley, 2016, pp27, 37.
112 Benoît, Jérémie, *Marengo: Une victoire politique*, 2000, p138.
113 Kennedy, *op cit*, pp132–33.
114 Broers, *op cit*, pp217–18.
115 *Ibid*, p172.
116 Robert Harvey, *The War of Wars*, Constable, 2007, p584.
117 Charles Esdaile, *The Peninsular War*, Allen Lane, 2002 p93.
118 Broers, *op cit*, p200.
119 Bell, *op cit*, p181: Munro Price estimates 1.4 million, *op cit*, p9; Kennedy 1.5 million, *op cit*, p167.
120 Bell, *op cit*, p181 has 5 million.
121 Frank McLynn, *Napoleon–A Biography*, Vintage, 1998, pp557–58.
122 Mansel, *op cit*, p121.

Chapter Five:
19th-Century Instability in France

The Bourbon Restoration 1815–30

France saw all kinds of progress after 1815, economically, internationally, socially and in particular culturally. For at least 70 years after 1815, however, French politics were dominated, and occasionally destabilised, by the competing claims of three dynasties, each with a competing set of beliefs and supporters, sitting alongside those who wanted a Republic. Each of these groups governed for a period, so their strengths and weaknesses played their parts in later contention. From 1815–30 the direct successors of Louis XVI reigned, and their followers, with support strongly in the Church and higher aristocracy and particularly in the west of France, became known as Legitimists. From 1830–48 the Orléans branch of the royal family reigned, with more of a liberal parliamentary regime; its followers, known as Orleanists, formed a new oligarchy, including wealthy bankers (often Protestant) and prosperous businessmen. Orleanists also provided key supporters of the subsequent imperial and republican regimes. And the admirers of the First Empire of Napoleon I were known as Bonapartists; their support waxed and waned during the 1815–48 period and after 1870, but they had their own regime in place from 1852–70 as the Second Empire, with Napoleon III presenting himself with some success as "the Napoleon of the people". In good times, followers of rival dynasties and even republicans supported whatever regime was governing. In bad times, or when a regime was toppled in the streets of Paris, as in 1830 and 1848, or when it was shattered by military defeat, as in 1870, it found itself abandoned even by nominal supporters. Thus both the regimes of 1830–48 and 1852–70 faced political opposition from the Right, in the shape of a rival dynasty, and the Left, in the shape of adherents of the Republic. And some of the Royalists supported a tradition hostile to the Republic as late as the Vichy regime of 1940–44.

In 1814, the Tsar was determined to depose Napoleon, but who should follow – Louis XVIII, Louis Philippe, Duc d'Orléans, or the infant King of Rome, already proclaimed Emperor under the regency of his mother, the Empress Marie Louise? France's eastern provinces, invaded by the Allies, showed no affection for the Bourbons, but Bordeaux had welcomed them. While the Army still favoured Napoleon, its leaders were divided.

After Napoleon briefly ousted Louis XVIII and was ousted himself after Waterloo, doubts were expressed about the Bourbons, so unceremoniously expelled. The Tsar openly argued that Louis Philippe should take over. Wellington opposed this, with typical acerbity: "He would simply be a usurper of good family." It was in haste to forestall such a candidacy that Louis XVIII returned "in the baggage train of the enemy" – a risky venture.[1] There was a suspicion that Louis Philippe had been conspiring against his cousins at the time of Napoleon's escape from Elba. Mansel quotes from one of "the strange, treacherous letters" Orléans "scattered far and wide during the Hundred Days", that Louis XVIII intended "undoubtedly to return political and public institutions, opinion, customs and above all etiquette ... to what they were before the revolution". He sent these letters to Talleyrand, Wellington, and Castlereagh "obviously in order to discredit the king in their eyes".[2]

The Allies wanted to ensure the stability of France and thus the peace of Europe. That, in the view of the British, who were listened to with respect, and of Tsar Alexander, meant a moderately liberal constitution. Of the French population of 30 million, however, just 90,000 were given the vote, in contrast to Britain, where 440,000 of a population of 20 million had votes, even before the 1832 reforms which added a further 216,000. The French monarchy did not have the confidence to follow this route.

It was noted that many mayors and prefects had welcomed Napoleon as he marched on Paris in early 1815, so Louis XVIII's government "did what every other nineteenth century French regime did on seizing power; it sacked its enemies and installed its friends in office". It was estimated that a third to a quarter of civil servants were affected.[3] And the army had been halved in size so there existed many demobilised, discontented and often unemployed ex-soldiers, mixing with Bonapartist former officers.

Of all political groups the ultra-Royalists were best organised, exercising a strong party discipline in votes and debates. Their effective leaders, varying in personality and political attitude, included Villèle and Chateaubriand. The moderate royalists divided into the Centre Right and the Centre Left. The former was usually led by the Duc de Richelieu, who was pragmatic but had no sympathy for the Revolution; he had spent 25 years in exile in Russia and tended to ally with the ultras. The Centre Left had leaders who were either nobles who had accepted office under Napoleon, or new men who had risen in his service. Finally there were the liberals, who were hostile to the restored Bourbons and tended to be anti-clerical. Several had close links with republican secret societies such as the *Carbonari*, which aimed at a popular revolt.

During the summer of 1819 various Bonapartists were allowed to return to France. This is unlikely to have compensated for the execution of Marshal Ney in 1815, the damage therein recognised by this remark by Louis XVIII: "By allowing himself to be caught he has perhaps done us more harm than even on March 13" when Ney welcomed Napoleon instead of, as he had promised, "bringing him back in an iron cage".[4]

The elections of 1818 had benefited the liberal opposition. Decazes, the royal favourite, was Minister of the Interior as well as of police: in November 1819 he became Prime Minister. This calm was shaken by the assassination of the Duc de Berri, the Comte D'Artois' younger son, on 13 February 1820. He was stabbed by a fanatical Bonapartist who planned to kill all the Bourbons: he chose Berri first because he was the only one capable of fathering an heir (the Duc d'Angoulême, his elder brother, was sterile). In fact, the Duchesse de Berri was already pregnant with Henri, Duc de Bordeaux, who was born on 28 September 1820. As Comte de Chambord he became the Bourbon claimant after Angoulême's death in 1844.

Decazes was blamed for this security failure and so eventually was sacked. In 1820 an organisation called *Bazar français*, consisting of various former officers or NCOs of the Imperial army, aimed at risings at various garrison towns in the north. La Fayette and other Liberal deputies "were cognizant of the plan". 138 were arrested, but the leaders escaped. A further plot was centred on Belfort and planned for 29–30 December 1821. It was postponed, then betrayed, and proved abortive. La Fayette was not prosecuted, but it was alleged he had had his general's uniform sent on for him to wear.[5] Other abortive risings under General Berton were planned to take place in February and June 1822, with the intention of proclaiming a provisional government consisting of various generals. Berton was arrested and, along with various others, executed in September 1822.

Despite these failures, there remained a fear that "Napoleon would return", Indeed, in every March between 1816 and 1825 there were rumours of this, some specific as to where he had landed and the number of troops with him (the latter varying from Turkish, Moorish, Persian, Chinese or Indian).[6] His death on St Helena in 1821 rendered easier the co-operation of all anti-Bourbon parties.

With a new electoral law favouring the most wealthy, the elections of November 1820 saw the Liberals losing heavily, going down to 80, while the ministry and the ultras rose to 190 and 160 respectively. The new prime minister was the ultra leader, Villèle, who held power for seven years. In the elections of March 1824 the royalists were massively successful; only 19 Liberals were returned, with La Fayette and other leaders defeated. Villèle was a master of opinion manipulation, through press censorship, purges of officials, last-minute revision of electoral rolls, and redrawing of constituency boundaries. These practices were never confined to France, and in France they continued until well into the 20th century. Yet his objective was to force through measures which were intended to benefit the nobility and the clergy. [7]

Smitten by a combination of diabetes, hardening of the arteries and finally gangrene, Louis XVIII died on 16 September 1824. Charles X's personality was not without attractions. He had never shared his brother's distrust of the Orléans family and one of his first acts was to give Louis Philippe and all members of his family the title of Royal Highnesses. But he pressed for the full ultra programme. The most significant was the indemnity law for the former émigrés whose ancestral properties had passed into other hands. While this ensured that the revolutionary land sales were not questioned, the means of funding the bill, reducing the rates on government bonds, was highly controversial and was rejected by the Chamber of Peers. A more complex package was eventually passed in April 1825, involving the payment of 630 million francs to 700,000 claimants. The largest payment, 17 million francs, paradoxically, went to Louis Philippe for the Orléans family's losses. [8]

The other great plank of the ultra programme, restoring the status of the clergy, was even more unpopular. There was opposition to the Catholic religious orders, especially the Jesuits, with their influence on schooling. So another bill, giving these orders the benefit of legal status, eventually passed the Chambers but was limited in scope. In April 1827 a carriage carrying the Dauphine (the Duchesse d'Angoulême) and the Duchesse de Berri was greeted with cries "*à bas les Jesuitesses*". [9]

There followed "the restoration's most notorious piece of religious legislation". This was the "law of sacrilege", with an ascending order of penalties. While the ultras wanted the death penalty for the profanation of the Host, they did not criminalise impious acts towards other Christian churches or groups. In fact, after its passage it was never once applied, but it alarmed public opinion.[10] A further act of Villèle's was the dissolution of the National Guard of Paris after a demonstration in April 1827. As a bizarre piece of negligence, they were allowed to take their uniforms and muskets home!

The elections of November 1827 saw the Liberals winning across Paris. More Liberals were elected across the country and the Government lost its majority. The crisis of the regime was now approaching. The King was reluctant to part with Villèle but was persuaded by Polignac and his faction to drop him in January 1828. As one historian comments: "when they [the Royalists] coalesced with the Liberals to bring about his [Villèle's] downfall they could not realise that they had driven from office the one man who, without violating the Constitution, was capable of governing in the interests of their party."[11] Villèle was succeeded by Martignac, a moderate who never enjoyed the confidence of the King, who chose Polignac to be his confidante.

Polignac was extreme over religion but had a Scottish wife, and from 1823 he had been ambassador in London and had developed a great admiration of English methods. "He believed it possible to form in democratic France a governing class, in imitation of the landed aristocracy which he had seen managing successfully local affairs in England." [12] In August 1829 Polignac became prime minister. Other appointments gave even greater offence: the new minister of the interior was La Bourdonnaye, an author of the White Terror on Bonapartists in 1815, while Bourmont, the minister of war, had deserted Napoleon's army on the eve of Waterloo and joined the Allies, subsequently appearing as the main witness in the trial of Marshal Ney. Meanwhile, the winter of 1829–30, like that of 1788–89, saw severe rain spoiling the harvest, while manufacturing was stagnating, leading to high unemployment.

To Charles's speech from the Throne on 2 March 1830, the Chamber made an address in reply that the King should only choose ministers who possessed parliamentary confidence. This was adopted by 221 to 181 on 18 March. Charles dissolved Parliament, with fresh elections timed for the end of June. He refused to recall Villèle because he knew that Villèle would not support the unconstitutional measures he was considering. France invaded Algeria at this time, capturing Algiers, a most momentous development, greatly influencing her place in the world over the next 130 years. It had no effect on public opinion: the crowds outside Notre Dame on 11 July, when Charles attended a victory *Te Deum*, were "pointedly silent, to the extent that the king himself was disconcerted". Chateaubriand remarked "Providence can at one stroke enlarge a kingdom and overthrow a dynasty."[13] In the elections, most deputies who had voted for the Address were returned, contributing to 270 seats for the Opposition. With only 145 seats, the Government was in a hopeless minority.

Then followed on 25 July the "Four Ordinances", dissolving the Chamber of Deputies which had not yet met and fixing a new date for elections, laying down a new, even more restricted, electoral law, and drastically limiting the freedom of the press, with threats to not only journalists and press proprietors but also to printing workers.

If this programme had been imposed in the late 1780s, it would have probably been accepted. But a lot had changed since 1789. A critical minister, Guernon-Ranville, declared "You need have announced merely that in future deputies will be appointed by the prefects." The reactionary Tsar Nicholas I told the French ambassador to tell Charles "were the Coronation oath to be violated, he must

Moenia Dardanidum – the wall of Troy (p11). Author.

The Ruins of Ani (pp75-6). Author.

Lord Bolingbroke (Chapter 3), The Miriam and Ira D. Wallach Division of Art, Prints and Photographs: Print Collection, The New York Public Library. Wikimedia Commons.

Francis Atterbury (p117), Wikimedia Commons.

Peckwater Quad, Christ Church, Oxford (p 121), Wikimedia Commons.

Canova's monument to the later Stuarts in St Peter's, Rome, (Chapter 3), Author.

Charles-Alexandre de Calonne, French Finance Minister, (Chapter 4), Wikimedia Commons.

Peter Stolypin, Prime Minister of Russia, (Chapter 6), Wikimedia Commons.

expect no assistance from Russia" and the reactionary but pragmatic Metternich told the French Ambassador in Vienna "I know well that the freedom of the press and your electoral laws are abominations, but any attempt to abolish them by a *coup d'état* will be fatal to the Bourbons."[14]

The outcome was a chapter of accidents and mistakes. Charles and Polignac were convinced that Paris would remain quiet. All four lieutenant generals of the Royal Guard were absent from their posts, along with other officers visiting the provinces in order to vote; it was claimed that half the senior officers were on leave.[15] So no troops had been concentrated, no plans made to occupy key points or arrest potential dissidents. Marshal Marmont, commanding the Guards, had heard late about the ordinances and spoke very bitterly of the government's conduct.

Adolphe Thiers and 44 Liberal journalists declared "the Government has forfeited its right to expect obedience. We intend to resist … The rule of law is at an end, and that of force has begun."[16] Marmont ordered out his troops on 27 July, and cleared the streets with some killed: this gave the opposition the martyrs it needed, and the corpses were paraded about. The crowds did not disperse and by 8am on the 28th 60 men from two regiments of the line had gone over to the insurgents. Others followed. Barriers were thrown up in the rear of the troops, gunsmiths' shops were looted, the tricolour hoisted. Former members of the National Guard either joined the rebels or handed over their guns. The government troops lacked food and water in very hot weather.

Marmont pressed the King to make a peaceful settlement – "tomorrow, perhaps, may be too late". Charles refused. The Swiss Guards abandoned the Louvre; their commander, the Comte de Salis, did not want them to suffer the fate of 1792.[17] Other troops retreated to the Place de l'Étoile; Marmont planned to resist there. A message came from the King at Saint-Cloud that the Duc d' Angoulême had taken command and wanted to retreat. This demoralised the troops and led to a violent exchange of words between Marmont and Angoulême.

Meanwhile, various suggestions were made to save Charles X: he should dismiss Polignac, withdraw the ordinances, and include some Liberals in a new cabinet under the Duc de Mortemart. The King was reluctant; delays took place. While he accepted these three decisions in the afternoon of the 29th, he only agreed at 7am on the 30th to written confirmation of them. Further delays accompanied the despatch of this information into Paris on the morning of the 30th, with the emissary told by a Liberal deputy, "you are too late."

In fact, the candidacy of Louis Philippe had been launched the previous evening. That same night, Thiers and Lafitte issued a proclamation stating that Charles has "shed the blood of the people" and setting out the case for the Duc d'Orléans, "a Prince devoted to the cause of the Revolution". Although Orléans had not assented on the 30th, "before midday [his] name was on every tongue".[18] Eventually, both Chambers agreed that Louis Philippe should become Lieutenant General of the Kingdom. Only on the evening of the 30th did Louis Philippe agree to go to Paris and accept this offer: on the 31st he went to the Hôtel de Ville where, with the collaboration of La Fayette, he took part in a "republican coronation", in which he was accepted by the crowd. In the circumstances, this was an advance, as the cities, especially Paris, strongly supported a republic, and his supporters had to calm an angry populace.

Meanwhile, Charles and the court retreated to Rambouillet, arriving as dusk was falling on the 31st. The only way of saving the legitimist principle was for Charles and the Dauphin to abdicate in favour of the young Duc de Bordeaux; this was done, and Louis Philippe was asked to proclaim the accession of King Henri V, and assume the regency. Louis Philippe was not prepared to co-operate: he acknowledged the abdication but made no mention of Henri V. This inaction "was never forgiven by the elder branch" of the Bourbons, and it started a "bitter feud" between it and the Orléans family which lasted much of the 19th century, playing into the hands, first, of the Bonapartists and then of the republicans.

Louis Philippe later claimed he would have preferred to act as regent for Henri V, but that this had become impossible after three days of fighting in which about a thousand people had been killed: the revolutionaries, now holding Paris, would never have accepted it. And there would have been constant political clashes between himself and Henri's family. Was his ambition simply to seize the crown? It appears that he asked the British ambassador to send one of his staff to Charles with the offer that Henri could remain in France, presumably as king, on condition that no member of his family stayed with him. Charles considered this offer but finally refused it: the Duchesse de Berri refused to be separated from her son, who was only nine. It was a somewhat unnatural proposal, and the British emissary "took a suspiciously long time to reach Charles": by this time (7 August), Louis Philippe was about to be crowned king.[19]

At first, Charles refused to leave Rambouillet but on 3 August, with the untrue rumour that the royal troops had murdered emissaries, a huge crowd of nearly 20,000 Parisians prepared to march there – repeating the pattern of October 1789. Charles and his family then fled to England.

Louis Philippe: the "July monarchy"

He began with clemency. Of seven ministers in Charles's last cabinet, only three escaped abroad. Four including Polignac were arrested, tried by the Chamber of Peers and found guilty of high treason. The King was determined to spare their lives so they received sentences of life imprisonment. The revolutionary mob was very violent towards them but they were protected and exiled after six years' imprisonment.

The same mob wanted a more radical constitution: "a popular throne surrounded by republican institutions."[20] On 7 August 1830, the deputies approved this. The monarch would now be prevented from assuming the emergency powers invoked in July 1830. Censorship was abolished, and Catholicism was no longer the state religion, but "the religion of the majority of Frenchmen". The Tricolour replaced the *Drapeau Blanc*. Changes were made to the electoral law, slight, but contrasted with recent franchise reductions: about 166,500 would now have the vote. On 7 August the King took the oath, and four veteran Napoleonic Marshals presented him with the royal insignia: the crown, sceptre, sword and the hand of justice.

Louis Philippe acted as his own prime minister, taking a considerable interest in foreign policy. He never tried to sustain a government that had lost the confidence of the Chambers; given time, Orleanist party politics might have evolved along English lines. This hope, however, was swept away in 1848.

There was expectation in army circles and among the poorer classes that he would wipe out the shame of the 1814–15 defeat by attacking those who had inflicted it. He had no plans of this nature, and, equally, he had to reassure France's former enemies that this was the case, a point which several, especially Metternich's Austria, doubted. The Austrian Emperor Francis later admitted that the only reason he had not gone to war with France in 1830 was that he could not afford to. When Louis Philippe was toppled by revolution in February 1848, the Tsar commented that he "has only received his just deserts; he has gone out by the same door by which he came in".[21] The Russian Princess Lieven, Metternich's former mistress and later Guizot's, wrote to Lady Palmerston in 1838 that the Tsar's "rage against Paris is stronger than ever, and I, who inhabit that evil city, am regarded as a rebel, and will probably be taken for a spy before long". And when Louis Philippe sought to marry his eldest son, Ferdinand Philippe, to an Austrian archduchess, Metternich persuaded the girl's father, who was delighted with the idea, to reject it, reminding him of the fate of Marie Antoinette.[22]

Risings in 1830 in Germany and Italy produced in France the expectation, always disappointed, that France would resort to armed intervention. Likewise, the revolt in Poland in 1830–31 produced demonstrations, and the news of the fall of Warsaw to the Russians in September 1831 saw several days of rioting in Paris.[23]

Significant sections of the French nobility and governing class retained Legitimist loyalties; most retired to their estates but some conspired. The real danger, however, did not lie with the Legitimists but with the Left. The Society for the Rights of Man was paramilitary; its members were armed and each section was required to drill and hold target practice. There were four serious republican risings between 1831 and 1834, two in Paris (and two minor ones) and two in Lyons. On 14 February 1831 the annual memorial service for the Duc de Berri, held for the first time since the July revolution, saw a Legitimist rally faced by a mob – the latter wrecked the church and the palace of the Archbishop of Paris, a noted Legitimist. His priceless library of manuscripts was thrown into the Seine, with the authorities, even the National Guard, doing nothing. This was followed by attacks on churches elsewhere in Paris and in the provinces. Another rising in Paris in June 1832 saw the King appeal to the National Guard with a "fighting speech" – a "decisive" act, as it "definitively rallied the National Guard to the regime". He continued to show himself on horseback, even at the risk of his own safety. The republican rebels were hemmed in near the Rue Saint-Denis, in the cloisters of Saint-Merri, where they were "finished off with artillery". The army and National Guard had combined casualties of 50 dead and 274 wounded, the republicans "perhaps 100 dead and 300 wounded". [24]

In February 1834 20,000 Lyons textile workers went on strike against pay cuts, leading to a rising in April with between 3000 and 6000 people taking up arms. The fighting lasted for four days, with the army using artillery to regain control: 130 soldiers, 170 insurgents and about 20 civilians died. A sympathetic rising took place at the same time in Paris, crushed by 35,000 soldiers and 5000 National Guards, with very few casualties. And in May 1839 there was a further attempt in Paris by the Society of the Rights of Man; this lasted one day, with 28 soldiers and between 15 and 40 insurgents killed.[25]

And the "Citizen King" faced several assassination attempts. Most notable was that in June 1836 using an "infernal machine", containing 25 musket barrels, which killed Marshal Mortier and another 17 people, wounded prime minister Broglie, with one bullet grazing the King's forehead. He faced four more serious attempts on his life over the next 12 years, and a total of seven: the writer Sophie Gay complained that "it is becoming rather monotonous". Around 1844 a package addressed to the King turned out to contain four live rattlesnakes.[26]

Republican and Legitimist newspapers attacked the regime with cartoons and virulent written attacks throughout the reign. Even so, French politics became more stable during Molé's ministry from 1837–39, then during those of Soult and Guizot to 1847 (coincidentally, Molé and Guizot, like Louis Philippe, all had fathers guillotined during the Terror). Confidence was such that Molé granted an amnesty to all political prisoners in May 1837 to celebrate the marriage of the King's eldest son. And in May 1840 the "return of the ashes" of

Napoleon I from St Helena was announced to the French Chamber; this took place, to massive public rejoicing in Paris, in December 1840.

The regime also withstood amazingly incompetent putsches by Louis Napoleon, the son of Louis Bonaparte who had been displaced by the Emperor as King of Holland in 1810. After a fiasco in Strasbourg in October 1836, he was exiled to America, where he did not remain. He attempted another coup in August 1840, hoping to subvert a regiment of the line in Boulogne with the aid of a London pleasure-steamer the *Edinburgh Castle* and a small eagle – allegedly a vulture. This was also a flop; he was tried by the Chamber of Peers and imprisoned in the fortress of Ham until May 1846 when he was able to escape disguised as a labourer. With his father now dead (and Napoleon II, the King of Rome, had died at the age of 21 of tuberculosis in 1832), he was the Bonapartist claimant, and the wealth he inherited from his mother helped to finance his rather more successful challenge to the Second French Republic after 1848.

Guizot brought political stability but refused compromise and ended by "isolating the Crown from the rest of the country".[27] This isolation was intensified by the King's personal losses. His eldest son and heir, Ferdinand Philippe, Duc d'Orléans, was killed in a coach accident in July 1842. Not only was he was very popular with the army and the public, the tragedy hit his father hard: otherwise, he would not have sunk into the "fatalistic indecision" that the rest of his family also showed in 1848.[28] Another key loss was the King's sister, Adélaïde, on whom he depended enormously over affairs of state: she died in December 1847. By then the King was in his mid seventies.

Between 1841 and 1845 bread prices reached their lowest level of the post 1830 period, and the French industrial revolution was taking shape, in textiles, mining, metals and chemicals. Guizot, however, failed to address the social issues of industrial areas, with no social legislation of any significance. Occurrence of political scandals and corruption "made it very easy for the reformers … to denounce the whole circle as rotten".[29] In 1846 the boom sharply ended and, with two bad harvests, the price of bread rose. Violent disturbances spread all over France; demand for manufactured goods slumped, with textiles hit especially hard. The railway boom of the 1840s collapsed and in numerous bankruptcies middle class savings were lost. Unemployment rose high: a survey by the Paris Chamber of Commerce indicated that 56 per cent of the Paris workforce was unemployed in the spring of 1848. By the end of 1847 substantial grain imports and a good harvest reduced bread prices. But the King was blamed for the earlier suffering.

Paris activists began a campaign for electoral reform. Popular banquets were used, 70 during 1847, with the tone becoming increasingly republican.

Following an outbreak of revolts in Italy, the atmosphere in early 1848 was tense, with many people leaving Paris for the provinces. A reform banquet was banned on 21 February and a trial of strength with the forces of order began. This time, unlike 1830, the latter seemed well prepared, with 31,000 regular troops around Paris. The most active dissidents, such as Ledru-Rollin and Louis Blanc, were absent because they believed that the political climate was not right for revolution.[30]

The three-day saga of the fall of the regime has many similarities to the July 1830 revolution: confused tactics, unreliable troops, a (probably accidental) excess of force coupled with divided and self-interested political leaders and a monarch who eventually lost his nerve. Crowds gathered on 22 February; that afternoon the first barricade was built and gun shops were looted. There was calm by midnight, but with crowds reassembling on the morning of the 23rd, the National Guard was called out. This was a mistake as by now three out of the four legions were sympathetic to the rioters, indeed, one prevented the regular cavalry from clearing the crowd from the Place des Victoires. At this news Louis Philippe "began to crumble", refusing to unleash the regulars on the National Guard.

He agreed to dismiss Guizot; this was well received and most believed the trouble was over. The King sent for Molé, who accepted the need to extend the franchise, but "his conviction that he was not the man for the job … was shown in his lack of energy" in trying to recruit allies, notably Thiers. This coincided with an accidental massacre in the Boulevard des Capucines; a crowd was pressing back troops: a random shot rang out, and the panicking troops fired two volleys, killing over 60 of the demonstrators and wounding over 80. That night over 1500 barricades were thrown up; on the 24th armed mobs attacked military outposts.

The King decided to send for Thiers and to put Marshal Bugeaud, loathed by republicans, in overall command of troops and National Guard. The 24th saw emerge a Thiers/Odilon Barrot ministry with an electoral and parliamentary reform programme, alongside Bugeaud's plan of street-fighting tactics, avoiding some of the mistakes of 1830. All went well, until one of Bugeaud's three large columns, under General Bedeau, aiming for the Place de la Bastille, was halted by a large barricade on the Rue Saint-Denis. There was a confusing pause, with Bedeau reluctant to fire on the National Guard, and, eventually, an even more confusing command to cease hostilities and retreat to the Tuileries. No one subsequently accepted responsibility for originating this command; the finger of suspicion points to Thiers and Barrot. It seems to have been communicated to all three columns, which became disorganised, demoralised and eventually disbanded. All this occurred early on the morning of the 24th.

Crowds advanced on the Tuileries shouting, "We don't want Thiers! We don't want Barrot! The people are masters," and then the fatal word "abdicate". Episodes of violence continued, with an officer and several soldiers killed on the Place du Palais-Royal. The King, Royal Family, and courtiers crowded in the Tuileries, witnessing a growing mutter for abdication, and silence to the King's question "is defence possible?" So he decided to abdicate in favour of his grandson the Comte de Paris, aged nine, but, curiously, refused to sign anything making the Duchesse d'Orléans, the boy's mother, Regent. Then they were all forced to evacuate the Tuileries, which was invaded and plundered.[31]

The end, on the evening of the 24th, took place inside the Chamber of Deputies. The Duchesse entered, accompanied by her two sons, the Comte de Paris and the Duc de Chartres, aged seven, and was greeted by cheers. One deputy, supported by Barrot, announced the establishment of a Regency. "The majority of deputies … were ready enough to accept"[32] this, but mob rule intervened. A republican moved the adjournment to oblige her to leave. She refused, there was growing chaos, and then armed National Guardsmen, workers and students invaded the Chamber, shouting slogans hostile to a regency, the regime, even the Chamber, and favourable to a Republic. Tocqueville asked the well-known poet Lamartine to speak to quieten the chaos; he replied, "I refuse to speak as long as that woman and that child are here." Subsequently, Lamartine did speak, declaring himself in favour of a Republic.[33] With violence threatening the Duchesse, her two small sons and their companions, they departed: the boys were for two days separated from their mother in the chaos.

In fact, over the three days, the death toll was low compared to that in 1830, when about 1000 perished: in 1848 it was 72 soldiers and 289 revolutionaries. However, the Tuileries, the Palais-Royal and the chateau of Neuilly (the summer residence of the Orléans family) were sacked in 1848, the latter being destroyed by fire. And there appears a contrast between the reluctance of monarchs, such as Louis XVI, Charles X, Louis Philippe, and in 1870, Napoleon III's Empress, to shed the blood of their subjects, with the ferocity of the Second Republic in suppressing the June Days revolt of 1848 (10,000 killed and injured, and 4000 deported to Algeria), and that of the incipient Third Republic in suppressing the Paris Commune in 1871 (between 10,000 and 20,000 killed, many in cold blood – the lower figure is more likely – and at least 1100 deported, usually to New Caledonia in the Pacific). On 24 February Thiers had urged Louis Philippe to withdraw with the regular troops and then take Paris by force (as Thiers himself did in 1871): the King refused and later remarked, on hearing of the June Days: "Republics are lucky: they can shoot people."[34]

The Second Empire

The 1848 Revolution, like those of 1789, 1830 and 1870, set the politics of Paris against those of the rest of France. The Constituent Assembly elections in April 1848, under universal male suffrage with 9 million eligible to vote, saw over 5 million voting for moderate republicans, while 1.8 million voted Royalist, either Legitimists or Orleanists. The political situation appeared inherently unstable, with Bonapartist agents infiltrating the national workshops, designed, somewhat ineffectively, for the unemployed. On 22 June the government decided to close these workshops, and this provoked a spontaneous workers' rising, recognised by both Marx and Tocqueville as naked class war.[35] Regular troops and bourgeois National Guards were used to suppress this (the June Days).

This combination of continuing economic misery and public disorder led to the election in December 1848, as President of the Republic, of Louis Napoleon Bonaparte, with over 5.5 million votes (74 per cent of the total). He appealed to the Right, as a guarantor of order and stability, and his name resounded to the rural population. Even the urban masses rallied to him as a contrast to Orleanism – he polled 58 per cent in Paris. General Cavaignac, the hope of the moderate republicans, despite his role in suppressing the June revolt, polled fewer than 1.5 million. The Parliamentary election of May 1849 saw a counterbalance; 3.3 million, or over 50 per cent of the vote, with nearly 500 seats, went to the two Monarchist brands, as opposed to 1.9 million (or around 200 seats) for republican socialists and only 800,000 for moderate republicans.

Louis Napoleon was frequently pressed by his supporters to mount a *coup d'état* to consolidate his position and avert disorder, or worse, from the "red republicans". While he went on well-received provincial tours, the royalist majority in the Assembly regarded his Presidency as a temporary necessity until a royal restoration; he was barred from running for re-election in 1852. He hoped to change this law, but in July 1851 the monarchists denied him the 75 per cent majority required. He again failed on 15 November to repeal the electoral law by 353 to 347. This determined him on a coup, eventually settling for 2 December – the anniversary of Austerlitz and of Napoleon I's coronation.

Planned by Morny and Persigny and aided by St Arnaud's troops, who occupied the Chamber of Deputies, other positions, and made nearly 80 arrests, the coup had clearly succeeded by 7am on the 2nd. What the plotters had not expected was widespread resistance – not only requiring further arrests of deputies included royalists like Tocqueville, Barrot, and Berryer, but fighting extending to the working-class areas of Paris, and some bourgeois districts. Those resisting in Paris were estimated at 1000. While the army commanders did their best to avoid civilian casualties, they included 400 killed, plus 30 soldiers.

Also most unexpected was the scale of the rising in the provinces, involving peasants and republicans in south-eastern France and some areas of the centre and south-west; all overpowered. 26,000 left republicans were arrested, although Louis Napoleon ordered the release of 12,000 within a matter of days.[36] 9500 were deported to Algeria and another 3000 imprisoned, while martial law was imposed on 32 departments until the spring of 1852. All this contributed to the success of a plebiscite on 20 December, with 7.5 million to 640,000 endorsing Louis Napoleon's actions; 1.5 million abstained. "If the *coup d'état* was a crime, France was less its victim than its accomplice."[37]

A new constitution, promulgated on 14 January 1852, confirmed "Prince Louis Napoleon Bonaparte" in office for ten years with substantial executive powers. A sweeping victory in the legislative elections on 29 February/1 March and another successful provincial tour, this time to the south and west which had displayed most opposition to the *coup d'état*, encouraged him to restore the Empire. Yet another plebiscite voted for this by nearly 8 million to 250,000, with nearly 2 million abstentions. In Reims, it was the workers who petitioned for a return to the Empire, while the middle classes remained aloof.[38] On 2 December 1852 he was proclaimed Emperor Napoleon III.

Napoleon III governed France for 21 years – longer than any other individual since. His political ideas were "essentially opportunistic", and he admired William III of England because he ended a century of revolution. Wisely, he stated, "possibly a greatest danger of modern times is this false opinion with which people have been indoctrinated, that a government can do everything."[39] Billault, Minister of the Interior , said "to speak little, to do much, ought to be the motto of the Napoleons, just as to speak much and to do nothing was ... at least the practice of the government of 1830."[40]

Proclaiming, in his Bordeaux speech on 15 October accepting the throne, that "The Empire means peace", he listed the "conquests" he wished to make, in political reconciliation, social care, agriculture, transport and commerce. Unlike Napoleon I who attempted very little for the economy, Napoleon III did much, pioneering new agricultural methods, where millions of acres of wasteland and swamp were reclaimed while corn and wheat production rose greatly.[41] In contrast to the July monarchy and the early decades of the Third Republic, the Second Empire was "a period of remarkable economic growth",[42] with full employment and expanding markets.

The July monarchy spent years consulting over railways but had only built 1931 kilometres by 1848; by 1870 almost 18,000 kilometres existed. The Paris Bourse became a leading international money market, and the Crédit Mobilier and Crédit Lyonnais developed. He negotiated free trade treaties with Britain,

Belgium, the German Zollverein, Italy , Switzerland, Spain, Austria, Holland and Portugal (in fact all the EU as in the mid 1990s except Scandinavia); in contrast, the Third Republic restored Protection.

The greatest visible tribute to the Second Empire is the achievement of Baron Haussmann in Paris, with the Emperor's full support. This was not only aesthetic – the rebuilding of Paris included 95 kilometres of broad new gas-lit streets, while public health improvements were achieved in the fields of sewage disposal, provision of clean drinking water, and welfare, medical services and shelters for the homeless. A register of thousands of historic monuments was drawn up, with hundreds saved and restored.

The Second Empire faced two challenges. One, perceived from the start and very pronounced, was instability or even revolution within France. Here, as we shall see, Napoleon and his chief colleagues achieved remarkable success. The second, less perceived because much harm turned out to be self inflicted, was in the field of foreign affairs. Mismanagement and ill fortune here brought the regime to an unexpected end in 1870.

The political success of the Second Empire had, in turn, two causes. First, political opportunism existed among various individuals and groups which were not, either in origin or belief, Bonapartist. This is illustrated by the Emperor's famous remark: "What a government is mine! The empress is a legitimist, Napoléon-Jérôme (alias Plon-Plon, his cousin) a republican, Morny Orleanist, I myself am a socialist. The only Bonapartist is Persigny, and he is mad." Second, there was the skill of Napoleon himself, his natural half-brother, the duc de Morny, and his long-standing fellow plotter, now Minister of the Interior, Persigny, in establishing what an esteemed historian of the period has termed "the political system of Napoleon III".

"The Orleanist party was essentially a politician's party," and was ready to rally to the Empire if its members could win back their jobs "or at least their influence". They were an intellectual and financial elite with very little influence on the masses.[43] In the Parliament of 1852 only one third of deputies might be described as Bonapartists; many of these had been Orleanist before 1848. In 1852 and after we see developed the concept of official candidates, men who would not only vote for the government but bring real strength to it. Many of them were "new men", many had helped in and after the *coup d'état*; most were recommended by influential men.[44]

The reason for the government's success in the first ten years of the Empire was that the mayors' authority was so great as to influence "floating voters" to vote the right way. After 1860 there were signs of "a new spirit", with even villages no longer following the mayors' advice. Thus we see a "decay of the system of managing elections".⁴⁵ And we also see the start of the "liberal Empire", with the legislature given more rights. The most important reason for this was that a despotic empire would collapse on Napoleon's death, so permanence needed to rely on institutions.

The Liberal Empire was based on a new party consisting of both opponents and supporters of the old regime. Émile Ollivier, now a republican deputy, imprisoned after the *coup*, announced his readiness to rally to the Empire if it became liberal. So he broke with the republicans and in the mid-60s began occasionally to support the regime in the Assembly. Further liberal moves only came after 1867 when the international situation became worrying. In addition, after the mid-'60s, Napoleon's health began deteriorating: he was aged over 50 and a stone in the bladder was diagnosed in 1865. He refused an operation.

France was now evolving political theories and practices which England had taken over 200 years to achieve. The final moves towards the Liberal Empire coincided with electoral difficulty. In the 1863 election no government candidate was elected in Paris; there was similar hostility in other large cities. By 1869 "the old system of managing elections was at its last gasp and … the will to make it work was slight and fitful". The Ministry of the Interior told prefects not to suspend mayors who refused to co-operate. "Renegade mayors who deserted to the opposition ceased to be uncommon."⁴⁶ A liberal press law enabled various powerful newspapers to display their hostility. Government candidates had to set up their own organisations. So none of the seats in Paris (where 333 candidates stood), Lyons or Saint-Étienne were contested by the Government, and other government candidates were "careful to conceal the fact".⁴⁷ The campaign was conducted with a violence unprecedented since 1848–49, with riots in Paris and 1000 arrests. The result was a nominal victory for the Government but the Opposition polled well. The real victors were those who were prepared to co-operate with a liberal empire. Negotiations between Napoleon and Ollivier lasted between October and the end of 1869. In January 1870, Ollivier formed a government which was responsible to Parliament as well as the Emperor.

In contrast to the elections, the ensuing plebiscite of 8 May 1870 was a triumph for the Liberal Empire, with 7.5 million positive votes. Gambetta, who had hailed Ollivier's government as "a bridge between the Republic of 1848 and the Republic of the future … it is a bridge we intend to cross", now admitted that the Empire was stronger than ever. Another republican deputy, Jules Favre, advised a young friend to stay at the Bar as "there was nothing more to be done in politics".⁴⁸

Foreign affairs

The Ollivier government was to face a massive crisis in foreign affairs, which had been steadily building up. France's position had initially appeared secure. Napoleon was keen to woo Britain and during the Crimean War (1854–56) there was close collaboration. The state visit to England in 1855 saw excellent relations established with Victoria and Albert. The Crimean peace was good for the prestige of France and its Emperor. After the war, France sought to facilitate her rather clumsy ambitions of aggrandisement which Britain did not support.

Napoleon had a deep-seated dislike of Austria, coupled with great sympathy for Italian nationalists. The latter encouraged his support by several assassination attempts on him, of which the Orsini bomb plot was the most serious: it galvanised him to "do something" for Italy. In the same month – March 1858 – that Orsini was executed, Napoleon indicated to the king of Sardinia (whose territory included Piedmont, Savoy and Genoa) and his chief minister, Cavour, that France was ready to ally to drive the Austrians out of northern Italy. In July the pact of Plombières was made: Sardinia would make gains in northern Italy, there would be a new kingdom of central Italy under the Duchess of Parma, and a seriously reduced area round Rome under the Pope. These three states, plus Naples, would form a federation headed by the Pope.

Austria was, as so frequently, very clumsy, and rejected the proposal for an international congress on the Italian question. War began in early May 1859, but was not a walk-over. The French encountered mobilisation and logistical difficulties which were to prove fatal when repeated in 1870. Greater Austrian incompetence ensured their defeat at Magenta on 4 June and, at greater French cost, at Solferino (24 June). Considering his casualties, the Austrians falling back on their fortresses of the Quadrilateral, and a fear of Prussian intervention which the French had no reserves to combat, Napoleon speedily concluded an armistice (12 July). After this, Austria ceded Lombardy, retaining Venetia, while France received Savoy and Nice, as agreed.

Disappointed, the Italian nationalists pursued their revolutions in central Italy and Naples and by February 1861 they and Garibaldi had liberated the whole of Italy, except for Venetia and an area round Rome, where the Pope was defended by a reinforced French garrison, greatly irritating the nationalists and their supporters in France.

Bismarck, after 1862 Minister President and Foreign Minister of Prussia, exploited French expansionist ambitions in his skilful handling of Napoleon before Prussia's Seven Weeks' War with Austria in 1866. In October 1864 he hinted that France might obtain Belgium and Luxembourg if she helped Prussia. In October–November 1865 at Biarritz, Bismarck held nine conversations with

Napoleon, Drouyn and Rouher (the French Foreign and Prime Ministers), along with the Italian Ambassador Nigra. From Bismarck's and Nigra's accounts, it appears that Bismarck was trying to persuade France to endorse his plan for a larger North German Confederation under Prussian leadership; in return, he hinted again at Belgium. The conversations were inconclusive.[49]

This coincided with a more elaborate French diplomatic programme, in part designed to help the Poles, who had risen in revolt against the Russians in January 1863. In accordance with his (in the event, quite rash) ambition to redraw the map of Europe, Napoleon hoped for a European Congress, designed to break the 1815 settlement. Britain vetoed a congress.

After 1864, the international situation worsened. This was partly bad luck, including Austria's clumsiness in incurring the Seven Weeks' War with Prussia, lost by her in that short time. It was also a consequence of varying rash initiatives, all inspired by Napoleon's attraction to the "grand redrawing of the European map which he dreamed of".[50] Napoleon could not resist dabbling. As the Austro-Prussian war began, he hinted that the 1815 Vienna settlement might now be reversed. He then wrote an open letter to Drouyn, stating that France would remain neutral, but might have to intervene if the European balance were to be upset. At a council of ministers on 5 July, Drouyn, the Empress, and later Persigny, put on pressure for such military intervention (Rouher and the Minister of the Interior opposed this).[51]

Eventually, Napoleon decided against intervention and any speculation was speedily terminated by a truce in Germany on 22 July, followed by a peace treaty which gave Prussia 4 million new subjects in northern Germany. Sad attempts followed to obtain territorial "compensation". Benedetti, French ambassador in Berlin, persisted in seeking an alliance (for which Prussia now had no need) and submitted, on 29 August, a proposal accepting further unification in Germany in return for Prussian agreement to the French acquisition of Luxembourg and, eventually, Belgium. Bismarck did not reply, but kept the draft treaty, which he published in the London *Times* in 1870 at the outbreak of the Franco-Prussian war, as evidence of French imperialism.[52]

French aggrandisement plans were not confined to Europe, and there were modest successes, in Algeria and Indo-China. Napoleon strongly supported Ferdinand de Lesseps's idea of a canal into the Red Sea; work begun in 1859. It was completed in 1869: on 17 November the Empress, in the Imperial yacht, headed some 40 ships which sailed through this "Suez Canal".

The most ambitious, and eventually disastrous, venture was in Mexico. Here Napoleon hoped to found a large commercial empire, also designed to act as a counterpoise to the USA, preoccupied during its Civil War between 1861–65.

French forces were engaged in 1861–62, initially with British and Spanish cooperation; the other two withdrew when the extent of French ambitions became apparent. Reinforced to a strength of 40,000 the French captured Mexico City in 1863. A provisional government offered the throne to the Archduke Maximilian, brother of the Austrian Emperor. Facing guerrilla war, after costly reverses, with the threat of American intervention, French forces were withdrawn in 1866, and Maximilian was betrayed and executed in June 1867.

The end in 1870

In the mid-1860s France had 85,000 troops in Algeria, 30–50,000 in Mexico, and several thousand in Indo-China and elsewhere in Asia – leaving around 150,000 for the defence of France. Prussia had 750,000 available including reserves.

France suffered from a lack of trained reserves as a result of weaknesses in the conscription system. Attempts were made to reform this after 1866. The republicans and the Orleanists were hostile to a standing army in peacetime. The public were reluctant to be conscripted, especially as the regime argued that the new order in Germany was not a threat. Even the military, committed to the idea of a professional army, opposed. The legislature, with its greater powers, was able in 1867–69 to emasculate the various proposals, including those from the War Minister, Marshal Niel, for a Mobile Guard. So there was no trained reserve, and no expert general staff; army commanders had been trained in Algerian warfare but were not ready for European conflict.[53]

France was understandably alarmed by the prospect of Prince Leopold, a relative of King William of Prussia, being offered and then accepting (on 2 July 1870) the throne of Spain: if he faced internal troubles Prussian forces might go to Spain. Napoleon, Ollivier and the new clumsy and pro-Austrian Foreign Minister, the Duc de Gramont, were tempted by the opportunity of humiliating Prussia and especially Bismarck. On 6 July Napoleon and Gramont issued a statement which implied war if the candidature were not withdrawn. On 12 July, Leopold's father renounced on his (absent) son's behalf; Thiers, Guizot, and foreign observers saw this as a very fine French diplomatic victory.

Napoleon's ill-health prevented him asserting himself for peace. Benedetti was asked to seek an assurance from King William that he would veto any future Hohenzollern candidature for Spain. This led to the encounter on the 13th in Bad Ems, where the king declined Benedetti's request for guarantees and refused a further audience. The episode was exploited by Bismarck into the provocative "Ems telegram". In Paris, at a council of ministers Gramont threatened to resign if war was not declared. Other ministers resisted him. Napoleon welcomed the suggestion of an international conference, but Ollivier, fearing the mood of the deputies, rejected this. The war party, both at Court and in the Assembly, was rampant and a further council of ministers opted for war.

If France had obtained early successes, the regime's hope that Austria, Italy or even some of the south German states might join on France's side might have progressed. However, powers like Britain and Russia, not wishing for a French invasion of Germany, sympathised with Prussia, and the south German states firmly sided with Prussia. The French had the chassepot rifle, and (very few) *mitrailleuses* – early machine guns – but their artillery had not advanced much since Waterloo, while Prussia had more accurate, faster firing and longer range (4 miles) Krupp breach-loading guns. The war proved from the start a speedy disaster. Prussia and her allies greatly outnumbered the French, whose mobilisation was chaotic. They were defeated in three separate battles on 4 and 6 August. Napoleon's health became steadily worse and he panicked, ordering the whole army to retreat to Châlons, then changed this to Metz, with resulting confusion. If he had accepted advice to return to Paris, the regime might have survived and the generals coped better. The Empress, however, bullied him into staying with his forces, while Ollivier was forced to give way to the Comte de Palikao. Ironically, the last pre-Republic prime minister was one with a title derived from an obscure victory in the recent Chinese war!

The inconclusive battle of Vionville-Mars-la-Tour (16 August) and the French defeat (both battles seeing heavy Prussian casualties) at Gravelotte-Saint Privat, saw the French performing well, but let down by their commanders. They fatally fell back on Metz where they were besieged (Bazaine, a weak commander, eventually surrendered there on 29 October). The Châlons army, under Marshal MacMahon, with Napoleon, advanced towards Metz. Somehow the French ended up in Sedan by the Belgian border. If it had tried earlier, MacMahon's Army might have escaped. Once it was bottled up, the Emperor felt he had to stay with it, despite plans to enable him to escape. As Ducrot, one of the abler French generals, said, *"Nous sommes dans un pot de chambre, et nous y serons emmerdés."* No translation is required: they surrendered on 2 September.

With the Emperor captive, Eugénie was left in charge in Paris. Certain individuals might have averted revolution: Thiers was one, but he had always opposed the Empire and was not going to save it now. The able general Trochu, now governor of Paris, was another, but he was ignored both by Eugénie and Palikao, so he "washed his hands" of the threat of revolution and concentrated on the external defence of the city. Eugénie rejected proposals to transfer the government to a provincial city; she thought this would mean civil war. She refused to defend the Tuileries palace – this also would have meant bloodshed.

Politicians like Thiers frustrated her hope of remaining as regent for the Prince Imperial. A combination of radical deputies and the usual Paris mob produced a proclamation of the Republic on 4 September. Eugénie escaped in a cab, helped by the Austrian and Italian ambassadors. We read of the occupants of the palace being advised to remove their uniforms before going into the streets.[54]

After 1871

An armistice was signed in late January 1871, with elections on 8 February to produce a government which could make peace. Extraordinarily, these returned a massive victory for the Royalists, both Legitimist and Orleanist (182 and 214 seats respectively) because they were believed to favour peace, against 222 republicans of various shades and only 20 Bonapartists. The strife between the Legitimists and Orleanists, however, saw the opportunity of another Restoration pass. As President, Thiers saw the writing on the wall, declaring "I found the Republic already made. A monarchy is impossible because there are three dynasties for a single throne."

The anonymous Paris correspondent of the London Rothschilds reported to his employers in October 1871 the result of a hypothetical plebiscite worked out by various eminent public servants: 3 million would vote for the Empire, 2 million for a republic, 2 million for a Legitimist monarch and 1 million for an Orleanist monarch. The correspondent himself, although an Orleanist, thought Napoleon III would obtain between 5 million and 6 million votes.[55] In fact, Napoleon, a very sick man, died in January 1873, but Bonapartists hoped that the Prince Imperial might sustain this popularity.

Thiers famously summed up the situation: republicanism was "the form of government that divides France least." In 1873 he was ousted and succeeded as President by Marshal MacMahon who was privately a Legitimist and wanted to facilitate the restoration of the monarchy. In May 1877, MacMahon controversially forced the resignation of a republican prime minister, and appointed Broglie, an Orleanist, in his place. Facing condemnation, MacMahon dissolved the Assembly. The elections of October 1877 gave the republicans 313 seats over 64 Royalists and 104 Bonapartists. After republicans obtained a Senate majority in January 1879 elections, MacMahon resigned. On 1 June 1879, the Empire's last hope, the Prince Imperial, was killed fighting in Zululand alongside British forces.

With Royalists then in a majority in the Assembly, a pact was made in 1873 by which the Orleanists accepted the childless Comte de Chambord as Henry V, with the Orleanist claimant, the Comte de Paris following after his death. Chambord, however, would not accept the national flag, the tricolour, to which the remaining groups were devoted, so there was no restoration.

A further underlying Legitimist weakness was the position of the Church. A sharp division arose between liberal Gallican Catholics (such as Broglie and other Orleanists) and the Legitimists who were allied to the Church which, by the 1870s, was committed to ultramontanism: Papal dominance. The Papal encyclical *Quanta Cura* of 1864 had condemned "modern" errors, such as liberalism, individualism, liberty of conscience, progress, and the secularism of the State. The Syllabus of Modern Errors and the Decree of Papal Infallibility cemented the Papacy among the forces of reaction. This led to Gambetta's slogan in 1876 "Clericalism – there is the enemy" and Jules Ferry's 1882 bill, banning clerical supervision from all state primary schools.

Divisions continued for decades, enhanced by the clericalism issue. Elections confirmed that republicans did not enjoy overwhelming power: those of 1885 saw the Right polling 600,000 votes less than the republicans, but securing only 202 seats. This sufficiently alarmed the Government as to prompt it to expel from France, in 1886, the Comte de Paris (Chambord having died in 1883) and all other heads of former ruling houses together with their heirs, and to decree that no member of their families should join the army or navy, occupy any public office or be eligible for Parliament.[56]

The Dreyfus affair, which lasted from 1894 to 1906, whatever its detailed merits (Dreyfus was innocent of the charges against him), has been described by a Rightist partisan as "a battle between two philosophies, two traditions: the one Catholic, conservative and nationalist, the other anti-clerical, individualistic and pacifist. All France was divided into two camps … A feeling of common danger united the parties of the left, even … the socialists, in the defence of the Republic … The victors had been seriously alarmed, and they determined to use their strength in the political field to try to crush their adversaries once and for all."[57] This led to a further attack on the Church's influence in education under Émile Combes.

Action Française, an extreme nationalist newspaper founded in 1899 and its supporters announced their conversion to the cause of monarchy in 1904. They never had influence in parliament, which they affected to despise, but their violent attacks on the Republic and their leaders, especially Charles Maurras, "were to exercise a considerable influence for the best part of forty years".[58] These reverberated into the 1930s, including the clashes in early 1934, when *Action Française* and the Leagues which it spawned organised large demonstrations in Paris over the dismissal of a Right-wing Prefect of Police. On 6 February 1934 the police opened fire, killing 14 rioters and injuring over 600. Many on the Left thought these riots indicated "a definite plot on the part of the Right to overthrow the Republic". If the government had not ensured the guarding of the Chamber of Deputies, "there might well have been a repetition of the scenes of February 1848 and September 1870."[59]

More tragic were the failure to resist German expansion and the wish by the French Right, under Pierre Laval, to work closely with Mussolini's Fascist Italy – all against the background of the "Popular Front", allying left Radicals, Socialists and Communists, and triumphing in the May 1936 elections. An inefficiently armed and politically divided France went into the Second World War, experiencing total defeat and the formation of the collaborationist Vichy regime, which in various ways rejected the inheritance of the Third Republic. Vichy and its supporters were almost totally discredited in 1944–45, but the real healing of the longstanding fissures in French politics probably did not arrive until sustained economic growth took place after 1945 and the semi-monarchical Fifth Republic under General de Gaulle was established in 1958.

Under Macron in the 2020s, France faces a further challenge from the Right, with limited inspiration from the 19th century, and rather more provocation from uncontrolled immigration.

FOOTNOTES

1 Munro Price, *op cit*, p83.
2 Mansel, *op cit*, pp199, 247.
3 Mansel, *op cit*, pp283, 327.
4 Munro Price, *op cit*, pp92–93.
5 Mansel, *op cit*, p393.
6 Adam Zamoyski, *Phantom Terror: The Threat of Revolution and the Repression of Liberty 1789–1848*, William Collins, 2015, p130.
7 Munro Price, *op cit*, pp110–11.
8 *Ibid*, p117.
9 Major John Hall *The Bourbon Restoration*, Alston Rivers 1909, p388.
10 Munro Price, *op cit*, pp118–9.
11 Hall, *op cit*, p398.
12 *Ibid*, p429.
13 Quotes respectively Munro Price, p138; J Lucas-Dubreton, *The Restoration and the July Monarchy*, Heinemann, 1929, p158.
14 These quotes Hall, *op cit*, pp449–50.
15 Lucas-Dubreton, *op cit*, p158; Munro Price, *op cit*, p145.
16 Lucas-Dubreton, *op cit*, p160.
17 Marmont quote, Hall, *op cit*, p461.
18 *Ibid* p471.
19 Munro Price, *op cit*, pp182–83; he concludes "we shall never know the truth".
20 Munro Price, *op cit*, p186.
21 Zamoyski, *op cit*, pp444 and 487.
22 *Ibid*, pp446, 468.
23 *Ibid*, pp384, 404, 412.
24 Munro Price, *op cit*, pp234–5, Furet, *op cit*, p332.
25 Munro Price, *op cit*, p243.
26 Zamoyski, *op cit*, pp419, 424.
27 Munro Price, *op cit*, pp295–96.
28 *Ibid*, p311.
29 J P T Bury, *France 1814–1940*, Routledge, 1985, p64.
30 Zamoyski, *op cit*, p480–81.
31 This account based on Munro Price, *op cit*, pp350–59 , Lucas-Dubreton, *op cit*, pp360–63 and Zamoyski, pp480–85.
32 Bury, *op cit*, p66.
33 Lucas-Dubreton, *op cit*, p363.
34 Bury, *op cit*, p132; Lucas-Dubreton, *op cit*, p377.
35 James McMillan, *Profiles in Power: Napoleon III*, Longman 1991, p31.
36 Alan Strauss-Schom, *The Shadow Emperor – A Biography of Napoleon III*, Amberley

Publishing, 2018, p161; also Furet, *op cit*, pp435–6.
37 F A Simpson, *Louis Napoleon and the Recovery of France, 1848–56*, 1951, p163.
38 McMillan, *op cit*, p51.
39 Theodore Zeldin, *France 1848–1945*, OUP, 1973, hereafter *France*, quotes from pp510, 537.
40 T Zeldin, *The Political System of Napoleon III*, Macmillan 1958, hereafter *System*, p68.
41 Strauss-Schom, *op cit*, pp426–27.
42 McMillan, *op cit*, p137.
43 Zeldin, *System*, pp155–56.
44 *Ibid*, p15.
45 *Ibid*, pp91–92.
46 Quoted, *ibid*, pp135, 93.
47 *Ibid*, p139.
48 Theo Aronson, *The Fall of the Third Napoleon*, Cassell, 1970, p47.
49 McMillan, *op cit*, pp76, 101.
50 *Ibid*, p103.
51 *Ibid*, pp105–07.
52 *Ibid*, pp112–13.
53 Strauss-Schom, *op cit*, p380.
54 Aronson, *op cit*, pp199–200.
55 *Ibid*, p33.
56 Bury, *op cit*, p169.
57 Charlotte Touzalin Muret, *French Royalist Doctrines Since the Revolution*, Columbia University Press, 1933, p218.
58 Bury, *op cit*, p205.
59 *Ibid*, p267.

Chapter Six:
The Russian Revolution

"Had it not been for the Russian Revolution, there would very likely have been no National Socialism, probably no Second World War .... and certainly no Cold War"
(Richard Pipes, *Three Whys of the Russian Revolution,* Pimlico, 1998, p3; later cited as *Three Whys*)

"Heads must roll, blood must flow .... The strength of the French Revolution was in the machine that made the enemies of the people shorter by a head ... No intermediate policy exists ... We're introducing the dictatorship of the proletariat." (Trotsky during the October Revolution, Robert Service, *Trotsky: A Biography,* Pan Macmillan, 2010, henceforth referred to as Service, *Trotsky,* pp172, 190)

The present author follows the examples of Sean McMeekin and Tony Brenton in giving dates for Russian events up to 1918 according to the Julian calendar, as used by the Russian empire. This was thirteen days behind the Gregorian calendar used in the West. In 1917 this is particularly important. However, dates of importance in European history, in this case mainly events in the weeks before the outbreak of war in 1914, are given in both forms with a slash, Julian followed by Gregorian. In mid-January 1918 the Bolsheviks switched to the Gregorian calendar which is then applied.

A recent historian of the Russian Revolution has described how the majority of western scholars writing over the later twentieth century "about Communism and the Soviet Union have been in varying degrees sympathetic ... inclined to stress the positive achievements of post-1917 Russia and to explain its failures either by the legacy of Tsarism or by foreign hostility ..." Adding that "the prevailing view among Western historians is that the fall of Tsarism as well as the triumph of Bolshevism were preordained", he declares: "My thesis is precisely the opposite to that advanced ... which, by now, is virtually obligatory in Western universities."[1]

The work of other recent historians, on which this present chapter is built, indicates a similarly revisionist view. Dominic Lieven points out that "most" British or American historians of Russia "were liberals or socialists" and thus "their sympathy and interest were largely directed towards individuals or groups which shared these loyalties in pre-revolutionary Russia"[2] If the politicians thrust into power by the 1917 February Revolution, such as Kerensky, had shown "more competence and fortitude" in suppressing Bolshevik subversion, Lenin would "merit, at most, a footnote" in history, while the Bolshevik corruption of the Russian army in the summer of 1917 was "an audacious, chancy and close-run affair."[3]

In 1881–85 Russia was responsible for 3.4 per cent of global industrial production – less than a quarter of the German share and much less than half that of France. By 1913 Russia produced 5.3 per cent, nearly the same as France and more than a third of Germany's. As the world's fifth largest economy, with annual growth nearing a stupendous ten per cent, in the early 20th century Russia was a substantial net importer of both people and capital. Neither was true after the Revolution.[4]

The conventional picture is of a poverty-stricken peasantry facing famine. Bad harvest years could bring famine, for example 1892 when half a million died, mostly of cholera. By 1914, Russia was not only feeding herself, but had just replaced the USA as the world's leading grain exporter. While Russian agriculture was less efficient than that of France or Germany, Russian farms were much larger, and in 1900 Russian peasants had more ample and healthier diets than a large proportion of the German population of the time. A German study in 1987 concluded that the Russian peasant's diet in 1900 was roughly comparable to that of the West German population in the early to mid-1950s. And between 1863, when Tsar Alexander II emancipated the serfs, and 1915, Russian nobles sold over 60 per cent of the land remaining to them.[5]

The myth that the Tsarist regime was the epitome of oppression, harshness and cruelty is greatly exaggerated. Only the worst criminals, such as assassins, were given the death penalty: between 1825 and 1917 only 6300 were executed, including those executed for murder. Most political subversives suffered "administrative exile" in Siberia, where conditions in the 1890s were nowhere near as harsh as under Communism in the 1930s and after. They received visits and books: the state gave them a monthly stipend, enough for subsistence, and they were allowed to seek gainful employment, for example as tutors or using other skills. They took part in much political discussion and disputation. Trotsky was able to play croquet in Siberia: for him, "Siberia was like a free revolutionary university of the *taiga*."[6] As Lieven states, "Educated Russia was European in its culture, values, dress, and even, in some aristocratic circles, in its preference for using foreign languages." [7]

Tensions existed, as in all other late 19th century societies, between the elite and the mass of people. And the bourgeois entrepreneurial class was quite small in 1900, often foreigners or from non-Russian minorities such as Jews, Poles and Armenians. As an indication of trouble ahead, revolutionary socialist doctrines and groups had deeply infiltrated the Russian educated classes, just as educated France had been infiltrated by revolutionary ideas before 1789.

Various "what if" questions arise: what if Stolypin, the one statesman who showed any capacity to challenge the opposing forces of reaction and revolution, seen as an "authoritarian moderniser", had not been murdered in 1911? What if Rasputin had not been recuperating from an assassination attempt at the time, and had succeeded in persuading the Tsar not to mobilise in July 1914, thus bringing Russia into war?

And what if Nicholas II, who was, like Louis XVI, conscientious and hard-working, had been competently supported by a private secretariat. None existed, not even a private secretary; extraordinarily, he stamped his own envelopes and wrote notes ordering carriages to be made ready. As Lieven has pointed out, this absence meant that important documents were not summarised or digested, but presented "virtually at book-length". It contrasted with Stalin's arrangements: in the 1920s and 1930s he was supported by an "immensely powerful personal secretariat packed by ambitious, able and ruthless clients".[8]

In the earlier part of his reign Nicholas was served by some competent ministers. However, the Tsar was expected to rule as well as reign. Nicholas disliked confrontation, and thus tended to agree with people to their faces and then do otherwise, thus winning him a reputation for "being untrustworthy and indecisive".[9] There were also, unfortunately, relatively few competent ministers after 1914, and rivalry tended to blunt the effects of the best.

And two linked questions. How far did the occurrence and then failure of the 1905 revolution immunise Russia for several years against a repetition; and how far were the destructive and tragic developments in 1917 avoidable? There can be no doubt that the educated middle class, whatever its discontent with the regime, had been seriously frightened by the extremism and violence of the 1905 revolutionaries.[10] To some extent, they were comforted by the constitutional innovations after 1905, just as many peasants welcomed Stolypin's land reforms, and the whole country benefited from economic growth. The events leading to the two revolutions of 1917 display the themes of this present book, "chance, mistiming, incompetence", as well as "the decay and abdication of authority".

Towards the 1905 revolution

Alexander II (1855–81) had initiated various reforms, notably the emancipation of the serfs. Described by Lieven as "a remarkably peaceful process imposed from above on the landowners, which granted much better terms to peasants",[11] this did not prevent that Tsar being assassinated, just as he was about to bring elected representatives into central government. There was an inevitable reaction under Alexander III (1881–94); the small provincial assemblies called *zemstvos*, created by his predecessor in 1864, saw their power curtailed. The secret police – the

Okhrana, was strengthened, with informers and double agents making deep inroads into the terrorist underground.

The forces preparing for revolution consisted of Marxists, in the innocuous-sounding Social Democrat Party, and non-Marxists in the Socialist Revolutionary Party (hereafter SR); the latter tended to be more popular among the Russian people. The Social Democrats split in 1903 into Mensheviks and Bolsheviks (these terms mean "minority" and "majority", true for the voting at that particular congress in 1903, but for much of the time until October 1917 the two groups varied in strength). Mensheviks, led by Martov, and including Trotsky, were slightly more moderate, being prepared to work with other opposition groups and through trade unions; the Bolsheviks, led by Lenin, advocated armed revolution to establish totalitarianism. The SR Party was undoubtedly violent, responsible for a terrorist campaign of assassination of ministers (three killed between 1901–04), police and officials.

Nicholas II inherited from his father as minister of finance one Sergei Witte, originating from a Baltic German family. Witte held this position, which included responsibility for industry, commerce and transport, from 1892 to 1903, after which he held a less powerful role as chairman of the Committee of Ministers until 1905. He pursued a policy of rapid industrialisation, including the encouragement of investment from foreign capital, entrepreneurial talent and technology, and typified by the construction of the Trans-Siberian railway, starting in 1891. This brought enormous economic benefits with the industrial and agricultural development of Siberia and migration to it from western Russia. It also produced the expansionism and clumsy diplomacy which resulted in the Russo-Japanese war, starting in February 1904.

Witte's policies had met increased opposition from forces fearing the changes that industrialisation was bringing. Among these was a great increase in industrial unrest, involving strikes. An influential report on strikes written in 1898 by General A I Panteleev, employed by the Ministry of the Interior, correctly attributed most strikes to the "exploitation of the workers by the manufacturers [who] … making a huge profit, pay the labour force little and besides, with rare exceptions, do almost nothing for the improvement of the way of life of the workers and their families". Another official, Zubatov, believed that many strikes resulted from minor infringements of workers' rights. He had imaginative ideas of allowing workers to organise themselves to defend their interests, under police supervision, and for a while the state intervened early in disputes and adjudicated between workers and their employers. The ultimate, somewhat far-fetched, ideal, was to create "a loyal labour movement … a major weapon in the state's hands, a force with which the financial and industrial elites could be balanced".[12] The alternative was demonstrated by the Odessa general strike of 1903 and revolutionaries obtaining control over the government-run unions in St Petersburg in early 1905.

Zubatov's union scheme was launched in 1900–01 with great initial success in Moscow, where he and it enjoyed the protection of the Governor-General of Moscow, the Grand Duke Sergei, the Tsar's uncle, assassinated in 1905. It also progressed in western Russia, but was opposed by senior officials in the Ministry of the Interior.

Witte was sympathetic to cheap credit for peasant farms. This encountered the difficulty that most peasant farms belonged to the village community, the commune; they thus could not be sold, mortgaged, or act as security for loans. By 1902 he was pressing the Tsar for change: "for the success of the market economy it is necessary to raise the whole economic standard of living and this is only possible if peasant life is rearranged on the basis of individual property and communal possession is abolished."[13] The issue was complex and, not surprisingly, the Tsar was cautious. Substantial reform would, in fact, be headed by Stolypin, after Russia had experienced defeat in war and revolution.

As a third strand of discontent, alongside the industrial and rural masses, came the non-Russian nationalities, and not only the Poles who had revolted in 1863–64. Infringements on Finnish autonomy threatened revolt, hence the assassination of Governor-General Bobrikov in June 1904. As General Alexander Kireev, a loyal but critical servant of the Romanovs, remarked in his diary "thanks to Bobrikov … we have created a new Poland at the gates of Saint Petersburg! And it would have been so easy to avoid this."[14]

Tsar Nicholas had great ambitions for the Far East, including occupation of Manchuria and designs on Korea. Witte was seeking a shorter railway link, across northern Manchuria via Harbin, to Vladivostok, while a number of nobles close to the Tsar had obtained a large timber concession on the river Yalu, on the border between Korea and Manchuria.

Japan's concern about Korea, and clumsy, wavering and ambiguous Russian diplomacy led to Japan's surprise attack on the Russian Far East fleet in Port Arthur in February 1904. For Russia, this war was a disaster from start to finish, partly because of the inadequacy in military and naval preparedness. Witte could not avoid the Tsar's wish to build battleships, but he cut back resources for the crews' training and upkeep.[15] Other factors were also the vast distances for reinforcements to travel, the rivalries between the various Russian commanders, and the Japanese talent for speedy and effective victories, often at great cost, on land and sea. These included the Yalu, April 1904, Liaoyang August 1904, the fall of Port Arthur, January 1905, Mukden, 5–26 February 1905, culminating in the destruction of almost the entire Russian Baltic fleet at Tsushima in May 1905 (the light cruiser *Aurora,* of significance in the 1917 October Revolution, was one vessel to escape). Peace was made in September, when Japan was exhausted. With high-quality Russian reinforcements on their way to Manchuria, the tide might have turned, and the army was dismayed by the outbreak of peace. Lessons were obviously learned for use in 1914, and there is a parallel with Britain's dismal experience in the Boer War of 1899–1902 and her performance in 1914. But by late 1905, Russia was well on the way to revolution.

After students had assassinated one Minister for the Interior in 1901, Nicholas appointed V K Plehve to that post. A strong reactionary, he stimulated Russification campaigns in Finland and Poland and his known anti-semitism encouraged pogroms on the Jewish community. The most notorious of these was that in Kishinev in April 1903, which resulted in 47 deaths and over 1000 mostly Jewish homes destroyed. On 28 July 1904, Plehve was assassinated by a SR bomb.

Surprisingly, he was succeeded by a liberal: as Governor-General of Vilna, Prince Peter Svyatopolk-Mirsky had implemented reforms which had allowed more rights to national minorities and ceased anti-Jewish pogroms. As minister, he made further attempts at liberal reform, including permitting members of the *zemstvos* to discuss broader policy issues, which had not been permitted previously. He proposed the inclusion of elected members to the State Council, measures to extend freedom of the press, and broaden the authority of local self-government. This programme was discussed by the Tsar, ministers and senior officials in December 1904, with the Tsar, under conservative pressure, rejecting the key proposal for what he termed " a representative form of government". Svyatopolk-Mirsky told the Tsar "If you don't carry out liberal reforms … then change will come but in the form of revolution."[16]

The Ministry had lost control over the workers' trade union groups in the capital, where they were led by a priest, Father Gapon, who was moving to more radical ideas. On 9 January 1905, Gapon led a vast demonstration (numbering an estimated 150,000) to the Winter Palace to demand reforms, including the calling of a constituent assembly.

"Like Communist regimes in the late 1980s, the Tsarist government, having always banned demonstrations, had no experience of dealing with them and no policemen trained to handle them." So the army was used, in what became known as "Bloody Sunday". As Peter Durnovo, former head of the Tsarist Police Department, commented, while Cossacks and cavalry would disperse a crowd with few or no deaths by using whips and the flats of sabres, "the mistake had been to summon infantry units" which fired on the unarmed demonstrators, killing at least 200 and wounding about 800.[17]

The government sought to respond by a combination of concessions and repression. Neither, initially, were sufficient. Nor was a manifesto in early March announcing that a consultative elected assembly would be called. Terrorism mounted during 1905: according to the government's own estimate, 3600 imperial officials were killed or wounded that year alone.[18] Peasants throughout Russia and Ukraine – especially in what is now eastern Ukraine–attacked the estates of landowners, burning manor houses and destroying crops. June 1905 saw the mutiny at sea on board the battleship *Potemkin,* with seven of the ship's 18 officers killed, including the captain. A Soviet was formed and the ship sailed to Odessa to provoke revolution. Riots and looting took place there; then, with the city under martial law, the crowds were bloodily crushed and the *Potemkin* sought refuge in Romania. These events were immortalised in Eisenstein's Bolshevik propaganda film released in 1925.

Almost all Poland and half of Russia were affected by strikes by the autumn of 1905. The universities reopened in early September, becoming centres for revolutionary agitation. On 6 October the Moscow railway union came out on strike, this extending by the end of the month to the railways nationwide and to post, telephone and telegraph workers. The Tsar was persuaded to create the post of prime minister. Witte was the obvious candidate and insisted on his right to choose ministers and determine policies.

The Tsar issued the October Manifesto on 17 October: it offered civil liberty concessions, with the elected assembly already promised now "guaranteed the opportunity of real participation in control over the legality of actions of the authorities appointed by us". This State Duma would also need to approve all laws. Witte made the Tsar put the whole country under martial law, with troops told to fire on "any crowd using arms". [19]

Opposition and revolutionary leaders were not expecting revolution (their surprise was to be repeated in February 1917). Milyukov, the liberal leader, returned from abroad only in April. Chernov, the SR leader, Martov, the Menshevik leader, and Lenin, the Bolshevik leader, who spent the year in London, returned only in November. However, Stalin was active in the Caucasus (in February 1906 he organised the assassination of General Griazanov, who had previously crushed the revolution in Tiflis/Tbilisi), and Trotsky and Parvus supported the general strike in St Petersburg. In early December, the Interior Ministry, now headed by the able Peter Durnovo (Lieven calls him "resolute, self-confident and very intelligent" with an "acute sense of tactics and timing"[20]) began arresting executive committee members of the St Petersburg Soviet. Eventually, 260, including Trotsky and Parvus, were arrested.

The Moscow Soviet called for an armed revolt on 6 December. The regular army, headed by the Semenovsky Guards, stormed the rebellious city areas, crushing both resistance and the Soviet, with around 1000 revolutionaries and strikers killed. Lieven states that "in the winter of 1905–6 the regime came closer to collapse than at any other time", but that winter saw a turning point.[21] In March 1906 Witte, Durnovo and the army chiefs agreed to send troops into the Russian interior, depleting forces in Poland and other border regions, where the rising had been suppressed: Witte was confident that Germany would not take advantage of the situation to attack. Control was then reasserted over the railways and telegraph, with punitive columns fanning out. The revolutionaries lost morale and momentum.

Strikes declined; unlike the case before 1905, these no longer had much support in the propertied classes or even the intelligentsia, who felt "increasing horror and resentment … as the revolution of the masses grew more radical and violent." Unpaid volunteers came forward to break the post and telegraph strike.[22] Terrorism replaced striking and revolution: in 1906 288 police and gendarmes were killed, and 383 wounded. By 1907, some 4500 police and officials had been killed since the start of the Russo-Japanese war in 1904, with a similar number of civilians, whether terrorists or bystanders. Another estimate states that the SRs murdered over 7000 persons between 1906 and 1909, of whom 2600 were officials. Under Stolypin as Minister of the Interior, commencing in April 1906 up until April 1907, military courts in the field hanged about 1000 terrorists.[23] Trotsky, Parvus and Lenin went back into exile.

In mid-January 1906, Witte reported to the Tsar that while the urban revolution had been defeated, the peasant rebellion was still raging. He encouraged the adoption of a proposal by the Minister of Agriculture for partial expropriation of private land. This had been vigorously opposed in the Council, and the Tsar rejected it. It was argued that compensation could not be afforded, it would not bring any easy economic gains, and it would whet political appetites. After he had used his diplomatic and financial skills to negotiate a large foreign loan in April 1906, Witte concluded he had lost the Tsar's confidence, and resigned.

The actual constitution was not as radical as some had hoped: as established at the end of April 1906, the Duma had veto power over legislation only through its upper house, which was the appointed State Council. Duma deputies had power to question ministers, but not to appoint them, and the Tsar was given power to dissolve the Duma and rule by emergency decrees when the Duma was not sitting.

The Kadets (the Constitutional Democrats, a liberal party) dominated the Duma because the socialist parties had boycotted the elections. The Kadets in

October 1905 had called for universal male suffrage, government responsibility to the Duma, expropriation of much gentry land and an amnesty for all political prisoners. None of these were acceptable to the government. Perhaps as an indication of the regime's confidence returning, this Duma was dissolved in July 1906. Mutinies at the Baltic fleet bases of Kronstadt and Sveaborg were swiftly and ruthless suppressed.

Stolypin

By this stage, the tragic hero of the pre-war Empire was in charge – Peter Stolypin. His "far-sighted" land reforms contributed to the "remarkable recovery" of the country after 1905–06.[24] He became Interior Minister in April 1906, then combined this with chairman of Council of Ministers – the equivalent of prime minister – in July. Since 1903 he had been a vigorous and effective Governor of the disorderly Saratov province, a SR stronghold, surviving several assassination attempts. He was "neither a Petersburg bureaucrat nor a member of the capital's high society" but the fact that he came from an old and wealthy family of the provincial landowning nobility ensured good relations with members of the new parliament and the Tsar.

Combining them with fierce measures against terrorists, he started reforms. In the spring of 1907 he pressed through the second Duma measures to protect citizens from arbitrary arrest, develop a progressive tax system and extend insurance benefits for state workers. He initiated a new franchise to ensure that the third Duma, elected in autumn 1907, would be more pliant. However, his ambitious proposal to grant civil equality to Jews and other minorities failed because of opposition from the Tsar.

In his earlier career in Poland and Lithuania he had appreciated the political value of private landholdings of the western type, in contrast to the commune-dominated farming in central and southern Russia. As Governor of Kovno he had made some progress in consolidating peasant holdings. As prime minister, his major reform was to enable peasants to consolidate into private farms their share of the narrow strips hitherto widely distributed under village communal cultivation. They were offered easier terms for credit from a Peasant Land Bank. Over the next decade about 2.5 million peasants took advantage of this. He also developed incentives to cultivate state-owned farmland in Siberia and Central Asia, and 3 million peasants responded positively to this. These measures, also expanding the cultivated acreage and increasing agricultural productivity, gave Russia an export surplus of 13.5 million tons of grain in 1911, and over 20 million tons in 1913. These paid for investment into industry, while industrial workers saw their wages rise in these years.

Might the Revolution have been prevented by Stolypin's programme of reform? His attempt to transform the Russian peasantry into "a flourishing agrarian bourgeoisie" appears to have established his lasting reputation in Russia. He has been seen as the progenitor of a patriotic conservative consensus sought by many Russians in the early 21st century. An opinion poll to find the greatest Russian, organised by the state-controlled TV station *Rossiya* in December 2008 was responded to by more than 50 million people. Stolypin came second only to Prince Alexander Nevsky; Stalin was in the third place, with Peter the Great and Lenin behind.[25]

It has been claimed that the peasants were not greatly attracted by these reforms and that Stolypin's farmsteads were established in significant numbers only in the Baltic provinces where there was a German influence. The rate of privatisation had slowed significantly even before this reform retrospectively passed the Duma in summer 1910. Over half the land sold through the agency of the Peasant Land Bank was bought by village communes and co-operatives. The consolidation of a family's land into one enclosed farm was often difficult and proceeded slowly. Thus in 1916 61 per cent of all households still held land in communal tenure. This still meant that between a quarter and a third of all formerly communal land was now owned outright by peasants and between 1905 and 1914 about one fifth of all noble-owned land was sold to peasants. Peasant consumer and trading co-operatives "mushroomed."[26] Despite these reservations, the Bolsheviks recognised the effectiveness of Stolypin's policy; hence their long and eventually murderous persecution of the better-off peasants, known as kulaks.

Stolypin recognised that the fruits of his programme would take years to appear. In a newspaper interview in 1909, he suggested that 20 years of peace would be necessary. He was emphatic about keeping out of wars, for example the diplomatic crisis of 1908–09 over Austria's annexation of Bosnia. His American biographer Abraham Ascher speculated that he would have tried to keep Russia out of war in 1914.[27]

Tensions with the Tsar grew because Stolypin tried to conciliate the westernised groups – "educated society" – that Nicholas distrusted most. The Orthodox hierarchy were suspicious of his desire to extend the rights of other religions. Industrialists complained about his welfare legislation. Above all, the landowning aristocracy opposed his plans further to democratise local government, fearing this might increase their tax burdens. Not only did he arouse resentment and suspicion in St Petersburg, sadly, he attracted hostility from his two most effective predecessors: Durnovo and Witte. The latter pursued a vendetta reaching its zenith in 1911. It is reminiscent of the feuding between Louis XVI's reforming ministers.[28]

Stolypin wanted to extend Alexander II's *zemstvos* to the western borderlands, which had hitherto been excluded because of a fear they would be dominated by Polish landowners. Reactionary forces among noble landowners derailed this. The bill passed the Duma, by 165 votes to 139, but after the Tsar told members of the State Council to vote as their consciences directed, the bill fell by 92 to 68. Stolypin was "enraged", feeling "personally humiliated" by "deliberate sabotage" of government policy.[29] He threatened to resign unless the Tsar agreed to pass the bill using emergency powers. Very reluctantly, the Tsar agreed.

It remains a mystery whether there was any regime involvement in Stolypin's eventual assassination in Kiev on 1 September 1911 (he died of his wounds four days later); his assassin was a paid *Okhrana* informer, from a wealthy Kievan family of Jewish origin, long assimilated into the Russian elite.

Stolypin's successor was Vladimir Kokovtsov. Clever and hard-working, he had none of Stolypin's charisma. He enjoyed less support in the Duma and under him, the government ceased to attempt any further coherent reforms. Ministerial rivalry continued: Kokovtsov's enemies included Alexander Krivoshein, Minister of Agriculture, who secured Kokovtsov's removal in February 1914. He was succeeded by the aged Ivan Goremykin, with Krivoshein dominating the government in 1914–15. However, Krivoshein carried forward the Stolypin land reforms and co-operated successfully with the *zemstvos*. The latter were well funded from the centre in their efforts to improve rural life in general, and this saw a notable expansion of primary education; by 1914 roughly three-fifths of Russian children attended school, with further expansion planned.[30]

As a warning, there was serious labour unrest in the spring of 1912, and a strike at the Lena gold works in north-east Siberia saw the army firing into the crowd, killing 270 and wounding 250. There was a fierce public reaction: after five years of industrial peace, this incident set off a renewed wave of strikes, increasing in scale right up to the outbreak of war.

Even so, the chances of revolution in 1914 were described as "very slim" after several years of good harvests. The army seemed very firm: troops brought into St Petersburg to deal with a general strike in July 1914 "appeared completely loyal" and the strike collapsed. After 1907 most educated Russians "had turned their backs on revolutionary socialism".[31]

The War 1914–17

Stolypin opposed war, arguing that to adopt anything other than a defensive policy would be evidence of "an insane government" which would "put the survival of the dynasty at risk". The more sensible conservatives "were deeply fearful of the domestic consequences of any war with Germany", expressing these views, however, not in the press or the Duma but in private conversations with senior officials. Not all were sensible: Alexander Guchkov, political leader of the Octobrists (moderate reformers), urged the Balkan Slavs towards war in collaboration with Nicholas Hartwig, Russian minister in Belgrade.[32]

Durnovo sent a memorandum to the Tsar in February 1914 stating that a great European war was now likely. In his view, contrary to the conventional wisdom at the time, it would not be a short one. Russia was ill-equipped for such a war: he pointed to the inadequacy of strategic railways, the shortage of rolling stock if the demands of war were to be met, the lack of heavy artillery and machine guns, and the consequences of the closure of the Baltic as well as the Black Sea on imports of war materials and exports of grain. The government would be blamed for all shortcomings, he argued: it should not take these risks. His warning that "the army, having lost its most dependable men, and carried away by a primitive peasant desire for land, will find itself too demoralised to serve as a bulwark of law and order" proved prophetic. Durnovo was out of power, however, and there is no evidence that his wise warnings were heard by war-hungry ministers such as Krivoshein and Sazonov. And the Tsar might be justly blamed for the heavy expenditure after 1905 on building Dreadnought battleships for the Baltic fleet – which had very little effect in 1914 – at the expense of heavy artillery and modern communications technology for the army.[33]

However, in the years before 1914 Germany was increasingly concerned by the rapid growth of Russian economic and military strength and the development of Russia's railway network making for speedier mobilisation. The Balkan Wars of 1912–13 greatly strengthened Austria-Hungary's enemy, Serbia. As Lieven adds, Durnovo's memorandum did not offer "a convincing strategy for reconciling Russian and German interests" where they were increasingly liable to conflict in the Habsburg lands, the Balkans and the residue of the Ottoman empire. A war with Germany would wreck Russia's links with her main trading partner which was also the "key bulwark of European conservatism".[34]

A contentious figure, but one with enormous influence over the Tsar and Tsarina, Grigory Rasputin consistently warned Nicholas and Alexandra against going to war. At the vital moment, he was recuperating in Siberia from an assassination attempt and was not able to see them in St Petersburg. He sent a telegram warning that war "would mean the end of Russia and yourselves". It arrived too late to be heeded.[35]

In the event, after the assassination of the Habsburg heir Archduke Franz Ferdinand and his wife in Sarajevo on 15/28 June 1914, the pressures on Russia to go to war became tremendous. It is to the credit of the Tsar that he resisted them until the last minute. Tension mounted, leading to Austrian mobilisation on 12/25 July; and finally Austria's declaration of war on Serbia on 15/28 July. Lieven describes those factors which "screamed out for a strong Russian stance" – such as "concerns over the balance of power … holding the allegiance of clients and allies … the decision makers' own sense of honour and fear of being branded as cowards".[36]

Some key ministers took a hawkish approach. Sazonov, the foreign minister, warned that if Russia allowed the destruction of Serbia's independence, her position in the Balkans "would collapse utterly". What would be the effect on possibly friendly Romania, on Bulgaria, greedy for Serbian territory, and on undoubtedly latently hostile Turkey? Others, such as the army and navy ministers, were not particularly hawkish: they gave realistic estimates of Russia's strength, with the former, Sukhomlinov, asking that Sazonov be told that "even with the support of France we would find ourselves until 1917, and perhaps even until 1918, in a position of indisputable inferiority with respect to the combined forces of Germany and Austria". Maklakov, the minister for the interior, as late as 16/29 July 1914 warned how greatly revolutionaries would welcome war.[37]

The final decision was determined by the technical issues of mobilisation in such a vast country and the timing of moving reservists from very distant parts towards the frontier. Significantly, the Tsar refused to see his military chiefs, all pressing for the mobilisation order. He did see Sazonov, who he thought was uncommitted. Sadly, this was not so, and only on the afternoon of 17/30 July did Nicholas consent to general mobilisation. In the hours before the German declaration of war on Russia (19 July/1 August), he joined his wife and daughters in church: "he prayed very hard that God would spare his people this war, which seemed so close and unavoidable".[38]

The early months of the war in 1914 were moderately successful for Russia: the Austro-Hungarians in Galicia were overwhelmed, but after the two armies invading East Prussia were defeated (Tannenberg and the Masurian Lakes), the battle of Lodz against the Germans in November was inconclusive. However, Russia incurred heavy casualties, estimated at 300,000 per month in killed, wounded and prisoners. The defeats of 1915, which saw Russia losing all Poland as far as Vilna and Brest-Litovsk, and the carnage of 1916 added to this. In 1915, between May and November inclusive, Russian casualties totalled 2 million, including 1 million prisoners. The cadre of professional officers which had saved the imperial government in 1905–06 had been destroyed by 1917: the 40,000 officers of 1914 "were more or less completely wiped out", and officer casualties, including newly commissioned ones, had reached 60,000 even by mid-1915. Not only did Russia lack experienced officers, even more she lacked NCOs who could link them with the men. Lieven contrasts the German army in 1914, which had 65,000 long service NCOs, with 8500 in the Russian army.[39] Thus "the gap between the Russia of the officer class and the Russia of the private soldiers widened throughout 1915".[40]

In the spring of 1915 it was clear Russia faced a severe munitions crisis that contributed to the reverses of that year. Ministerial tensions resulted, and further defeats in January and February 1915 coincided with an espionage crisis. One Colonel Myasoedov was accused of spying for the Austrians and was made a scapegoat for the recent defeats; after a rapid trial by a special military tribunal in Warsaw on 18 March, he was convicted of various offences and hanged. This affair shook politics, and Kerensky wrote a "private" letter – widely circulated – to Rodzianko, the Duma president, claiming that "in the bowels of the Ministry of Foreign Affairs a tight organisation of real traitors has been calmly and confidently at work". This led to "a wave" of Germanophobia and anti-semitism, with a riot in Petrograd on 29 May, and the looting of nearly 500 German-linked businesses, while 750,000 Jews and Germans were expelled from their homes behind the front lines.[41]

The Tsar and Tsarina were concerned at the popularity of the supreme commander, the Grand Duke Nicholas. So he was also dismissed at this time, and the students of Petrograd university reacted by going on strike.[42] The Tsar assumed supreme command in the west, and this, it seems, "did lead to the better co-ordination of military and civil authority." The Tsar's chief of staff, General M V Alekseev "proved far more competent" than the Grand Duke and the previous chief of staff, Yanushkevich.[43]

Panic in Petrograd greeted reports from headquarters that Kiev would be lost and Petrograd might be abandoned. In fact the front stabilised, small counter attacks took place, and there was a great improvement in military supplies thanks to effective collaboration between the Ministry of War and Russian industry. The Germans "were full of admiration for the 'brilliant conduct' of the Russian retreat", which led the Germans into a barren area, making their supply problems "overwhelming".[44] This helps to counter the frequent suggestion that Russia should then have made peace; quite apart from betrayal of the western allies. The Bolsheviks feared not only that Nicholas II might make a separate peace in 1915–16, but that, failing to do so, he would be pushed aside by the anti-socialist parties in the Duma, under Guchkov and Milyukov.[45]

What McMeekin terms the "liberals' shadow government" now emerged. The new war minister, General A A Polivanov, convened a "special conference" of bankers and industrialists to carry forward military procurement, under a "War Industries Committee", chaired by Guchkov in Moscow – away from the Stavka headquarters in Mogilev and the ministers in Petrograd. These liberal leaders were suspicious of the Tsar's circle, which they believed wanted to end the war in order to preserve autocracy. As well as Guchkov, the "plotters", according to a document obtained by German intelligence, included Kerensky, Prince G E Lvov, a senior Kadet leader, and Milyukov. Several of these and others belonged to a secret Masonic order; and most became Ministers after the February revolution. They took charge of the war effort in 1916 and production in all sectors surged – rolling stock, boots, uniforms and all kinds of armaments, especially shells: 28 million 3-inch rounds were produced in 1916, after only 11 million in 1915. In 1916 Russia was turning out four times as many artillery shells as Austria-Hungary, and half as many again as Germany.[46]

1916 saw great successes on the Turkish front, under the talented General Yudenich: Erzurum fell on 3 February, and this was followed by Trabzon, Bitlis, Mush and Erzincan, leaving open the way to Ankara and central Anatolia. In Poland, Brusilov punched a hole nearly 30 miles deep in the enemy front at the end of May. But by September, with the Germans reinforcing the Austro-Hungarians, the Russians there had incurred a million casualties, as against 1.5 million, predominantly prisoners, on the German-Austrian side. If Brusilov had called his offensive off in early summer, he would have conserved lives while consolidating an advanced defensive line. His success brought Romania into the war on the Allied side at the end of August; a dubious gain, as she was swiftly defeated.

Military censors' reports, only recently discovered, show that, far from falling, morale in the Russian army ranks in the winter of 1916–17 was rising, partly because the Russian troops were better fed than the Germans. Letters from troops on the northern sector of the front expressed hopes of defeating the Germans in 1917. Morale in the southern sector, on account of Brusilov's heavy casualties, was less high. With the Ottoman fleet incapacitated for lack of fuel, the Russians were planning an amphibious descent on the Bosporus in 1917. Their Black Sea fleet had far better morale than the Baltic one, after successes in 1916, in which it sank four German submarines, three Turkish torpedo boats and three Turkish gunboats along with 3000 colliers.[47]

The home front was a less happy affair. The railway system was under enormous strain, having to supply food, forage and fuel to both Petrograd and the front. Windfall profits for the few sat alongside the people as a whole suffering from increasing food and fuel prices. The wheat harvest was lower in 1916 than in 1915, owing to poor weather, and the peasants withheld grain from the market.

Richard Pipes wrote "I know of no belligerent country in Europe during the First World War where there was as much tension between government and educated society as in Russia."[48] It did not help that the Tsarina was originally German and that in 1916 the prime minister was one Boris Sturmer. Ministerial instability worsened. The last prime minister in Imperial Russia, appointed on 29 December 1916, was the septuagenarian Prince N D Golitsyn, who "often fell asleep during meetings".[49] In mid-August Guchkov wrote to General Alekseev, chief of staff at the Stavka, making copies for his political allies. This letter denounced most ministers, claiming that "the home front is in a state of complete disintegration … the rot has set in at the roots of state power."[50]

The Duma, reconvened on 1 November, saw Kerensky describing the ministers as "men suspected of treason, these fratricides and cowards". He pointed at Rasputin as the regime's pro-German conspirator. More damaging still, because it came from a reputed moderate, was Milyukov's speech the same day. Elements in the government had been intriguing for a separate peace with Germany, he claimed, with "wild allegations" directed at ministers and others. He quoted from an Austrian newspaper about a pro-German "clique said to gather around the Tsarina". Were, he asked, government blunders caused by "stupidity or treason"? He added phrases such as "sinister rumours of treachery and treason" and "occult forces fighting for the benefit of Germany". Millions of copies of this "dangerous and irresponsible speech", with its "enormous impact on public opinion", were printed and circulated.[51]

In early December in the Duma a reactionary deputy, V M Purishkevich, called for Rasputin's death. Then he, along with Prince Felix Yusupov, husband of the Tsar's niece, and the Tsar's first cousin, Grand Duke Dmitri, brought about, on the night of 16–17 December, the complex assassination (by poison, stabbing, shooting and drowning) of Rasputin.

The February revolution

1916–17 saw a more savage winter than usual, with temperatures in northern Russia staying well below zero (Fahrenheit; thus –18° Centigrade) for weeks and blizzards disrupting supplies of food and fuel, hence rocketing prices in Petrograd. Prominent figures openly praised Rasputin's murderers and the pursuers of spies were now targeting the Tsarina. Faced with all these political and economic crises, the Tsar's mood was described as "fatalism", "lethargy" and "passivity". Rodzianko, Guchkov and others began plotting to depose him. Milyukov and Rodzianko were reluctant to see the removal of the dynasty, fearing worse from more radical elements. So Guchkov obtained pledges of support from the left-wing Kadet Nekrasov and the chairman of the War Industries Committee in Kiev, Tereshchenko, who all thought that the best approach was to force the Tsar to abdicate in favour of his haemophiliac son, Alexis, with Nicholas's brother, the

Grand Duke Michael, designated as regent. If soundings in the army proved positive, Guchkov planned to strike in March or April 1917. Others such as Prince Lvov, not a Duma deputy but powerful as leader of the Union of *Zemstvos*, wanted the Grand Duke Nicholas to take over. The latter, now Governor of the Caucasus, at headquarters in Tiflis, was approached by the mayor thereof at a New Year's Day reception with an outline of Lvov's plan "for a bloodless palace coup". The Grand Duke replied that neither the army nor the people would support overthrowing the sovereign in wartime.[52]

The tinder existed in Petrograd, with militant workers in hundreds of factories and inactive army rearguard units and new recruits crammed into overcrowded barracks. No one guessed what was about to happen – not the regime, nor the liberals, nor the Allied ambassadors, not even the German agents who had subsidised numerous strikes in the city in the previous year. On 22 February 1917, the temperature rose to well above freezing for five days. People ventured out and took part in large demonstrations over a lock-out at the Putilov works. Perhaps because of a wish to avoid another "Bloody Sunday", the Cossacks did not intervene. On the 24th, more were on strike and more violent persons joined the crowds. By the 25th, food shops were looted, crowds were estimated at 200,000, carrying placards attacking the war and the "German woman" (the Tsarina). On the 26th troops at last spread out to clear the central areas. There were arrests and firing involving the Pavlovsky Guards regiment and two inexperienced companies of Volynsky Guards; about 40 civilians were killed.

Overnight, protestors persuaded first one, then more guards regiments to disobey orders to fire on demonstrators. On the morning of the 27th, the commanding officer of the Volynsky company was shot dead in a brawl with his men over the previous day's incident. Men knew they would be viewed as collectively guilty, so closed ranks behind the mutineers. At dawn on the 28th the barracks of a loyal unit was surrounded by mutineers; when the unit's commander tried to speak he was shot dead. Mutineers were encouraged by the singing of the *Marseillaise* and the waving of red flags, with police stations set on fire, uniformed police lynched, shops and liquor stores looted, the Arsenal stormed for weapons. About 8000 hardened criminals were freed from prisons. The *Okhrana* headquarters was stormed and police files were burnt. The events were similar to, but more serious than, those in Paris in 1830 and 1848.

As word of events in Petrograd circulated, there was a violent naval mutiny in Kronstadt, where several officers were killed, including Admiral Viren. This spread to Reval/Tallinn and Helsinki, and around 100 officers, mostly Baltic Germans, were lynched.

While ministers panicked, the opposition leaders were divided. Rodzianko had ostensibly remained aloof from the plotting of Guchkov and Lvov and was "the only credible opposition figure trusted, to some extent, by the Tsar".[53] The Tsar ignored Rodzianko's advice on the 26th to appoint a "government of public confidence". On the afternoon of the 27th, Rodzianko telegraphed the Tsar at Mogilev, insisting "tomorrow will be too late". Kerensky and other left-wingers wanted to welcome the revolution, but Milyukov, Lvov and Rodzianko opposed this. Rodzianko and Golitsyn, still prime minister, advised that the Council of Ministers should resign in favour of a parliamentary ministry, and a popular general be appointed military dictator of Petrograd with authority to use force to put down street disorders. The Tsar endorsed the second proposal, and ordered General Ivanov, popular owing to his successes on the Galician front, to advance with reliable forces equipped with machine guns.

Prince Golitsyn tried, on the Tsar's orders, to prorogue the Duma but the deputies refused to disperse. In parallel with France in 1789, they went to another chamber and set up a "temporary committee" under Rodzianko claiming to be the de facto government. During Tuesday, 28 February, the Duma building was taken over in chaos by workers, soldiers and students. Kerensky was in a strong position, as a member of the temporary committee and vice chairman of the new "Petrograd Soviet of Workers' and Soldiers' Deputies". He saved many Tsarist officials from mob lynchings by "arresting" them in the Duma building. The Soviet was dominated by Mensheviks and SRs, while its newspaper, *Izvestiya*, was edited by Lenin's close friend, Vladimir Bonch-Bruevich.[54]

On 1 March, *Izvestiya* published instructions from the Soviet to the Petrograd garrison, known as Order No. 1. This told soldiers to seize weapons and ammunition. While this "order" did not apply to the army as a whole, news of it was circulated and widely implemented. A radical sailor stated: "Educated folk will read it differently. But we understand it straight: disarm the officers".[55]

Early on Tuesday, the 28th, the Tsar left Mogilev by train, preceded by an armed escort train, aiming for Tsarskoe Selo but going the long way round, via Smolensk, so as to leave the direct line via Vitebsk open for Ivanov and his force. He was out of touch with the generals in Mogilev and the politicians in Petrograd, and he was also delayed by threats of revolutionaries attacking the line. By the evening of Wednesday 1 March he had reached Pskov, still 200 miles short of Tsarskoe Selo.

The 'Tsar' Michael episode

People did not expect the Romanov dynasty to end. The consensus, extending to many liberals and other non-extremists, was that if Nicholas was removed from the throne, thus conveniently removing the unpopular Tsarina, he would be succeeded by his 12-year-old son Alexis with Nicholas's younger brother Michael as regent. Michael was described as " a war hero, a cavalry commander holding Russia's two highest battlefield awards … known to be sympathetic to a constitutional monarchy on the British lines; the army held him in high regard and he would also be a popular choice in the Duma …" The alternative, it seemed, would be left wing extremists taking over the streets.[56]

There is even now, with more material at hand, a confused picture of these few days which saw the end of the rule of the Romanov dynasty which had reigned since 1613. There were no legal precedents for what was happening; just as the Petrograd Soviet itself "was *sui generis*", so no existing law "gave Rodzianko the authority to issue government decrees, however 'provisionally.' He was making things up as he went along." While Alekseev, chief of staff at the Stavka, believed that Rodzianko recognised the "necessity of maintaining the monarchical principle in Russia", there is no evidence of Rodzianko stating this, and he now appointed A A Bublikov, a radical leader, as minister with responsibility for the railways and, importantly, the telegraph lines that ran alongside them and conveyed information and propaganda to all Russia. [57]

During 28 February Rodzianko (in Petrograd) and Alekseev (in Mogilev) agreed on the terms of an abdication manifesto which would implement the Alexis-Michael solution. Alekseev agreed to call off the Ivanov force, as he thought Rodzianko had Petrograd under control. The latter admitted that he was "far from having succeeded" in achieving this.[58]

Alekseev was determined that trouble in Petrograd should not undermine the front-line armies before their planned spring offensive; hence his support for "regime change". He put this to the Tsar late on 1 March and to various commanders and admirals. By now, "most of the leading generals had lost faith in Nicholas's leadership or his ability to organise the rear for victory over Germany".[59] The first replies reached the Tsar via Alekseev on the 2nd: from Grand Duke Nicholas in the Caucasus, General Brusilov, and General Evert, commander of the western front. Others also responded: Grand Duke Sergei Mikhailovich, inspector of artillery, and Admiral Nepenin in Helsinki (who was to be lynched on 4 March). All supported abdication in the interests of retaining military discipline.[60]

Nicholas II signed the draft manifesto of abdication around midnight on 2–3 March. Lieven states that General Ruzsky, commander of the northern front headquartered in Pskov, "browbeat" the Tsar and "controlled the flow of information to him".[61] If Ruzsky had known that Rodzianko, for all his claims, was ineffective in face of the Petrograd revolutionaries, things might have been very different. Rodzianko refused to go to Pskov, where late on the 2nd the Tsar was visited by Guchkov and another Duma member. Nicholas told them that he had changed his mind about abdication; he would pass the throne directly to Michael, so he himself could remain to care for Alexis (a doctor had just informed him that Alexis's haemophilia, which had never been made public, was incurable). Despite Guchkov's doubts, the Tsar insisted and signed the new act of abdication at 11.50pm on the 2nd (backdated to 3.05 pm). And the Tsar named Lvov, not Rodzianko, as chairman of the Council of Ministers; this was later confirmed, of his own volition, by Michael.

Rodzianko told Ruzsky not to publish the latest abdication manifesto; the Petrograd crowd might "perhaps reconcile themselves to the regency of the Grand Duke" but not to him as Tsar. There was undoubtedly a concern over how he as Tsar might discipline mutineers and this made the Petrograd Soviet hostile to his accession. There was, however, clear evidence of support for Michael as Tsar, from people in Petrograd streets, with the front line troops cheering, while a *Te Deum* was sung for him at Pskov.[62]

The politicians – Rodzianko, Lvov, Milyukov and Kerensky, as well as Golitsyn, other ministers, members of the temporary committee and Guchkov (who was late) all met Grand Duke Michael in Petrograd at 10 am on the 3rd. Most insisted on his abdication from a title he had not yet accepted; if he refused, they claimed that none of them would serve as ministers. Michael was then closeted with Lvov and Rodzianko (sadly, excluding his real supporters in this group, Milyukov and Guchkov). Michael agreed not to accept the throne but demurred at the word "abdicate". Legal questions were raised, for example, could Tsarevich Alexis be lawfully bypassed and, indeed, could the throne ever be legally "vacant". The result was a manifesto, drafted with legal advice, which would make Michael emperor without saying that he accepted the throne. He stated that he was willing to assume "supreme power" but only "in the event that such is the will of our great people, upon whom it devolves by a general vote, through their representatives in the Constituent Assembly …" Thus he vested his powers in the new Provisional Government and would wait until a future Constituent Assembly voted for a constitutional monarchy and elected him. "Meanwhile, he would not reign, but neither would he abdicate." His manifesto said that the throne had been "thrust upon me" and instead of commanding, he "beseeched" the citizens to obey the Provisional Government. It was, however, signed "Michael" that is, as Tsar, not "Michael Alexandrovich", the terminology appropriate to him as Grand Duke. In a moment of brutal realism, Nicholas II retorted "His manifesto ends up by kowtowing to the Constituent Assembly, whose elections will take place in six months. God knows who gave him the idea of signing such rubbish."[63]

Michael was placed under house arrest on 21 August 1917, on the orders of Kerensky. After Russia had been declared a Republic on 1 September, he was released. He was imprisoned again after the Bolsheviks took power, and eventually murdered by them near Perm on 13 June 1918 – a few weeks before his brother, the ex-Tsar, and his family, perished.

The announcement of Michael's "abdication" was forwarded to front commanders at 2am on the 4th, asking soldiers to transfer their allegiance to the "Provisional Government". A further episode saw the removal of Grand Duke Nicholas, who had just been re-appointed by Nicholas II as commander-in-chief. On 3 March, the Petrograd Soviet ordered the arrest of all members of the Romanov dynasty. On 11 March, Prince Lvov, who had become chairman of what was now termed the "Council of Ministers of the Provisional Government", formally deprived the Grand Duke of the command.[64]

The Provisional Government did not allow Nicholas II's final address, intended for the troops, to be published. Indeed, on 7 March he was placed under arrest and he and his family were not to be free again. Lieven reports restrictions on his movements in Tsarskoe Selo, while during the next month he and Alexandra were kept apart and not allowed any conversation in private. And this was months before the eventual murderers of the Imperial family obtained control in Russia.[65]

The Liberal failure to consolidate February

Soviets were spreading through the army and navy, but many of the rank and file were saddened by the Tsar's abdication and confused by the various political manifestos. The officers were hostile to the Petrograd Soviet, which through Ispolkom (its executive committee) decided in April to send political commissars to the front. The war minister, Guchkov, then sent his emissaries to the front, creating tensions between the two groups.[66]

Thus the loose grouping which formed the Provisional Government had several disagreements over policy. An early casualty was Milyukov, who had become foreign minister. On 5 March, he said that the Provisional Government would honour Russia's agreements with her allies, implying readiness for spring offensives. The Petrograd Soviet disowned this statement. Then on 11 April he said Russia remained committed to its pledges to the Armenians and the Slavs in Austrian Galicia. This, resonant of Russia's annexationist ambitions, came shortly after a Russian naval squadron, consisting of two battle cruisers, three sea-plane carriers, and six destroyers arrived at the mouth of the Bosporus with attendant dogfights with German and Turkish seaplanes (22 March). Milyukov was denounced by Lenin in *Pravda* and Victor Chernov, leader of the SRs, called for his resignation." Kerensky forced Milyukov into handing a more ambiguous statement to Allied diplomats.

Lenin had only just returned from exile in Switzerland and used this episode to attempt a coup. With cabinet backing, Kerensky told Kornilov, a popular general just appointed commander of the Petrograd military district, not to use force against demonstrators. There was a clash on 21 April between armed Bolsheviks, including Kronstadt sailors, and Provisional Government loyalists: a few were killed, but the government won back control. Once failure was known, the Bolshevik central committee disowned further action.

With Ispolkom asserting its control over the garrison, the government "failed to issue so much as a peep to defend Milyukov against the mob". Kornilov was disgusted by this and asked to be relieved: he was sent to take over the 8th army in Galicia. On 1 May Ispolkom voted to allow members of the Soviet to enter the cabinet; Chernov and the pro-war Menshevik leader, Tsereteli, did so. In the reshuffle, the foreign ministry went to Tereshchenko, a Kadet but closer to Kerensky's position on the war than Milyukov's, while Kerensky took over the war and navy portfolios. Milyukov and Guchkov, the war minister, both resigned.[67]

Before seeing how Kerensky threw his opportunity away, what of Lenin and the Bolsheviks?

V I Lenin

Lenin was hardly prepared for what was about to happen. In Zurich on 9 January 1917 (OS), he told a meeting of young socialists "we old-timers may not live to see the decisive battles of the coming revolution".[68]

Winston Churchill's immortal words aptly describe what was to happen. Referring to the "desperate stakes" facing the German war leaders in early 1917, with the USA about to enter the war against them, he continues "it was with a sense of awe that they turned upon Russia the most grisly of all weapons. They transported Lenin in a sealed truck [sic] like a plague bacillus from Switzerland to Russia."[69] Catherine Merridale has recounted[70] the negotiations between Lenin and his associates and the Germans for financial and administrative support in organising this journey. The German officers in charge were personally briefed by Ludendorff. Lenin and his party left Zurich on (Western) Easter Monday, 27 March (all dates in OS), crossed to Sweden in rough seas on the 30th, left Stockholm for Finland the next day, eventually arriving in Petrograd late at night on 3 April, the Orthodox Easter Monday.

After his arrival a message was sent from the political section of the German General Staff in Stockholm (which controlled the spies in Russia) to the German

Foreign Office: "Lenin's entry into Russia successful. He is working exactly as we would wish." What was this work? Nearly a year later, in March 1918, just before the humiliating treaty of Brest-Litovsk was signed, the German diplomat Paul von Hintze declared: "What do we want in the East? The military paralysis of Russia. The Bolsheviks are taking care of this better than any other Russian party, without our contributing a single man or a single penny …"[71]

That was not entirely true. With the German money brought by Lenin to Petrograd in spring 1917, the Bolsheviks bought a private printing press for 250,000 roubles or about $12.5million in modern money, after promising the owner they would retain the staff at full pay, that is 30,000 roubles monthly, or $1.5m. This explains why Lenin was able to promote his anti-war policy through *Pravda*. Thanks to the millions of marks sent by the Germans to help peace propaganda, and transferred through Alexander Helphand-Parvus, the Bolsheviks, even with a minority of places in the Soviets, were rapidly able to set up a large number of newspapers. It "stretches credulity" that Lenin did not know about the German help.[72]

But what else did Lenin stand for? Most of his ideas about the Revolution were set out in the *April Theses* of 1917. He was sympathetic to the view of Nicholas Bukharin, a Moscow revolutionary theorist, who noted how the advanced capitalist countries in wartime had both developed state power and suborned their socialist parties to maintain working class support for the war. So Lenin saw that it would be naïve to leave intact existing state institutions, such as the civil service and army: they had to build a new revolutionary state. He was also convinced that the existence of the Soviets would prevent the socialist revolution from taking the path of compromise, and that a Europe-wide socialist revolution was imminent.[73]

As well as rule by the soviets, Lenin wanted the nationalisation of large-scale industry, banks and agricultural land. He argued that the revolutionary socialist regime would not survive unless it used violent methods: hence the "dictatorship of the proletariat" and "class struggle". So the former upper and middle classes should lose their civic rights. The need for class struggle would diminish as these classes ceased to be a threat, and the lower social orders would get accustomed to running the economy, which would expand. According to Lenin, a kitchen maid could be entrusted with decisions previously undertaken by ministers, hence he might achieve the state's "withering away".[74]

Lenin had avoided the discussion of state terror in his books and wrote "glancingly" about it in 1917. But he was clearly inspired by the parallel with France in 1793: "The enemies of the people … in the 20th century are not the monarchs but the landlords and capitalists as a class … The 'Jacobins' of the 20th century would not set about guillotining the capitalists … it would be enough to arrest 50–100 magnates and queens of bank capital … for a few weeks so as to *uncover their dirty deals* …"[75] Lenin was convinced that the mass of the people would be on the side of the Bolsheviks, so repression would not need to be so long or so severe as it had been in France!

Lenin's tactic was to keep probing the defences of the Provisional Government by way of large demonstrations involving armed soldiers and sailors. Kerensky had to navigate a difficult course. In early May he sacked seven army commanders, 26 corps commanders, and 69 divisional commanders, including Alekseev who was replaced by Brusilov.

While the planned naval strike against the Bosporus would have been popular, the French were insistent on an army offensive on the Eastern front: after the failure of the Nivelle offensive in mid-April, and the mutinies which followed, their position was desperate. So Kerensky as war minister toured the front in late May, making rousing speeches whose effect was speedily lost.

Brusilov's original plan was to launch the Galician offensive on 10 June, but new recruits had arrived from Petrograd, infected by Bolshevik ideas. The attack was launched on the 16th, two days after a mass meeting attended by 12,000 guardsmen passed a no-confidence vote in the Provisional Government and condemned the planned offensive. The 11th army, heavily infected by Bolshevism, refused to advance. Ignoring warnings, Brusilov urged further attacks – some units mutinied and when loyal units continued attacking they incurred heavy casualties. By early July, the offensive had ground to a halt, with losses of nearly 40,000 officers and men.

The government now planned to arrest 28 leading Bolsheviks in Petrograd. This leaked; Lenin fled to Finland. On 2 July the Bolsheviks arranged a demonstration directed at the sympathetic First Machine Gun Regiment, which was threatened with being sent to the front. Trotsky, still nominally a Menshevik (he and his group joined the Bolsheviks a few weeks later), spoke. There is evidence that he attacked Kerensky and even said "kill Kerensky". A rising took place with shooting and looting in Petrograd. Lenin returned from Finland and gave Bolshevik support: 10,000 people took part in this rising. Ten-rouble notes were passed to those joining and helping. The Bolsheviks are described as being "on the cusp of victory" but "with Lenin failing, for whatever reason, to take charge and give instructions", by nightfall on 4 July the crowd had become "a directionless rabble", and slowly dispersed.[76]

At this stage, the mood was turning against the Bolsheviks. That same evening the Justice Minister Pereverzev with loyal officers discussed the evidence for a treason trial using the Parvus/Stockholm connection and the German money.

Loyal troops stormed the Bolshevik headquarters at the mansion built for Mathilde Kshesinskaya, the Tsar's mistress before he married, where they found more evidence and "seditious literature"; they smashed the *Pravda* printing press. In total 2000 Bolsheviks were arrested, including Kamenev, Kozlovsky and Lenin's wife. On 6 July the Provisional Government charged 11 Bolshevik leaders with high treason and organising an armed uprising. Most were not in custody; Lenin, having shaved off his beard, along with Zinoviev, escaped back to Finland which by now was seeking independence from Russia.

The "Kornilov Affair"

Ministerial confusion continued. The Kadet leaders, Lvov, Nekrasov and Tereshchenko, criticised Pereverzev for revealing the evidence before the culprits had been arrested. Kerensky sided with them and sacked Pereverzev. Lvov, who had ostensibly been head of the government, resigned in favour of Kerensky who was thus now minister-president of the "Government of the Salvation of the Revolution", as well as war and navy minister.

After the failure of the Galician offensive, Kornilov was appointed Commander-in-Chief, having required the restoration of discipline and an end to political interference. In the event, Kerensky could not keep these promises because he was dependent on the executive committee of the Soviet, which regarded all attempts to restore military discipline as "counter revolutionary". On 8 August the Ministry of War gave Kerensky lists of left-inclined and right-inclined persons, all to be arrested; he agreed to the arrest of the latter but not of the former.[77]

Kerensky summoned an All-Russian Conference in Moscow in mid-August, including ministers, the Moscow and Petrograd Soviets, former Duma deputies, trade unions, *zemstvos*, clergy, retired commanders, and representatives of the Allied armies – a total of 2400. Kornilov's speech received a boisterous reception from officers, liberal politicians and representatives of commerce and industry; the Soviet representatives were silent. A Cossack general, Kaledin, called for the removal of the Soviets: the Left thought he had spoken on behalf of Kornilov. Kerensky's doubts were kindled: "the documentary record (and Kerensky's subsequent behaviour) leaves no doubt that he believed, by late August 1917, that a counter-revolutionary plot was brewing". Kerensky "came to view the general as a rival who wanted to replace him".[78]

The Austro-Germans had avoided attacking in 1917, taking the view that a quiet front would encourage subversion. Rumours circulated round the Stavka at Mogilev of an intended Bolshevik rising, and Kornilov spoke to many who came there of his intention to deal with the Bolsheviks. Indiscreet conversations and suspicions that Kornilov intended to overthrow the Government were reported to Kerensky. Kerensky called an emergency cabinet meeting at midnight on 26 August. Savinkov, the acting war minister, tried to persuade Kerensky that there was no conspiracy.[79] He was ignored: Kerensky was given dictatorial powers, and relieved Kornilov of his command. *Izvestiya* of the 29th reported that Pavel Milyukov had offered his services as intermediary between the two: Kerensky rejected this on the ground that "there can be no talk of reconciliation".[80]

An angry Kornilov ordered a punitive detachment of four Cossack regiments to move on Petrograd under General Krymov. Krymov found no Bolshevik rising when he arrived on the 31st, and Kerensky relieved him of his command: Krymov shot himself. On 1 September, General Alekseev arrived in Mogilev to accept Kornilov's surrender. Kornilov was imprisoned with thirty officers known to be loyal to him. He then escaped to help found the Volunteer Army after the Bolshevik revolution and was killed by a shell in the civil war in April 1918.

Richard Pipes describes the Kornilov affair as "a tragedy of errors … misunderstandings with a dire result". None of the participants wanted its outcome: "yet they made it all but inevitable". He adds "there is no evidence of a Kornilov plot, but there is plenty of evidence of Kerensky's duplicity." McMeekin states "what transpired … could be played for farce, were the consequences not so catastrophic." The main consequence was that the army leadership was so disaffected with Kerensky that hardly any units (except the Women's Death Battalion, with a few Cossacks, officers and army cadets) considered intervening in late October when the Bolsheviks mounted their decisive coup in Petrograd.[81]

Kerensky encouraged this hostility by making peace with the Bolsheviks and releasing those arrested in July.[82] Despite the search of the Kshesinskaya mansion finding evidence of plans for a Bolshevik uprising, on 8 September Kerensky abolished the counter – intelligence unit that had conducted this investigation. And he even allowed the Bolsheviks to rearm to help defend Petrograd against "Kornilovites"; thus the Bolsheviks seized 40,000 rifles from a government arsenal.

After the Kornilov affair, there was a sharp leftward turn among the troops who suspected that their officers supported Kornilov. Soldiers' assemblies passed resolutions for peace, and the rate of desertion rose rapidly. Facing further German advances, the Stavka ordered the evacuation of Reval/Tallinn, the last major fortress before Petrograd. Kerensky then proposed that the government be evacuated to Moscow. The news leaked, and the Bolsheviks accused Kerensky of planning to surrender Petrograd to the Germans.[83]

As a background, the economic situation was dire, with monetary inflation "meteoric" alongside plummeting industrial production. Food supplies to towns continued to run short. The central state administration steadily disintegrated, with the Soviets acting as if they wielded formal power, the workers' control movement spreading, with workers taking over factories. Peasant attacks on rural manors became frequent.

The Bolshevik coup

Lenin had appeared to have lost his nerve in July when he almost succeeded in defeating the Government. Subsequent events led him, back in Finland, to conclude that all chances of revolution were over. However, fortune's wheel was turning. The Government failed to establish the Constituent Assembly which would have given Russia a legitimate authority. In March it was hoped that the Assembly would be convened by June. If elections had taken place in the summer of 1917, the SRs would have triumphed. Various elements wanted delay: the right-wing parties wanted revolutionary zeal to calm down, and the SRs wanted elections after the harvest. In June the plan was for elections on 17 September, with the Assembly meeting on the 30th. After the July rising this slipped, with a decision on 9 August for the elections to be delayed to 12 November, with the Assembly due to convene on 28 November. The delay was fatal.

Lenin arrived incognito in Petrograd between 7 and 9 October, attending the meeting of the Bolshevik Central Committee on the 10th. Encouraged by recent Bolshevik successes in both the Moscow and Petrograd Soviets, he declared that "the majority is now with us," adding "History will not forgive us if we do not assume power now".[84] Waiting was "senseless" as he believed that the Bolsheviks would never win a national election in which peasants – sturdy supporters of the SRs – would vote, in contrast to urban soviet elections. Trotsky proposed seizing power in the name of the Second Congress of the Soviets which would meet on 25 October, and this was carried by the Committee by ten votes to two.[85]

News of the coming coup became widespread. Lenin wanted insurrection, but Kamenev and Zinoviev opposed as they did not believe Europe was ready for revolution. Typical of his use of extremist language, Lenin denounced them in the Bolshevik press as "strike-breaking" and "blackleg".[86] Both perished in Stalin's Great Purge of the late 1930s. Further discussion took place on the 16th, with Lenin declaring "The situation is plain: either a Kornilovite dictatorship or a dictatorship of the proletariat and the poorest strata of the peasantry." He "pulled off his wig" in frustration at opposition; this diminished overnight, the final vote being 19 to two with four abstentions.[87]

The insurrection was to be organised through the Military Revolutionary Committee (Milrevkom) of the Petrograd Soviet. Commissars were sent to all military units in and near Petrograd, instructing them to ignore government orders unless countersigned by Milrevkom. This neutralised the garrison of 240,000 men. Hours before the coup, Lenin was nearly arrested near the Taurida Palace, only escaping because he convinced the police that he was a "harmless drunk."[88]

It was a "classic modern coup d'etat accomplished without mass support ... [a] seizure of the nerve centres of the modern state, carried out under false slogans in order to neutralise the population at large."[89] Just before dawn on 25 October units of Milrevkom took over key points bloodlessly. Cossacks and officer cadets alike failed to resist, respectively resulting from declared neutrality and Bolshevik subterfuge. Seeing the outcome, at 11.30 am on the 25th, Kerensky left Petrograd in a car lent by the US embassy, ostensibly to rally supporters at the front. Too late, he was now denouncing the Bolsheviks having only weeks before concentrated on Kornilov. The ministers were hemmed in at the Winter Palace, with a few guards, including the Women's Death Battalion: the latter numbered 137. The Bolsheviks threatened to shell the palace; in fact the light cruiser *Aurora*, whose role was so significant to Eisenstein and the Bolshevik myth-makers, and whose captain had been killed by mutineers during the February Revolution, fired only blanks as it lacked live ammunition. The cadets and Cossacks abandoned their posts, but the women resisted. A number suffered rape or physical or verbal abuse in the Bolshevik attack, but were released after intervention by Lady Buchanan, the wife of the British Ambassador, and the British military attaché, General Sir Alfred Knox. The ministers, who had been hoping Kerensky would return with reinforcements, were arrested at 2.10 am on the 26th.[90]

Hitherto, the Mensheviks and SRs at all key moments had supported the Bolsheviks because, they claimed, they did not want to lose the gains of the revolution hitherto. After the storming of the Winter Palace and the arrest of ministers, the Mensheviks and most SRs left the government and stopped co-operating. Trotsky denounced them: "Your role is played out: go where you ought to go, into the dustbin of history."[91] Similar language was used by Voroshilov in a 1934 letter to Stalin, referring to Trotsky, Kamenev and Zinoviev: "horrible little individuals, traitors, finished people. This poisonous and miserable scum ought to be annihilated".[92]

Brest-Litovsk

The new government, largely composed of Bolsheviks and Left SRs, known as Sovnarkom, announced the suspension of hostilities on the Eastern front. The All-Russian Congress of Soviets met on 25 October and announced the abolition of the landed property of the gentry, the Imperial family and the Church, declaring that "the right of private ownership of land is abolished forever".

From 29 October there was a railway strike in protest at the coup; it was broken by January 1918. There were also strikes by government employees and a bank strike. To crush these the Cheka, the first Soviet secret police organisation, was formed under Felix Dzerzhinsky "to combat counter-revolution, speculation and sabotage". The seizure of Petrograd had been relatively easy; it was not so elsewhere. The pro-Kerensky military were stronger in Moscow; the Bolsheviks took the Kremlin but were soon expelled. By the close of 2 November Kerensky supporters there had surrendered after fierce fighting and much damage to buildings, including the Kremlin.

The Assembly elections started on 12 November with voting taking two weeks: it was cleanly and well organised, with more than 40 million voting, around 50 per cent of those qualified. The Bolsheviks took only a quarter of the votes, though significantly they took 70 per cent of the military vote in Moscow and Petrograd. The main winners were the SRs, who obtained 40 per cent.

Before the count was complete, Sovnarkom announced indefinite postponement of the Assembly's opening. Some non-Bolsheviks demonstrated on the day of the original opening (28 November); the Bolsheviks responded by arresting the Kadet leaders. The opening was then set for 5 January, with the Bolsheviks concentrating troops in Petrograd. There was chaos, with Bolsheviks jeering all non-Bolshevik speakers. The chairman adjourned the assembly shortly after 4am on the 6th. The following day the Taurida Palace was closed and surrounded by troops: the session had lasted less than thirteen hours.[93]

On the still active Galician front, a poll of the Special Army found few supporting Lenin; a soldiers' committee denounced the Bolshevik seizure of power. The neighbouring 11th army, however, saw fraternisation with the Germans across the lines as early as 28 October. A circular was sent on 13 November from Berlin warning German diplomats to "conceal their glee" at public events over the recent developments. Meanwhile a Foreign Ministry sympathiser gave Trotsky the keys to the filing cabinet holding the secret treaties with the Allies. He denounced these and details were gradually published. And for delaying the opening of armistice talks with the Germans, General Dukhonin, who had been made Commander-in-Chief by Kerensky in August 1917, was sacked by Lenin on 9 November. He was replaced by Ensign Krylenko "almost certainly the lowest-ranking officer ever to command the armies of a great power." Dukhonin was subsequently lynched by Krylenko's men.[94]

Krylenko became Chairman of the Revolutionary Tribunal in May 1918, after abolition of the post of Commander-in-Chief. Trotsky ordered that Admiral Shchastny be tried for having refused to scuttle the Baltic Fleet. After a trial prosecuted by Krylenko, the Admiral was sentenced , "to be shot within twenty-four hours". To complaints that Lenin had already abolished the death penalty, Krylenko declared "Executions have been abolished. But Shchastny is not being executed; he is being shot." In his turn, Krylenko was shot in Stalin's Great Purge in July 1938. [95]

During the peace negotiations at Brest-Litovsk, the Bolsheviks played for time, in the spirit of Trotsky's slogan, "no war, no peace", while hoping for revolutions in Germany and Austria. The Germans knew how weak the Russians were; at the end of February 1918 they occupied Estonia and then sent much harsher peace terms. Their advance continued, occupying Minsk, Pskov, and Kiev and bombing Petrograd on 2 March. Lenin forced the terms through the Central Committee by 116 votes to 85, with 26 abstentions, and the treaty was signed on 3 March. It was "draconian": the Bolsheviks had to evacuate Finland, the Baltic States and Ukraine – where they were forced to recognise a separatist regime based on Kiev. Russia lost 1.3 million square miles, with 62 million people, a third of its agricultural capacity and three quarters of its iron and coal production.

Southern Russia would not stay a vacuum: Austro-German forces seized Odessa in mid-March, then Nikolaev and Kherson, then Crimea, occupying Sevastopol on May Day, and then Kharkov and the Donbass region, while a German force was in Georgia by July. The Kadet leader, Milyukov, who had fled to Ukraine, opened contacts with the Germans in Kiev, while General Anton Denikin's Volunteer Army did so in the Don region. And the Trans-Siberian railway was occupied by liberated Czech prisoners from Penza to Vladivostok.

In an agreement signed on 27 August, the Bolsheviks agreed to pay Germany 6 billion marks of "reparations" (equivalent to $1.4 billion at the time, and $140 billion today).[96] While they agreed to recognise Georgia as a German satellite and to ship 25 per cent of future Baku oil production to Germany, the Germans promised to evacuate White Russia, Rostov and part of the Don basin. In September, the Bolsheviks shipped to Berlin the first two of five planned reparations, including 100 tons of gold.

The German Foreign Office wanted to co-operate with the Bolsheviks against threatened Allied intervention in northern Russia. On 6 July assassins, hired by the leader of the Left SRs, previously allied to the Bolsheviks, murdered Count Mirbach, the German Ambassador in Moscow. So Ludendorff planned for his forces, on their way to counter the Allies in Murmansk and Archangel (where there were now 40,000 British troops), to occupy Petrograd and forcibly remove the Bolsheviks. Only the collapse of Bulgaria after 15 September, threatening the whole German hold on the Danube basin, caused him to call this plan off on the 27th.[97]

It was a narrow escape for Lenin. Within six weeks Germany had collapsed. The armistice with the Western Allies invalidated the treaty of Brest-Litovsk, but this did not bring peace.

Civil war

"The civil war did not occur by accident." In the winter of 1917–18 the vast majority of the people supported either the Mensheviks or the SRs, both of whom throughout 1917 had been "partly guided by their fear of and revulsion for civil war". A coalition of these parties, resting on the Constituent Assembly as the only legitimate authority, might have made counter-revolution inconceivable. Lenin, unlike some other Bolshevik leaders, would not accept such a coalition: he "pursued policies which, as he well knew, made civil war inevitable". While the Whites, the anti-Bolshevik forces, often acted with "chaotic brutality", especially towards Jews, they refrained from ordering the extermination of whole families, children included, of rival politicians. The Reds' "cold-blooded rationalisation of class terror carried the world into a new dimension of political crime".[98]

This account will use the terms "Reds" and "Whites", although the latter term was a Bolshevik insult, implying a link with the French Bourbons. The White leaders, who wished to restore the Constituent Assembly, but not necessarily the Tsardom, did not accept the name.[99]

At various times, but without co-ordination between their armies, the Whites advanced towards the Red centres of Moscow and Petrograd from the west, east and south. The Reds benefited from a more unified command and more favourable geography as their central bases gave access to the core of the Russian railway network. The Whites, by contrast, had to rely on Cossacks, Ukrainians, and Baltics, and obtained weapons only with difficulty. The Reds took over the bulk of the Tsarist arsenal – 18,000 machine guns, 430,000 mid-range or light guns, 500 Vickers heavy guns and 2.2 million rifles.[100] It was only a matter of time before the Reds overwhelmed the Whites by sheer strength. And they also benefited from Trotsky's skilful command as War Commissar.

50, 000 in the officer corps joined the Volunteer (White) Army. But because the Western Allies seemed a threat, thousands of veteran officers joined the Red Army out of misplaced patriotism.

Counterfactually, had Britain, France, the USA and Japan intervened in strength in the winter of 1918–19, this would have been decisive. There were various reasons they did not, the main one being that they were exhausted, with likely domestic political resistance to large scale intervention in Russia. In late autumn 1919 came Lloyd George's sudden abandonment of the Whites, announced, without giving his Coalition ministerial colleagues notice, at the Lord Mayor's Banquet on 9 November. This had a devastating effect on White morale.

The French became most involved because of the size of the Russian debt to French bondholders, of which there were over a million. They intervened in some strength with Balkan allies in south Ukraine during the winter of 1918–19. The troops under French command were mostly Greeks, Romanians and colonials from Senegal, with little enthusiasm for Russia or its climate; mutinies resulted. They made humiliating withdrawals from Odessa in March 1919 and Sevastopol in April.

In November 1918 the Provisional All-Russian Government vested power in Admiral A V Kolchak. He was "neither an effective military commander nor an astute politician".[101] After he was declared "Supreme Ruler" in March 1919, his army began attacking in the southern Urals, helped by the Czech Corps, 50,000 strong. Kolchak advanced on Samara and Kazan, but then was forced back to the Urals. On 14 November the Reds captured Omsk, Kolchak's headquarters, without resistance; by now they outnumbered the Whites two to one on that front. Kolchak gave up the title of Supreme Ruler in favour of General Denikin, another White leader. In January 1920 Kolchak's train was halted at Irkutsk and he was held by the Czechs, handed over to the Reds, tried and shot on 6 February. He was the only one of the senior White leaders to be captured and killed during the civil war.

From the south, Denikin's Volunteer Army, reinforced by Don Cossacks and Baron Peter Wrangel's Caucasian Army, advanced, taking Tsaritsyn (now Volgograd) with 40,000 prisoners and then Kharkov in late June, and rapidly in the autumn taking Kiev, Kursk, Voronezh and Orel, 250 miles from Moscow. During 1919, Ukraine had around six partisan armies, ranging from those under right-wing Cossack hetman Petliura to left anarchists under Makhno.

Meanwhile, Yudenich attacked from Estonia and by mid-October 1919 was eight miles from Petrograd. There Trotsky, dashing about in his armoured train, haranguing troops and carrying out mass executions of deserters, managed to repel him. After the Reds offered peace and recognition to Estonia at the end of August 1919, Estonia withdrew support from Yudenich. Likewise Polish Pilsudski refused to help Denikin who did not support Polish independence. Thus the Reds were able to transfer troops and Trotsky's crack Latvians routed Denikin's western flank near Tula (120 miles from Moscow), while Budennyi's cavalry threatened them from the south-east. By December 1919 the Reds were driving Denikin towards Kharkov. There were tensions between Denikin and Wrangel; the latter left Russia in February but returned on request after a demoralised Denikin resigned his command in April 1920. Wrangel, now the White commander, regrouped in the Crimea, restored discipline and pledged to leave the peasants with the land they had been promised in the Revolution, but the Red forces were too powerful. In November 1920, the last White troops, with some lucky civilians, left Sevastopol: thousands of men, women and children left behind were massacred by the Bolsheviks.[102]

Now Pilsudski, the Polish leader, invaded: his forces captured Kiev easily in early May 1920. A month later, however, they were routed by Budennyi and the Reds advanced on Warsaw. Lenin's aim had been to race for Berlin, fondly expecting the German proletariat to rise. Tukhachevsky claimed he would bring Communism to London and Paris "over the corpse of White Poland on the road to worldwide conflagration".[103] Instead, the Reds were defeated in the Battle of Warsaw in August.

If the Reds had won the battle of Warsaw, it is unlikely that world capitalism would have toppled. What actually happened was minimal. The Spartacists attempted a rising in Berlin in January 1919; their leaders Rosa Luxemburg and Karl Liebknecht were executed after it was suppressed. Other revolutions were attempted in March 1919 in Munich, which speedily failed and more significantly, in Hungary under Bela Kun, also in March. There a Red Terror took place. Banks and industry were nationalised and the large estates seized, accompanied by considerable violence, with Catholic priests hanged. It was crushed in August 1919, following a Romanian invasion. Kun organised the Red Terror in the Crimea in 1920–21. During Stalin's Great Purge of the late 1930s, Kun was accused of Trotskyism, arrested, tried, and swiftly executed.

Terror, looting and the attack on the Church

As the Bolshevik regime came under both internal and external pressure, it resorted to terror. As it ran out of money, it looted Russia. And looting the Church led to resistance from Church supporters.

The economic consequences of the Revolution were massive. Banks, factories and farms were nationalised in December 1917: the great banks had been "the lifeblood of the pre-war economy", financing railway construction, timber, mining and manufacturing.[104] By 1919, industrial production had fallen to 26 per cent of the 1913 level; by 1920 to 18 per cent. Oil production was down to 42 per cent, coal to 27 per cent, iron ore to 2.4 per cent. Agriculture declined less but was down to 38 per cent in 1920. The collapsed production of locomotives, from 1000 annually in the years before 1917, down to 40 in 1919, wrecked transportation. So food supplies to Petrograd and Moscow were further squeezed; they became "ghost towns", with the pre-war population of Petrograd of 2.5 million down to 750,000. Moscow fared little better.[105]

Trotsky was enthralled about the use of terror, stimulated by the example of the French Revolution. Years later, in 1940 shortly before he was murdered in Mexico by Stalin's assassin, he claimed: "we too stood for terror but for mass terror realised by the revolutionary class." Before the October Revolution during demonstrations against the Provisional Government, he told the Kronstadt naval garrison "… heads must roll, blood must flow … the strength of the French Revolution was in the machine that made the enemies of the people shorter by a head …" As soon as he had power after October 1917 he openly called for the application of mass terror against "enemies of the people", adding: "No intermediate policy exists. There is no going back. We're introducing the dictatorship of the proletariat. We'll force people to work."[106]

In 1924, he declared: "The party in the final analysis is always right because the party is the sole historical instrument given to the proletariat for the solution of its fundamental tasks."[107] His ally, Grigory Zinoviev spelt out: "We must carry along with us 90 million out of the 100 million of Soviet Russia's population. As for the rest, we have nothing to say to them. They must be annihilated."[108]

State terror seems to have been accelerated by the assassination attempt on 30 August 1918 on Lenin by Fanny Kaplan in Moscow, with one bullet puncturing his lung. On the same day the head of the Petrograd Cheka was assassinated. Meanwhile, the Tsar, the Tsarina and their family had been murdered on the night of 16–17 July, according to the most recent research, on Lenin's personal orders. A Right SRs rising in Yaroslavl, led by Boris Savinkov, Kerensky's acting war minister during the Kornilov affair, was brutally suppressed by 21 July, after days of shelling of the city: 428 of Savinkov's supporters were shot. Savinkov escaped into exile, but was lured back to the Soviet Union in 1924, tried and sentenced to death. This was commuted to ten years' imprisonment; he committed suicide, or was murdered by the OGPU, successor to the Cheka, in the Lubyanka, in May 1925.

Lenin telegraphed the Bolsheviks of Penza on 10 August 1918 over the revolt of "kulak districts", ordering: "You must make an example of these people. Hang (I mean hang publicly, so that people see it) at least one hundred kulaks, rich bastards and known bloodsuckers …" These words were kept secret during the Soviet period. If his views were doubted, he had also stated: "Surely you do not imagine that we shall be victorious without applying the most cruel revolutionary terror?" And Trotsky announced on 31 August that various deserters had been shot, including the "cowardly liars who played sick". A Sovnarkom decree on 5 September legalised summary executions and the establishment of concentration camps near all military fronts.[109]

On 4 September, the day after Kaplan's execution, Jakov Sverdlov, the chairman of the Bolshevik Central Executive Committee, announced the reprisals known as the Red Terror. The soviets would launch "merciless mass terror against the enemies of the revolution", while anyone spreading rumours against the regime "will be arrested immediately and sent to a concentration camp", while "all persons participating in White Guard organisations, conspiracies and rebellions must be executed by shooting …" Dzerzhinsky added: "We stand for organised terror. This should be frankly admitted. Terror is an absolute necessity during times of revolution …"[110]

The Cheka took thousands of captives from the middle and upper classes, from former tsarist officials, landowners, priests, lawyers, bankers and merchants. Some were immediately shot, others kept as hostages. Across the country nearly 15,000 executions took place in the first two months of the Terror. Among tsarist officials executed on 5 September was A N Khvostov, former Minister of the Interior. By 1920 there were 84 concentration camps containing "class enemies".[111]

Lenin overrode Zinoviev and Bukharin who tried to moderate the powers of the secret police. When Zinoviev tried to restrain attacks on middle-class people in Petrograd, Lenin "was incandescent": no class enemy, he said "should be allowed to feel safe under Soviet rule". As the Cheka alone could not do everything, the workers "had to be let loose".[112]

In an echo of the Paris September Massacres of 1792, tribunals were set up in Moscow's prisons "which summarily executed hundreds of suspected spies". The following, from G I Petrovsky, the People's Commissar for Internal Affairs in 1918–19, might easily have come from Hitler or Himmler: "No weakness or indecision can be tolerated during this period of mass terror." And it was Petrovsky who declared in the face of Ukrainian famine: "We know that millions are dying. That is unfortunate, but the glorious future of the Soviet Union will justify that." Other thugs declared their own vileness. Martin Latsis, a Cheka commander, explained: "We do not wage war against individuals. We are exterminating the bourgeoisie as a class," adding "As far as the bourgeoisie are concerned, the tactics of mass extermination must be introduced." As for the Ukraine, I I Rheingold, a very un-Wagnerian Bolshevik official, proclaimed: "Sooner or later we will have to exterminate, simply physically destroy, the Cossacks, or at least the vast majority of them," while an anonymous Bolshevik order called for "… the complete, immediate and decisive destruction of the Cossackry as a specific cultural and economic group … and the formal liquidation of the Cossackry."[113]

Members of the former middle class saw their homes confiscated and possessions seized, while they were placed in the lowest category for food rations – bordering starvation – and forced to do heavy labour, frequently with fatal consequences. Obtaining accurate totals of those who perished during the 1918–21 Red Terror is difficult. Martin Sixsmith gives an estimate of half a million killed in the three years to 1921, while 1 to 2 million fled abroad. Sean McMeekin states that nearly 15,000 perished in the first two months alone after Kaplan's assassination attempt.[114]

As in France in the 1790s, the Church became a target. Russian churches were filled with millions of vessels made out of precious metals, especially silver, as well as icons and other artwork. Icons and service books were destroyed for scrap metal in such a clumsy way that these objects yielded 40 or 50 times less than their original worth.[115]

An argument later given for the need to loot the Church was "famine". Patriarch Tikhon asked Lenin for permission for the Church to buy food supplies directly and set up relief points in famine areas. Lenin seems to have taken offence at this intervention and arrested the leaders of Tikhon's famine relief committee, exiling them to the far north. While Tikhon was subjected to house arrest and "deposed" on 12 May 1922, Metropolitan Veniamin was arrested as a counter-revolutionary, tried and executed with three other clergy on 12–13 August 1922.

Regarding priests resisting church confiscations, Lenin ordered Molotov: "We must put down all resistance with such brutality that they will not forget it for decades."[116] According to Soviet sources, nearly 700 clergy and parishioners were killed attempting to protect church property between February and May 1918. Lenin's fear of the peasantry caused him to slacken his attack on the Church later in 1918. By 1921 the peasants had been devastated by famine so the attack was renewed. In February 1922 the Bolsheviks started a national anti-religious campaign, using machine guns and artillery in various conflicts. Show trials ensued in Moscow and Petrograd in April 1922, with many executions, Lenin wanting to be informed "on a daily basis" how many priests had been shot. The best estimates of clergy casualties between 1917 and 1921 are around 1500, with the regime itself estimating that at least 28 bishops and 1215 clergy were killed, as well as around 20,000 parishioners.[117]

As Lenin's health declined, Trotsky took over the responsibility for raiding Church treasures. By spring 1922 over a thousand violent clashes had occurred between Trotsky's raiders and Church defenders, both in the countryside and in cities such as Rostov on Don, Smolensk, Novgorod, Moscow and Petrograd. McMeekin estimates that by April 1922 the Petrograd looters had collected 30 tons of silver, about 145 pounds of gold, 3690 diamonds, and that by June 1922, the provincial looting teams had taken a quarter ton of gold, 167 tons of silver, 12,124 diamonds and brilliants, and 48 pounds of pearls.[118]

So widespread were the Bolshevik expropriations that Russian children played a game called "Search and Requisition". Many believers, even those sympathetic to Bolshevism, "had a profound attachment to church property", and a majority of the later Soviet population self-identified as religious "even in the forbidding context of the official Soviet census of 1937".[119]

In the process of looting privately owned bank accounts, the Bolsheviks encountered problems in accessing the safes in bank vaults, where the metallic doors had so rusted that they could not be opened. The Bolsheviks also seized Armenia's national church treasure brought to Moscow for safekeeping in 1915 and the Romanian gold reserve and other Romanian treasures sent to Russia in 1916.[120]

The revenue raised by the sales of purloined gold and other precious metals abroad in 1921 (about $200 million, or the equivalent of $20 billion in 2009) was devoted not to famine relief but to the purchase of expensive military aircraft and other weapons for use in the civil war, as well as luxury food for the Bolshevik leaders. The latter also used over 16,000 gold roubles on spare parts from London for their fleet of Rolls-Royces. In 1927–28, the Soviet government started major sales of paintings by European Old Masters, along with rare Caucasian and Persian carpets and even the crown the empress Alexandra had worn at her 1894 wedding. McMeekin also records the role of Armand Hammer, petromagnate and later philanthropist, in selling "Romanov treasures" to the American wealthy during the 1930s.[121]

This passage from the closing paragraphs of *Heist* should stand, as McMeekin intended ("so few people know the first thing about it") as a memorial to all who suffered from the Revolution: "Who will speak for the pre-Revolutionary Russian aristocracy, the icon artists and icon worshippers, the … merchants, bankers, army officers, … the town artisans and peasant kulaks … the émigré intelligentsia, who lost their homes and their entire beloved civilisation? The patrimony of Russia belonged above all to them … until it was robbed from them at gunpoint, laundered by cynical middlemen and finally scattered to the four corners of the earth."[122]

Lenin: the end

On the eve of the 1920 harvest, with the Whites largely defeated, grain requisitions by armed procurement squads caused large scale revolts in Russia, Ukraine, the Caucasus and west Siberia. "The Civil War was extended by nearly a full year" as a result of this.[123] In February 1920 Trotsky had proposed the partial repeal of these requisition measures, pointing out the vicious cycle created of peasant hoarding, state violence, reduction of the sown area and rebellions. Lenin rejected this, indulging his vituperation towards the kulaks.[124]

Lenin's policy, and drought led to harvest failures and famine in 1921, with several million dying (the figure of 5 million is given), largely in Ukraine. Thus the New Economic Policy (NEP) replaced the draconian measures of War Communism. While famine relief largely came from American and West European charities, "without the NEP, the Soviet state would have been overwhelmed by popular rebellions". On 8 March 1921, Lenin told the Tenth Party Congress about the NEP; then, fearing that they might think he "was going soft," he added "The peasant must do a bit of starving so as to relieve the factories and towns from complete starvation … "[125]

March 1921 saw the revolt of the previously hard-line naval garrison in Kronstadt, demanding an end to terror, grain requisitions and one-party rule. Lenin demanded ferocious reprisals and Trotsky vowed the rebels would be "shot like partridges".[126] Of the survivors over 2100 were executed and another 6500 sent to prisons or concentration camps mainly in the North where nearly three quarters would die in a year. The Red Army suffered 10,000 casualties in suppressing the revolt.

A large revolt also occurred in Tambov province, involving 50,000 peasant partisans. General (later Marshal) Tukhachevsky was sent to suppress it in May 1921, with an army of 100,000 and a vast number of imported armaments, including aeroplanes and poison gas bought by Zinoviev in Germany. Tukhachevsky ordered: "The forests where the bandits are hiding are to be cleared out by the poison gas … calculated so that the layer of gas penetrates the forest and kills everyone hiding there." 15,000 peasants were shot or gassed and another 50,000 sent to forced labour camps. (Tukhachevsky became one of the leading victims of Stalin's Great Purge in 1937–38).[127]

While Kamenev pushed for justice to be formal and open, Lenin said that "bandits" should be shot on the spot and "the speed and force of the repressions" should be intensified. He declared, "the greater the number of the representatives of reactionary clergy and reactionary bourgeoisie we succeed in shooting on this premise [ie treason], the better."[128] Bukharin and Karl Radek promised that if the Mensheviks and SRs were put on trial, they would not be executed: Lenin denounced these two for making unnecessary concessions. He obtained a show trial of the SRs, but not one of the Mensheviks and, against his wishes, the death penalty was not imposed. In contrast, the Politburo sanctioned the executions he had wanted of Orthodox Church personnel.

Lenin suffered a massive stroke in May 1922, with his whole right side rendered immobile. Recognising Stalin's unscrupulous ambition as General

Secretary, with control over party membership, Lenin proposed, in his political testament in January 1923, "to comrades that they should devise a means of removing him from this job", and appointing someone who "should be more tolerant, more polite and more attentive towards comrades".[129] With this testament unpublished, on 21 January 1924 Lenin died.

Opinion outside Russia is relatively tolerant of Lenin and Trotsky, undeservedly so, as the evidence cited above indicates.

Aftermath: Stalin and the spread of Communism

Stalin is still revered by many in Russia, largely on account of his wartime leadership. Outside Russia, he would adorn a monstrosity pinnacle adjacent to Hitler, with equal monstrosities such as Mao Tse-Tung only omitted because less is popularly known about them and their victims.

Stalin deliberately ordered the killing, torturing, and deporting to the gulags of some hundreds of thousands of "comrades". Official records indicate nearly 682,000 executed in 1937–38, but other estimates put the total number of "political" deaths between 1930 and 1953, including deaths in detention, at between 1.5 and 1.7 million, while an estimated 18 million passed through the gulag system. For example, of the 2000 who attended the 17th Communist Party Congress in 1934, 1100 were arrested, and by 1939 two thirds of those arrested had been executed.[130]

The total dying in the 1932–33 Ukraine famine was between 2 and 4 million, and the total perishing through the collectivisation of agriculture between 1928 and 1940 could amount to 10 million.[131]

After 1939 these excesses were not confined to Russia, but accompanied the establishment of Communist regimes in all the East European "satellites" following their occupation by the Red Army. Over 20,000 Polish army officers, political leaders, government officials, doctors and intellectuals were murdered in Katyn forest and elsewhere in spring 1940.[132] Various estimates of the numbers of Poles deported to Siberia or killed during the war years exist: in 2009, the 70th anniversary of the Soviet invasion, the Polish Institute of National Remembrance, using sources revealed since the fall of Communism, estimated a total Polish civilian death toll of 150,000.

Similar excesses occurred in the other East European countries "liberated" by the Red Army in 1944–45. In attempting to take over Greece, the Greek Communists were involved in two civil wars, one in 1944–45, ending with intervention by British forces, and a longer and bloodier one, between 1946 and 1949. The casualties incurred during the Soviet suppression of revolts in East Germany in 1953, Poland in 1956 and Czechoslovakia in 1968, in full glare of the world's media, were relatively slight. In the notorious case of Hungary in 1956, however, 2500 were killed and 20,000 wounded, with 229 executed afterwards, 22,000 imprisoned and 200,000 became refugees.

These last paragraphs exclude the spread of Communism to China, North Korea, Vietnam and Cambodia. While these resulted more from intrinsic circumstances, Lenin's and Stalin's Soviet Union played a key role in bringing these various regimes to life, as it did with Castro's Cuba, Mengistu's horrible regime in Ethiopia, and elsewhere. Without Soviet support for extreme nationalists in Southern Africa, including Rhodesia/Zimbabwe, these countries might have developed more balanced black-white partnerships, perhaps with benefits elsewhere in Africa.[133] Together, all these form the heritage of the events of 1917, as does Putin's invasion of Ukraine in 2022.

FOOTNOTES

1 Pipes, *Three Whys, op cit*, pp7–8.
2 Dominic Lieven, *Nicholas II, Emperor of All the Russias*, BCA, 1994, p247, hereafter Lieven, *Nicholas*.
3 Sean McMeekin, *The Russian Revolution: A New History,* Profile Books, 2017, pp*xv–xvi*, hereafter McMeekin, *Revolution*.
4 Dominic Lieven, *Towards the Flame: Empire, War and the End of Tsarist Russia*, Allen Lane, 2015, p67, hereafter Lieven, *Flame*; McMeekin, *Revolution, op cit*, p12.
5 Lieven, *Nicholas, op cit*, pp16–17.
6 McMeekin, *Revolution, op cit*, p20; Service, *Trotsky, op cit*, pp60, 66.
7 Lieven, *Nicholas, op cit*, p18.
8 *Ibid*, pp116–17.
9 Lieven, *Flame, op cit,* pp92–93, 97.
10 See for example, Lieven, *Flame, op cit*, p167.
11 *Ibid*, p61.
12 Both quotes, Lieven, *Nicholas, op cit*, pp78–79.
13 Quoted, *ibid*, p84.
14 Quoted, *ibid*, p87.
15 Lieven, *Flame, op cit,* p85.
16 Lieven, *Nicholas, op cit*, –37.
17 *Ibid*, pp139–40.
18 McMeekin, *Revolution, op cit*, p37.

19 Quotes, Lieven, *Nicholas, op cit*, p146, and McMeekin, *Revolution, op cit*, p42.
20 Lieven, *Nicholas, op cit*, p150.
21 *Ibid,* p149.
22 *Ibid,* p150–51.
23 McMeekin, *Revolution, op cit*, pp45–46.
24 *Ibid*, p*xvii*.
25 Simon Dixon, "The Assassination of Stolypin", in Tony Brenton, editor , *Historically Inevitable? Turning Points of the Russian Revolution,* Profile books, 2016, pp29–30, hereafter Brenton, ed.
26 Lieven, *Nicholas, op cit*, pp183–84.
27 Dixon, *op cit*, p39.
28 See Chapter Four.
29 Lieven, *Nicholas, op cit,* p180.
30 *Ibid*, p184.
31 *Ibid*, p186.
32 Lieven, *Flame, op cit,* pp109, 112, 172, 174.
33 Lieven, *Nicholas, op cit*, pp196 and 205; Lieven, *Flame, op cit,* p103.
34 Lieven, *Flame, op cit,* p305.
35 McMeekin, *Revolution, op cit*, p59.
36 Lieven, *Flame, op cit,* pp319, 321.
37 *Ibid*, pp323–24.
38 McMeekin, *Revolution, op cit*, p59; Lieven, *Flame, op cit*, pp327, 337.
39 McMeekin, *Revolution, op cit*, p64;

Lieven, *Flame, op cit,* p162.

40 Norman Stone, *The Eastern Front 1914–1917,* Hodder and Stoughton, 1975, pp166–67.

41 McMeekin, *Revolution, op cit,* pp66–68.

42 Stone, *op cit,* p187.

43 Lieven, *Nicholas, op cit,* p213.

44 Stone, *op cit,* pp183–84.

45 Robert Service, *Lenin: A Biography* Pan Macmillan, 2010, p239, hereafter Service, *Lenin.*

46 McMeekin, *Revolution, op cit,* pp70–72; McMeekin, *History's Greatest Heist – The Looting of Russia by the Bolsheviks,* Yale UP, 2009, p*xxi,* hereafter McMeekin, *Heist.*

47 McMeekin, *Revolution, op cit,* p92.

48 Pipes, *Three Whys, op cit,* p25.

49 McMeekin, *Revolution, op cit,* p84.

50 *Ibid,* pp76–77.

51 *Ibid,* pp77–78; the last two quotes Lieven, *Nicholas, op cit,* p228.

52 McMeekin, *Revolution, op cit,* pp84–87.

53 *Ibid,* p101.

54 *Ibid,* p112–13.

55 Quoted, *ibid,* p114.

56 Donald Crawford, "The Last Tsar", in Brenton, ed, *op cit,* p67.

57 McMeekin, *Revolution, op cit,* pp106–07.

58 *Ibid,* pp108, 112.

59 Lieven, *Flame, op cit,* p352.

60 Crawford, *op cit,* pp75–76; McMeekin, *Revolution, op cit,* p115.

61 Lieven, *Nicholas, op cit,* p232.

62 Crawford, *op cit,* pp79–81.

63 *Ibid,* pp87, 90.

64 McMeekin, *Revolution, op cit,* pp116–22.

65 Lieven, *Nicholas op cit,* pp234–36.

66 McMeekin, *Revolution, op cit,* pp138, 148.

67 *Ibid,* p145 for the words quoted; the whole episode, pp140–46.

68 Service, *Lenin, op cit,* p234, last quote McMeekin, *op cit,* p129.

69 Winston Churchill, *The World Crisis,* Volume V, Butterworth, 1923–31, p73.

70 Catherine Merridale, *Lenin on the Train,* Penguin Books, 2017 chapter 5.

71 Both quotes, *ibid,* pp241, 253.

72 McMeekin, *Revolution, op cit,* p132; Service *Lenin, op cit,* p294.

73 Service, *Lenin, op cit,* pp240–41.

74 *Ibid,* p295–96.

75 *Ibid,* p297; emphasis in original quotation.

76 McMeekin, *Revolution, op cit,* pp167,172.

77 Richard Pipes, "Kornilov Affair", in Brenton, ed, *op cit,* p111.

78 McMeekin, *Revolution, op cit,* p184; Pipes, "Kornilov Affair", *op cit,* p111.

79 McMeekin, *Revolution, op cit,* pp186–88.

80 Quoted, Pipes, "Kornilov Affair", *op cit,* p120.

81 Pipes, *Three Whys, op cit,* pp50, 109; McMeekin, *Revolution, op cit,* p187.

82 McMeekin, *Revolution, op cit,* p193.

83 *Ibid,* pp204–05.

84 Quoted Orlando Figes, "The 'Harmless Drunk': Lenin and the October Insurrection", in Brenton, ed, *op cit,* p129.

85 McMeekin, *Revolution, op cit,* pp202–03.

86 Figes, *op cit,* p132.

87 Service, *Lenin, op cit,* p305.

88 Figes, *op cit,* p123.

89 Pipes, *Three Whys, op cit,* p60.

90 McMeekin, *Revolution, op cit,* p206.

91 Quoted Figes, *op cit,* p138.

92 Quoted Service , *Stalin, A Biography,* Pan Macmillan, 2010, p339.

93 Tony Brenton, "The Short Life and Early Death of Russian Democracy January 1918", in Brenton, ed, *op cit,* p157.

94 McMeekin, *Revolution, op cit,* p227–28.

95 The Krylenko episode from Robert Conquest, *The Great Terror: A Reassessment,* OUP, 1990 p249.

96 McMeekin, *Revolution, op cit,* p263.

97 *Ibid,* pp263–68.

98 This argument, with quotes, from Lieven, *Nicholas, op cit,* pp248–49.

99 McMeekin, *Revolution, op cit*, p285 footnote.
100 *Ibid*, p286.
101 Evan Mawdsley, "Sea Change in the Civil War", in Brenton, ed, *op cit*, p214.
102 Martin Sixsmith, *Russia, A 1000 year Chronicle of the Wild East,* BBC Books, 2011, subsequently *op cit*, p228.
103 Quoted, *ibid*, p227.
104 McMeekin, *Heist, op cit*, p25.
105 McMeekin, *Revolution, op cit*, pp275–77; also McMeekin, *Heist op cit,*.
106 Quoted in Service, *Trotsky, op cit*, pp90, 109, 113, 172, 190.
107 Quoted, *ibid*, p323.
108 George Leggett, *The Cheka: Lenin's Political Police,* Clarendon Press, 1981, p. 114.
109 McMeekin, *Revolution, op cit*, p266–7; Leggett, *op cit*, p57; Service, *Lenin, op cit*, p365.
110 Martin Sixsmith, "Fanny Kaplan's attempt to kill Lenin, August 1918", hereafter Sixsmith, "Kaplan", in Brenton, ed, *op cit*, p193.
111 McMeekin, *Revolution, op cit*, p301.
112 Service's paraphrase, *Lenin, op cit*, p401.
113 Fred E. Beal, *Proletarian Journey,* Hillman-Curl, Inc, 1937, p310; Bruce Lincoln, *Red Victory: A History of the Russian Civil War*, Simon and Schuster 1989, p160; Peter Holquist, *Making War, Forging Revolution: Russia's Continuum of Crisis, 1914–1921,* Harvard University Press, 2002, pp166, 192, 194–95.
114 Sixsmith, "Kaplan", *op cit*, pp193–4, 195–6; McMeekin, *Revolution, op cit*, p265–67.
115 McMeekin, *Heist, op cit*, p90.
116 Quoted Sixsmith, "Kaplan", *op cit*, p198.
117 McMeekin, *Heist, op cit*, p83.
118 McMeekin, *Revolution, op cit*, p331.
119 Catriona Kelly, "The Bolsheviks and the Church", in Brenton, ed, *op cit*, pp248, 254, 259.
120 McMeekin, *Heist, op cit*, pp32, 66, 86.
121 *Ibid*, pp77, 219.
122 *Ibid*, p221.
123 Erik Landis, "Fate of the Soviet Countryside", in Brenton, ed, *op cit*, p219.
124 Service, *Lenin, op cit*, p399.
125 Quoted *ibid*, pp422, 426, respectively.
126 Quoted McMeekin, *Revolution, op cit* p317.
127 McMeekin, *Revolution, op cit*, p319, *Heist, op cit*, p165.
128 Service, *Lenin, op cit*, pp441–2.
129 *Ibid*, p469.
130 Sixsmith, "Kaplan", *op cit*, p317.
131 *Ibid*, pp260, 263.
132 See George Sanford, "The Katyn Massacre and Polish-Soviet Relations, 1941–43", in Journal of Contemporary History *2006,* Vol 41 (1) pp95–111.
133 See Nicholson, *op cit*, pp64, 236–38.

Chapter Seven:
Britain in Europe: From Churchill's Zurich Speech to the fall of Thatcher 1945–90

"I don't like it. If you open that Pandora's box, you never know what Trojan 'orses will fly out." (Ernest Bevin, Foreign Secretary, re Britain in 1949 possibly joining the Council of Europe, which he mistakenly thought would be a supranational body; quoted in *Britain & Europe In a Troubled World,* Vernon Bogdanor, Yale UP, 2020, p43)

"There is a total gulf in politics today ... between those who were brought up in the 1930s and served in the war, and those who didn't. It's a very strange and almost indefinable difference". (Lord Whitelaw, interview in *Woman's Own,* 7 May 1988, quoted by Peter Hennessy, *Never Again: Britain 1945-51,* Penguin, 2006, p4)

A constitutional revolution?

Irrespective of the merits of the UK joining and remaining in the European Community, David Cameron's voluntary decision in 2013 to propose an in-or-out referendum was a prime example of governmental abdication of authority.

A referendum might have been feasible to endorse a Government decision, backed by Parliament, to leave the EU, thus reversing the decision of the 1975 referendum. Even so, the device is a dubious one, condemned in one quotation by two quite contrasted but highly respected political leaders: Margaret Thatcher observed in 1975, "Perhaps the late Lord Attlee was right when he said that the referendum was a device of dictators and demagogues." Referenda (called "plebiscites") were used by Napoleons I and III to cement their power. The device obtained some UK legitimacy when used in the context of Scottish and Welsh devolution. The liberal intelligentsia which normally governs this country has denied the public a referendum on capital punishment, fearing what the outcome might be.

If enough people really gave priority to leaving the EU, over and above other desirables, the constitutional method, however difficult, would be to elect a majority of MPs committed to voting for EU exit. That is how the leaders of Tariff Reform in the early 20th century hoped to succeed.[1] In his darker moments, Cameron feared that something like this might happen, starting with the Carswells and Recklesses (where are they now, one might ask?) He feared that an upsurge for UKIP might damage the Conservatives. He insulted UKIP's leaders, rather than treating UKIP as another opposition party. Nor did he for a moment contemplate the idea that Brexit pressures might be frustrated by cross-party coalitions, in the national interest, such as happened after 1846 and in 1931, as well as during war-time in the 20th century.

So these final two chapters are a history of how British political leaders failed to embrace the European opportunity when it was first offered, and when they might have moulded it to suit Britain's traditions. And then how other (Conservative) leaders were bullied by feuding and occasionally mutinous MPs. The political significance in Conservative ranks of the single currency issue will become apparent; even after it had lost relevance in the early 2000s, it had clearly succeeded in poisoning the well.

And significantly, once the Gaitskell "thousand years of history" lament, Wilson's shilly-shallying and the 1983 Footite "leave the EEC" manifesto, were each left behind, the Labour Party remained largely immune to the strife which beset the Tories. Perhaps this indicates Labour's obtaining political maturity, though respect is owed to Labour opponents of EEC membership including Douglas Jay, Peter Shore, Bryan Gould, and Tony Benn. Tory divisions were the main contributing factor to their rout in the 1997 general election, at a time when the UK economy was in remarkably good shape. Continuing argument contributed to substantial electoral defeats in 2001 and 2005. Most Conservative leaders after Eden saw their careers damaged and sometimes terminated by the Europe issue.

This chapter will describe British perceptions of the weaknesses in the original structure of the EEC, ensuring from the start a lack of enthusiasm in the UK towards the political case for involvement. For supporters, who throughout the UK's 43 years of membership, 1973–2016, were frequently exceeded by opponents according to opinion polls, the case for membership remained overwhelmingly commercial. Thus Mrs Thatcher supported the EEC as essentially a trading framework and "neither shared nor took very seriously the idealistic rhetoric" of others in Europe.[2]

The geopolitical dimension

Whatever interests Britain may have outside Europe – and these were and are considerable – within Europe she has been seen as one leg of a three-legged stool, the other two legs comprising France and the major power to her east, whether this was the Holy Roman Empire, the Habsburg realms, or, since the mid-19th century, Germany. For two centuries after the 1660s, Britain had looked to this third leg to help counterbalance an overmighty France. Subsequently, Britain was obliged to aid France against Germany. Every UK town and village has memorials to those who served and died in the two great wars in which Germany was the enemy. And visits to UK military or naval museums, or to many churches and stately homes, will see evidence of the earlier warfare against France.

As the late Sir Crispin Tickell, who as a diplomat assisted the 1970–72 successful negotiations on entry and was later *chef de cabinet* to Roy Jenkins as President of the Commission, stated shortly after the 2016 vote to leave "We realised that if the French wanted us in to counterbalance the Germans and the Germans wanted us in to counterbalance the French, it was important that we should play a strong political role."[3]

Harold Macmillan recognised in August 1950 that "the French are beginning to see that to federate with Germany and Italy would be to put France, in due course, under German control … What an opportunity for British diplomacy, if it existed."[4]

The great Disraeli had also recognised this challenge, declaring in 1879 that "if that country" – he did not name Britain – "from a perverse interpretation of its insular geographical position, turns an indifferent ear to the feelings and the fortunes of Continental Europe, such a course would, I believe, only end in it becoming an object of general plunder." Margaret Thatcher, always attracted by telling epigrams, used the same quotation in launching the Conservative campaign for a Yes vote in the 1975 EEC Referendum.

This warning was also expressed by that traditional Imperialist, Julian Amery, in his maiden speech in the House of Lords in the Second Reading debate on the Maastricht Treaty Bill on 8 June 1993: "I cannot help thinking that if we were to withdraw from the Maastricht Treaty Germany would lead a smaller Europe. I have been taught by history that a Europe united without us could one day become a Europe united against us. Let us not run that risk unless we have to."[5]

Early British reservations

To understand what went wrong after 1990, it is necessary to go back more than 40 years previously.

Britain had a different constitutional history, with Parliament beginning by the 13th century, and gradually asserting itself. And Britain was never ruled or occupied by Fascists or Nazis, whereas all the other original EEC members had to regain their freedom after 1945.

However, Jean Monnet in August 1943 told the French National Liberation Committee, "There will be no peace in Europe if the states are reconstituted on the basis of national sovereignty … The European states must constitute themselves into a federation." In Bogdanor's view, those Monnet targeted "were the elites, who would construct Europe by stealth, using economic means to lock nation states together", while the people "would be almost unaware of the process until it had become irreversible".⁶ This might have been tolerated in the deferential Europe of the 1950s where unelected officials had great prestige. It has had decreasing power since.

Monnet's judgement was not even then unchallenged. In a 1962 booklet, Sir John Biggs-Davison quotes as a chapter heading the words of Michel Debré, first Prime Minister (1959–62) of the French Fifth Republic: "The reality of Europe is the Nation. Europe herself is not a Nation."⁷

So Monnet drafted the Schuman Declaration in 1950 stating "Europe ... will be built through concrete achievements which first create a *de facto* solidarity". This would involve the pooling of coal and steel industries (the ECSC), essential for fighting war, and the "setting up of common foundations for economic development as a first step in the federation of Europe".

With Marshall Aid after 1947 the Americans sought a Europe which "could ... cease to be a drain on the US economy while becoming an ever more effective buffer against Soviet expansion". The Organisation for European Economic Cooperation (OEEC) was set up to administer Marshall Aid. For these reasons "the record does indeed show that the pressure was on from Washington to lever Britain into an economically united Europe".⁸

Monnet was very much aware of British opposition to federalism, which "no doubt, explains why he and Schuman gave London no advance warning of the Coal and Steel plan for fear that the British would seek to pluck out its federalist entrails before negotiations with Germany, Italy and the Benelux countries even began".⁹ This "plucking out" opportunity was later recalled by Macmillan and others. So the British government ensured that the Council of Europe was and remained an "innocuous and purely advisory body" to the detriment of what later might have become an alternative approach for Britain, in contrast to what was then on offer; the ECSC.

Harold Macmillan, speaking for the Conservative opposition, drew on his own memories of Stockton and unemployment in the 1930s: "Our people are not going to hand over to any supranational authority the right to close down our pits or steel-works." But he was critical of Labour's generally negative view and became a keen supporter in 1947 of the British Committee of the European League for Economic Co-operation (ELEC). In his diary for 7 April 1947 he set out his aim: "we hope, by detailed study of ... trade relations ... and of monetary policy (including widening and strengthening of the sterling area) to prove our case that Europe and the Commonwealth should be complementary and mutually supporting in a dollar-dominated world." In 1949 Macmillan became one of six Conservative delegates to the Consultative Assembly of the Council of Europe, established that year. When divisions opened between those wanting co-operation and the federalists who wanted formal integration, he strongly opposed federalism."¹⁰

In August 1950, Macmillan and Eccles, on behalf of the British Conservative delegation to the Council of Europe, proposed a non-supranational element to the ECSC: the French rejected it. So a supranational ECSC was firmly in place when the Conservatives returned to office in October 1951. An indication of the grandiose ideas already existing came from the head of the British delegation to the Coal and Steel High Authority: the ECSC would "result in a single market with its accompanying measures of a common currency", from there the movement to "a common foreign policy and common budget for all but local requirements would be almost inevitable".¹¹

And Macmillan criticised the later initiative of the European army "to be accompanied by all the paraphernalia of the Coal and Steel plan; committees of ministers, parliamentary bodies and all the other 'organs' which the French love so much".¹²

Churchill's opportunity: Eden's dilemma 1945–55

Speaking as Foreign Secretary at Columbia University in January 1952, Anthony Eden referred to "the frequent suggestions that the United Kingdom should join a federation on the continent of Europe" commenting, "This is something which we know, in our bones, we cannot do." Eden's biographer, David Dutton, seeks to defend him from the charge, frequently made later, of allowing his scepticism to delay or frustrate any effective British involvement during the early 1950s. Perhaps the most damning remark came from Lord (Roy) Jenkins: "he, more than anyone else, was responsible for allowing Europe to be made without us in the crucial years from 1951 to 1956."¹³

Eden's vision was complex. As Foreign Secretary, and as Shadow before 1951, he believed that Churchill and Macmillan indulged in confused thinking and language, with outbursts of enthusiasm tempered by contact with reality: Dutton refers to Churchill's "visionary phase" during the war, with Eden having to "pour cold water" on his outbursts. "Too much attention had been paid to the grand flourishes" of Churchill's earlier statements "and too little to the small print"; thus he had "created expectations which he never tried to fulfil on returning to power".¹⁴

Eden's first objective was an effective world organisation, with US and, if possible, Soviet involvement. This, he hoped (somewhat unrealistically) would take care of the European problem. He feared British emphasis on Europe might encourage American isolationism and provoke Russia. With Churchill, he was anxious to provide an effective British commitment to the defence of Western

Europe, not only against Soviet Communism, but against a revived Germany. Even Boothby, a Euro-enthusiast, warned that a European army without British or American participation "must sooner or later be directed by a revived German General Staff". And like others, Eden saw the threat that a British entanglement in European plans might have for the Empire and Commonwealth. Few anticipated how quickly the Commonwealth would decline in Britain's economic and commercial life: in 1955 it provided nearly half of Britain's imports, took over half of her exports, and two thirds of her investments. Dutton quotes Oliver Harvey, then ambassador in Paris: "without the Commonwealth, Britain would be a doubtful asset to western Europe".[15]

What of Churchill? In that decade after 1945, he had the opportunity to promote a sensible future for Britain's association with a newly liberated Europe. After a promising start, the eventual verdict on his achievement must be somewhat negative.

In wartime, he responded warmly to the opportunity presented by hoped-for victory. In a presentation to a Royal Historical Society conference in 2000, the historian John Barnes stated: "The ambiguities of Churchill's position are well known and contributed, it could be said, to the suspicions felt by Paul Spaak, Jean Monnet and others about the consequences of including Britain in the building of the European Community."[16] However, even in the dark days of August 1940, when Britain's own survival was in doubt, Churchill wrote in a Cabinet paper: "After the last war people had done much constructive thinking … Something of the kind would have to be built up again: there would be a United States of Europe, and this Island would be the link connecting this Federation with the new world and able to hold the balance between the two."[17]

Before the war, Churchill had known Count Richard Coudenhove-Kalergi (1894–1972). The Coudenhoves were a wealthy Flemish family who fled to Austria during the French Revolution, while the Kalergis were a wealthy Greek family from Crete, tracing roots to Byzantine royalty; all appropriate connections for this present volume. Coudenhove had worked with others on the Continent, and with the British Imperialist, Leo Amery, through the Pan-Europa Society, founded in 1922. This author's earlier book[18] describes the collaboration between the great Franco-German duo, Briand and Stresemann, during the late 1920s and early 1930s, with Amery attending a Pan-European conference in Berlin in May 1930 where "my chief part was to make quite clear both our sympathy and our inability to take part in any Pan-European union". These earlier efforts were stifled by the Slump of 1931 and the coming to power of Hitler in 1933, but as late as 1938 Coudenhove, Churchill and Amery were discussing the subject together, with Amery describing Churchill as "an out and out European" while his own view was "we are not European though a useful link between Europe and the new world outside." This last point was echoed in Churchill's 1940 paper.

Planning and work on this subject continued before and after D-Day, with Churchill, in a Cabinet meeting of 9 May 1944, explaining his concern about Europe – "the storm centre, the place where the weather comes from", adding, that he could not "ignore the probability that the United States Government would be under strong and continuous pressure ... to withdraw troops from Europe" when the war ended.[19]

In his dramatic Zurich speech of 19 September 1946 ("Let Europe Arise") he declared "we must build a kind of United States of Europe". He did not specify what this meant, but he clearly envisaged Britain as a catalyst and partner.

An enticing counterfactual is revealed in a post-Zurich exchange Churchill had with General de Gaulle, like him, then out of office. De Gaulle replied that "if French support was to be won for the idea of European union, France must come in as a founder partner with Britain", with these two countries reaching "a precise understanding with one another upon the attitude to be adopted towards Germany".[20] Tugendhat adds that if Britain had been "on the inside" of the EEC when de Gaulle returned to power in 1958, the "approach of the two countries towards the federalist ambitions of the others would have been very similar".

In 1946, Churchill found himself collaborating with Leo Amery, whose reservations continued. To Lord Vansittart, former head of the Foreign Office, Amery wrote (2 February 1946): "No group system can live unless based on a real collective patriotism. It would weaken the patriotism of the Empire here, and even more in the Dominions, if this country by itself joined a European union ..." To a critic of the European campaign he wrote (20 June 1947): "It is perfectly true that if Europe ever got so far as to draft a federal constitution or a customs union we should be at the parting of the ways ... If meanwhile more moderate inter-European preferential schemes came into being we might even come into some arrangements on certain lines which would not interfere with the development of Empire preference."

However, he threw his weight into the European campaign after Churchill's Zurich speech, meeting for a planning lunch at Chartwell, on 30 September 1946, with Churchill, Duncan Sandys, Boothby and Julian Amery. Explaining his role, Amery later recorded in his diary for 11 December 1951 that "a United Europe is for us partly a matter of sympathy like Italian unity a century ago, partly also a practical need for our defence and prosperity." At a conference in Brussels a few days later (diary, 15 December 1951) he pointed out that "the only real solution ... was to widen the conception of unity to that of Europe and the

Commonwealth as a twin constellation. They welcomed this eagerly and I was most effectively backed by Giscard d'Estaing, the very clear-headed leading French delegate ..."[21]

Amery died in 1955, before he could witness the Suez disaster, the weakening of Dominion bonds which Suez and American-led international trade policy was to cause (the trade preferences negotiated with the Dominions at Ottawa in 1932 by the mid-1950s already had less than one third of their original value), and also before the beginning of the collapse of the colonial empire and the economic revival of Europe. Each of these strengthened the attractions of Europe.

Churchill regarded Britain as inevitably involved with whatever emerged in Europe. "We here in Great Britain have always to think of the British self-governing Dominion ... It is necessary that any policy this island may adopt towards Europe and in Europe should enjoy the full sympathy and approval of the peoples of the Dominions. But why should we suppose that they will not be with us in this cause? They feel with us that Britain is geographically and historically a part of Europe and that they also have their inheritance in Europe. If Europe united is to be a living force, Britain will have to play her full part as a member of the European family. The Dominions also know that their youth, like that of the United States, has twice in living memory traversed the immense ocean spaces to fight and die in wars brought about by European discord in the prevention of which they have been powerless ..."[22]

Unlike Amery, Churchill gave little thought to the economic underpinning of European structures. He deliberately avoided constitutional definitions. What was ingenious about Amery's existing and Macmillan's evolving concepts was that they wanted a body whose economic ties rested on a preferential relationship and whose constitutional form (assuming it had to be tighter than the loose Commonwealth arrangement) was confederal rather than federal. However, the French thought the only way to prevent a recrudescence of German ambitions was to bring them into supranational arrangements. As Dutton remarks, Macmillan's ideas "overlooked the very strong commitment on the Continent to proceed along federal lines", with no indication apparent that the Continentals would accept an "inter-governmental approach".[23]

Macmillan and Amery, in seeking to integrate the Commonwealth and Europe economically by means of preference, believed they had Churchill's backing. But Churchill had clearly not accepted the idea that an economic entity must underpin the whole: he had opposed, during the first 30 years of the 20th century, an Imperial economy based on tariffs and preference. The Amery-Macmillan alternative probably could only have been brought about in the late 1940s or very early 1950s, before Continental views hardened. And no attempt was made to educate the Conservative Party in these matters, with nothing relevant appearing in the Conservative manifestos for the 1950 or 1951 general elections.

So Churchill's government, elected on 25 October 1951, continued Labour's detachment from the Europe project. Churchill's last major pronouncement on it was a Cabinet paper of 29 November 1951, where he ranks at third place in terms of objectives a "United Europe, to which we are a separate closely – and specially – related ally and friend", beneath the Commonwealth and the "fraternal association of the English-speaking world", including the USA. But the most significant part of the paper is the passage which follows dealing with the Schuman plan for coal, steel, and eventually, wider economic union. "I never contemplated Britain joining in this plan *on the same terms* as Continental partners. We should, however, have joined in all the discussions, and had we done so, not only *a better plan would probably have emerged, but our own interests would have been watched at every stage.* Our attitude towards further economic developments on the Schuman lines resembles that [which] we adopt about the European army. We help, we dedicate, we play a part, but we are not merged and do not forfeit our insular or Commonwealth-wide character."[24]

In 1950, the French government declared that France would only agree to German rearmament within the framework of a completely integrated European army: the European Defence Community (EDC). Churchill had been persuaded in the autumn of 1951 that, although he disliked it, the EDC plan was the only one on offer and that the British might involve themselves both with it and the ECSC/Schuman project by treaties of association.

Macmillan's diary traces the retreat beginning in the early weeks of the Churchill government, noting the views of powerful colleagues. "Churchill wd like, obviously, to be loyal to the European movement … Salisbury and Lyttelton, for different reasons, are temperamentally opposed … Many in the Cabinet will fight" the two on-going projects. Macmillan himself "said that I thought the Schuman plan wd collapse and that de Gaulle wd [not] like the European army … with all its political paraphernalia. The way would then be open (and the last opportunity presented) for Britain to give a lead to Europe. The subject dropped; but in a certain atmosphere of doubt."[25]

On 29 November 1951, Macmillan recounts: "Eden has stated definitely in Rome … that we shall not join the European army. Maxwell-Fyfe has stated definitely in Strasbourg that we may do so. Reynaud says that no French assembly will vote for a European army in which Britain is not represented. But how can Britain be represented in the devitalised and denationalised army which Pleven and Monnet plan to make …" Since both plans were "doomed", Britain should take the lead: "if we stated our terms, they wd be accepted".[26]

In his memoirs, Macmillan revises his tone, describing the apparent Eden-Fyfe clash as "an unhappy misunderstanding", with Fyfe, the Home Secretary, giving an "authorised" statement and Eden replying to questions at a press conference: he thought Eden's words were "rather frigid sentiments [which] seemed to many unhelpful or even contemptuous".[27]

Five days later, at Cabinet, Eden explained that, since the (Labour) government had refused to take part in the negotiations on the European army and political co-operation, "it was too late to do so now". In fact, writing to Eden on 21 December, Macmillan stated "If we had been 'in' on the Schuman Plan or European Army Plan two years ago, we might have moulded both to our liking", but it would be "impertinence" and "folly" to "butt in at the last stage of the negotiations".[28] Macmillan told the Cabinet "that I thought the present position tragic, but that, in view of what Eden had said, we must accept it". He thought that both the Schuman and the army plans "might break down". His memoirs reiterate this point: "if we could not kill EDC openly, we need not strive to keep it alive. When EDC was dead and buried, we should then be in a position to take the initiative in organising an alternative system. I was convinced that if we stated our terms they would be accepted."[29]

Again in his memoirs, Macmillan described his alternative approach, about which, after consultation with Maxwell-Fyfe, he had written to Eden early in 1952. Highly ambitious, but at this point Britain was entitled to be ambitious, it recognised that "federation was not the only form of constitutional association between states. There could be a confederation, based on continuous consultation between Governments; a Consultative Assembly … European currencies could be linked individually or collectively to sterling; a European preferential area could be created, interlocking with our own system of Imperial Preference; and specialised but not supranational authorities could be set up for such matters as defence and heavy industry. We could certainly participate in a European army …" This latter would contain "national units of at least divisional strength, in which the joint command would be responsible, as in the NATO concept, to the different national governments". These were radical ideas, yet consistent with British traditions, but "if we did nothing, the French, German and Italian federal system – 'Little Europe' – might … come into being – but without Britain".[30]

Looking back twenty years after the event, Macmillan "never understood why Anthony Eden stood aloof". Could Macmillan have challenged Eden more forcefully than he did? Eden's biographer, David Dutton, has told the present author "I don't think Eden and Macmillan were ever close enough in personal terms to be entirely frank with one another in correspondence or conversation." In those years, Macmillan was some way down the ministerial pecking order, at

Housing. In addition to the difficulty of mounting a full-scale opposition to government foreign policy fronted by Churchill and Eden, Macmillan was politically ambitious. As Dutton adds "Macmillan was, I think, guilty of what a later generation might call 'cakeism'. Many would have seen his idea of 'confederation' as hair-splitting."

So Macmillan seems to have kept his stronger views to himself. He describes a turning point during the next few weeks; in fact, the last opportunity for Churchill to have a chance of influencing the course of European unity in a way more consistent with Britain's traditions than the route later taken. The Cabinet discussion on 18 February 1952 heard that "The French are ready to jettison any or all of the complicated constitutional machinery … round the conception of the European Army, if only they can get the British in … Churchill seems to make no effort for the European conception … Eden, therefore, and the FO, and the majority of the Cabinet – all of whom have always been against the European movement – are taking full advantage of C's strange unwillingness to defend the idea … wh he did so much to promote…" A further Cabinet on 13 March, with Eden absent convalescing from 'flu, saw Macmillan develop his argument "without any assistance. Salisbury restrained, but very hostile. Maxwell-Fyfe loyally favourable, but not powerful in his discussion. The rest, largely ignorant … Churchill, clearly uneasy, did nothing at all to help." Macmillan "seriously contemplated" resignation: but this would be "no good and wd delight those who are against us."[31]

Cabinet on 5 April saw more evidence that the French Assembly would reject the EDC "unless Britain is more directly associated". A further Cabinet on 15 May saw "a very painful discussion" about Europe, Salisbury "being almost a disciple of Beaverbrook in his isolationism … the PM is puzzled and unhappy".[32]

The timing was important. Churchill anticipated that he might stay as Prime Minister for only a year. He had just had another stroke and his wife was urging him to go to the Lords. Eden expected him to retire at any time after his election victory in late 1951; it was thought he might do so after the new Queen's coronation in June 1953. His own performance, in Parliament and elsewhere, was very variable. Why take a gamble, especially as Eden's attitude had substantial Cabinet backing. Talking to Macmillan on 1 September 1953 Churchill "said he supposed I felt he had rather let down the European movement. But it was inevitable. We had got in too late, and things had hardened."[33]

As Barnes comments: "It is easy to see why Churchill was persuaded that it was better to let matters run on … Hindsight suggests that this may have been a mistake, that when the EDC treaty failed to secure ratification in France, and WEU [Western European Union] was revived, it was too late for the latter to become an alternative model to Schuman and economic union when the European states came to consider their future. But it is possible that it was already too late in the autumn of 1951, that no move on Britain's part could have changed the course that European integration took. To be able to act, Churchill would have needed more support in the Cabinet and the Conservative party than he was likely to be able to muster."[34]

With the Churchill government standing aloof, the Continentals signed the draft treaty for a European army (the EDC) on 27 May 1952. The French asked the British to associate with this force, to hold the balance against Germany and to avoid rejection by the French Assembly, where it was opposed by both the Left and the Gaullist Right. As expected, without this British commitment, at the end of August 1954 the French Assembly rejected EDC by 319 to 264.

On 28 September 1954 Eden chaired a conference in London, which agreed that the German Federal Republic, with the occupation regime removed and sovereignty restored, should enter NATO. In late December, the French Assembly voted for this and accepted German rearmament, insisting that it should be specifically within the orbit of the Western European Union. The revived WEU, including Britain and the future Six, would be an intergovernmental body co-ordinating national armies, with its own permanent secretariat and a consultative assembly of parliamentarians. Macmillan welcomed this development: "the federal system of EDC is dead; the confederal system of Western European Union is very much alive."[35]This was premature; the WEU was never built upon. An Anglo-ECSC agreement on association was signed in London in December 1954, by Monnet and Sandys, the British Minister of Supply, but it was overtaken by events.

From Messina to Rome

In April 1955 Eden succeeded Churchill as Prime Minister. The Cabinet Committee on Relations with the Coal and Steel Community met only twice during 1955.[36] The meeting at Messina of the foreign ministers of the ECSC Six was designed to "relaunch" Europe after the EDC imbroglio. Rather ambitiously, it aimed to establish "a united Europe by the development of common institutions, the gradual fusion of national economies [and] the creation of a Common Market". The strongly pro-British Belgian foreign minister, Paul Spaak, was put in charge of a committee to take this forward. He invited the British government to send a representative. Macmillan was just taking over as Foreign Secretary. Butler, still Chancellor (but with the economy encountering "overheating") said that Eden was "bored" by the Messina plans, "even more bored than I was". On 21 June 1955 at a dinner of the OEEC, Butler referred to the conference as "some archaeological excavations" in an old Sicilian town that need not concern Britain.[37] A senior French official recalled being told by London over the telephone that Messina was a very awkward place for a Minister to get to. Indeed, Messina was about as far from Britain as one might reach within the territories of the Six.

However, Mr Russell Bretherton from the Board of Trade was sent, under the "prevailing Whitehall assumption that Britain could always associate herself with whatever emerged from Europe, if only because the continuing mutual suspicions of France and Germany made a British presence desirable to both parties".[38] Professor Dutton has told the present author: "Eden thought he had 'won' after setting up WEU. He completely underestimated (as did others) the speed with which the European movement would pick itself up from the ground. By the time that the penny dropped, it was too late for Britain to engage with this new impetus – and Eden's thoughts were focussed on the Middle East."

Many years later, Lord Thorneycroft (President of the Board of Trade in 1955) regretted that no Minister had represented Britain at Messina. "Opinion in Cabinet was too strongly adverse to Europe to commit a Cabinet minister to these negotiations at that time. I wish I *had* gone. It has had the biggest effect of any lost opportunity."[39]

However, on 29 October 1955 Bretherton, about to be withdrawn from the Spaak committee, warned London that, contrary to their hopes and expectations, the movement towards European economic integration was unlikely to collapse. While Britain took no part in negotiating what became the Common Market under the Treaty of Rome, ratified in May 1957, the Macmillan diary traces progress on Britain's alternative approach during 1956. On 4 September, now as Chancellor of the Exchequer, he "had a long talk" with Spaak "about OEEC, the Messina plan and the possibility of British association (what we call Plan G)" – the European Free Trade Area proposal. The next day Plan G was discussed by the Cabinet's Economic Policy Committee, with all the ministers present, except Home, "enthusiastic for this great venture". When it came to full Cabinet on the 14th, "all the younger men" took a favourable view, but Home put the Commonwealth difficulty, Butler "was on the whole against", as was Salisbury.[40] On 26 November (after the Suez crisis) Macmillan announced the intention to begin negotiations for an industrial free trade area.

Eden resigned in January 1957, and Macmillan became Prime Minister. His scepticism as to whether the Six would keep to what they had signed was widely shared. He sought to transform the project into "something intergovernmental", proposing a Free Trade Area, with free trade in industrial goods among all the 17 OEEC members. It would not include agriculture, so cheap food from the

Commonwealth would not be excluded. The opposition of the Six to this proposal was led by France even before de Gaulle came to power in May 1958. De Gaulle then increased this hostility.

Macmillan's rather hysterical reaction is displayed in a minute sent only to Heathcoat-Amory as Chancellor and Selwyn Lloyd as Foreign Secretary on 24 June 1958: "I feel we ought to make it quite clear to our European friends that if Little Europe is formed without a parallel development of a Free Trade Area we shall have to reconsider the whole of our political and economic attitude towards Europe … I doubt if we could remain in NATO …" And he "would be inclined to make this position clear to both de Gaulle and Adenauer".[41] Macmillan told Adenauer on 9 October 1958: "No British Government could continue to take part in the military defence of a continent which had declared economic war upon her. The United Kingdom would become isolationist." It is not clear how this impressed Adenauer.[42]

Reginald Maudling, seen then and later as a potential Prime Minister, joined the Cabinet in late 1957, and was given the task of persuading the Six to abandon their customs union proposal in favour of the free trade area. His lack of international experience led him to underestimate the task and he aroused anger by seeking to play off the Germans against the French. In November 1958, de Gaulle's Minister of Information, Jacques Soustelle, told the Press that France "contemptuously rejected" the Maudling plan. Members of the OEEC who were not in the Six, viz the three Scandinavian countries, Switzerland, Austria, Portugal and the UK now planned how to cope with the Six: the European Free Trade Association (EFTA, the Seven), resulted. In November 1959 Maudling signed the EFTA Convention in Stockholm.

The Macmillan bid and its rejection

During the first four years of Macmillan's premiership the British view of the EEC changed, influenced by various factors, principally Britain's need for a "place in the sun" as a post-Suez substitute for Empire. Of growing significance, "joining Europe" was felt to be good for the Conservatives. But were these motives likely to lead to a satisfactory outcome for Britain's long-term interests?

Back in 1956, Macmillan, as Chancellor, and Thorneycroft, President of the Board of Trade, argued to Cabinet that Commonwealth trade would in all probability decline. Thorneycroft had worked on trade policy alongside another European enthusiast, Sir Frank Lee, Permanent Secretary at the Board of Trade. Lee became Joint Permanent Secretary at the Treasury in early 1960 and the Lee Report of June 1960 (*The Six and the Seven: The Long-Term Objective*) was crucial in convincing Macmillan to seek membership of the EEC.

Macmillan had asked "What has changed since Ministers decided against joining the Common Market in 1956 and again in 1959?" He posed four tests (with the replies given to him summarised in parenthesis): it was doubtful that the EEC would see the light of day (it had done so, and Western Europe was no longer weak economically); Britain could always make her own terms (the Free Trade Area negotiations proved that wrong); it had been thought that joining the EEC would weaken relations with the USA (the USA now attached importance to the EEC's development); and it had been feared that joining would weaken links with the Commonwealth (remaining outside the EEC might be more damaging to Commonwealth relations).[43]

Macmillan also saw Britain as the link between Europe and the USA, but was aware of American perceptions of Britain's weakness. This was illustrated by the full context of Dean Acheson's famous later remark at West Point in 1962 "Britain has lost an empire and not yet found a role". Acheson had added: "the attempt to play a separate role ... apart from Europe ... based on a 'special relationship' with the United States ... based on being the head of a Commonwealth, which has no political structure, or unity, or strength ... this role is about to be played out."[44]

Party political considerations were decisive. During 1960 what Nora Beloff called the Conservative party's "thinking apparatus" (she meant the Conservative Research Department, headed then by Sir Michael Fraser) "had come to believe that a bold bid for Europe could give the party the new look it needed to win another election" – the fourth in a row. Taking account of the views of industry, commerce, and key newspapers, one unnamed key adviser in the autumn of 1960 stated that the EEC "was precisely the new challenge the Party needed", whereas Labour was "insular enough to be relied on to resist".[45] And there was movement in Europe: Chancellor Adenauer, previously opposed to Britain joining the Six, now agreed with his deputy, the Economic Affairs Minister Dr Erhard, to support Britain's application.

So on 27 July 1961 the Cabinet formally decided to apply for EEC membership. While this was approved by the Commons, over 20 Conservatives abstained; 49 Conservative MPs had already signed a motion expressing a fear that Britain's sovereignty might be threatened. Butler, in practice, and soon in title, Macmillan's deputy, was unattracted by the European idea. He was concerned both about a foreign body controlling the British economy, and over the consequences for farmers.

Macmillan's biographer refers to a curious piece of evidence. By-election reverses, starting with the dramatic loss of Orpington to the Liberals in March 1962, produced Macmillan's "night of the long knives" in late July 1962. A press indiscretion by Butler had speeded up the ministerial sackings that Macmillan was considering, and on 1 August the latter told Selwyn Lloyd, just brutally sacked as Chancellor of the Exchequer, that "he had been rushed. One day he would tell me the conspiracy again [sic] him which had forced his hand ... Butler had been plotting to divide the party on the Common Market, and bring him down." Macmillan's diary for 21 August 1962 describes Butler dining with Macmillan at Bucks Club, and after listing the disadvantages of EEC membership, saying "he had decided to support our joining the Common Market. It was too late to turn back now. It was too big a chance to miss, for Britain's wealth and strength."[46] So at the 1962 Conservative Party Conference it was Butler who retorted to the Labour leader Hugh Gaitskell's lament that the Conservatives were abandoning "a thousand years of history" with the immortal sally "for them, a thousand years of history; for us, the future!"

In fact, Lord Hailsham, Lord President of the Council, and leadership candidate in 1963, "seemed the likeliest rallying point for any resistance." Instead of plotting a coup in 1961–62, however, Hailsham simply absented himself from the 1962 Party Conference, which displayed great support for the EEC application, on the grounds that his wife was expecting a baby.[47]

If the 1990s pattern were to have been rehearsed in the 1960s, Macmillan's predecessor, since 1961 Earl of Avon, "was by far the Government's most eminent opponent" on the issue. However, despite "friendly overtures", offering publicity and funding, from Lord Beaverbrook, the leader of Conservative opponents of EEC membership, Avon, "even if he had desired to, would hardly have had the physical strength after his grave illnesses to go back into the fray".[48]

Avon in October 1962 told Lord Chandos (Oliver Lyttelton, Colonial Secretary in the early 1950s) that "the British people should know where they are going before they wake up and find themselves where they do not want to be". Further exchanges then took place between Avon, Chandos, Lord Salisbury (hostile to Macmillan since resigning in 1957) and Lord Boyd of Merton (Alan Lennox-Boyd, Colonial Secretary 1954–59), leading to Chandos and Boyd meeting Macmillan in October 1962 to express their concerns. "To Eden's dismay", Macmillan "largely succeeded in reassuring his visitors", but as Salisbury told Avon, "I wish I trusted him more; but I'm afraid that he is a very slippery customer." Avon concluded, "I myself doubt if the experiment of the Six can succeed without federation and ... we shall be faced with that decision in a few years' time ... I am sure that it must be federation in the sense of one Parliament, one foreign policy, one currency etc."[49]

Given these critics, reinforced in November 1962 by the loss in a by-election of the safe Conservative seat of South Dorset (with the intervention, as Anti-Common Market candidate, of Sir Piers Debenham, obtaining over 5000 votes), it is not surprising that Macmillan failed to take the advice, given earlier by Lord Kilmuir, the Lord Chancellor, and warn his party and the country that accession to the EEC carried serious implications for national sovereignty. Lord Tugendhat not only criticises Macmillan over this, but believes it "set a precedent for successive governments to be less than honest with the British public about EEC issues and … their constitutional implications".[50]

It is doubtful whether openness over these matters would have led to the "full-hearted" consent – those oft-repeated words – of the British public then or later. As was clear in 1960, and, as we shall see, continued to be clear, there remained serious differences between the way the British viewed the European venture and the aspirations of the Continental political elite. Lord Tugendhat has told the present author "I am sure you're right that neither Macmillan's nor Heath's colleagues would have swallowed the full Monnet vision."

Even during the earliest negotiations in Brussels, the only exceptions on Commonwealth trade that the Six would concede was for a group of African and Caribbean countries to be associate members. Other, more advanced, Commonwealth countries would be treated as "third", that is, foreign, countries.

De Gaulle warned Macmillan in June 1962 that "the thought of choosing between Europe and America is not yet fully developed in your mind". After by-election reverses, he believed that Macmillan was on his way out. Though he was angered by Macmillan's visit to Nassau in late 1962, for the Polaris missile agreement with Kennedy, the key issue for de Gaulle was the Common Agricultural Policy (CAP) "without which, he believed, there would be riots in Paris". Tugendhat quotes Robert Marjolin, the French vice-president of the newly-formed Commission: "I was convinced that if there was no agreement on a common agricultural policy, France would pull out of the Common Market." Britain joining the EEC would delay CAP agreement and threatened to "upset the delicate economic balance of the bargain between French agriculture and German industry upon which the EEC was based". For Gaullists and Christian Democrats on the Continent, a powerful agricultural sector, with a sizeable peasant community, formed essential traditional sources of military recruitment, electoral stability and a counterbalance to urban-based socialism and communism.[51]

On 14 January 1963, the day negotiations in Brussels restarted after the holiday, de Gaulle was as offensive as a friend and ally could be in his Élysée press conference. Britain "was insular … maritime … linked … to the most diverse and often the most distant countries; she pursues essentially industrial and commercial activities, and only slightly agricultural ones". With her loyalties to the Commonwealth and the USA, she had failed to put "Europe" first, "without restriction, without reserve, and in preference to anything else" (almost the words from the marriage service).

Sir Michael Fraser, Director of the Conservative Research Department, wrote that "Europe ... was to be our *deus ex machina:* it was to create a new contemporary political argument with insular Socialism; dish the Liberals by stealing their clothes; give us something *new* after 12–13 years ... give us a new place in the international sun. It was Macmillan's ace, and de Gaulle trumped it."[52]

Waiting – 1963 to 1970 – *L'Affaire Soames*

Labour Prime Minister Harold Wilson decided after the July 1966 economic crisis to apply to join the EEC. The prospects were not helped by the 18 November 1967 devaluation of the pound. Another de Gaulle press conference (the "second veto") followed on 27 November. Having regretted Britain's lack of engagement with the European project, de Gaulle suggested that this application was because of "the great economic, financial, monetary and social difficulties with which Britain is at grips", adding that success required a "radical transformation" to address Britain's chronic balance of payments problem, its sources of food supply, as well as the external liabilities of sterling resulting from its being one of the world's reserve currencies. In de Gaulle's view, Britain joining would lead to the "break-up of the Community", as Britain's economy and policy "does not at present belong to Europe as we have started to build it". He would not stand by during "the destruction of an edifice that has been built at the cost of so much hardship and in the midst of so much hope."

De Gaulle resigned as President in April 1969 after losing a constitutional referendum and was succeeded by Georges Pompidou. During the debates on UK entry during the summer of 1971, under Edward Heath, Sam White, the notable Paris correspondent of the London *Evening Standard*, declared "M Pompidou is no more wedded to the Common Market as it exists than was General de Gaulle" when the latter earlier proposed to the British Ambassador, Sir Christopher Soames, "that Britain and France should discuss the creation of something new".[53]

This episode had become known as *L'Affaire Soames*, and the present author remembers conversation about it with Julian Amery, at the time preparing to fight (successfully) the Brighton Pavilion by-election on 27 March 1969. He was a member of Amery's electoral team, staying during March with it and the family with Amery's father-in-law Harold Macmillan at the latter's house, Birch Grove, in Sussex, and witnessing dinner-table conversation. The view they held was that *L'Affaire Soames* was a missed opportunity of a deal with de Gaulle which might have suited Britain.

The present author is grateful for information from Anthony Teasdale, academic, special adviser to the Foreign Secretary 1988–90 and the Chancellor of the Exchequer 1996–97, and recently Director General of the European Parliament Research Services,[54] with recent update to the author from retired diplomat Sir Roger Carrick, who served in the British Embassy in Paris at this time.

On 4 February 1969 de Gaulle spoke at a private lunch without officials to the British Ambassador, Sir Christopher Soames and his wife Mary, Churchill's daughter, about "what he saw as the increasingly integrationist direction of the Six". De Gaulle went on to propose a "wider, looser grouping", involving the Six and the seven members of the European Free Trade Association, which included Britain. According to Soames's report, the whole would be run by a directory of the largest countries, viz France, Germany, Italy and the UK. De Gaulle suggested "far-reaching bilateral talks" between France and the UK.

The opportunity – if it was genuine – was doomed by circumstances. Teasdale and Carrick agree that the Wilson government "did not want to be seen as part of a French plot against the other member states, all of which had supported Britain's two applications" to join in 1961–62 and 1967. "Diplomatic shock waves" were generated as the British government, on 12 February ("somewhat maladroitly", without informing Paris), told other EEC members and the USA of de Gaulle's initiative. The press had heard about the Soames lunch by 17 February, by which time the French government was accusing the British of betraying its confidence and distorting what de Gaulle had said. Carrick describes "the leak … of the fact of de Gaulle's initiative to European capitals and to Washington" as looking "fairly inept now." Soames was then told by the French that no bilateral talks were now possible. Even if anything had come of the "offer", it would have been terminated by political and physical mortality. Eighteen months after his resignation, de Gaulle died in November 1970.

"The Terms" – commonwealth and sovereignty

Edward Heath, elected Prime Minister in June 1970, was supported by a united Cabinet in renewing the application in 1970. There followed two years of negotiations but despite the belief that Pompidou was an improvement on de Gaulle, it seems that Heath had had to make a commitment, implying lasting consequences both for British interests and Continental expectations. Pompidou declared in a television interview that he had asked Heath whether Britain, an island, "had decided to moor herself to the continent and if she was therefore ready to come in from the wide seas which had always drawn her", adding that Heath's response had "convinced him that his views were in line with France's own conception of Europe". The average French viewer hardly attached much significance to the "wide seas" issue – indeed, France herself retained considerable extra-European attachments, but this aspect was clearly one of the essential dogmas of the new Europe.[55]

The Treaty of Accession was signed in January 1972; the European Communities Act obtained Royal Assent on 17 October 1972, and the UK's membership of the EEC came into effect on 1 January 1973.

In 1971–72 the present author collaborated with Sir John Biggs-Davison MP over Britain joining the EEC. They were friends, initially in the late Sixties through the Monday Club, the then powerful "ginger group" on the Conservative Right, until his early death in 1988, when they were both in the Commons. John was greatly admired by one of the three dedicatees of this book, David Levy, and was later a member of the 1922 Committee Executive. Never in Government, owing to his persistent independent-mindedness, John was a great campaigner for "lost causes", including the Portuguese role in Africa, which collapsed in 1973–74, and Catholic Unionists in Northern Ireland; he also had a sneaking regard for the French monarchists. But he held to his views bravely and persistently and if attention had been paid to them the European cause in Britain might have assumed a wider attraction, going beyond the "HeathCo" commercialism satirised by *Private Eye* at the time. He is cited in some detail here because his reservations echoed those of the present author and because they largely arose from the lost opportunities of the 1945–70 period.

As a strong supporter of the "old" Commonwealth, Biggs-Davison in 1957 wrote: "London should become the centre of a world system of sovereign nations based on the Commonwealth, the Sterling Area and those European institutions which are flexible enough to allow our full co-operation."[56] At that time, the Commonwealth was still (just) a viable entity of British power.

In the summer of 1971, shortly after Coudenhove-Kalergi had addressed the Monday Club on the subject, Biggs-Davison and the present author had an exchange on the doorstep of Julian Amery's home, 112 Eaton Square, London; at the time the author was working on L S Amery papers there. In his juvenile enthusiasm, he regretted that Coudenhove had not addressed the detailed commercial issues facing the UK over EEC entry. Biggs-Davison retorted "Don't you think we should get our ideals straight first?" He scornfully dismissed the trade issues as "taking in each other's washing machines".

He had his own clear views of what form European unity should take. The title he gave to one pamphlet, an early draft, with his own manuscript amendments, which this author possesses, is significant: *A European Alternative to the Common Market*. He also possesses a final copy of his undated pamphlet, *Great Britain, Great Europe*. Both documents coincided with the debates on the principle of Britain joining the EEC, on the terms negotiated by the Heath government, during the summer of 1971. In *Great Britain, Great Europe*, Biggs-Davison declared "This great Europe ends neither at the Channel nor at the Pyrenees, nor yet at the Berlin Wall and the Communist watch-towers."

He developed this: "in a sense Europe extends to the Antipodes and to the Cape of Good Hope", since the Commonwealth "has been colonised from the Continent as well as from the British Isles", and forces, significantly though not entirely, from the "old" rather than the "new" Commonwealth, "twice … flocked unconscripted to the rescue of Europe". Europe, he declared, "is the fount and matrix of the civilisation which binds the white Commonwealth, and white southern Africa, to what is the most creative of continents and the spiritual power-house of the world".

He believed that the arrangements negotiated for New Zealand's dairy products were only a first step towards lasting links with Europe: "A Europe that means to count again in the world cannot yield her stake in Australasia to Japan and the USA". Declaring that "Europe is an oceanic as well as a continental concept," he added: "Europe … reaches from the North Cape to the Cape of Good Hope but also from Australia to Argentina." Latin America was largely the creation of "Iberian Europe", and France, Germany and Britain also had cultural and commercial links there. "Like Black Africa", he harshly but realistically remarked, "Latin America is the name of an incoherence [and] needs help from Europe".

It is worth adding that the British and French overseas empires were sharply contrasted. The former, in the shape of the "old Commonwealth", retained through ethnic and other links, close ties with Britain. While France worked hard to ensure her former colonies, especially in Africa and the Pacific, were deeply involved in the EEC, her links with these were manifestly failing by the 2020s.

These views, not confined to the Conservative Right, were key themes in a letter published in *The Times* on 12 October 1971, on the eve of the crucial 1971 Conservative Party Conference, expecting to debate EEC entry before it was put to Parliament. The letter was deliberately intended to show support for entry from significant members of the Monday Club, in contrast to others on the Right who, deferring to Enoch Powell (not a Monday Club member, but with substantial influence there) were opposed to entry. The present author (drafter of the letter and the penultimate co-signatory) trudged round central London assembling the signatures of senior Club figures, including two MPs (Biggs-Davison and Geoffrey Stewart-Smith), and Horace Cutler, then Deputy Leader, later Leader, of the then Conservative-held Greater London Council. The letter stated that Britain wanted to "secure Continental recognition of the need to establish enduring political and economic relations with the Commonwealth realms of European settlement".

As indicated above, the sovereignty implications of the EEC had never been secret. The present author recalls during the 1971–73 entry debates his own arguments over the sovereignty issue with Richard Ritchie, a close friend and collaborator of Enoch Powell. A little later, in about 1977, he recalls his Research Department colleague, Michael Portillo, assisting John Biffen in a pamphlet which, rather optimistically, took the view that enlargement from the original Six, which was already occurring, might avert the drift to Brussels centralisation. Perhaps that is happening, decades later, but it is ambiguous.

The author's view then and later, widely shared across the political domain, was that these issues would be sorted by negotiation, nuancing, or obstruction, as necessary. This reflected the view of Julian Amery, then a leading Monday Club figure and a Minister. In 1993, the day after Baroness Thatcher delivered in the House of Lords a diatribe against the drift of European policy towards federalism, and in particular the Maastricht Treaty, Lord Amery made a more historical assessment:

"The alternative (to rejection) is to ratify the treaty and press on with our vision of a Europe of states. For that we are uniquely qualified. It is often forgotten that the federal idea was rather popular in Britain ... in 1902 the Balfour Government actually proposed to the colonial Prime Ministers ["colonial" was then the word for what very soon became "Dominions"] that we should have a federation of the Empire with a federal government, a federal parliament ... They turned it down. Instead they offered us the closest co-operation in all spheres of government. They lived up to their word. In World War I they sent men and money ... When we went off the gold standard [in 1931] all except Canada adopted the sterling system. In World War II they were even more magnificent than they had been in World War I. And in the aftermath of the war, when the lend-lease had stopped, they stood by us. We could justly claim that the old Commonwealth was a superstate in almost every respect. Yet it was based entirely on intergovernmental co-operation. It was a union of states which had themselves rejected the federal idea."[57]

Back in 1971, the support of right-wingers including Amery and Biggs-Davison, alongside others (mainly back-benchers) such as Jock Bruce-Gardyne, Airey Neave, John Peyton, Nicholas Ridley, Duncan Sandys, Norman Tebbit and Patrick Wall was to help decisively in winning Parliamentary approval for the principle of entry on 28 October 1971 and then for the legislation which implemented this. The issue was to prove divisive for both main political parties:

Labour's partisan whip against entry "on Tory terms" was defied by 69 Labour MPs who voted with the Heath Government. A smaller number of Conservatives voted against the principle of entry. Their well-established leaders, Enoch Powell, Neil Marten, Sir Derek-Walker-Smith, and Teddy Taylor, were joined by a significant number of Tory "knights of the shire" (such as Bullus, Kaberry, McAdden, More, Nabarro, Harmar-Nicholls, and Turton), as well as more vociferous backbenchers, Bell, Biffen, Body, Fell, and Soref, and others who became influential, such as William Clark, long-standing chairman of the backbench finance committee, Angus Maude and Sally Oppenheim, both frontbenchers under Mrs Thatcher, as well as other emerging euro-sceptics, such as Toby Jessel, Roger Moate, David Mudd and Peter Fry. A large tranche of Ulster Unionists, then taking the Conservative whip, voted against the principle of entry.

The 1975 referendum, "our money" and "slippery slope"

Wilson's Labour party campaigned in the two 1974 elections on a policy of renegotiating the "Tory terms" and then putting them to a referendum. The "renegotiation" made hardly any difference to the terms of membership, and the outcome of the referendum, in June 1975, was influenced by two key factors. First, Britain's economic situation was dire, with inflation at 26 per cent, and the trade unions seen as overpowerful. So there was a vote for safety. Second, continued EEC membership was supported by political leaders who were respected: most leading Conservatives, including Margaret Thatcher, just elected party leader, and Labour moderates including Denis Healey as Chancellor and James Callaghan as Foreign Secretary. Leading Labour figures who were disliked or distrusted, Michael Foot and Tony Benn, campaigned to leave the EEC, as did Enoch Powell. The result was 67 per cent support for remaining in the EEC, on a turnout of 64 per cent.

Thatcher's position at this point is interesting. She supported membership because she saw the EEC as a bulwark against Communism and because it promoted free trade. Significantly, in March 1975 she told London University students that "political and economic power in the world today is based on … populations the size of America, Western Europe, the Soviet Bloc and now Japan. Where power resides, there must British influence be exerted."[58]

Various contentious aspects of EEC membership were not changed by the Wilson "renegotiation." These mainly involved Britain and her new partners having different agricultural support systems. In 1961 Britain imported more food than all the Six together. The EEC funded its budget through levies on imported agricultural products – a punitive measure directed at countries not pursuing self-sufficiency. In 1970 the Six agreed that these levies should go direct to Brussels and thence to member states according to the size of their agricultural sectors. This fund would then pay out to producers to subsidise exports. Britain had to inherit this arrangement. Large financial distortions resulted, making Britain by 1977 the second largest contributor after Germany.

Should Heath and Rippon have made more difficulty over this in the 1971 negotiations? It was not done, and the Six were determined not to alter their rules to suit British convenience. Nor did the 1974–79 Labour government attempt a revision, partly because of Britain's desperate economic weakness.

Mrs Thatcher was determined to get "our money" back. Threats and blandishments took place, with serious talk of withholding the money, and more realistically a threat that Britain would block new endeavours until the matter was settled. Eventually the June 1984 European Council at Fontainebleau agreed a 66 per cent reduction of the net British contribution: Thatcher had wanted 70 per cent, while the French and Germans were hoping to stick at 60 per cent.

In recent years agriculture only accounted for 33 per cent of the European budget, with greatly increased spending on regional policy, and the environmental, tourism and cultural sectors. But the eccentric system of raising revenue (unrelated to GNP), and Britain's continuing high contributions caused lasting resentment, and played well with the "out" campaigners in 2016. And the gap between the rules and ambitions of the EEC/EU and what Britain might tolerate was still large.

The 1980s became the era of "slippery slope" European politics: the Eurocrats forged ahead with their plans while reassuring British politicians, officials and diplomats. Thatcher was advised to put up with what officials called the "windy rhetoric" in order to get concrete gains. Her biographer remarks "The trouble was that the windy rhetoric usually meant something important to the men who uttered it."[59]

Thatcher's relations with Chancellor Kohl were never particularly good and were not helped by his post Milan European Council press conference in July 1985 where, according to the telegram from Sir Julian Bullard, British Ambassador in Bonn, Kohl stated: "He could not accept that Europe should degenerate into an elevated free trade zone ... the mission of the founding fathers had been to slowly dismantle national sovereignty ... At the end a European federal state could arise."[60]

Her biographer argues that "broadly speaking" she was "deceived", adding that she "must also have been self-deceiving". Most of her officials and, with very few exceptions, her ministers failed to tell her that Europe was "not, for the most part, going her way, and it was never at any time likely that it would".[61] In 1985

Jacques Delors was agreed on as President of the Commission, where he reigned with great power for ten years. She was told by Geoffrey Howe, then Foreign Secretary, and by French sources that he would be very strict over Budget matters. So she supported the nomination: no one warned that he would try to move Europe in a direction "that was anathema to Mrs Thatcher". A few years later, in 1990, Delors told the European Parliament that he wanted Europe to become a "true federation" by 2000. Even Mitterrand, watching it on TV, exclaimed "That's ridiculous! ... No one in Europe will ever want that. By playing the extremist, he's going to wreck what's achievable."[62]

In the decade after 1986, as a Conservative candidate and then, after the 1987 General Election, an MP, the present author attended meetings of a group of 16 newly elected Conservative MPs and a similar number of new West German Christian Democrat MPs. Known as the "Dresden Circle" (in early 1987 they visited the memorable city of Dresden, still in Communist East Germany, and partly ruined), the group was established under the auspices of the Konrad Adenauer Foundation, closely linked to the Christian Democrats, and subsequently met every year, sometimes at Adenauer's summer villa, Villa La Collina, in Cadenabbia, on Lake Como, and after 1990 sometimes in Eastern Europe. Their gathering in September 1990 was multinational, with representatives from France, Poland and other Eastern European countries, celebrating the largely peaceful and successful revolutions against Communism. One of their number was Alain Lamassoure, a Deputy of the *Giscardien* UDF in France, later a Minister and a MEP. He spoke good English and had an attractive sense of humour, which made him popular with the British. Suddenly, in a discussion on the events in Eastern Europe, he broke into an impassioned *"Ou était l'Europe?"* What role had "Europe" played in the events of that year; the implied answer being, "much less than he would have wished".

This brought home to the present author the rather proselytising style (resembling that of a schoolmate who would ask him, "Are you saved?") of the supporters of "European union". The British looked down their noses at this somewhat alien emotion, without attributing any sinister significance to it. The British number of 16, selected by their German hosts without particular emphasis to their opinions on Europe, included at least three stolid opponents of European integration. One of these, Roger Knapman, a consistent Maastricht treaty rebel at Westminster, was later leader of the UKIP party (2002–06) and a UKIP MEP (2004–09). The remainder varied in their opinions.

An important question arises. How often then and later did senior British Ministers, not including Mrs Thatcher who was *sui generis*, warn their European counterparts: "you know that our government, and British people generally, will not follow you down a centralising, federalising route – and I personally share that view?" The author fears that none of the Dresden circle, as he recalls, said this in their formal discussion sessions, though some might have done so privately. This may well have been out of politeness – they were guests – or simple friendliness. The author recalls the German host and organiser of these meetings saying to him, at midnight, just as the news that the Maastricht treaty had, by a hair's breadth, obtained a slight majority in the French referendum in September 1992, "now we can get on and build Europe". He should have questioned what he meant and warned him that there were limits to their enthusiasm. When British ministers, such as John Major, did so warn, the Continentals tended to believe that he was arguing "merely to appease party opinion, and not out of conviction. So they listened politely and took no notice of what I was actually saying."[63]

The Single European Act and its aftermath

The Single European Act, signed in early 1986, aimed to establishing a single market in the EEC by the end of 1992. It also codified European political co-operation, implying a European common foreign and security policy, as well as another long-standing ambition, "the progressive realisation of European Monetary Union (EMU)".

The bulk of the British business community – and Margaret Thatcher herself – were strongly in favour of the "Single Market" as such. A British Commissioner, Lord Cockfield, had drafted the initial European White Paper on the subject. Britain had long been irritated by obstacles to free trade in manufactures. These were now to be cleared, and progress towards free trade in services was also expected, although obstacles to the latter took time even to start to diminish.

Thanks to Thatcher's support and that of a united Government, only 17 Conservative MPs rebelled against the 1986 European Communities (Amendment) Act. These opponents, in the key divisions on Second Reading on 26 April 1986, the guillotine on the Committee stage on 1 July, and Third Reading on the 10 July, were mostly a predictable group. They were led, however, by two highly distinguished opponents of EEC membership: Powell himself, now representing a Northern Ireland constituency, and Sir Edward du Cann, predecessor of the present author as MP for Taunton. Du Cann had been a minister, Chairman of the Conservative Party, Chairman of the Public Accounts Committee (1974–79), and long-standing Chairman of the Conservative backbenchers 1922 Committee (1972–84). He was a long-standing opponent of UK membership of the EEC, speaking and voting against the legislation in 1972 and speaking for a "No" vote in the referendum of 1975. In opposing the Second

Reading of the Bill on 23 April 1986, he declared: "If there were a genuine spirit of working together in foreign affairs, perhaps one could say that we should move on to other things ... In endeavouring to press on too early with such important constitutional changes, we risk ridicule."[64]

Nearly ten years later, in his autobiography, he was more nuanced, emphasising the attractions of the Commonwealth, the Far East and South America as "vast potential markets", adding "Nor do we need to tear ourselves apart over the issue of a single European currency" as "it will be some years before the conditions for it exist".[65]

Delors and the 1988 Bruges speech

There was a hope that the Single Market would be developed by the Council of Ministers on confederal lines. Instead, under Delors, the Commission took over; he told the European Parliament on 6 July 1988 "ten years hence 80 per cent of our economic legislation, and perhaps even our fiscal and social legislation as well, will be of Community origin".[66]

After his re-election in May 1988, Mitterrand became "so concerned about the impact a unified ... Germany might have on Europe that he became determined to extract a firm date from Germany for economic and monetary union" in return for French support for unification. Meanwhile, starting in 1979, the European Exchange Rate Mechanism (ERM) linked the values of member currencies within slightly variable bands; it "was an attempt to use the reserves of one or more countries in order to defy the market – an attempt that failed lamentably, with deep ill-feeling all round", not only in the UK but in other countries, on Black Wednesday in September 1992.[67]

Delors spoke to the British TUC conference on 8 September 1988 – a provocative venue – calling on the British labour movement to support the Commission in building a "platform of guaranteed social rights". This was seen by many as a bid to strengthen trade union power, which the Thatcher government had spent the previous nine years weakening. Afterwards, her occasional economic adviser, Professor (Sir) Alan Walters passed to Mrs Thatcher a letter from the economist Bernard Connolly. Connolly believed that Delors's advisers feared Britain might obtain "the lion's share" of US and Japanese direct investment. So they wanted Britain in the ERM (and, subsequently, in a single currency) "to stifle favourable supply-side changes".[68]

This all helped to fuel Margaret Thatcher's Bruges Lecture of 20 September 1988. What was seen as a major battle-cry was this: "We have not successfully rolled back the frontiers of the state in Britain, only to see them re-imposed at a European level, with a European super-state exercising a new dominance from

Brussels". In fact, neither Delors nor the Blair Labour government, elected in 1997, made any attempt to reverse Britain's labour market reforms, apart from the modest removal of Britain's opt-out from the "social chapter" of the 1992 Maastricht treaty.

The speech in its entirety reads as a call to reform. There was no hint that the UK should consider departure. In 1988, it was clear to her and most Conservatives that the UK's presence in the EEC helped head off undesirable tendencies there, both directly by resistance and the final threat of veto, and indirectly by encouraging resistance from other Member States.

So the Bruges speech makes clear Thatcher's recognition that "Our destiny is in Europe, as part of the Community" and that "we British are as much heirs to the legacy of European culture as any other nation". This she derived through British history and European political philosophy, where "classical and medieval thought" led to "that concept of the rule of law which marks out a civilised society from barbarism", and Christianity, where "we still base our belief in personal liberty and other human rights". Typical Thatcher boldness (perhaps to 2024 readers) lay in her reference to "how Europeans explored and colonised and – yes, without apology – civilised much of the world", and to her hailing, while Communism still appeared to hold sway over Eastern Europe, "Warsaw, Prague and Budapest as great European cities".

But there were warnings. "Europe never would have prospered and never will prosper as a narrow-minded, inward-looking club …" She continued: "To try and suppress nationhood and concentrate power at the centre of a European conglomerate would be highly damaging and would jeopardise the objectives we seek to achieve. Europe will be stronger precisely because it has France as France, Spain as Spain, Britain as Britain, each with its own customs, traditions and identity. It would be folly to try and fit them into some sort of identikit European personality …" In her concluding passages, she declared "Let Europe be a family of nations … doing more together but relishing our national identity no less than our common European endeavour."

The speech has usually been cited by Eurosceptics as a founding text for their cause. Thus the fanatical Eurosceptic Daniel Hannan (later an MEP and in 2020 a peer) said that, before Bruges, Euroscepticism "was a cause like Esperanto or naturism. It just wasn't serious, it wasn't real." Bruges and Delors began to change things.[69]

Nigel Lawson: ERM and EMU

Just before the 1987 election, David Norgrove, Mrs Thatcher's private secretary, warned her of the pressures building from the Chancellor, Nigel Lawson, and other Cabinet members, for ERM entry. In one discussion, Lawson admitted to her that "he was not himself a great believer in UK membership of the European Community, but this was one of the few areas where membership had benefits to offer": it was helpful for the management of sterling and thus the control of inflation.[70]

Thatcher had been isolated on ERM at a Cabinet meeting on 13 November 1985 (apart from John Biffen, a longstanding free-floater and Eurosceptic); others, even Norman Tebbit (party chairman) and Willie Whitelaw, urged joining the ERM. She summed up against entry, to the irritation of most of those present, while Lawson considered resignation. According to David Norgrove, "it was clear that she would resign rather than join." The matter was never really discussed again between her and Lawson.[71]

Writing about his Chancellorship some six years later, Lawson described his policy of "shadowing the deutschmark" (DM) between early 1987 and early 1988: "the main purpose … was to arrest the fall in sterling". He describes how in an interview with Simon Jenkins in *The Times* (29 June 1991, after her fall), Thatcher admitted that she had known about his DM policy, "claiming … that her decision to allow it was her 'great mistake' ". The ending of the DM policy, via the uncapping of the pound in March 1988, "coupled with her adamant refusal to contemplate" British membership of the ERM, "removed a major plank of my counter-inflationary policy", with it becoming "increasingly clear that Margaret preferred the advice of an academic economist observing the British economy from 3000 miles away to that of her Chancellor of the Exchequer".[72]

And pressures on Thatcher over ERM entry built up before the EEC Madrid conference in June 1989, with Howe prepared to resign if she refused it. Professor Walters came to her aid by defining the changes that were needed before entry: complete abolition of all exchange controls in the EEC and deregulation and mutual recognition of all financial and capital markets across it: quite a mountain to climb. After one joint minute by Howe and Lawson on 14 June, another was sent on 23 June – two days before Madrid. If she made the right move on ERM, they said, it would be the key to "kicking Stages II and III (of EMU) into the long grass". Howe and Lawson refused to accept separate phone conversations with Thatcher, so the three met on the Sunday morning, the 25th. Howe made it clear he would resign if she did not agree and Lawson said he would follow. In fact, she only agreed to spell out the conditions on which the UK would enter the ERM; she did not give a date. She set out what became known as the Madrid Conditions, following Walters's proposals but including the requirement that UK inflation should be falling. "Privately, following Walters, she had little expectation that her conditions would be met."[73]

Lawson admitted that a resignation over the absence of a date would "have been bizarre and incomprehensible".[74] Post Madrid, things moved rapidly. In the last week of July, Thatcher moved Howe from the Foreign Office to Leadership of the House; with much less power he was given the title of Deputy Prime Minister. John Major became Foreign Secretary.

The resignation on 26 October 1989 of Lawson, a real heavyweight, contributed to Thatcher's fall a year later. It is certainly possible to speculate whether his resignation was caused by communication failures: was Number 10 really aware of the impossible position he felt Walters had placed him in? Or was it stress from the declining economic situation on his side and exhaustion, having just flown back from the Commonwealth conference in Kuala Lumpur, on hers? What is clear, from his voting for Heseltine in the two 1990 leadership elections, his memoirs, and her *obiter dicta*, is that their once firm alliance had terminated in considerable ill-will.

Sterling had fallen sharply during 1989, and he argued "It was when sterling was weak that the Walters view, which was widely taken by the markets to be that of Margaret, too, that sterling should be free to 'find its own level', was most damaging." What proved fatal were further Walters interventions, deliberate or not. The *Financial Times* of 18 October had extracts from an article by him scheduled to appear "in an obscure American academic journal", attacking the ERM and any thought of sterling entering it. The same newspaper reported a Walters speech "that sterling needs to fall to avoid a severe recession in the UK". Lawson added: "What made my job impossible was Number 10 constantly giving the impression that it was indifferent to the depreciation of sterling. I cannot recall any precedent for a Chancellor being systematically undermined in this way."[75]

Lawson and Moore describe in detail the meetings and exchanges on this last day, 26 October, and Lawson's private thoughts. Thatcher was determined to keep Walters; Lawson was determined to resign if she would not remove Walters: "she said everything except the one thing that would have persuaded me to stay".[76]

Reactions tell us much. The *Sun*, responding to Bernard Ingham's "black propaganda machine", had the headline "Good Riddance", whereas the *Economist* declared. "the day Nigel Lawson said 'enough' may be the day that Mrs Thatcher's term of office started to draw to its close." Interviewed many years later by Moore, Lawson said that Walters "had a certain extremism about him which you often find with people from very poor and socialist backgrounds who have seen the light of market economics". And Lord Whitelaw commented to Lawson: "She could so easily have got rid of Walters, but increasingly I fear that she simply cannot bring herself to be on the losing side in any argument. That failing may ditch us all."[77]

Lawson's resignation speech in the Commons on the 31st made clear his views that full UK membership of the ERM "would signally enhance the credibility of our anti-inflationary resolve in general … He added: "There is also a vital political dimension … It is vital that we maximise Britain's influence in the Community so as to ensure that it becomes the liberal free-market Europe … I have little doubt that we will not be able to exert that influence effectively … as long as we remain largely outside the EMS."[78]

Lawson was always an impressive figure: the present author recalls his fascinating talks to the Oxford Blue Ribbon Club in the mid-sixties. In 2016 he prominently supported the campaign to leave the EU, but his earlier reservations on the way Europe was going are worth heeding. He declared them at the end of his memoirs, adding that he had been "a committed supporter of closer European unity, with Britain playing a leading part in it" since he had been at Oxford in the early 1950s. However, "You do not make a nation simply by decreeing it to be one … saw the European Community as an inspired constitutional innovation; providing as it did for the most intimate form of co-operation between the various nation states of Europe, without becoming a federation … It is the height of folly to seek to destroy this unique and careful balance between international co-operation and national sovereignty."

He added that it would be "far too risky" to take "a more relaxed attitude towards EMU, confident that it will eventually collapse under the weight of its own absurdities and self-contradictions", adding: "It is hard to overstate the capacity of old men to become intoxicated by ideas whose consequences they will never live to see …"[79]

In the wake of Lawson's resignation, a Conservative backbench MP did what up to then had been considered unthinkable: Sir Anthony Meyer challenged the Prime Minister for the Conservative leadership. Meyer directed his attack mainly over Europe: "Never has Mrs Thatcher's insistence on the retention of every scrap of national sovereignty seemed so dangerously unwise … The only safe haven for a united Germany, is a closely integrated Europe … This concept is utterly alien to Mrs Thatcher … And it is vital to the survival of us all."[80] In the election on 5 December 1989, 60 Conservative MPs (or 16 per cent of the parliamentary party) declined to vote for her. She won by 314 to 33, with 24 spoilt papers and 3 abstentions.

In his report on this contest, George Younger, who had headed Thatcher's campaign, warned her "at least 40 who voted for the Prime Minister did so very reluctantly (and) cannot be counted on another time."[81] Lobbied by Chris Patten to vote for Thatcher, which the present author did, he implored Patten to ensure reasonable funding for local government as the poll tax arrived, otherwise it would be a disaster. That funding did not appear, and it was a disaster, with the burden exacted by it in many areas being around 30 per cent more than previously exacted by domestic rates.

In his very balanced biography, her admirer Charles Moore makes this crucial critical judgement on the ERM issue: "She never found – indeed, never, after the painful meeting in November 1985, really sought – a way of exploring and agreeing the matter with the Cabinet. Instead, she spent virtually her whole period in office sniping at her own government's declared policy until, just before the end, she succumbed, ungraciously."[82]

The fall of Mrs Thatcher

The year or so before Thatcher's fall saw her engaged in a campaign, which so far as they were aware of it, must have damaged her colleagues' trust in her judgement. This was her opposition to German reunification. Few expected events in East Germany to move so fast, when in early November 1989 developments enabled East Germans to pass to the West. In her talks with Gorbachev in Moscow in late September 1989, according to Charles Powell's note, she said "in practice we would not welcome it at all," to which Gorbachev replied "They did not want German reunification any more than Britain did." Hurd comments: "My officials were warning that we seemed to be more pro-Russian than the Russians ... in danger of seeming to prefer Europe as it was, divided and half-Communist ..."[83]

Mitterrand's view is perplexing – almost behaving as an *agent-provocateur* – and reinforcing Thatcher's reservations. So during the European Council in Strasbourg in December 1989, he told Thatcher that he "did not think that Europe was yet ready for German reunification". Then Mitterrand decided to back reunification, having exacted progress to EMU from Kohl. So Thatcher was isolated and John Major perceived that her hostility to reunification, which she could not stop, prevented Britain from exploiting the considerable German doubts about the single currency. "Whereas our influence on most matters carried weight, we were listened to politely on EMU and then ignored."[84]

One aspect of Thatcher's concerns included fears of a German threat to Poland's post-1945 western border, which gave Poland lands which had previously been German for several hundred years. This was assuaged by assurances from Kohl in early March 1990. Such concerns might seem incredible, but the present author recalls, as one of several Conservative candidates attending a German briefing on reunification in March 1987 in Detmold, seeing in the room a large map prominently displaying the 1937 eastern border. The German defence to his query was that there had been no peace treaty to amend the borders!

A sad consequence was the notorious Nicholas Ridley interview with Dominic Lawson in the *Spectator* of 12 July. Ridley described EMU as "all a German racket designed to take over the whole of Europe", adding "the idea that one says 'OK we'll give this lot our sovereignty' is unacceptable to me … You might just as well give it to Adolf Hitler." The Chief Whip told Thatcher that if Ridley did not resign, his views would be taken to be hers (Moore adding, in parenthesis "which, to a large extent, they were"). Ridley did resign, thus depriving Thatcher of the most important of her Cabinet allies.[85]

To be fair to Ridley, before the *Spectator* interview, but when "he was getting very exercised about Nigel Lawson et al trying to get Mrs T to agree to us joining the ERM", he was asked what made him change his mind about Europe, having been a keen supporter of original EEC entry. "He said that he hadn't changed his mind. He still believed in a united Europe, but a single currency could only come about once, with free movement of people, goods etc, our economies had become much more closely integrated. It was no good trying to force currency alignment on economies which were still so different." At the interview he is said to have had only one glass of wine "but he had a weak head and this might have been enough to loosen his tongue."[86]

Shortly after becoming Chancellor, Major presented to Cabinet a paper, drawn up under Lawson's auspices, on "competing currencies", designed to be an alternative to EMU. By strange coincidence, this had been agreed at a meeting on 25 October 1989 between Thatcher, Lawson, Major and Ridley – the very day Lawson decided to resign; the "currencies" meeting was sandwiched between their unsatisfactory exchanges over Walters. It was a concept similar to Major's later proposal for the hard ecu. The latter would be a common currency which could co-exist with existing currencies, giving business and consumers a choice over a long period, thus letting the market determine whether a single currency should evolve. Thus it had both political and economic advantages.

As Major explains, Mrs Thatcher "appeared to have no idea of how committed our partners were" to the single currency; she was also confident it would not work, and therefore saw no early need to confront them. When he presented the idea to ECOFIN, the EEC's monthly meeting of finance ministers on 13 November 1989, in his words it "came too late and was seen in Europe as a wrecking tactic". As Hurd remarks "I do not know whether it would have worked if we had introduced it earlier and pushed it harder." And he quotes a Spanish minister: "Good proposal, wrong country."[87]

Major believed Thatcher's "No" tactic "would not stop them going ahead and

… only deprive the UK of any influence over their plans". He wanted her to be "more subtle" in her opposition. Hurd agreed: "her tactics, in particular her occasional rough and overstated arguments, would produce the wrong results." Her approach produced strange effects: Hurd describes how, on 29 October 1990, the day after the disastrous Rome summit, her great admirer Alan Clark came to Hurd's room "to say that Margaret Thatcher must go and I should take her place". This encounter, Hurd states "is not recorded in his published diary". So her manner, while contributing to her fall, also did not assist British purposes in the EEC.[88]

Major and Hurd formed what Charles Powell called "a bond of steel" about the ERM and Powell agreed to help persuade her: "I thought entry was wrong, but politically necessary. I thought it was essential to preserve her." As Lawson declared in the Commons debate on 23 October 1990, after ERM entry, "had we joined five years ago there would have been no danger of confusing the ERM and the EMS with EMU".[89] Having lost one Chancellor, Thatcher could not afford to lose another, and at this stage she saw Major as her likely successor at the top.

With business clamouring for relief, what clinched ERM entry was the opportunity to make a simultaneous interest rate cut (by 1 per cent). Entry was announced on 5 October, with Britain joining at DM 2.95. Bill Keegan of the *Observer* stated, presciently, that this was too high a rate. Mrs Thatcher herself had wanted a higher rate, and the Banque de France and the CBI wanted the rate to be DM 3.00. The European Commission and the Bundesbank had "severe reservations" about the rate (the Germans "certainly thought that it was too high and unsustainable"). A senior member of Delors's staff in Brussels produced a paper warning the Commission that it would not be long before Britain would have to devalue within the ERM.[90]

The economic circumstances were not attractive: by September 1990, UK inflation had reached 10.9 per cent – the highest level for eight years, in spite of interest rates at 15 per cent, while manufacturing labour productivity in Britain still lagged 20.4 per cent and 17.4 per cent behind German and French levels respectively. Newspapers such as *The Times*, the *Sunday Times*, *Telegraph* and *Sunday Telegraph*, welcomed UK entry, in sharp contrast to their hostility to it two years later. Parliament was calm, though Major's Parliamentary Private Secretary, Tony Favell, resigned in protest.

As an admirer of Heseltine at that time and a sceptic of Thatcherite economic policy especially in the early 1980s (both these views were later somewhat revised), the present author recalls his dismay when Heseltine announced in the spring of 1990 that he would not challenge the leadership "this side of an election". This was at a time when the poll tax was inflicting devastation on the Conservatives in the local elections. During that summer recess, as he spoke with constituents and worked his garden, he gloomily counted the odds: a recession which by then was unavoidable, the poll tax, higher than originally predicted, which also seemed irremovable, and an increasingly unpopular Prime Minister. Europe did not feature in that equation, nor did he expect things would change so rapidly.

The 27–28 October 1990 Rome European council was a disaster: the Italian Premier, Andreotti, and Thatcher disliked each other and disagreed deeply on European policy. Powell advised her to "build tactical alliances on the practicalities involved"[91] – something the British are usually good at – and thus avoiding an 11 to one split. She did not do this and the split became reality. Thatcher and Mitterrand had good personal relations, and she gave him lunch at the British Ambassador's residence, the Villa Wolkonsky. He affected to agree with her insistence on Britain's right to issue its own currency; "that was where France stood too: a common currency, not a single currency". This was not French policy, however, and he was of no use to Thatcher during the Council.[92]

After Rome, she made a prepared Commons statement in line with policy, then in response to provocation from Neil Kinnock, "she lunged into that now-famous unscripted outburst". She quoted Delors who had wanted the European Parliament to be the democratic body of a future European state, the Commission to be its executive and the Council of Ministers to be its Senate, to which her response was "No, No, No". That response would and did command large Conservative support. More damaging to her relations with Major was her admission about the hard ecu that "in my view, it would not become widely used throughout the Community". In Major's words, "she had wrecked months of work and preparation".[93]

Howe resigned the next day. Various factors led to his devastating resignation speech two weeks later, on 13 November, which immediately produced Michael Heseltine's decision to stand for the leadership: the sharp, condescending tone Thatcher adopted to him, often in front of colleagues and, more immediately, the typical claims by what Lawson terms "the Number 10 black propaganda machine" that his resignation was merely over a matter of style.[94]

Howe's resignation speech is well known. He specifically responded to Thatcher's point on the hard ecu: "It was remarkable – indeed, it was tragic – to hear my right hon Friend dismissing, with such personalised incredulity" the hard ecu. "How on earth are the Chancellor and the Governor of the Bank of England, commending the hard ecu as they strive to, to be taken as serious participants in the debate against that kind of background noise." This led directly to his famous line on cricket bats "broken before the game by the team captain". Major's later comment on this passage was "I could only agree".[95]

Europe was the occasion of the Heseltine challenge and the fall of Thatcher. There were three underlying factors, however, each more powerful than theological disputes about Europe. First was the recession. Second, there were the electoral shocks: the loss of the Eastbourne by-election on 18 October 1990. And third, Thatcher had been Prime Minister for over 11 years and the same style which had irritated her EU partners and Cabinet colleagues also irritated many electors, including many Conservatives. As Lawson put it in his memoirs, she was seen as "disagreeably strident, excessively authoritarian, and unbearably bossy," adding "it was she herself – not Geoffrey, not Michael, not me, and not a disloyal Cabinet – who was the author of her own misfortune".[96]

Immediately after the Howe resignation speech, Heseltine asked this author (while approaching many others) for support. He replied "but I thought you had ruled out a challenge". He replied: "any Chancellor will tell you that changing circumstances alter policies". Shaken but excited, the author promised his support. He preferred Heseltine's interventionist economic policy and had admired his domination of the front pages after his Westland resignation, and Taunton's constituents had worshipped him when he visited Wellington during the 1987 election campaign. However, the author came to value hugely what Thatcher had achieved. Also in retrospect, he now considers that John Major's Baldwinesque approach, after the turmoil of the Thatcher revolution, was preferable to Heseltine's Bonapartism (the author was critical of him over coal mine closures in late 1992 and, later, over Post Office privatisation). Events, fanned by a vicious Press, were to mangle John Major worse than the 1930s Press Lords with Stanley Baldwin. Would events have transpired differently under a Heseltine premiership? Some Eurosceptics believe he would have cajoled them, and some Europhiles believe he would have compelled obedience. The author doubts it would have been so simple.

The first round took place on 20 November, when Thatcher led by 204 to 152, two votes short of the total required by the rules. After meetings and intrigue, she decided not to contest the second ballot and resigned as Prime Minister on the morning of the 22nd. While Douglas Hurd entered the fray against Heseltine, supported by MPs like Chris Patten and Tristan Garel-Jones, both close to Major, many across the party, not all Thatcherites, looked to Major to be a unity candidate to beat Heseltine. He thus attracted support from various individuals, some of whom, like Peter Lilley and Norman Tebbit, were later critical of his Europe posture. Having asked Norman Fowler to manage Major's campaign, and finding he was already committed to Heseltine, Norman Lamont, with whom Major's relations later became very difficult, assumed this role, "at the request of the team", but "not without a little dissent", as Major remarked. As Major later wrote: "Because Margaret favoured me in the campaign, many of her followers backed me. She and her allies, however, deceived themselves if they thought I would pursue unchanged policies."[97]

The second stage of the leadership contest displayed some curious cross currents in politics and the press, with later implications for the Europe issue. Nigel Lawson continued to back Heseltine, this causing "a humdinger of a row with Norman Lamont" – "a particularly intemperate telephone call" in Lawson's words, when he made a public declaration of support. Despite the Eurosceptic and Thatcherite views of its proprietor, Rupert Murdoch, the *Sunday Times* under Andrew Neil backed Heseltine, while the later strongly Eurosceptic *Telegraph* backed Hurd. As his biographer remarked of Major, "he would evoke a peculiar scorn in many intellectual commentators, notably Simon Heffer, Paul Johnson and William Rees-Mogg", but, surprisingly, also Europhiles such as Max Hastings. While Heseltine persuaded some right-wingers, including Edward Leigh and Neil Hamilton, to vote for him (they thought Mrs Thatcher had been betrayed by plotters), she herself gave a lunch for the No Turning Back Group, "strongly pleading with doubters like Michael Forsyth and Michael Brown to vote for John Major".[98]

Major secured 185 votes to 131 for Heseltine and 56 for Hurd; Heseltine conceded, and was appointed Environment Secretary. Hurd remained Foreign Secretary. Major considered Chris Patten, Kenneth Clarke and John MacGregor for the vacant Chancellorship, with Lamont going to Trade and Industry ("my initial inclination"), eventually appointing Lamont for continuity's sake ("the most controversial appointment of my premiership" with "many colleagues … critical at the time"). Whether the course of the next few years would have been less turbulent is anyone's guess; a strongly Europhile Chancellor such as Clarke, who eventually succeeded Lamont in May 1993, might have created earlier what Major termed "a deep and widening fissure in the party" on European policy.[99]

FOOTNOTES

1 See the present author David Nicholson's *Crisis of the British Empire*, Halsgrove, 2017, Chapters Three and Six.
2 Tugendhat, *op cit*, pp 37, 171.
3 *Guardian*, 25 June 2016.
4 Peter Catterall, ed *The Macmillan Diaries: The Cabinet Years 1950–57*, Pan Macmillan, 2004, pp17–18, 43.
5 House of Lords Hansard, 8 June 1993, col 736.
6 Bogdanor, *op cit*, pp9 and 119.
7 Biggs-Davison, John, *The Walls of Europe*, Johnson, 1962, p13.
8 Peter Hennessy, *Never Again: Britain 1945–51*, Penguin edition, 2006, p293.
9 Peter Hennessy, *Having it so Good: Britain in the Fifties*, Allen Lane, 2006, pp284, hereafter

Henessy, *Fifties*.
10 Catterall, *op cit*, p61; D R Thorpe, *Supermac: the Life of Harold Macmillan*, Chatto and Windus, 2010, pp256–57.
11 Quoted David Dutton, *Anthony Eden: A Life and Reputation*, Arnold, 1997, p302.
12 Catterall, *op cit*, diary for 22–24 November 1950, p30.
13 Bogdanor, *op cit*, p14; *Observer*, 12 October 1986, quoted, Dutton, *op cit*, p281.
14 Dutton, *op cit*, pp282, 292.
15 Quoted, *ibid*, pp296, 288.
16 John Barnes, *Churchill and Europe*, January 2001, unpublished background text for his presentation, p1.
17 Quoted by Barnes, *op cit*, p6, from Jock Colville, *The Fringes of Power*, pp215–16.
18 Nicholson, *op cit*, pp176–77.
19 Quoted Barnes, *op cit*, p16.
20 Quoted Tugendhat, *op cit*, p6, from Martin Gilbert, *Winston Churchill*, Vol VII *Never Despair, 1945–65*, pp286–87.
21 These extracts from the diary and letters are in *The Leo Amery Diaries*, Vol II, *The Empire At Bay 1929–45* edited by John Barnes and David Nicholson, Hutchinson, 1988, pp1058–60.
22 Quoted, Barnes, *op cit*, p37.
23 Dutton, *op cit*, p299.
24 Quoted, Barnes, *op cit*, p45, present author's italics.
25 Diary, 25 November 1951, Catterall, *op cit*, p119.
26 Diary, 29 November 1951, *ibid*, p120.
27 Harold Macmillan, *Tides of Fortune 1945–55*, Macmillan, 1969, hereafter Macmillan, *Tides*, p463.
28 Dutton, *op cit*, pp297–98.
29 Diary, 4 December 1951, Catterall, *op cit*, p121; Macmillan, *Tides*, p466.
30 Macmillan, *Tides*, p469.
31 Catterall, *op cit*, p144.
32 *Ibid*, pp 156, 162.
33 *Ibid*, p262.
34 Barnes, *op cit*, p46.
35 Diary, 24 October 1954, Catterall, *op cit*, p363.
36 Hennessy, *The Prime Minister: The Office and its Holders since 1945*, Penguin, 2001, p211.
37 Thorpe, *op cit*, p311.
38 Dutton, *op cit*, p307.
39 Quoted Hennessy, *Fifties*, p399, from his interview with Thorneycroft for the Channel Four TV Series, 29 July 1993; emphasis in original.
40 Hennessy, *Fifties*, p392; Catterall, *op cit*, pp593, 599.
41 Quoted Hennessy, *The Prime Minister*, p268.
42 Thorpe, *op cit*, p413.
43 Hennessy, *Fifties*, p615; Thorpe, *op cit*, pp324, 468, 514–5, 618.
44 Quoted Bogdanor, *op cit*, p53.
45 Nora Beloff, *The General Says No*, Penguin, 1963, pp95–96.
46 Quoted Thorpe, *op cit*, p524, from Lloyd's account; Macmillan's diary for 21 August 1962, quoted by Hennessy, *The Prime Minister*, p269.
47 Beloff, *op cit*, pp108–10.
48 *Ibid*, p134.
49 David Dutton, "Anticipating Maastricht: The Conservative Party and Britain's First Application to Join the European Community", Contemporary Record, Vol 7, No 3, Winter 1993, pp530–31, 534–35.
50 Tugendhat, *op cit*, pp34–36]
51 Robert Marjolin, *Architect of European Unity*, Weidenfeld and Nicolson, 1989, pp313, quoted Tugendhat, *op cit*, p45; Bogdanor, *op cit*, p65; Thorpe *op cit* pp534–37.
52 Thorpe, *op cit*, p536–37, citing David Butler file of interviews for his book on the 1964 General Election.
53 *Evening Standard*, 11 June 1971.
54 Anthony Teasdale, co-author *Penguin Companion to European Union* 2012.
55 The Pompidou quote from Bogdanor, *op cit*, pp27–28, citing Sir Stephen Wall, *The Official History of Britain and the European*

Community, vol 2 *From Rejection to Referendum, 1963–75*, Routledge, 2013, p406.
56 Quoted, Kevin Hickson, *Britain's Conservative Right Since 1945: Traditional Toryism in a Cold Climate*, Palgrave Macmillan, 2020, pp67–68.
57 House of Lords Hansard, 8 June 1993, col 737.
58 Quoted, Tugendhat, *op cit*, p81.
59 Charles Moore, *Margaret Thatcher: The Authorized Biography*, Allen Lane, Vol II, 2016, pp389–90.
60 Quoted, *ibid*, pp401–02.
61 *Ibid*, pp393–94.
62 Moore, *op cit*, Vol II, p392 and Bogdanor, *op cit*, p127.
63 John Major, *The Autobiography*, HarperCollins, 1999, p270.
64 House of Commons Hansard, 23 April 1986, col 946.
65 Du Cann, *Two Lives*, Images Publishing, 1995, pp275–77.
66 Quoted, Moore, *op cit*, Vol III, Allen Lane, 2019, pp143–44.
67 William Keegan, *The Prudence of Mr Gordon Brown*, Wiley, 2003, pp82, 93, 94.
68 Moore, *op cit*, Vol III, p148.
69 Michael Mosbacher and Oliver Wiseman, *Brexit Revolt: How the UK Voted to Leave the EU*, New Culture Forum, 2016, p10.
70 Moore, *op cit*, Vol III pp95, 97–98.
71 Moore, *op cit*, Vol II pp419–21.
72 Nigel Lawson, *The View from No 11*, Bantam, 1992, pp783–800.
73 Moore, *op cit*, Vol III, pp313, 316, 318–20.
74 Lawson, *op cit*, p935.
75 *Ibid*, pp949–50, 955–57.
76 *Ibid*, p963.
77 Quoted, Lawson, *ibid*, p968–69; Moore, *op cit*, Vol III, p339.
78 House of Commons Hansard, 31 October 1989, col 208.
79 Lawson, *op cit*, pp1030–33.
80 Quoted Moore, *op cit*, Vol III p353 from *The Times* of 30 November.
81 Quoted, Moore, *ibid*, Vol III, p356.
82 *Ibid*, p733.
83 Quoted Moore, *ibid*, Vol III, p478; Douglas Hurd, *Memoirs*, Little, Brown, 2003, p383.
84 Moore, *op cit*, Vol III, pp501–2, 507; Major, *op cit* p150.
85 *Ibid*, pp551–52.
86 This paragraph private information to present author.
87 Major, *op cit*, p139; Hurd, *op cit*, p397.
88 Hurd, *op cit*, pp398–99; Major, *op cit*, pp142, 148.
89 Moore, *op cit*, Vol III, pp563, 581; Lawson, *op cit*, p1009.
90 Major, *op cit*, pp163–64; Keegan, *op cit*, p95.
91 Moore's paraphrase, *op cit*, Vol III, p639.
92 *Ibid*, p641, quoting Powell's note.
93 Major, *op cit*, p176; Commons Hansard, 30 October 1990, cols 873, 878.
94 Lawson, *op cit*, p999.
95 Commons Hansard, 13 November 1990, col 464; Major, *op cit*, p180.
96 Lawson, *op cit*, pp1000–01.
97 Norman Lamont, *In Office*, Warner Books, 2000, p21; Major, *op cit* pp190–01.
98 Major, *op cit*, p194; Lawson, *op cit*, p1004; Anthony Seldon, *Major: A Political Life*, Orion, 1999, p203; Lamont, *op cit*, p27.
99 Major, *op cit*, pp202, 205–06.

Chapter Eight:
Europe: The Unravelling 1990–2016

"John Major isn't the Tory Party's problem. The Tory Party is John Major's problem."
(Tony Blair, May 1995, quoted Seldon *John Major,* subsequently *Major,* p551)

"The trouble is that, when Margaret leaves, she will leave the Conservative Party divided for a generation." (Lord Whitelaw to Robin, later Lord Butler, Cabinet Secretary, winter 1987–88, quoted Charles Moore *Margaret Thatcher,* Vol III, *Herself Alone,* p38)

"By leaving the EU we have removed the principal voice against its integration into a single state … We have also guaranteed that we will have absolutely no influence over what it does." (Lord Sumption, *Sunday Times,* 27 August 2023)

After Thatcher's fall, many ardent supporters remained loyal to her and to her dissident approach on Europe. So Lord Whitelaw's warnings of division were intensified by the continuing looming of EMU. By the early 2000s, EMU had become a red herring; in the meantime, as the first part of this chapter will show, it wreaked havoc on Tory unity. The present author was an MP during the start of this process, and offers some personal recollections.

Maastricht and the 1992 General Election

Unity was not helped by Thatcher's accepting the chairmanship of the Eurosceptic Bruges Group, nor, perhaps, by the "fateful" headlines (as he later described them) produced by Major's speech to the German Konrad Adenauer Foundation in Bonn in March 1991: "I want us to be where we belong, at the very heart of Europe." Lamont "did query the phrase" but Major and Sarah Hogg, the head of his Policy Unit, "were obviously keen on it." Meanwhile, the hardline Thatcherites – Tebbit, Cash and Gardiner – formed a backbench support group. When Thatcher wanted to attack the plans to replace the poll tax, she was reminded "Europe is the big issue".[1]

As the key European conference at Maastricht approached, the media reported Thatcher's lecture tours in the United States, expressing hostility to joining a single currency. Thatcher was still in the Commons, and in a speech on 26 June on the preparations for Maastricht, she warned of the EU's habit of exploiting "vague commitments" so that they became "highly specific and damaging proposals". And, along with other Eurosceptics, she began to question whether an opt-out on EMU would hold.[2]

At the start of the Maastricht negotiations a MORI poll in September 1991 indicated that half the electorate would increase their support for Major if he stood up to the Eurosceptics and only five per cent would decrease support. Major described the original Dutch proposal for Maastricht as "catastrophic", including new Community powers on foreign affairs and home affairs, more authority for the Court of Justice and power for the European Parliament to overrule decisions by national governments. It was savaged by a number of member states: even Mitterrand was appalled, saying, rather oddly (and privately) to Major that the Parliament "has no legitimacy and will not have for a hundred years".[3]

The main issue at Maastricht was the single currency "no longer a vague ambition but an explicit proposition". Writing in 1999 Major could see longer term advantages of currency union but, he added, in 1991–92 "it was all too early", with member states "far apart in economic efficiency and development". He feared, all too justifiably, that concentration on EMU might delay or obstruct the admission of the former Communist Central and Eastern European nations.[4] Thus, most did not join the EU until 2004, with Bulgaria and Rumania doing so in 2007, and Croatia in 2013 – all obliged in principle to join the single currency. The small ones (the Baltics, Slovakia, Slovenia, Croatia) have since done so, but the more significant (Poland, Hungary, Romania, the Czech Republic) by 2024 have not.

Chancellor Lamont was firmly opposed to joining the single currency, telling the Bruges Group back in November 1990 that there were few examples in history of a currency union without a political union, thus "a single currency means a single government". He wrote that the single currency at that time "seemed a very distant and theoretical prospect to Conservative MPs"; Major himself "frequently made clear to the author that he did not believe the single currency would actually happen".[5]

By 1999, when he wrote his book on the 1989–97 period, Lamont was well on the way to adopting a radically hostile position to EU membership itself. "In my opinion it was a fatal error to believe there was a way of reconciling Britain's view of Europe with those of other countries. That delusion was longstanding …" In addition to the political/constitutional objections, Lamont cited various economic objections to EMU, which Major and others warmly shared. The lack of convergence in the EU was "spectacular", with inflation varying from two per cent to 23 per cent, short-term interest rates from nine per cent to 19 per cent, and budget deficits from three per cent to 19 per cent of GDP: high deficits in one country might force up interest rates throughout the single currency area. Lamont says that he "firmly supported strong convergence criteria", whereas in

1998, when it was decided which currencies qualified to join the euro, "the Germans along with the Commission and everyone else acquiesced in fudging the figures".[6] This led to the price which Greece and other Mediterranean countries paid in deflation and high unemployment in the 2000s.

There can be no arguing with Lamont's statement that "the reality was that Germany was determined to have the euro for political reasons, even if it meant the inclusion of countries such as Italy about which there were real reservations." Further evidence of euro-fanaticism came from Wim Kok, then the Dutch Finance Minister and later Prime Minister, who said of a proposal, supported by Lamont, that national parliaments should vote on national moves to the single currency, "if we let Parliaments interfere in this matter then they may vote against the single currency and Europe will never find its destiny."[7]

Lamont adds that during the Maastricht negotiations "for the first time I heard European politicians openly and enthusiastically arguing for the creation of a European state", though never using that expression in public. He describes how an un-named senior official from one of the EU countries most keen on the euro told him "that he agreed with almost every economic point I made against the single currency" but it was going to happen.[8]

Major held a Commons debate on 20 November 1991 to gain approval for Britain's negotiating stance. This obtained a majority of 101, with only six Conservative MPs voting against. The apparent perversity of those who voted for the stance and then, in 1992–93 against the resulting Treaty and legislation might be excused by the ERM fiasco in late 1992; it was more likely encouraged by the vulnerability of the Government's majority after the 1992 election. In the 1991 debate Margaret Thatcher advocated a referendum before joining any single currency. In 1991 this was "strongly opposed" on constitutional grounds by Clarke, Hurd, and, interestingly given his views on EMU, by Portillo.[9] After the 2016 referendum, with Portillo interviewing Michael Gove on TV, both agreed that they would not have wanted that "in-or-out" referendum, but both acknowledged that if it had taken place, they would have voted to leave the EU.

Britain's currency opt-out was relatively easy because the principle had been accepted beforehand. The proposals for a Social Chapter in the Treaty threatened to undermine or even reverse the Thatcher reforms to trade union law, and here there was more of a struggle. There were two communications with Howard, the Employment Secretary, in London as to whether he would accept a compromise. His response to both was negative, and he told friends he would consider resigning. So the Chapter was signed by the other eleven but not by the UK.

The UK press ranging from the *Telegraph* to the *Economist* welcomed the outcome, as did backbench meetings. In place of the 40 dissenters anticipated by Richard Ryder, the Chief Whip, only seven including Tebbit, Biffen, Budgen, Favell and Richard Shepherd voted against, while certain others including Thatcher herself, her PPS Gerald Howarth and Teresa Gorman abstained. Teddy Taylor, a strong Eurosceptic voted with the Government. Might the Bill have been whipped through in early 1992, with the Government's large majority? Failure to do so was one of Major's "biggest mistakes", according to Tristan Garel-Jones The excuse given was that there was great pressure on Parliamentary time because of the imminence of the Election, and that splits would have looked bad. However, a tight majority after the Election might well have been predicted.[10]

In Major's biographer's view, "there were harbingers" of trouble. Simon Heffer in the *Spectator* declared: "nothing happened at Maastricht to keep Britain off the conveyer belt to federalism; indeed, quite the reverse." Judith Chaplin, Major's political secretary, wrote in her diary that if the rest joined the single currency Britain would have to join. To the Right, "Major was not trusted, because his stance at Maastricht was seen as more a negotiating position than a position resting on firm personal or philosophical convictions".[11]

Seldon remarks on how Thatcher felt generally, harping on rumours of betrayal in the first ballot in 1990. The present author recalls being approached then by PPSs of senior ministers, all of whom were later part of Major's campaign team, with several of the PPSs becoming ministers, each asking "If Thatcher is beaten in the first round, whom will you back in the second – Major or Heseltine?" Did Major know of these preparations? At her December 1991 Christmas party "attendees described the atmosphere as 'like a government in exile'".[12]

Charles Moore traces Thatcher's growing disillusion with Major over Europe. An indication as to how far she was diverging came in this statement to Sir Teddy Taylor, "I have always felt that the best answer for us was to be a kind of free-trade and non-interventionist 'Singapore' off Europe, seeking contact and understanding with the growth areas of the world." She feared this might prove "perhaps too revolutionary even for my fellow Eurosceptics".[13]

However, there was "barely a mention of Europe" during the 1992 Election campaign.[14] The economic background was not good: while inflation had fallen to below three per cent, unemployment was over 2.5 million and 75,000 people had lost their homes through repossessions in the previous year. The result was perhaps a surprise: but despite a lead over Labour of seven per cent in voting, the overall Conservative majority was a tight 21. This was later sliced away through by-election defeats and defections.

Before the 1992 election, with advice from the whips, Major had concluded that most of the 50 or so MPs retiring were loyalist or pro-European in outlook:

Black Wednesday

Chris Patten believed in pressing ahead with the Maastricht Bill before the summer recess, before opposition had time to harden. It would have coincided, however, with the economic traumas building up and especially the French referendum. Patten, defeated at Bath and now off to govern Hong Kong, thought Major's failure to do this was a "major mistake". [16]

The Maastricht legislation process was made immensely more difficult by a series of events culminating in the politically damaging exit from the ERM in October 1992. The Second Reading of the Maastricht Bill on 21 May 1992 saw 22 Conservative MPs voting against. This was followed by the rejection of the Treaty in the Danish referendum on 2 June: Lamont told an adviser at "prayers" (the name given to early morning ministerial meetings), "It's the best result ever". Better than the election result, he was asked: "Much better". This, from one of Seldon's unattributed "private interviews" is almost incredible, showing even at that stage a hard-line Lamont. Lamont's own more cautious account states that backbenchers "equated Maastricht, the ERM and the recession and they made a dangerous cocktail".[17]

Major told the Commons that the committee stage of the bill would be temporarily suspended. He would not abandon the Treaty. Portillo and Lilley, members of the Cabinet, attended a meeting of junior ministers to discuss their concerns over it. The day after the Danish referendum, Michael Spicer, later chairman of the 1922 committee, and a long-standing, discreet but strong Eurosceptic, initiated with several backbenchers a Commons Early Day Motion calling for a new approach to Europe. Bill Cash encouraged people to sign – saying "Number 10 wants you to sign". This was not so but 69 signed on 3–4 June, while Kenneth Baker, sacked after the Election, called for the government to "think again" and predicted that the Bill would be defeated. Gerald Howarth, who had lost his seat in the 1992 Election, telephoned new members inviting them to meet Margaret Thatcher so she could persuade them to vote against the Bill. Major believed that her role was crucial to stoking the revolt.[18]

The next cause of instability was Mitterrand deciding to call a referendum on Maastricht although not obliged to by law.

Major considered that there was "no inevitability about the earthquake" known as Black Wednesday. This was optimistic. As Kenneth Clarke points out in his autobiography, Major and Patten had persuaded Lamont to "sign up to a significant increase in public spending as part of our election manifesto", causing "quite excessive increases in public borrowing".[19] Thus the pound sank from DM2.91 in May to 2.81 in July; in August it was close to the ERM floor of DM2.778. Lower US rates in December 1991 meant a weaker dollar and hot money flowing to the DM, putting more pressure on sterling, while Germany's problems of reunification – high expenditure on former East Germany and thus higher inflation – produced a tough line from the Bundesbank. "All Europe suffered and grumbled, but the Bundesbank offered no policy change." On 16 July, two days after Major complained to Kohl about damaging suggestions from Bundesbank officials that the other countries could always devalue, the Bundesbank raised its rate from 8 to 8.75 per cent. Lamont noted that many Germans, keen to keep the DM, would welcome the end of Maastricht; Dr Helmut Schlesinger, President of the Bundesbank "deeply disliked Maastricht".[20]

Meanwhile, "perceptive investors" such as George Soros, "calculated that the British economy was not strong enough to cope with" the extent of deflation needed to keep sterling above the floor set by the ERM – so they sold sterling.[21]

Major and Lamont both knew that an interest rate rise might be lethal to getting Maastricht through the Commons. On 28 July they both decided against devaluation or leaving the ERM. During August fear of a No in the French referendum increased (a French poll forecast 51 per cent No). The French wanted to keep the franc strong so would not agree to a vague offer by Dr Schlesinger that the Bundesbank might cut rates if a parallel realignment could be arranged. According to Lamont, the French regarded this as "absolutely unthinkable".[22]

Lamont's account constantly reiterates the need for interest rate cuts during 1991–92, facing the reality that "of course, we were constrained by the ERM". He admits that both the Treasury and he had "underestimated the sensitivity of the economy to interest rates".[23]

Lamont chaired the meeting of EU Finance Ministers (ECOFIN) at Bath on 5–6 September, described by a central bank governor as "the most ill-tempered meeting I have ever attended". Italy had pushed up its interest rate to 15 per cent, with crippling effects on industry and little help for the "crumbling" lira. Along with France, she pressed Germany for a rate reduction. Major told Lamont and Burns, Treasury Permanent Secretary, that "it was a choice between a crisis now and a slow death later, and his inclination was to have the row now." France, Italy, Denmark and Ireland were happy to keep the Germans in the meeting until there was movement, with Lamont asking Schlesinger four times to cut rates. Unfortunately and bizarrely, the Royal Bath Hotel meeting room was required at 7pm for a dance. The outcome consisted of ambiguous words in the communique, with Schlesinger "quickly and unhelpfully" saying that this represented "no change in our policy". Strangely, later that evening, both Schlesinger and Duisenburg, the Dutch central bank governor, separately told Burns that "we should have opted for parity adjustments". Lamont remarks "It was difficult to know what weight to give" this.[24]

Major records that the Germans had "deeply resented" Lamont's style of chairmanship at Bath which had required Schlesinger "to be physically restrained from walking out". Lamont points out that the tension was not just between Britain and Germany but between Germany and "particularly the French, Italians and Irish", while "other countries … sometimes afraid to speak bluntly to the Germans, often expect the British to do it for them".[25]

The Germans claimed that devaluation of sterling was inevitable. Speaking to the Scottish CBI in Glasgow on 10 September, Major robustly defended the exchange rate in contrast to "the soft option, the devaluer's option, the inflationary option"; he admits that this was against the advice of his key assistant, Sarah Hogg, who urged "be softer, less definite".[26]

On 13 September Italy devalued, with the lira leaving the ERM within days: Germany responded by a trivial rate cut of 0.25 per cent. On Tuesday the 15th the *Handelsblatt*, a German newspaper, trailed remarks by Schlesinger: "further devaluations are not excluded". This required a "swift and authoritative rebuttal" from the Bundesbank, but it issued a "non-denial, confusing, lukewarm and late" which was "worse than nothing at all". Lamont gives details about the vain efforts that evening to secure a retraction, while sterling fell below the ERM floor in New York.[27]

Next day was Wednesday 16 September. Lamont describes Schlesinger's remarks as "every bit as bad as I feared … deliberately calculated to damage our position … such a cavalier way … effects … bound to be devastating". Clarke states that the run had started the previous afternoon; "Sarah Hogg was afterwards quite scathing about the lack of overnight preparation that the Treasury and the Bank of England had made for that morning's market opening." Intervention proved to be totally insufficient, so at 11am interest rates went up by two per cent. This had little effect, and by the afternoon Lamont was proposing the temporary suspension of sterling's membership of the ERM. Hurd, Clarke and Heseltine were summoned.

According to Lamont's account, Heseltine and Clarke wanted a further increase in rates; he thought this would be ineffective, but eventually conceded it. Clarke proposed a "deliberately dramatic increase", then "to leave the ERM if it became clear after about half an hour's trading that it had not worked". At 2.15 pm a three per cent rise to 15 per cent was announced, delayed until the next morning. This had no effect on sterling. At the same time Major told Kohl that unless European central banks bought sterling or interest rates fell across Europe, the pound would leave the ERM. With the French franc believed to be next in line, Bérégovoy, the French Premier – as finance minister an old ally of Major's – said the French could not accept a realignment then as their referendum was only four days away: he said sterling should leave the ERM. Consultations with other central banks were taking place, with Lamont stating that "at one point we thought we might get the whole ERM suspended … the Italians and the Portuguese were sympathetic to that". Clarke remarks that these calls "seemed to me to be hopelessly belated"; Major and Bank Governor Leigh-Pemberton "should have been in steady personal contact with these figures both before the crisis and as soon as it had begun". A further meeting at 5pm led at 7.30 to Lamont announcing the suspension of sterling's ERM membership and that the rate rise to 15 per cent would not proceed. Clarke says that he and Heseltine wanted rates to go back to ten per cent, with Lamont insisting on 12 per cent, only agreed "after a rather fierce exchange".

Lamont points out – a riposte to the myth-makers – that "reserves can be, and were, rebuilt". He explains Schlesinger's role, with his "irresponsible and inexcusable "remarks, one of a series made by officials and board members of the Bundesbank, not intended deliberately to undermine the British position but resulting from strains between the Bundesbank and the German government. The Treasury compiled a list of the Bundesbank's misdemeanours and the redoubtably-named German Ambassador, von Richthofen, called on the FCO's Permanent Under-Secretary with a detailed rebuttal, then refuted by the latter. "Sharp words" were exchanged between Major and Kohl, with a "crisp letter" sent from the Governor of the Bank of England to Schlesinger. With the franc under pressure, for Euro-political reasons "the Germans supported the French, and fought the speculators in a way they had not done in the case of sterling". The franc's value survived, but with interest rates rising to 13 per cent after their referendum, while Britain was able to cut hers by a full point on 22 September, and another full point on 16 October, to eight per cent. Within days Spain, Portugal and Ireland reintroduced temporary exchange controls. Within weeks the peseta and escudo devalued. And these other countries, like Britain, spent almost all their reserves.[28]

The press held that the second, albeit brief, rate rise did all the damage: business confidence in some cases did not recover for months. As Lamont acknowledged, however, thanks to the ERM, the UK had "massively and rapidly reduced inflation more than we had anticipated".[29]

The French referendum result – 50.8 per cent, a majority of just over half a million, voting for Maastricht – was the "worst conceivable result for Major".

Lamont remarked: "To my surprise he told me that he was desperately hoping for a French 'No' ." This would have sunk Maastricht, Major believed. He implied that the French cheated: "they found Cook County", said one observer recalling the dodgy result that gave Kennedy victory over Nixon in 1960. Kenneth Clarke suggests the exertion of "a certain amount of indirect influence on the results declared from the French overseas territories" if the result was likely to be tight on the mainland.[30]

Getting Maastricht through Parliament

Major later reflected on Maastricht, "it was always too soon for British public opinion, always a treaty too early". In his view, after Black Wednesday "many Conservatives threw logic to one side; emotional rivers burst their banks". The malcontents had various motives: genuine concerns over the Maastricht Treaty, wider hostility (then carefully disguised) to British membership of the EU, or simply removing Major from the leadership. Major paraphrases the view of James Cran, a rebel MP "Maastricht was worth a battle, it did not justify a war". Cran made a similar remark to the present author, after Maastricht had passed: "I fought a battle; they (the hardcore rebels) want to fight a war." A carefully organised faction, with its own headquarters at Lord McAlpine's Great College Street house, and unofficial whips, co-ordinated opposition, with finance from the late Sir James Goldsmith. According to Major, in 1993 McAlpine, formerly the Party Treasurer, suggested Kenneth Clarke be leader, in 1994 he suggested Heseltine: both strong Europhiles. Then he left for Goldsmith's Referendum Party.[31]

Opposition was fuelled by the newspapers then owned by Rupert Murdoch (*Times* and *Sun*) and Conrad Black (*Telegraph* and *Spectator*); the former was not a British citizen, and the latter had Canadian and British citizenship, renouncing the first in 2001 in order to take a seat in the Lords, upon ennoblement by William Hague. Peter Stothard, the new editor of *The Times*, was a strong Eurosceptic, and while Max Hastings, the *Telegraph's* editor, was not; he despised Major. Charles Moore, editor of the *Sunday Telegraph* and the new *Daily Mail* editor Paul Dacre were all vehemently against the Treaty.

The rebels collaborated with the Labour whips – George Gardiner often drove into the Commons with Derek Foster, Labour's chief whip. Tugendhat cites John Biffen's recollection of the cordial relations between the two (Conservative) sides in 1972 contrasting with the bitterness of 1992–93.[32]

The "paving motion" to resume progress on the Maastricht Bill was carried on 4 November by only 319–316; 26 Tories voted against the Government and seven abstained. The Bill saw 200 hours of debate in Commons, in which 600 amendments and new clauses were debated. "The rebels wasted huge tracts of time on artificial debate."[33] Agreement was made with Labour to have a specific vote on the Social Chapter after completion of the Bill, but before it became operative. Thus the Commons Committee stage ended on 22 April 1993. The Government defeated a demand for a referendum by 363 to 124, with Labour support; John Smith agreed with Major that Parliament had the constitutional authority to ratify the Treaty. Third Reading took place on 20 May, two days after the Danes, on a second referendum, gave the Treaty a substantial "yes" vote. The Bill obtained support from some Labour MPs and all the Liberal Democrats, except Nick Harvey, and passed by 292 to 112. 46 Tory MPs voted against it, including such names as Bendall, Bonsor, Boyson, Butcher, (John) Carlisle, Fry, (Harry) Greenway, Hawksley, Jessel, Lord, Pawsey, Robathan, Skeet, Townend, and Wilkinson: indication of quite widespread dissent.

On 14 July 1993, the House of Lords rejected a referendum on the Treaty, proposed by the distinguished historian Lord Blake, by 445 votes to 176. In his maiden speech in that debate, Lord (Nigel) Lawson declared: "Without monetary union the Maastricht Treaty is not, in my judgment, of any greater constitutional importance than the Single European Act ... However, should there come a time when this or any future British Government are so unwise as to conclude that this country should participate in a European monetary union, with all its political consequences, that would be a decision of such momentous constitutional significance as to warrant ... a prior referendum of the British people. Unless and until that time arrives – and for a number of reasons I rather doubt that it ever will – I do not believe that the case for a referendum is made."

Lady Thatcher stated: "In 1972, at the very big meeting just before we went in ... progressive realisation of economic and monetary union was decided on ... All this was decided. It was in Eurospeak before we entered in 1973. So often, when the new Eurospeak declarations came up, and I said, 'I want to get that out,' they said, 'You can't. Your Government has already agreed it.'"

The late (and great, although the present author often disagreed with him) Lord (Ralph) Harris of High Cross indicated changes of view among younger Conservatives: "During the last three years, the Oxford Union has rejected European political integration on four occasions with large and increasing majorities. The Campaign for an Independent Britain has become Oxford's second largest and fastest growing political organisation. Over the last two years it has numbered among its members a majority of Union officers and every President and officer of the Oxford University Conservative Association. A similar situation exists in universities across the country."[34]

On 22 July, as agreed, the Commons voted on the Social Chapter, with the rebels voting with Labour to incorporate it. The Government was defeated by eight, and the following day (a Friday) a motion of confidence (endorsing the Government's position on the Social Chapter) was carried by 38. In Cabinet, Redwood, Portillo and Lilley opposed this tactic – they would happily have seen the bill fail. None resigned.

As we shall see, Major was dogged by misfortune, much of it not his fault. Harm was done that very Friday evening, when recording an interview with Michael Brunson. Thinking the microphones were silent and chatting to Brunson, Major said "we don't want another three more of the bastards out there," the reference being to those who might have resigned from the Cabinet.

Division and misfortune 1993–95

Earlier, at the European Council at Edinburgh in mid-December 1992, Major encouraged the start of negotiations for enlargement with Austria, Sweden, Finland and Norway (this last later failing after a referendum).

A parenthesis on enlargement, which the present author spoke about in a Commons debate in late 1989. He pointed to a problem and an opportunity: "We do not want a return to Balkanisation … In the two or three years before those countries were swallowed up, first in Nazi and then in Communist tyranny … the Poles and Hungarians took slices of Czechoslovakia and the Hungarians and Bulgarians took slices of Romania. The borders of eastern Europe and the Balkans have no great certainty or legitimacy," lacking in historical, geographical or ethnic respects, and sometimes all three. Enlargement offers "tremendous scope for developing the European Community as a sort of commonwealth of nations in Europe … I hope that the Community can rise to these challenges."[35] Hitherto, this has been achieved, but in recent years the dominant liberal ideology in Brussels, especially over non-European migration, has been resisted by several of the new member states.

Returning to 1993: relations between Premier and Chancellor had worsened since Black Wednesday. Lamont was damaged by various accidents and anecdotes – rather like Major, he was "unlucky". He was attacked for his "singing in the bath" claim after Black Wednesday, and his *"je ne regrette rien"* remark during the Newbury by-election. Newbury was lost on a 28 per cent swing, while 500 seats were lost in the simultaneous county council elections. William Rees-Mogg declared in *The Times* on 10 May – Major "cannot speak … has a weak Cabinet … lacks self-confidence … no sense of strategy or direction … his ideal level of political competence would be deputy chief whip".[36] One is tempted to ask what Rees-Mogg would have made of the recent administrations adorned by his son.

So Major moved Lamont from the Treasury on 26 May, offering him the post of Secretary of State for the Environment and keeping Dorneywood, both of which Lamont declined.

In his Commons speech on 9 June Lamont robustly defended his record, and implicitly, that of the Government. "This recession was not caused by Britain's membership of the exchange mechanism"; it "began before we joined the ERM ... it has its origins in the boom of 1988 and 1989." As Chancellor, "I accepted the policy, believed that it could be made to work"; it "enabled us to get inflation down dramatically".[37]

Who should be Chancellor? Howard was opposed to joining EMU which would have created tensions with the powerful Europhiles in the Cabinet. However, the appointment of Clarke as Chancellor meant that the Party was then unable to unite by ruling out adherence to the single currency during the next Parliament. While it was not possible, in early 1993, to foresee the full horror of what was to face the Conservatives, it might well have been predicted.

What might have served at this point is the appointment of a Royal Commission or a similar body, to examine and take evidence, from all quarters, on whether the UK joining a single currency made economic sense, and in what conditions. The present author served for a time on the secretariat of the 1965–68 Royal Commission on Trade Unions and Employers Associations. The process of taking evidence and carrying out research undoubtedly educated public and political opinion, and it also quite clearly kicked a vexatious issue into the long grass for a period. For the process to command respect, the Commission should have had t be balanced by adherents of the single currency, opponents thereof, and respected individuals who had no clear position, with the possible exclusion of hard-liners. And the secretariat would have needed to be independent of ministerial interference. The final decision on publishing, implementing or rejecting the conclusions would, of course, be taken by the Government of the day, with the support of Parliament.

With such an inquiry in place, it would not have mattered if the Chancellor were Howard, counter-balanced by powerful Cabinet Europhiles, or Clarke, counterbalanced by ministerial and backbench Eurosceptics. The existence of the inquiry would, at least temporarily, have shut down divisive controversy and policy declarations.

It was not to be: the single currency issue remained the elephant in the room until Gordon Brown's burial of it in 2003 – a decision so well prepared that it was received virtually without public dissent from Labour's Europhiles.

Major continued to appeal to the sceptics. At the end of September 1993 he wrote in the *Economist*: "It is not for Europe to attempt to supersede nations ... The Treaty of Rome is not a creed. It is an instrument ..." Regarding the single currency, he reiterated: it was "by no means certain to go ahead". Too many things needed to be clarified, including whether the other economies would have converged. "No one knew." The article "did serve substantially to delineate his thinking on Europe for the following four years"; it sadly had little impact on the rebels.[38]

Major's William and Mary Lecture at Leiden on 7 September 1994 was well received in the party and press. "He dismissed as outdated the original vision of the founders" of the EC in the 1940s and 50s, seeking "a new vision and new role for Britain", dismissing French notions of a "permanent hard core of inner EU nations", praising flexibility as "perfectly healthy" and calling for wholesale reform of the CAP and curbs on some Commission powers.[39] He was encouraged in December 1994 by "Delors' last testament" at the European Council in Essen. "He said, in effect, that his vision of Europe had been mistaken". It should not involve "bind[ing] yet more areas of domestic policy into centralised decision-making." The priority was to "embrace the new democracies"; such "enlargement, to perhaps twenty-five nations, was necessary and inevitable, and it would make tight centralisation impossible."[40]

Yet, as Major recognised, the others still talked in private about a federal destination, even though in public they were reassuring towards nation states.[41]

This was encouraging, but various misfortunes intervened Three unexpected deaths produced dramatic by-election defeats in 1993–94: Newbury, Christchurch and Eastleigh. With the Liberal Democrats gaining each of these, as well as their substantial advances in local elections, the Tories faced a war on two fronts, as Tony Blair followed the deceased moderate John Smith as Labour leader in July 1994. Other heavy by-election defeats followed – each caused by death – Dudley West (December 1994), Littleborough and Saddleworth (July 1995), Staffordshire South-East (April 1996) – each lost to Labour, and Perth and Kinross (May 1995) to the SNP.

Seldon describes the next phase as "Regaining the Initiative: October–December 1993". This was frustrated. The Blackpool Conference speech had the theme "Back to Basics" – intended to address issues that really concerned and affected people. Unfortunate wording implied a moral crusade, which Major (by no means a puritan) abhorred. In Number 10 Nick (later Lord) True, who had crafted much of the speech, was in favour of the moral thrust, and spinning by Tim Collins led to talk of a "war on permissiveness".[42] In early 1994, "events boomeranged", with varied personal affairs involving MPs Tim Yeo, Edward Hartley Booth and Michael Brown, and Lord Caithness. And the "cash for questions" issue started when the media enticed certain MPs to agree to ask parliamentary questions in return for cash payments. The English word "sleaze" conveniently incorporates both sexual misdemeanours and dubious business practices.

A leadership election 1995

There were rumours of a leadership challenge in the summer of 1993, averted when Heseltine had a minor heart attack in Venice. Portillo and Redwood were then thought too junior, though there was, strangely, talk of a Clarke-Portillo challenge. A contest would have happened in 1994 if the June 1994 European Parliament elections had seemed disastrous. Although the Conservatives held only 25 per cent of the national vote, Major was given credit for a good campaign. That Tory 25 per cent is almost on a par with their vote in subsequent Euro-elections: 25.9 in 2004, and 27.4 in 2009.

However, there were further rumours of a Heseltine-Portillo deal, with Portillo as Chancellor. Portillo was believed to be cultivating support, behaving "like a man with an acute sense of his own destiny". At the 1994 Party Conference Portillo's speech was seen as a great success, with applause organised by his helpers spread around the hall. At a fringe meeting of Conservative Way Forward, however, he disappointed the hardliners by not following Lamont's call to consider leaving the EU.[43]

In November 1994 the future EU financing deal agreed at Edinburgh in 1992 came before Parliament. While the main Bill was approved by 285 with Labour support, eight Tories abstained on a Labour amendment and lost the whip, with Richard Body resigning the whip in support. In one of his regular *Sun* columns, Lord Tebbit declared that the whipless MPs had his and Baroness Thatcher's full backing. Some weeks later they were readmitted in the expectation, indicated by Michael Spicer, that they would toe the line. Then they held a "cocky, unapologetic press conference". Tony Blair produced one of his best lines: "John Major isn't the Tory Party's problem. The Tory Party is John Major's problem."[44]

To underline this, Hurd reports a "long but ... fruitless talk" with Portillo in mid-February 1995, trying to find "where he thought the ... Party could realistically pitch its tent on Europe". He reports in his diary "V. hard. Has no tactic to remedy present disastrous strife ... Unwilling to help me find common ground ... Polite but uncompromising."[45]

In the May 1995 local elections the Conservatives lost 2000 seats. Then, on 13 June, Major met with the Fresh Start group, with 50 or so MPs present. John Townend, Chairman of the backbench finance committee, was "intemperate to a degree" others, including Lamont, were "aggressive and hostile". "In exasperation at the questions, he [Major] snapped that he didn't believe that the public cared much about Europe anyway." This led to heckling. His biographer states that Major did not judge the mood right: he was looking "shattered by the most unruly and disrespectful meeting he was to attend as premier". According to Graham Bright, his PPS, "it would seem that (this) meeting proved the last straw." Kenneth Baker demanded that Major be moved. Even Gillian Shephard "let it be known" that she would be interested in being a compromise candidate.[46] Major faced the likelihood that Lamont, at least, would challenge in the autumn. Hence his decision to resign as leader and force an election – in his words: "it is time to put up or shut up". He was "not prepared to see the party I care for laid out on the rack like this any longer".

That decision on 22 June was announced to the 1922 Committee of backbenchers. Lamont reports that at the announcement "one Major supporter" said that he (Lamont) turned as "white as a sheet".[47] That "one" was probably the present author who was briefly interviewed on the evening TV news: he had assumed that Lamont was taken by surprise. The following night, at the Gaudy dinner for his contemporaries at Christ Church, Oxford – always an occasion of enjoyable festivity – his observations were eagerly solicited.

Lamont's account of his attempts to find a candidate to oppose Major or support himself is instructive. He phones Portillo, who says that even if Major wins narrowly, ministers such as himself might refuse to serve, adding "one way or the other I am convinced that this is the end for Major." Redwood resigned from the Cabinet and stood against Major. Lamont argues, "The Redwood Campaign had been planned a long time ago, possibly many months previously."[48]

Major lists Lord Cranborne, David Davis, Michael Howard, Anne Widdecombe and Sir Archie Hamilton as key supporters and planners of his campaign. These turned out in 2016 to be Brexit sympathisers. Michael Heseltine remained loyal, although certain of his lieutenants, including Richard Ottaway and Keith Hampson, put out feelers on his behalf. These were not followed up so Major assumes they were discouraged by Heseltine himself. And while various young apparatchiks, including Georges Osborne and Bridges assisted Major, another, Steve Hilton, helped Redwood: a foretaste of Hilton's turning on Cameron during the 2016 referendum.[49]

Having expostulated to a friendly journalist about the contest, the present author was invited to write an article supporting Major for the *Sunday Telegraph*. This appeared alongside one supporting Redwood by Nick Budgen. He was telephoned at breakfast by a grateful Major!

Trevor Kavanagh of the *Sun* encouraged a Portillo intervention. While Portillo assumed Redwood would withdraw if Major withdrew after a disappointing first ballot, Redwood invited Portillo to join his campaign. Portillo refused and Redwood's campaign team made it clear he would not make way for Portillo in a later ballot. To a report of Portillo's team installing telephone lines, his backers said this was private enterprise, not apparently sanctioned by Portillo. Redwood "frankly considered himself the better man" compared to Portillo whom he "considered a bit flaky and hot-headed".⁵⁰ Baroness Thatcher stood by Major – though McAlpine and Tebbit wanted her to support Redwood. Perhaps she feared a Heseltine leadership emerging.

Hints were given to right wingers of an imminent ruling out of Britain joining a single currency until 1999 or later and a Eurosceptic replacing Hurd at the Foreign Office. The former was attempted but resisted by Clarke, while Rifkind, who became Foreign Secretary, was a very mild Eurosceptic.

Much of the press was foul about Major during the contest: the Murdoch press predictably so. Rothermere allowed the *Evening Standard* to support Major. A non-Eurosceptic editor, Max Hastings (*Daily Telegraph*) came under pressure from the proprietor Conrad Black, hence a very hostile editorial on Major. The *Sunday Telegraph* supported Redwood.

Lamont, who backed Redwood, describes the difficulty in winning over Portillo supporters. The Major campaign talked up Redwood's prospects with Portillistas who knew this could be fatal to their candidate. Alan Duncan was persuaded by William Hague (Redwood's successor as Welsh Secretary), and with John Whittingdale and Bernard Jenkin voted for Major. Redwood himself believed that several Portillistas declined to vote for him at the last moment, fearing he was doing too well. He added: "If (Portillo) had come with me, we would have done it easily between us. He spoke for at least twenty votes." ⁵¹

The result on 4 July was 218–89, with 20 abstaining. Major admitted he had hoped for 230 votes or more, deciding he would resign if he got 215 or fewer. Lamont was therefore right in thinking that if the Portillistas had voted for Redwood the outcome would have been fatal for Major.⁵²

"A period of political calm" 1995–97

Major "hoped we had entered a period of political calm". However, Conservative fortunes hardly moved and then plunged, with new outbreaks of sleaze. And as one of Major's allies remarked: "You cannot deal with unreason, and on Europe there was no middle ground, no meeting point with them ... Whatever they may have said, most of them wanted us out of the EU, but they didn't say that because that was beyond the pale."⁵³

So disunity remained. Margaret Thatcher indicated that she would not campaign for any Conservative candidate who was opposed by a Goldsmith Referendum Party candidate. Hitherto the Cabinet Europhiles had resisted the notion of a referendum before any move towards a single currency. The Party Chairman Brian Mawhinney warned that, without one, Goldsmith's Referendum Party could cost the Tories up to 20 seats. Howard, Lilley and Forsyth all supported it, and Clarke saw he had lost after a Cabinet discussion on 7 March

1996; he ensured, however, that the offer should only apply to the next parliament.

And there were defections, not overtly on the Europe issue, but influenced by demoralisation and frustrated ambition. In October 1995 Alan Howarth, to Labour; then Emma Nicholson to the Liberal Democrats on New Year's Eve, while Peter Thurnham resigned the whip in February 1996, and sat as a Liberal Democrat from autumn 1996. Howarth and Nicholson, but not Thurnham, obtained peerages from their new parties. And at the end of July 1996 David Heathcoat-Amory resigned as Paymaster General in protest at the Government's compromise position on the single currency.

The biggest, and most unexpected, disruption of political calm came in March 1996 when a possibly over-reacting Department of Health admitted a "small, but unproven, risk" that BSE in cattle could cause CJD, a usually fatal disease in humans. The reaction across the EU was hysterical especially in Italy and Germany, and the EU placed a temporary ban on the export of British beef products not only to EU markets but to the rest of the world. As Major added "it was not banned for use in Britain, only everywhere else ... to enable the rest of Europe to continue exporting."[54]

This did have the effect of converting the present author from relative Europhilia towards clear opposition to the single currency. Thus he was one of the 66 Tories voting on 23 April 1996 for Iain Duncan-Smith's private member's bill to overrule certain decisions of the European Court. He also voted, on 11 June, for Bill Cash's private member's bill, to provide for a referendum on any wide-ranging changes in our EU membership. The bill was backed by 95 MPs, mostly Conservative.

On 20 May a minority of member states led by Germany, Austria and the Netherlands blocked a vote in favour of the Commission's proposals for eventual lifting of the ban on gelatine, tallow and semen from Britain. Facing outrage across the Conservative party, Major decided that the UK would withhold its consent from decisions that required unanimous approval. This forced the issue of beef to the top of the agenda for the European summit at Florence at end of June, where there was an agreement, and Major ended his veto. The agreement was not implemented by the EU; as Major angrily describes, "it was a vintage bit of backstabbing by anonymous Commission officialdom." A selective cull of cattle, required by the EU, began early in 1997. The entire export ban was not lifted until 1 August 1999; in Germany's case, even later. "In the two years before the 1997 General Election the UK beef market shrank by a third."[55]

After the 1996 Conservative party conference, Labour's opinion poll lead fell from 23 to 14 per cent. Then a claim by the Conservative Central Office that

Clarke was the obstacle to any change of European policy produced a further row, and the Labour lead shot up. So the single currency haunted the Government until Election Day. A large number of Tory MPs and candidates, including some ministers, were expected to declare their opposition to it in their election addresses. So Major and Clarke met and agreed a change of "nuance". Major told the Commons on 23 January 1997 "It is very unlikely but not impossible that the single currency can proceed safely on 1 January 1999, but if it did proceed with unreliable convergence we would not of course be part of it." Commentators regarded this as the Cabinet's "most sceptical stance yet" over EMU. It was, however, too late to avert the outward and visible display of division, while the phrase "proceed[ing] with unreliable convergence" was unlikely to commend itself on the doorstep.[56]

Senior ministers' speeches were examined by the press for evidence they were preparing for a leadership contest after defeat. "Friends" of Michael Howard suggested he had "no problem " with the idea of leaving the EU. A Rifkind speech in Zurich stated that the single currency would be divisive within the EU, and in February 1997 after another speech in Bonn he told an interviewer he was personally "hostile to a single currency".[57] On New Year's Day 1997 Stephen Dorrell, the Health Secretary, normally a strong Europhile, commented about renegotiating Britain's relations with Brussels.

Just before the Election Paul Sykes, a multimillionaire, offered Eurosceptic candidates up to £3000 towards their election expenses. The *Sun* newspaper endorsed Goldsmith after he had said he would spend £20 million on his campaign. The targeting of his candidates was erratic: while not opposing Lamont, they opposed Heathcoat-Amory, Howard and other sceptics. During the campaign, Major made a dramatic appeal at a press conference to his Party "do not bind my hands when I am negotiating on behalf of the British nation." The present author was disappointed that this did not mark a more decisive policy shift on EMU, however belated.

Apart from Europe, the campaign was heavily influenced by the renewed sleaze issue – the "cash for questions" case of Al Fayed, Ian Greer and Neil Hamilton. And tactical voting completed the Tory rout, so 43 per cent, 31 per cent and 17 per cent voting turned into a disastrous 418, 165 and 46 seats for the three main parties. The results did not discriminate between rebels and loyalists – Teresa Gorman lost on a 17.6 per cent swing against her in Billericay, while Lamont in Harrogate and Portillo in Southgate had crushing defeats. The present author's Parliamentary career ended but only on a 4.6 per cent swing.

And despite everything narrated above, the Major government had a sound economic record after 1992, with inflation below four per cent for four years, and growth at two to three per cent a year. If keeping Major was the main obstacle to Tory revival in the mid Nineties, why did a succession of other leaders not budge the polls or the election results over the next decade?

Tory doldrums 1997–2005: Hague 1997–2001

In contrast to previous Tory election disasters, in 1906, 1945 and 1966, where the defeated leader – Balfour, Churchill, Heath – continued, leading towards victory or at least substantial advance in the following election, the defeats of 1997, 2001 and 2005 each resulted in the resignation of the leader and a succession struggle. Nor was there a speedy return to good fortune. Peter Snowdon expresses the widely held, and probably just view, that the Tories "retreated to the margins of political debate, choosing a succession of unelectable leaders."[58]

The supporters of the various candidates in the June 1997 Conservative leadership election, showed Kenneth Clarke's supporters were predictably Europhile, but sadly, for his future leadership prospects in 2001 and 2005, they were largely old guard, and even more sadly, they included three who later defected to Labour, mainly on the Europe issue: Peter Temple-Morris (in 1998), Shaun Woodward (in 1999) and Quentin Davies (not until 2007). In the last stage of this leadership contest, having concluded that "this was an elimination contest to see which Eurosceptic was eventually going to defeat me", Clarke first offered to stand down in Michael Heseltine's favour ("I believed he was less unpopular than me with the right wing") then, when Heseltine's doctors vetoed it ("twenty years later, Michael remains remarkably healthy"), he launched into "our last desperate idea of the Clarke-Redwood pact". In fact, Clarke asserts, the two usually agreed on domestic and economic matters, and "we solemnly agreed that Europe was to be an open issue with no binding party policy", thus attempting "to reduce Europe's profile in the party's campaigning". Whether this civilised approach would have survived is highly debatable, but it speedily ran into trouble with Redwood supporters. Baroness Thatcher, who had earlier preferred Howard, joined Hague's victorious campaign (he won by 92 votes to Clarke's 70), haranguing Redwood supporters one by one. And if he had won, Clarke later reflected, he would have had to lead the party through "five stormy and divided Europe-obsessed years".[59]

Strong Eurosceptics Lilley and Howard became Shadow Chancellor and Shadow Foreign Secretary, with Redwood and Duncan Smith joining the Shadow Cabinet. This endorsed Hague's pledge not to join any single currency either during the 1997 Parliament or its successor. Thus two Europhile front benchers, Ian Taylor and David Curry, resigned – and some months later, Stephen Dorrell followed them.

Two Conservative MEPs, John Stevens and Brendan Donnelly, left the Conservatives and formed the Pro-Euro Conservative Party (PECP) in January 1999. They were able but their initiative was doomed. Stevens obtained 3.8 per cent of the vote in the Kensington and Chelsea by-election in November 1999 when Michael Portillo was elected. Neither was elected in the June 1999 European elections, their party only obtaining 1.4 per cent of the vote. It was dissolved in December 2001. And Bill Newton Dunn, a Conservative MEP from 1979–94, re-elected as one in 1999, joined the Liberal Democrats in 2000, while James Moorhouse, a Conservative MEP from 1979, joined the Liberal Democrats in October 1998 but retired in 1999.

There was (very limited) traffic by former Tory MPs into UKIP, the party whose later prowess pushed Cameron towards his EU referendum: Roger Knapman, who as an MEP was to lead UKIP, Piers Merchant, who failed to secure election as a UKIP MEP in 2004, and Neil Hamilton, eventually elected as UKIP to the Welsh Assembly. These elections were governed by PR, hence their relative success; all three attempted Westminster seats as UKIP candidates and, as these are determined by first-past-the-post, all failed. The Blair government's introduction of PR for European Parliament elections meant, for the first time, the election of three UKIP MEPs in 1999, giving UKIP "an institutional foothold, access to European Parliament funds and a career trajectory for aspiring politicians".[60]

A reader ignorant of recent political history might, on visiting the experiences of the Major government, consider that to have been the nadir of Tory fortunes. But this continued for over ten years, partly as a consequence of the economic success of the various Labour governments. However, the divisions and unattractiveness of the Tories cannot be ignored.

Bale cites research published by himself and Nick Sparrow showing that "there was no reservoir of hidden Conservative support just waiting to be tapped by a more robustly right-wing, eurosceptic stance". Tory abstention in 1997 was "no more than three quarters of a million, whereas defections to Labour and the Lib Dems ran at something like 3.5 million".[61]

The Conservatives did better in the 1999 local elections than the polls forecast, and the skilful slogan "In Europe, not run by Europe" gave them 34 per cent in the European Parliament elections in June, well ahead of Labour but on a dismal 24 per cent turn out. Hague appealed, somewhat ambiguously, at the 1999 Conference "Come with me, and I will give you back your country." In his speech to the Party's Spring Forum in early March 2001, just before the General Election, Hague not only repeated this pledge eight times but added a more unambiguously sinister warning that under further Labour government, Britain would become a "foreign land". Hague insisted that these remarks referred to the influence of the EU – probably correctly, as his new speech writer was the fanatically Eurosceptic MEP, Daniel Hannan (a Johnson-appointed peer in 2021). Journalists claimed that Nick Wood, Hague's press spokesman, had briefed that Hague was talking about the impact of immigration.[62]

The sorry saga of the Hague leadership is narrated in Simon Walters' *Tory Wars*. The *dramatis personae* include several talented Tory men and women, many of whom served in previous and later governments but who in the years 1997–2005 failed to display loyalty, unity, discipline or restraint. Their contests had little relationship with the Europe issue, but they help to explain the party's continued exclusion from any proximity to power.

The General Election on 7 June 2001 saw another Labour landslide, with a nine-point lead in the popular vote. Hague resigned, and the ensuing leadership election saw much evidence of hostility to Portillo, considered the favourite. His leading supporters included keen Europhiles: Dorrell, Soames, Yeo, Willets, and Lidington but the "anyone but Portillo" group included Liam Fox, David Davis, Michael Ancram and Eric Forth. Clarke came first in the final MPs' vote, with Duncan Smith beating Portillo into third place by one vote. In his autobiography, Clarke declared: "If Portillo and I had got through to the final stage, the Conservative party would have been required to choose between two of its more unpalatable prejudices … whether the party was more Europhobic than homophobic, or vice versa. Faced with the choice at that time, they would almost certainly have plumped for me."[63] Clarke brutally continues: "Most members of the general public and the majority of voluntary (party) members had never heard of Iain Duncan Smith and knew nothing about him." Yet on 13 September he was declared the winner of the membership's vote by 155,993 votes to Clarke's 100,864.

Duncan Smith and Howard 2001–05

In the 2001 election the Tories had polled 1.2 million fewer votes than in 1997. While polls showed Clarke twice as popular with the public as Portillo and four times as popular as Duncan Smith, 86 per cent of Conservative Party members told ICM in August 2001 that Europe was very or quite important in deciding their leadership vote, with 58 per cent thinking it likely that Clarke would split the Party, and only 18 per cent thinking the same of Duncan Smith.[64]

None of the Tory MPs most associated with the Clarke campaign (Tyrie, Curry, Maples, and Ian Taylor) was given a job by Duncan Smith. Howard was Shadow Chancellor and Duncan Smith's campaign manager Bernard Jenkin went to Defence. Dominic Cummings, previously with Business for Sterling, and subsequently highly notorious, became the Party's Director of Strategy, resigning after only eight months.

However, "a determined attempt was made to downplay the European issue".⁶⁵ After increasingly poor performances against Blair at Commons Question Time, and by-election disappointments, opposition to Duncan Smith built up before and at the 2003 Party Conference. After it the very Eurosceptic (later funder of UKIP) Stuart Wheeler, a spread betting millionaire, declared that he and other donors would withhold donations until the very "weak" leader was changed. So the whips encouraged MPs to send in the letters demanding a confidence vote. 25 were needed, 41 went in; the vote was 90 to 75 against Duncan Smith. After this, Howard was drafted in as leader without a contest: the reaction heard by the present author was that "the grown-ups are back in charge".

Clarke, Hague and Portillo chose not to serve under Howard but, with Major, the first two agreed to join an advisory council. Some balance was attempted, such as the inclusion of David Curry (he resigned in less than six months). Similarly, Howard decided not to press MEPs to leave the Christian Democrat dominated European People's Party-European Democrats (EPP-ED) group – to the annoyance of hard-line Eurosceptics and in contrast to Cameron later.

In April 2004 Howard launched a petition for a referendum on the proposed European constitutional treaty. Polling research made it clear that this did not interest voters and disputes over this advice caused ICM to decide to end its professional relationship with the party. Even Michael Portillo, writing in the *Sunday Times* on 6 June 2004 criticised the Tories for thinking "that Europe is their secret weapon, despite an abundance of evidence that it is their curse."⁶⁶

The fear of UKIP was pronounced, with a YouGov poll in late May suggesting it might obtain 20 per cent in the 2004 European elections (in fact, it obtained 16 per cent, against a disappointing 26.7 per cent for the Tories). Howard denied that any of his MPs backed withdrawal from the EU when clearly some of them did, and he withdrew the whip from four Tory peers who expressed support for UKIP.⁶⁷

Liberal-progressive commentators disapproved of Howard over his emphasis – he had been a tough Home Secretary – on immigration control. In 2005 – as a further foretaste of 2017 and 2019, the Conservatives ran a General Election campaign picking up support from lower social groups but losing votes of the professional middle class. Between 1992 and 2005, Tory support fell by 18 points to 36 per cent among AB voters. ⁶⁸

In the General Election of May 2005, the Tories gained 32 seats, taking them to a total of 198, against Labour's reduced total of 355, with the Liberal Democrats on 62. In view of previous expectations, they were disappointed with the result. Howard indicated his wish to resign, but to assist the younger generation of David Cameron and George Osborne, he delayed the contest to autumn.

Blair and Brown in Government and the EU 1997–2010

This tracing of Britain's gradual disillusionment with the EU is intended to be seen mainly from a Conservative standpoint, leading to the debacle in and after 2016, but the Labour governments experienced developments which did not help to diminish Tory scepticism. Most significantly, however, under Labour Britain did not join the euro, and unlike the Tory 1990s experience, this was achieved without political carnage. How did this happen?

There were plenty of respectable economists in favour of EMU "but their arguments tend[ed] to be influenced by political considerations; demonstrating beyond a reasonable doubt that the economic benefits outweigh the costs is trickier". The fear of joining the euro at the wrong rate and wrong time "overwhelmed [Brown's] innate pro-Europeanism" when he became Chancellor.[69] And both Brown and Blair recognised the strength of the Eurosceptic press and public opinion polls showing opposition to EMU.

Blair also wanted to lead in Europe: he was "the most instinctively pro-European Prime Minister since Edward Heath".[70] During the summer of 1997, Brown heard from his key lieutenant, Ed Balls, and other Treasury officials that "Britain's entry in January 1999 was neither feasible, on technical and economic grounds, nor desirable, on political grounds."[71] Even during the 1997 election campaign "Labour was half-hoping that the single currency issue would be postponed anyway: thus Blair could not understand why the Conservatives were so obsessed by the issue".[72] As Brown attended the regular meetings of ECOFIN, he saw the desire of his fellow EU finance ministers to harmonise European taxes "which was anathema to him".[73]

An early flashpoint was triggered on 26 September 1997 by a report by Peston in the *Financial Times* stating that the Government was about to announce that sterling would join early after the 1999 euro launch. The pound fell, reinforcing the view that entry would require devaluation. Blair and Brown agreed to rule out Britain joining in the first wave, and it was agreed that Brown would talk to Philip Webster of *The Times*, trusted by both camps. This produced a front-page headline on 18 October: "Brown rules out single currency for lifetime of this Parliament". As Webster admitted "the headline was stronger than the story but I still felt it stood up."[74]

There was an entertaining footnote. Surprised at the *Times* headline, and failing to reach Brown or Alastair Campbell, Blair finally contacted Charlie

Whelan, Brown's "press officer he [Blair] had tried to have sacked" on his mobile outside the Red Lion pub in Whitehall. He asked Whelan what was this "about us not going into the euro in our first term"? Whelan replied, "Well, I've agreed it with Alastair and Gordon. What's the problem?"[75]

In the Commons on 27 October Brown rejected the constitutional objections: "If … the single currency is successful and the economic case is clear and unambiguous, the Government believes that Britain should be part of it." He established five economic tests, the most important being the need for a sustained period of economic convergence between the eurozone members.

Doubters on the euro issue included senior ministers such as Prescott, Blunkett, Straw and Beckett. Mandelson, a crucial supporter, had to resign in December 1998 over Robinson's help with his house purchase (this was his first resignation; after being reappointed he fell for the second time in January 2001 over the Hinduja passport). By the end of 2000 European leaders had a "more jaundiced view" of Britain, with one senior German minister remarking that he expected Hungary to be in the eurozone before Britain, a clear example of German humour as Hungary is still outside the zone in 2024. And increased scepticism was encouraged by Balls, pointing to the strength of the British economy in contrast to lower growth in the eurozone caused by the fiscal rules of their Growth and Stability Pact. So the European Central Bank policy "that preventing inflation was more important than stimulating growth was, Brown and Blair agreed, folly".[76]

After re-election in 2001, Blair planned a two-year campaign for a British referendum on joining. His blasé optimism over the outcome is remarkable. He concentrated on the political case for the euro: one Treasury official described him as "pretty hopeless at economics", this being , in Seldon's words, "an open secret". Brown, on the other hand, became "increasingly concerned about the economics". In autumn 2002 the Commission called for eurozone countries to cut their budget deficits by 0.5 per cent a year. Brown riposted "I don't think the British public want the European Commission to cut £5 billion a year from (UK) spending."[77]

In his Cairncross Lecture in Oxford on 4 December 2002, Ed Balls, now Chief Economic Adviser to the Treasury, listed various historic mistakes over the exchange rate: the return to the gold standard in 1925, the failure to devalue in 1946 and 1964 only to be forced to in 1949 and 1967 and, finally, the ERM experience. He cited Blair's words in 2001 "we must not repeat the mistakes of the ERM and join under the wrong economic circumstances." Balls "hammer[ed] away at the Chancellor with his view that the euro decision could not be made merely for 'political' reasons and that the economics had to be right."[78]

On 11 December 2001, Blair's key lieutenant Anji Hunter had told a Treasury official that Blair, who believed the five tests were a smokescreen, would retire in favour of Brown so long as Brown delivered on the euro. Andrew Rawnsley reports that Blair asked Clare Short to convey this message to Brown, adding that Brown retorted "two other people have brought me this message from Tony … You can't arrange politics like this. And, anyway, he doesn't keep his word." Keegan asserts that Brown was "affronted and hurt" by these "deal" rumours which, Keegan adds, were "subsequently disproved by historians".[79]

Even so, Blair "repeatedly told his inner circle that he was absolutely dedicated to realising this ambition … indicating he would do it to other EU leaders." He surprised aides and ministers in a discussion shortly before Christmas 2002 by saying: "You know, this is more important than Iraq."[80]

The assessment of the five tests was a major operation. 25 Treasury officials worked on it full time, with another 100, including outside experts, involved. The final report contained the vital sentence "a clear and unambiguous case for UK membership of EMU had not been made and a decision to join now would not be in the national economic interest".[81]

Early 2003 was dominated by Blair implementing his promise to President Bush that the UK would support the USA in invading Iraq. Blair and Brown met on 1 April 2003 – just before the Budget. Blair said, "I don't accept it", hoping to revise the draft. Next day they collided, with Blair losing his temper (a "rare occurrence") and saying "you will have to consider your position", and Brown replying "I'll do just that", as he stormed out.[82] They drew back from the brink but Blair decided they should not "sneak out" the euro decision while the Iraq war was raging. So the announcement was delayed until 9 June 2003 when it was made clear that the first two tests – business cycle compatibility with the eurozone, and flexibility – had both failed. The third and fifth tests – effects on investment and growth and jobs, had passed "conditionally". Only the fourth – benefits for financial services – was passed unconditionally.

The Treasury agreed with Blair to have a further review at the time of the 2004 budget – but with the eurozone still performing worse than the UK, and with the wider fall-out from the Iraq war, including the David Kelly episode, Blair "lacked the heart to push for it".[83] The Iraq war's disastrous aftermath inflicted incalculable damage on the "New Labour" concept, and the discrediting of Blairism led, narrowly, to the election of Ed Miliband, rather than his brother David, as leader in 2010, thus to the election defeat of 2015, and then tragically to the election of Jeremy Corbyn as leader afterwards. This undoubtedly contributed to the outcome of the 2016 referendum.

Even after the prospect of Britain joining the euro received its quietus, the position of the UK within the EU was not helped by the latter's constitutional ambitions. At this stage, Blair was opposed to a referendum on the proposed constitution, seeing all the obvious risks. Straw "peppered Blair with personal minutes arguing the case", fearing the government would be forced to yield in worse circumstances. Blair agreed with Schroeder and Chirac to oppose a referendum. With decisions looming at the Dublin Council in June 2004, pressure mounted on Blair to have a referendum – from many Labour MPs and, obviously, from Michael Howard's Conservatives who wanted to "dish" the constitution and embarrass Blair. The Eurosceptic press joined the fray, with Murdoch's *News of the World* (28 March 2004) having the headline "Traitor Tony Blair is to let Britain be run by ten unelected bodies in his EU splendour"; the *Independent on Sunday* of 28 April revealed that Murdoch himself had argued for the use of "traitor".[84]

Blair then decided for a referendum, leaked to the *Sun* and *The Times*, thus "bouncing" the Cabinet. His retreat "was emboldening to his enemies and alarming to his friends", with Charles Clarke telling him "he was making a monumental error" and an even angrier Mandelson saying "he had made the single worst decision of his premiership".[85] While this view was patently exaggerated, Blair had opened the way for Cameron's disastrous decision a decade later.

This referendum was scheduled to take place in May 2006, with a bill introduced into the Commons in January 2005. To prepare a broad coalition for a Yes vote, Blair had meetings with Ken Clarke and Charles Kennedy, with plans to launch a campaign after the French and Dutch referendums. On 29 May 2005, the French voted No to the constitution by 55 per cent to 45 percent. On 1 June the Dutch voted No by 61 per cent to 39 per cent. The constitution was "dead in the water", with the European leaders deciding to hold a "period of reflection". Plans for a UK referendum were dropped.

Blair "would happily have kicked the constitution into touch for ever", but it lurked in his last months as Prime Minister in 2007. The Lisbon Treaty was signed there in December 2007. On becoming Prime Minister Brown, disliking its supranational elements, delayed assent until he obtained "an elaborate mechanism to ensure the opt-outs" in the fields of justice and home affairs "could not be overridden".[86]

Cameron in opposition 2005–10

The usual "churn" of retirements in the three elections since 1997 meant the older generation of Tory MPs had largely gone, and a new generation, very largely Eurosceptic, was displayed in the voting in the 2005 leadership election. In the first ballot of Conservative MPs on 18 October 2005, David Cameron came second, with 56 votes. After a disappointing Conference speech, the favourite, and by now very Eurosceptic, David Davis, with 62 votes had fewer than predicted. Another strong Eurosceptic, Liam Fox, was third with 42, while the traditional Europhile candidate, Kenneth Clarke, was eliminated with only 38 votes. In the second ballot on 20 October 2005, Cameron came first with 90, Davis second, with 57, while Fox was eliminated with 51. Cameron won the party membership vote, with more than twice as many votes as Davis. The MPs' votes indicate the strength of Euroscepticism – and Cameron himself was no Europhile.

Cameron promised during the campaign that he would pull the Tory delegation out of the EPP group in the European Parliament. Withdrawal took place in 2009, leading to an angry Angela Merkel withdrawing the head of the Konrad Adenauer Foundation office in London.

A notable casualty was Edward McMillan-Scott, a Conservative MEP since 1984, and leader of the British Conservative MEPs between September 1997 and December 2001, when he attended the Shadow Cabinet on European issues. He objected to Cameron's decision to withdraw from the EPP and protested more strongly when the composition of Cameron's new European Conservatives and Reformists (ECR) group was announced after the 2009 European elections. The new group was described, with modest exaggeration, by Liberal Democrat leader Nick Clegg, as "a bunch of nutters, homophobes, anti-Semites and climate-change deniers". In March 2010 McMillan-Scott joined the Liberal Democrats.

Lord Tugendhat regrets that from 2005 down to 2016, Cameron "would grumble and complain about the EU and call for its reform, but rarely say a word in its favour". However, on becoming leader, Cameron urged his party to "stop banging on" about Europe. During four years and more as Opposition leader, he managed to sustain this line – up to a point. For example, in the reshuffle in January 2009 Kenneth Clarke joined the Shadow Cabinet – the first time he had done so since 1997, and "the fact that Clarke was given a favourable welcome by the parliamentary party was an implicit recognition that Europe was no longer quite the obsessive issue …" However Cameron had promised a referendum over the Lisbon Treaty if it was signed but not ratified. As it had been ratified he had to appease his Eurosceptics, so at the St Stephens Club on 4 November 2009 he promised that his government would only transfer more powers to Brussels if sanctioned by a referendum. A Lords debate on subjecting the Lisbon Treaty to a referendum produced this from Lord (David) Howell, leading the Conservative response: "The world has moved towards the referendum mode … People are empowered, they have views and they wish to put those views forward … There will be a lot more of them."[87]

"The key reason why Cameron's premiership becomes so dominated by Europe is down to the Conservative Party itself and the rise of UKIP," declares his biographer.[88] Cameron loathed Nigel Farage and UKIP, describing it in 2006 as full of "fruitcakes, loonies and closet racists". This only served to provoke those sympathising with some of UKIP's views.

After UKIP had won 2.5 million votes in the 2009 European elections on a 35 per cent turnout, the then UKIP leader Lord Pearson offered Lord Strathclyde, Leader of the Lords, that if the Tories made a manifesto commitment to an In/Out referendum, UKIP would stand down in the coming general election and campaign for the Conservatives. Alarmingly, "Strathclyde was enthusiastic"; Cameron rejected the idea.[89] UKIP won only 900,000 votes and no seats in the 2010 Election.

Cameron in government

The Election of 6 May 2010 saw no overall majority, with the Tories as the largest party (306 MPs, to Labour's 258 and Clegg's Liberal Democrats at 57). If the numbers had been slightly better for Labour, there might have been a chance for Labour to have continued in government with Liberal Democrat support. In the event, this might have been better for Britain staying in the EU, although both Labour and the Liberal Democrats might have conceded a referendum, whatever its consequences, and, of course, such a Lab-Lib coalition might well have been overwhelmed in a subsequent General Election. There were negotiations on policy between Clegg and the other two parties. On the final day, 11 May, Clegg rang Brown at 6.50pm: "Gordon, we need more time. The Tory position on Europe is dreadful. They can't be trusted on Europe. You must not resign."[90] But Brown had had enough; with such ministers as Straw bitterly opposed to coalition, and pressed by Mandelson to end the talks, he went to the Queen to resign.

A new and unusual campaign for a referendum was launched in March 2011 – the People's Pledge. Its director was Mark Seddon, former editor of the left-wing *Tribune*, and it had support from MPs and others across the political spectrum. It proposed a series of constituency referenda to ask voters if they favoured one on remaining in the EU, paid for by the People's Pledge and verified by Electoral Reform Services. The first was in April 2012 in Thurrock, Essex, later very strong for UKIP. The turnout was 30 per cent (with 90 percent agreeing with the proposition). Two further referenda took place, in August 2012, in Cheadle and Hazel Grove, with turnouts of 35 per cent and similar results.

Further ones were cancelled once it became clear that Cameron would agree to an In/Out referendum.[91]

Cameron came to office "with little coherent plan for how to achieve" managing the EU issue. After a public petition in the autumn of 2011 calling for a referendum attracted 100,000 signatures, such a motion came before the Commons on 24 October. "Instead of letting the sceptics sound off in a vote that was not binding, Cameron unwisely turned the showdown into a trial of strength," and imposed a three-line whip. The motion was defeated by 483 to 111, with 81 Tories defying the whip, including 49 from the newly elected 2010 intake. One of Cameron's closest aides described this revolt as "the pivotal moment" pointing to the need for a referendum.[92]

The eurozone crisis and the Bloomberg referendum proposal

The referendum pledge in the January 2013 Bloomberg speech "gave the impression of a prime minister reacting to events rather than mastering them" while "the stellar rise of UKIP in 2013–14 threatened the most dangerous split on the right for generations." Bloomberg was "not a speech Cameron had wanted to make"; he had hoped the issue would calm down. He was irritated that "the advice he received before the 2010 election – that there would be no major treaty change in the next five years has turned out to be wrong."[93]

From the end of 2009 the EU endured what became known as the European sovereign debt crisis. Several eurozone states, particularly Greece, Portugal, Spain, and Ireland, were unable to repay or refinance their government debt or to bail out their over-indebted banks without the assistance of other eurozone countries, the European Central Bank (ECB) or the IMF. The Greek government revealed that its budget deficits were far higher than previously thought, called for external help and received an EU-IMF bailout package in May 2010. The crisis resulted in unemployment rates in Greece and Spain reaching 27 per cent and reduced economic growth throughout the entire EU. Some economists advocated the disbandment of the eurozone, or that Greece and the other debtor nations should leave it, default on their debts, and re-adopt their national currencies. EU leaders, Merkel and Sarkozy in particular, made it clear that they linked the survival of the euro with that of the EU. The justification of earlier British warnings about the weaknesses of the eurozone undoubtedly affected opinion in Britain about the EU.

To Cameron's dismay, the crisis produced a threat of a new treaty, with Merkel seeking one to meet German concerns about bailing out irresponsible eurozone members.

On top of this, 2012 was not a good year politically for Cameron's Government.

The spring saw the "omnishambles" Budget, which weakened Osborne. July 2012 saw a large Tory revolt against an elected House of Lords; this Bill's second reading passed by 462 to 124, but 91 Tories voted against it. A decision was later taken to drop the bill, whereupon Clegg claimed that the Conservatives had broken the coalition contract.

Cameron's personal position was further weakened by his promoting gay marriage (as an advance on the legal partnership of gay relationships). Graham Brady, Chairman of the 1922 Committee, thought it "caused more difficulty between Cameron and the parliamentary party than any other single issue over the five years … It felt …like the party was being bounced".[94] 136 Conservatives voted against second reading on 5 February 2013 (on a free vote but with pressure to support Cameron), and at third reading only 40 per cent of Tory MPs supported it. Given the strongly Christian views of Gary Streeter, MP and former opposition front bencher, it is not surprising that he should declare: "The UKIP vote is not just about Europe. It's also about a hard core of traditional Conservative voters saying, actually we don't like the kind of small-l liberal decisions this government is beginning to take. It offends us and we're going to protest and vote UKIP."[95]

The diary kept by the Liberal Democrat, David Laws, a minister during much of the period, drawing on conversations with Clegg and Conservative leaders, indicates the growing Tory panic. The entry for 12 April 2012 reports Clegg believing "that pressure for an in/out referendum" was increasing and "the risk of leaving the EU is getting quite high". Laws reports George Osborne thinking "that Conservative backbenchers are essentially 'unmanageable' on this [Europe] issue", with Osborne believing that while Europe used to be a distraction, it was now a "much more central issue in British politics, given the state of the Eurozone".[96]

An indication of Osborne intelligently seeking to avoid the electoral cataclysm was his asking Laws, in March 2012, if the two parties could make an electoral deal in 2015 "a sort of 'coupon election'", as had happened successfully in 1918. Laws was negative as it would mean his party being unable to contest Conservative seats.[97] Given the Conservative mood and underlying arrogance, they also were unlikely to have tolerated such a deal.

So the inevitability of an EU referendum strengthened. Hague "was the first to argue for" one. Tim Shipman records that a "senior Downing Street official" acknowledged that "the biggest advocate of the referendum was William Hague", whereas Osborne "thought it was a disastrous idea", and was "pretty hostile" in successive meetings, fearing that "several uncontrollable forces" might cause the vote to be lost. He was "the most outspoken opponent of the idea". In a pizza restaurant on 21 May 2012 in Chicago's O'Hare airport, Cameron, Hague and

Ed Llewellyn, Cameron's chief of staff, made the fateful decision: to reform the relationship with the EU and offer a referendum before the end of 2017. "This remains top secret," they agreed.[98]

On 7 November 2012 Merkel came to dinner in Number 10. Cameron explained to her that "the single currency was key because it changed everything", exacerbated by the eurozone crisis. He added that while some Tory MPs "never accepted his leadership and want to destroy him", the great majority are "terrified of their constituency associations". Seldon's judgement is that, while Merkel would try to help, "there are limits to what she can do, given Germany's multilateral relationships in Europe": this was "a caveat remembered more in Berlin than in London".[99]

By late 2012 some of Cameron's closest allies, "including Steve Hilton and Oliver Letwin", were "flirting" with leaving the EU. This was an odd couple: Hilton, Cameron's political strategist, was an eccentric genius; in the USA later he was an outspoken supporter of Donald Trump. In 2019, Letwin, having master-minded a cross-party motion to enable Parliament to vote to avoid a "hard Brexit", became with 20 other Conservative MPs a martyr to the subsequent Johnsonian purge. Gove, also not surprisingly, told *Mail on Sunday* journalists that on the current terms of membership, he would vote to leave the EU, but he opposed a referendum: he did not believe Cameron had thought through "what Britain would be outside the EU". He emailed Cameron before Bloomberg: "You don't need to offer a referendum."[100]

Cameron gave the Bloomberg speech on 23 January 2013. A senior figure in Number 10 regretted that the speech did not contain arguments like "We're going to have to compromise", adding "It was a huge error."[101] Laws records Clegg saying "Cameron may today have sown the seeds of a permanent split in his party over Europe. And if he thinks he can ever win over people like Liam Fox, he must be crazy … Never underestimate how short-termist and tactical he can be." As Farage put it, "The irony was that far from shooting the UKIP fox, all the Bloomberg speech did was feed it."[102]

Post Bloomberg: UKIP's momentum

Michael Crick describes Farage's talents, his communication skills, use of social media, bonhomie, and ruthlessness. Farage led UKIP for most of the period 2006–16, and "it was Farage who turned hostility to the EU from a cranky obsession into one of the great themes of our national life", as well as popularising the link between EU membership and mass immigration.[103]

Already in November 2012 UKIP had won second place, beating the Tories into third, in by-elections in Rotherham and Middlesbrough. The same pattern occurred in by-elections in Eastleigh in February 2013 and South Shields in April. The north-east had not been thought to be a good area for UKIP, but these results showed the willingness of Labour voters there to move Right (as displayed again in the 2016 referendum and also in 2019 by the Tory breakthrough in the Red Wall seats). Then the transitional controls on migrants from Romania and Bulgaria, which had dated from the two countries joining the EU in 2007, ended. UKIP predicted these migrants would compete for jobs and welfare, and the number of non-UK EU benefit claimants rose to over 300,000. "UKIP is thus able to roll together three toxic concepts – the EU, immigration and benefit cheats – into a single argument."[104]

The momentum continued with a *Times* article by Lord (Nigel) Lawson (7 May 2013) calling for the UK to leave the EU: any concessions Cameron might obtain would be "inconsequential". This fuelled an amendment by rebel Tories to the Address in reply to the Queen's Speech (an almost unprecedented move for Conservatives in government) regretting the absence of provision for a referendum. On 15 May, half the Tory backbenchers, 116 including 13 PPSs, voted for this, with the rest of the party including the front bench, abstaining. The amendment was defeated by 277 to 130 only by Labour and the Liberal Democrats uniting – a humiliating position for Cameron.

Then James Wharton, Conservative MP for Stockton South from 2010–17 and a Johnsonian peer from 2020, put forward a Private Member's Bill calling for a referendum. This received its second reading on 5 July 2013 by 304 votes to none, with the Conservatives supporting it, and most Opposition MPs abstaining. Having passed the Commons in November 2013, it had its Second Reading in the Lords (introduced by Lord Dobbs) on 10 January 2014, without a vote. In committee on 31 January peers voted by 180 to 130 not to allow more time for it, with the (defeated) Conservatives voting, in effect, to continue consideration.

In the European Parliament elections on 22 May 2014, with turnout under 36 per cent, UKIP came first, with 27.5 per cent of the vote and 24 seats, up by 11 and ahead of Labour on 20; the Tories went from 26 seats to 19, in third place, and the Liberal Democrats retained just one of their originally 12 MEPs.

2014 saw two Tory defections to UKIP: first, at the end of August, Douglas Carswell resigned and caused a by-election, having taken with him the detailed voting files of his Clacton constituency. Then, a month later, Mark Reckless, MP for Rochester and Strood, defected. In his by-election on 9 October, Carswell won with just under 60 per cent of the vote, with Reckless winning his on 20 November with 42 per cent. Carswell survived in the 2015 general election, later leaving UKIP and retiring; Reckless was defeated. Apart from Carswell, UKIP won no 2015 seats thanks to the electoral system, with Farage failing to win Thanet South by 2812 votes. UKIP obtained 13 per cent of the vote.

Polls and commentators had predicted a hung parliament. One source has a group of Eurosceptic Tory MPs gathering in Bernard Jenkin's Kennington kitchen, it seems just after the election, having "expected to be discussing an Owen Paterson [sic!] leadership bid in the wake of a Conservative defeat".[105] In fact, there was a surprise Conservative victory, with Conservatives gaining 27 seats from the Liberal Democrats, plus eight from Labour, while losing ten to Labour. This gave Cameron a slight overall majority – 330 seats compared to the 326 required. Labour saw its position in Scotland wiped out, with the SNP gaining 50 seats, 40 from Labour. The Liberal Democrats lost all but eight of their seats. The result clearly ruled out any continuation of the Conservative-Liberal Democrat coalition, and made an EU referendum inevitable.

After the 2015 election: the referendum

After the Election, Cameron was attacked "for allowing the country to believe that he will achieve more in his renegotiation … than he was ever capable of doing." He was also criticised by both Lynton Crosby and Andrew Feldman, key advisers, for "rush[ing] prematurely" into a referendum instead of leaving it to 2017, giving him more time to lobby the EU governments better. Tugendhat sums up: "He should have developed a case to convince people of the merits of membership in terms of British interests, shared values like those underpinning the relationship with the United States, and a vision of the sort of Europe he would like to see and Britain's role within it. He failed to attempt this until far too late …"

The problem Cameron encountered was that the new member states in Eastern Europe "stood staunchly opposed to compromise on the absolute free movement of people", while southern members were "suspicious of any reforms that might undermine the strength of the eurozone".[106] The press response to the outcome was cool, with the *Telegraph* arguing that the negotiation only proved that "the EU is arcane and sclerotic" and even the pro-Remain *Times* calling his deal "thin gruel".

The role of Boris Johnson was crucial to the outcome. The belief at the time was that he was balanced between the two sides, drafting articles for each view. A study of Tom Bower's recent biography shows that he felt no obligation of friendship or political alliance towards Cameron, whom he tended to despise, thinking he himself could do the job better. And his views were consistently Euro-sceptic. At a Party Conference fringe meeting in 2011 he called for a referendum on the Lisbon Treaty and, "for the first time, an in-out vote". His economic adviser as Mayor of London, Gerard Lyons, in 2014 told him that, since the EU refused to reform, Britain should leave; Johnson's own view was that there was nothing to fear about leaving the EU except "a great and glorious future". Key supporters, then and especially later, such as Lynton Crosby and Eddie Lister, told him that the Brexit campaign needed him as leader. While Ben Wallace and Jake Berry, close friends who promoted his Parliamentary ambitions in Uxbridge and South Ruislip, urged him to support Remain, Greece's plight after the Euro crisis "intensified" his "antagonism towards the EU". If Cameron's negotiation had produced more radical changes, Johnson might have hesitated. As it was, his personal ambitions coincided with his political beliefs.[107]

The actual Referendum contest is too well known (and painful) to dwell on. There were fond hopes that electors would follow the lead of respected politicians and that, with obvious omissions, Cameron's Cabinet would hold together. Neither occurred, and in the limited campaigning this author did he was equally dismayed by the Brexit opinions both of strangers and supposedly moderate and usually loyal Conservative old friends and neighbours.

The hope was that Labour votes would come to the rescue. But their leader Corbyn was a closet Leaver: 37 per cent of 2015 General Election Labour voters were estimated to have voted Leave.[108]

Not only did the Remain campaign never arouse urgency or emotion, it concentrated too much on economic arguments, leading to the "Black Day", 15 June, when Michael Howard and Iain Duncan Smith (both former leaders) and ex-Chancellors Lawson and Lamont all attacked George Osborne (and the Bank of England) for "hideous scaremongering". Thus, "Remain may have won the economic argument, but Leave won the immigration debate, and the latter trumped the former".[109]

Leave's "infamous" Breaking Point poster showing lines of migrants crossing the Croatia-Slovenia frontier at the height of 2015 migrant crisis was unveiled on 16 June. While this shocked "nice" people, most of the Leave politicians interviewed said immigration was the issue "most often raised on the doorstep". A Michael Ashcroft survey of 12,300 people after the vote endorsed this, with 33 per cent supported leaving so as to regain control of UK borders.[110]

The EU had prescribed a transition period from 2007 until 2011 for migration from the new member states; the Blair government, along with Ireland and Sweden, decided to open the borders immediately. Their forecasts were that only a few thousand EU migrants would arrive each year; in fact, over a million came into the UK in four years. The future minister Ed Balls, then working for Brown, later described this decision as "a failure of forecasting, of foresight, of politics and understanding", giving "rocket boosters to scepticism and hostility towards the EU".[111]

In January 2010 Cameron told Andrew Marr "we would like to see net immigration in the tens of thousands rather than hundreds of thousands" – that is, back to the levels of the 1990s. This was not delivered in the years before the Referendum (nor, palpably, since then). Consideration of the subject is usually, and unhelpfully, confused between East European (to which the UK had agreed by treaty) and non-European (usually not specifically agreed) sources of immigration. From 2011 European immigration continued to increase, with the eurozone crisis contrasting with British expansion.

As David Goodhart, in his very balanced study of the wider subject, acknowledges, Poles were not popular in parts of eastern England. Some non-European migrants were hostile to East Europeans: Goodhart cites Indians in Slough, Pakistanis in Peterborough "and Caribbeans everywhere", with Shaun Bailey, a black Tory London Mayoral candidate in 2021, claiming that a lot of black people "think that just when we were getting a foothold we have been pushed to the back of the queue again and these white Europeans have jumped ahead".[112]

Further thoughts on Brexit

In November 2010, Angela Merkel told the European Parliament that the Commission would become the government of the EU. The German-born Brexiter UK Labour MP Gisela Stuart later declared: "Voting to remain is not just about staying in the EU as it is today, but ... staying in as it will look in 2025 or 2035."[113]

Hence various wise but belated observations. Donald Tusk, then the Polish president of the European Council, said at Bratislava in September 2016: "It would be a fatal error to assume that the negative result in the UK represents a specifically British issue ... The Brexit vote is a desperate attempt to answer the questions that millions of Europeans ask themselves daily," including "the security of the citizens and their territory, protection of their ... cultural heritage and way of life". President Macron also admitted, in a BBC broadcast in early 2017, that the anxieties leading to Brexit were present in other European countries and if a referendum were to be held in France on continued membership, he could not guarantee a positive response.[114] Thus the European Parliament elections in May 2019 saw substantial gains for populist Right parties such as the French FN, the Italian League, the Swedish Democrats and the German AfD.

As Tusk acknowledged, concerns mainly related to security and cultural identity. Acting alone, the EU had failed to prevent ethnic cleansing of Muslims in Bosnia and Kosovo, requiring intervention through NATO by Britain and the US. Over the Ukraine crisis in early 2022, Germany's response was initially ambiguous, while German defence spending in 2019 was, at 1.2 per cent, well short of the required 2 per cent. Putin's folly dramatically reversed this for a time, but early 2024 sees signs of further European lukewarmth.

On cultural identity, two years after the Referendum, the historian Professor Niall Ferguson wrote: "Increasingly, I believe that the issue of immigration will be seen by future historians as the fatal solvent of the EU … Their argument will be that a massive *Völkerwanderung* overwhelmed the project for European integration, exposing the weakness of the EU as an institution and driving voters back to national politics for solutions."[115]

As described in these last two chapters, British attitudes to Europe since 1945 were characterised, at crucial points, by hostility, confusion, timidity and weakness. What might have worked to Britain's lasting benefit was lost through lack of interest in the 1945–57 period. The motives which prompted the application of 1961 were confused. Then, for the next 20 years Britain acted from an economically weak position. Britain welcomed the "Common Market" and especially the Single Market, but affected to ignore the associated political agenda, strongly held by the Continentals from the start and steadily pursued. Britain made no attempt to promote an alternative. Without such an alternative, a combination of vigilance and a preparedness to say no was needed, alongside effective campaigning against internal political dissent. The two decades after 1997 were not well used by the main British political parties.

There are various criteria by which the effects of Brexit might be judged.

First, UK leadership. The author originally asked himself, "Will Johnson and Co remain united and succeed in delivering a constructive Brexit?" As Johnson might acknowledge "*alea iacta est*" (the die is cast). The politics of the six years following the referendum vote might stand as "the Westminster Anarchy", with the May government seeing its various Brexit compromises defeated in the Commons, the dramatic intervention of the Supreme Court "Spider Woman" – Lady Hale, its President – over Johnson's prorogation, Johnson's purge of Tory MPs resisting a no-deal Brexit, his electoral triumph in December 2019, speedily followed by the unprecedented circumstances of the Covid epidemic. All culminated in the fall of Johnson and then, rapidly and bizarrely, of his successor, Liz Truss, in later 2022.

Second, economics. Some have argued that the UK, free of the rules and requirements of the out-dated EU economic model, might achieve a success which, within the EU, would have evaded us. Others argue the cost of disruption with our nearest and largest trading partner. The numbers change, distorted by the consequences of Covid. In particular, David Smith, Economics Editor of the *Sunday Times,* has consistently spelt out the costs. He declares that those who voted to leave the EU "hate being told that this has damaged UK growth, added to inflation and government debt, and hurt exports and investment". This is what "all the credible evidence shows, and we are only a little way through the process".[116]

Third, and most important, isolation. Would Britain, outside the EU, be more isolated than otherwise? The UK's membership of the EU did not diminish the UK's ability to work with such nations as the USA, Australia, Canada, New Zealand, Japan or India – rather the contrary. Brexit has also affronted Britain's many friends and admirers across Europe, and we have inevitably abandoned the various causes, stronger among the peripheral EU states and critical of EU establishment thinking, which we might have supported by remaining inside the EU. However, 2023 developments – the AUKUS agreement on nuclear co-operation, the "Windsor Framework" solution to the Northern Ireland Protocol and the August 2023 agreement for the UK to rejoin the EU "Horizon" science programme – are all welcome.

Fourth, immigration and demography. No political issue has been subject to such distortion and falsification, as that of migration – into the UK and, indeed, other EU countries. It was crudely and falsely exploited by the "Out" campaign during the 2016 referendum: the Turkish migrants lie. In fact, the Brexit claim that leaving the EU would reduce immigration has proved to be an even greater lie. The "Remain" campaign failed to respond to the concerns aroused, and thus the impression was given, particularly to voters in the north, that Brexit would prevent migrants from Eastern Europe competing with, and undercutting the pay of, local workers. In contrast to that, there was the view, held by many in Britain, including myself, that Poles, Hungarians and Czechs, let down by the UK and other Western countries in 1938–39, 1945, 1947 and 1956, made welcome contributions to Britain's economy and society, without appearing to be starkly "alien". Brexit has had no effect on the steady flow of migration, often illegal, from Africa, the Middle East and Asia: this has massively increased.

Linked to this is the cheerful expectation that the UK population will not only continue comfortably to exceed that of France, but will come to rival Germany's. This may look good to GDP-worshippers and large multinationals. It is less assuring to those who are concerned about the quality of life, "green-ness", overpopulation, congestion, transport, housing, and social services, especially in south-eastern England. And it raises the question of "how English is this rapidly increasing population?" That point will be developed in the Epilogue.

Fifth and finally, as befits a work with "civilisation" in its title, we should regret that Brexit has had sad consequences in the fields of artistic and musical exchanges and for university art history departments. The November 2023 *Burlington Magazine* editorial declared that, with the loss of home fee status producing average fees of £22,500 instead of £9,250, "the decline in European students studying art history in the UK is therefore a matter of considerable concern."

FOOTNOTES

1 Lamont, *op cit*, p35; Tugendhat, *op cit*, p121.
2 Commons Hansard, 26 June 1991, col 1028; Seldon, *Major*, pp244–45.
3 Seldon, *Major*, p243; Major, *op cit*, p270.
4 Major, *op cit*, pp271–72.
5 Lamont, *op cit*, pp11, 36, 111–12.
6 *Ibid*, p118.
7 *Ibid*, pp 118–20, 123.
8 *Ibid* pp124–26.
9 Major, *op cit*, p275.
10 Tim Bale, *The Conservative Party from Thatcher to Cameron*, Polity Press, 2010, p37.
11 Seldon, *Major*, p251.
12 *Ibid*, pp253–55.
13 Letter to Taylor, 14 October 1992, quoted by Moore, *op cit*, III, p803, also p824.
14 Major, *op cit*, p291.
15 *Ibid*, p347.
16 Seldon, *Major*, p296, from interview with Lord Patten.
17 Seldon, *Major*, p294; Lamont, *op cit*, pp199–201.
18 Major, *op cit*, p350.
19 Major, *op cit*, p312; Kenneth Clarke *Kind Of Blue: A Political Memoir*, Macmillan, 2016, p303.
20 Major, *op cit*, pp314–16; Lamont, *op cit*, p227.
21 Robert Peston, *Brown's Britain*, Short Books, 2006, p117.
22 Major, *op cit*, p320, Lamont, *op cit*, p152.
23 Lamont, *op cit*, pp151–54.
24 Lamont, *op cit*, pp233–38, Seldon, *Major*, pp310–11.
25 Major, *op cit*, p324; Keegan, *op cit*, p101; Lamont, *op cit*, p259.
26 Major, *op cit*, p326.
27 Major *op cit*, p 329, Lamont, *op cit*, p244–45.
28 The Black Wednesday episode is in Major, *op cit*, pp330–37, 340, Lamont, *op cit*, pp 240–66 and Clarke *op cit*, pp 304–06. The last point, about the reserves, is in Peter Snowdon, *Back from the Brink: The Inside Story of the Tory Resurrection*, Harper Press, 2010, p23.
29 Lamont, *op cit*, pp269–74.
30 Seldon, *Major*, p320; Lamont, *op cit*, p280; Clarke, *op cit*, p303
31 Major, *op cit*, pp338, 352–54.
32 Major, *op cit*, p371; Tugendhat, *op cit*, p136.
33 Major, *op cit*, p371.
34 These extracts from House of Lords Hansard 14 July 1993, cols 257, 282–3, 286, 296.
35 House of Commons Hansard, 1 December 1989, cols 994–96.
36 Quoted Seldon, *Major*, p372.
37 Commons Hansard, 9 June 1993, cols 281–85.
38 Quoted, Major, *op cit*, pp585–87; Seldon, *Major*, p393.
39 Paraphrase by Seldon, *Major*, p486.
40 Major's words, *op cit*, p522.
41 *Ibid*, p579.
42 Seldon, *Major*, pp403, 408.
43 Earlier quote, Andrew Grice, *Sunday Times*, 7 August 1994; Seldon, *Major*, p499.
44 Major, *op cit*, p605–06; Quoted, Seldon, *Major*, p551.
45 Hurd, *op cit*, p511.
46 Major, *op cit*, p615; Lamont, *op cit*, p433; Seldon, *Major*, pp562–65.

47 Lamont, *op cit*, p435.
48 *Ibid*, pp438–39.
49 Major, *op cit*, pp619–23; Bale, *op cit*, p57.
50 Seldon, *Major,* p575, the latter sourced from an unnamed "private interview".
51 Seldon, *Major,* p586; "Private information" to author: Simon Walters, *Tory Wars: Conservatives in Crisis*, Politico's, 2001, p16.
52 Major, *op cit*, p620; Lamont, *op cit*, p443.
53 Seldon, *Major*, p648; unnamed source, Snowdon, *op cit*, p30.
54 Major, *op cit*, p 651.
55 *Ibid*, pp656–57.
56 Seldon, *Major,* pp690–91, 697, 704, 720–21, 724.
57 Major, *op cit*, p700.
58 Snowdon, *op cit*, p*ix*.
59 Clarke, *op cit*, pp399–400.
60 Mosbacher and Wiseman, *op cit*, p23.
61 Bale, *op cit*, p72.
62 *Ibid*, p123, also citing Jo-Anne Nadler, *Too Nice to be a Tory*, Simon and Schuster, 2004, pp209–10.
63 Clarke, *op cit*, p416.
64 Bale, *op cit*, pp136, 138, 142.
65 Bale, *op cit*, p146; Snowdon, *op cit*, p91.
66 Quoted, Bale, *op cit*, pp211–12.
67 *Ibid*, pp213, 215.
68 Snowdon, *op cit*, pp160–61,169; Bale, *op cit*, pp243, 255.
69 Peston, *op cit*, pp179, 186.
70 Philip Stephens, *The Blair Government and Europe*, Political Quarterly 2001, Vol 72, p67.
71 Anthony Seldon, Blair, The Free Press, 2004, hereafter Seldon, *Blair,* pp318, 321.
72 Keegan, *op cit*, p315.
73 Peston, *op cit*, p198.
74 Quoted Seldon, *Blair*, pp322–23.
75 Whelan interviewed by Seldon in 2003, quoted *Blair*, p324.
76 Tom Bower, *Gordon Brown*, Harper Collins 2004, p 314.
77 Seldon, Snowdon and Collings, *Blair Unbound*, Simon and Schuster 2007, hereafter *Unbound*, pp205, 208; Keegan, *op cit*, p328.
78 Quoted Keegan, *op cit*, p322; Keegan, *op cit*, p311; Peston, *op cit*, p234.
79 Peston, *op cit*, p228; Andrew Rawnsley, *The End of the Party: The Rise and Fall of New Labour*, Penguin Books, 2010, p74; Keegan, *op cit*, p327.
80 Rawnsley, *op cit*, p190.
81 Peston, *op cit*, pp232, 234, 236.
82 Peston, *op cit*, p238; Seldon etc, *Unbound*, pp210–11.
83 Peston, *op cit*, pp243–45.
84 Rawnsley, *op cit*, p258; Seldon etc, *Unbound*, pp263–67.
85 Rawnsley, *op cit*, p259.
86 Anthony Seldon and Guy Lodge *Brown At 10*, Biteback 2010, hereafter Seldon, *Brown*, p68.
87 Tugendhat, *op cit*, p171; Snowdon, *op cit*, p338; Lords Hansard, 11 June 2008, col 634.
88 Anthony Seldon and Peter Snowdon, *Cameron At Ten*, William Collins, 2016, subsequently *Cameron*, p168.
89 Mosbacher and Wiseman, *op cit*, p27.
90 Seldon, *Brown at No 10*, p461.
91 Mosbacher and Wiseman, *op cit*, pp34–35.
92 Seldon, *Cameron,* p xxix; Tim Shipman, *All Out War: The Full Story of How Brexit Sank Britain's Political Class*, William Collins 2016, p7.
93 Seldon, *Cameron*, pp*xxx*, *xxxii*.
94 Interview with Brady, *ibid*, p280.
95 *Guardian*, 4 May 2012, quoted Tugendhat, *op cit*, p187.
96 David Laws, *Coalition Diaries 2012–2015*, Biteback, 2017, p5; Diary, 19 November 2012, *ibid*, p57.
97 *Ibid*, p3.
98 Shipman, *op cit*, pp3, 10; Seldon, *Cameron*, p259.
99 Seldon, *Cameron*, pp 262–65.
100 Shipman, *op cit*, p10–11.
101 *Ibid*, pp12–13..
102 Laws, *op cit*, p86; Mosbacher and

Wiseman, *op cit*, pp39–40.

103 Review of Michael Crick *One Party After Another: The Disruptive Life of Nigel Farage*, Simon and Schuster, 2022, by Dominic Sandbrook, *Sunday Times*, 6 February 2022.

104 Seldon, *Cameron*, p384.

105 Mosbacher and Wiseman, *op cit*, p53.

106 Seldon, *Cameron*, p 546; Tugendhat, *op cit*, pp175, 183; Mosbacher and wiseman, *op cit*, p71.

107 Tom Bower, *Boris Johnson: The Gambler*, W H Allen, 2021, pp186, 200–01, 232–33, 258–62.

108 Mosbacher and Wiseman, *op cit*, p126.

109 *Ibid*, pp100–01.

110 *Ibid*, pp110, 113, 117.

111 Ed Balls *Speaking Out: Lessons in Life and Politics*, Hutchinson, 2016, p185.

112 David Goodhart, *The British Dream: Successes and Failures of Post War Immigration*, Atlantic Books 2013, pp232, 213.

113 Bogdanor, *op cit*, pp120, 123.

114 Quoted, *ibid*, p115–16.

115 *Sunday Times*, 17 June, 2018.

116 *Sunday Times*, 27 August 2023.

Epilogue:
Migration and "Culture Wars"

"If we do not tackle this problem, the numbers will only grow. It will overwhelm our countries and our capacity to help those who actually need our help the most. If that requires us to … amend the postwar frameworks around asylum, we must do that."
(Prime Minister Rishi Sunak, in Rome, *Sunday Times,* 17 December 2023).

"Boris made a series of serious mistakes in the immediate aftermath of leaving the EU. We replaced freedom of movement for the EU with freedom of movement for the rest of the world. That was a fundamentally damaging decision."
(Robert Jenrick, former immigration minister, *Sunday Times,* 7 January 2024)

The diversity theme was impressively displayed at the King's Coronation. The human links the UK has with most parts of the world, largely derived from the former Empire, are certainly a powerful asset, and should, if sensibly handled, assist post-Brexit aspirations. Hitherto, relations among the various ethnic groups in the UK, including the majority host population, have been better than those in other countries, like France and the USA. And one factor promoting balance is that, not only does the UK contain sizeable communities from other European countries, from North America and Australasia, and the long-established Jewish community – Ministers and advisers of Jewish ancestry were crucial to the success of the "Thatcher revolution" – but the non-white communities are themselves diverse. We have Hindus, Sikhs and Muslims originating from the Subcontinent, Muslims and Christians from Africa, the Caribbean and the Middle East, and Buddhists and others from eastern and south-eastern Asia. And the UK has, for decades, attracted from all over Europe and beyond, distinguished leaders, innovators, creators and performers in business and the arts, just as we have in 2023 prominent Ministers of immigrant origin.

Thanks to this diversity and greater travel opportunities, as well as modern media, we have now a far greater knowledge of, and respect for, other cultures. This should build up a resistance against "fundamentalism" or exclusivity in religion and culture – such attitudes as "ours must overwhelm all the others", even to the extent of destroying their artefacts and persecuting or killing their adherents. While this resistance may be progressing in Britain and Europe, sadly fundamentalism and exclusivity are increasingly present in Asia and Africa.

However, all this in the UK might be put at risk, hence the warnings in this Epilogue. For several years immigration has been, in most people's view, excessive, with currently no clear hope of substantial diminution. And simultaneously – not perhaps overtly but potentially linked to migration – we have seen develop what are termed "culture wars". These started in America but have inevitably spread to the UK and elsewhere.

Previous culture wars did occur in the presence of a small migrant community, for example, the 1960–70s student disturbances. Mrs Thatcher's "swamping" remark of 1978 was perhaps premature, and it coincided with a period when personal abuse of non-white people was, sadly, all too common. That has largely evaporated, but recent immigration has surged out of control, undoubtedly fuelling cultural tensions.

Immigration "out of control"?

As this Epilogue was being drafted, official statistics confirmed that *legal* migration into the UK in 2021 and 2022 was four times what had been envisaged at the time of the EU referendum. Revised statistics published in late November 2023 showed net immigration was 672,000 in the year to June 2023, including 1.2 million incomers, mainly from outside the EU. Some of this was exceptional – genuine refugees from Ukraine and Hong Kong. Many others are students, controversially accompanied by large numbers of dependants; higher education has a, perhaps excessive, vested interest in the students, though not in the dependants. Much of the rest is to meet job vacancies, which under the UK's bizarre – or incompetent – recruitment, training and welfare system, are not filled by existing UK residents.

Clare Foges in mid-2022 cited work visas up by 50 per cent from 2019–20, study visas up 58 per cent, visas granted for family reasons up by 63 per cent.[1] The 2021 census shows 10 million people (15 per cent of the total) now in the UK born outside it, compared to 7.5 million (11.9 per cent) in 2011 and 4.2 million (7.1 per cent) in 2001.

One of Enoch Powell's wiser remarks on migration, alongside several foolish or exaggerated claims, was "numbers are of the essence". Yet many pundits regard the current inflow as inevitable. As Lionel Shriver provocatively wrote "We've been conditioned to regard minority majorities later this century as our destiny." Later, she stated that some commentators believe "the dilution of native populations is a conspiracy", adding "Me, I blame fecklessness".[2] White British are already in a minority in London, estimated at 37 per cent. Shriver describes recent Migration Watch assumptions and projections, calculating that if the same level of ingress is sustained, the UK's population will rise to between 83 (described as "optimistic") and 87 million ("more realistic") by 2046, requiring "between six and eight million new homes – the equivalent of 15 to 18 Birminghams".[3]

Apart from the consequences of over-population for congestion, transport, housing/planning/green belt invasions, health and social services, and schools – as well as population movement through "white flight" – the question must be asked "won't these much-increased numbers transform Britain culturally?" With small numbers overall, as in the 1990s, cultural assimilation might have been hoped for – but, surely, now that hope is diminishing. Quite apart from antagonism towards the "white British", how far will there be harmony among the various ethnicities? Already India's Prime Minister, while pressing for Britain to admit more Indian migrants, is complaining about UK-based Sikh conspiracies directed towards India. As Douglas Murray declares in the context of disturbances between local Indians and Pakistanis in Leicester, "if you import the world's people you import the world's problems".[4] A year later, the Leicester tensions are still of concern, fuelled, it seems, by recent migrants with links to Gujarat where Muslims have suffered from Hindu extremism. And nationwide tensions – pro-Palestinian marches and anti-Jewish incidents – followed the Hamas atrocities in Israel of 7 October 2023 and the Israeli military response. These produced the perhaps exaggerated headline "Marches show UK multiculturalism has failed" accompanying an Iain Martin *Times* article.[5]

The Powell numbers warning is of special relevance for the smaller nations of the British Isles. With populations of 5.4 million, 3.1 million, 1.9 million and 5.3 million respectively, Scotland, Wales, Northern Ireland and the Irish Republic would each find their specific cultures challenged if immigration continued to increase.

Shriver advocates speeding up applications from "proper political refugees" (Ukrainians and Hong Kongers) "while drastically reconceiving 'asylum', which is now a farce".[6] If possible, Britain should be sympathetic to refugees from Afghanistan and Iraq who result from the Blair government's "liberal imperialism" (heartily backed at the time by most Conservatives) and continued by the Cameron government. Such sympathy, however, must be coupled by a firm front towards migrants from elsewhere. And, of course, it is both ludicrous and offensive that arrivals, whatever their origin, previously resident in France should be termed "refugees" or "asylum seekers".

Incidentally, an unintended but disastrous consequence of that liberal imperialism was the removal of the secularist Saddam that left open the door for the fundamentalist ISIS terrorists. The present author would have liked to visit the sites in Syria and Iraq featured in Chapter Two of this book: even if these have survived, that would now be difficult.

Another own goal by the West was the removal of Gaddhafi from Libya, enabling that vast area to become a chaotic staging point for illegal migration across the Mediterranean. Somewhat extravagantly, Christopher Caldwell argued that the consequences of the 2011 invasion of Libya "will probably be seen to have posed a larger threat to the 'European way of life' than the invasion of Ukraine" in 2022.[7] He simultaneously referred to the rarely-mentioned (published 1973) novel *The Camp of the Saints*, by Jean Raspail, which predicted the collapse of Western civilisation from an overwhelming wave of Third World immigrants. An unbelievable nightmare scenario fifty years ago; now …

As William Hague argued (*We need migrants: This is only the start of the age of migration*), "we could introduce special visas for outstanding talent." This apart, Hague's was a contentious article, claiming inevitability for the migrant flood: "the need of European countries for migrants is inescapable". His arguments are plausible, but can and should be resisted (even in the difficult case of shortages of labour in the care sector, which will take longer to resolve). Over 20 years ago, Hague spoke of Britain becoming a "foreign land". Whatever he meant then, his implied 2023 migration policy would certainly deliver it.[8]

So in addition to "pull" to meet incompetently-created labour shortages, there is the "push" from economic migrants seeking that sanctimonious concept a "better life". To take the most alarming, and not very long-term scenario: the two areas where past and present population growth is huge and climate change (as well as wars) threatens, are the Indian Subcontinent and Africa. Are there any parts of the planet with agricultural potential which are currently under-populated? Two stand out: the USA, and with climate change, perhaps more of Canada; and Russia, Ukraine and adjacent territories. Within Western Europe the one fertile country with low population density is France. Massive migration into all these areas is … unlikely!

As emphasised by the "invasion" of Lampedusa during the summer of 2023, all Europe faces the migration threat, not just the UK, although we seem to be a preferred ultimate destination, probably owing to language and our believed welfare weaknesses. The 5th-century Roman Empire became incapable of resisting migration. If needed, more ruthless and well-equipped modern states will resort to firmer methods: a *Times* leader referred to "more aggressive naval patrolling and even military interventions at embarkation points to destroy smuggling operations and boats".[9] Australia and Denmark have actually halted illegal immigration. So, eventually, African and Asian population pressures will have to be resolved by the people and authorities in those continents. With liberation over 60 years ago from colonial power, the salvation of those countries now more obviously rests with those who belong there. Nor should Asians and Africans deprive their homelands of their talents and work. The "first world" might help financially, but the "third world" is not short of valuable resources with financial potential. That potential will require good governance, an end to corruption, a more even spreading of the benefits – and more effective curbing of population growth.

Much of the inter-ethnic harmony which has been achieved in the UK will be jeopardised if large-scale migration continues. That is why long-standing immigrant communities should support limitation. As Douglas Murray argues, "mass migration … damages a country for two reasons … it allows the immobilisation of a percentage … of the local population, who will find certain jobs beneath them. Second, it allows the country to change beyond all recognition." As *Spectator* editor, Fraser Nelson, declared, employers prefer "cheaper, foreign-born workers over investing in training locals". And "why do we think a million more people are going to end up on disability benefits? Why in Britain, not anywhere else?"[10]

So long-term failings in UK government, business and society have rendered the UK especially vulnerable to migration. And great government embarrassment – with great public anger – has accompanied the grotesque imitation of the Dunkirk evacuation – the constant illegal migration via small boats crossing the Channel. As William Hague acknowledged, on "the specific problem of illegal migrants arriving on our beaches, most voters never realised that leaving the EU meant we could no longer even try to return migrants to the first safe country they entered in Europe". However, as a *Spectator* leader acknowledged, "our neighbours have a vested interest in interrupting the chain of migration towards Britain." Lionel Shriver is right to describe the illegal flow as "a sideshow", with the magician's audience "distracted by one motion while the trick is slyly performed with another", that other being "soaring" legal migration.[11]

Not surprisingly, practically all democratic European countries now have powerful populist right-wing parties (liberals use the word "extreme"), strongly opposed to continuing immigration. In some, like France and Germany, the drift to the Right has been fuelled by riots and criminal acts by immigrants. Sweden, especially, is a shocking and compelling example. As Jonathan Miller wrote "Sweden has let in more refugees and people claiming to be refugees, as a share of the population, than any other European country. It is coping with the consequences … [it] has become one of the most violent countries in Europe, as measured by gangland shootings", many in heavily immigrant communities.[12]

The failure to tackle immigration might result, in any or all of these countries, in power passing to demagogues with unattractive agendas going beyond the migration issue.

Culture wars

Tensions raised by the migration issue are sharpened by campaigns, accelerating in 2020, against various respected figures in British history, such as Cecil Rhodes, Sir Francis Drake, Captain Cook and Admiral Lord Nelson. Disgracefully, the St Paul's Cathedral visitors' website attacked Winston Churchill as "an unashamed imperialist and white supremacist" (these terms were removed after protests). *History Reclaimed* refuted any connections Nelson had with slavery or the slave trade, pointing out that his victory at Trafalgar, "by confirming Britain's naval primacy … made it easier for Parliament" in 1807 to abolish the slave trade.

History Reclaimed, "an independent group of scholars from seven countries and several ethnicities", declares: "The abuse of history for political purposes is as old as history itself. In recent years, we have seen campaigns to rewrite the histories of Western democracies so as to undermine their solidarity as communities, their sense of achievement, even their basic legitimacy. There have been calls to abolish national days in Canada and Australia … Slavery – despite being almost universal until the early 19th century – is cast as the original sin of Britain and the United States, supposedly shaping their societies and creating their prosperity. Figures central to their histories are stigmatised as racists or for having connections, however distant, with slavery." Thus the current Australian High Commissioner in London has since called for Australia Day on 26 January 2024 not to be celebrated as usual.

The demolition of statues, removal of inscriptions, and rewriting of history creates anger and division. While many of these campaigns' leaders are left-wing whites, they seek to – and need to – exploit black or Asian support, if they can.

The Black Lives Matter movement was triggered by a (white) US policeman killing, while arresting, black George Floyd in Minneapolis in May 2020. One of Tom Bower's many criticisms of Boris Johnson in his, on balance, quite sympathetic biography, is that Johnson "failed to deliver a defining speech to answer the culture war inspired by the Black Lives Matter movement who had pulled down a statue in Bristol, daubed the word 'racist' on Winston Churchill's statue in Parliament Square, and disputed the traditional interpretation of British history. At critical moments, the student of ancient Greece and Rome was unable or not minded to deliver a memorable oration about his values and his vision."[13]

The statue in Bristol was of Edward Colston, benefactor to the city and slave trader. Stained glass windows in St Mary Redcliffe dedicated to Colston have since been removed and replaced by ones of a black Jesus on a slave ship and Jesus with Mary and Joseph on a cross-Channel migrant boat.[14] Charles Moore reminds us of the failed attempt by Jesus College, Cambridge, to remove from its college chapel the 17th century memorial to the benefactor, Tobias Rustat, on account of his slavery connections. This, despite the lavishing of "a six-figure sum of college [charitable] money on going to law";[15] sadly, this is a fraction of the seven-figure sum spent by Christ Church, Oxford in recently removing its Dean.

Patrick West remarked "The culture wars are really taking place, whether the left likes it or not ... The consequences of wokery are having a tangible effect in the USA – which always heralds what is to come – where withdrawal for support and funding of the police has grown at a time of rising crime in Los Angeles, San Francisco and even now New York ... Its advance in the UK has been ... as insidious as it has been invidious. For years now we have seen people lose their jobs, been silenced, or been (sic) investigated by the police for saying something 'inappropriate' online. We live now in a culture ... in which people are terrified to speak their minds on a day-to-day basis."[16]

As Professor Robert Tombs, Founder Editor of *History Reclaimed*, stated "Those of us old enough to be untouchable can speak our minds, but younger colleagues often tell us shamefacedly that they are constrained by concern for their careers."[17]

The termination of Nigel Farage's bank account by Coutts gave alarming evidence of how wide culture wars have spread. As Allison Pearson commented: "HR departments have been totally captured by Equality, Diversity and Inclusion (EDI), a virulent virus from the US ... Those of us who thought that the 'culture wars' were just something being waged by Leftie teachers will have realised that the woodworm of woke is gnawing away at the foundations of all our institutions."[18]

An early and major example of the UK lurching into culture wars was the reaction to the work on the British Empire by Nigel Biggar, Regius Professor Emeritus of Moral and Pastoral Theology at Oxford. As he told Matthew Parris, what "colleagues in Oxford and elsewhere ... did was to respond with abuse and aggression", with Priyamvada Gopal, Professor of Postcolonial Studies in Cambridge, tweeting in December 2017 over Biggar's proposals "We must shut this down." In consequence, Biggar believes he "lost the co-operation of one of the most eminent historians of empire, John Darwin ... I'm certain he took fright", adding "I've had to meet junior research fellows in Oxford in secret because they didn't want to be seen in public with me".[19]

Biggar remarked that the 2015 "Rhodes Must Fall" agitation in Oxford involved "several hundred students ... some were even Rhodes scholars", while simultaneously, in the homeland of one of RMF's leaders, Jacob Zuma and the ANC "were busy looting the state, driving South Africa to the verge of collapse".[20]

A YouGov poll shows US respondents think 41 per cent of their countrymen are black, when the real figure is 12 per cent; they think 29 per cent are Asian (real figure 6 per cent); 39 per cent Hispanic (real figure 17 per cent). Similarly in the UK: YouGov respondents estimated that 20 per cent of the UK was black (real figure 3 per cent), 15 per cent Muslim (real figure 4 per cent). This should not surprise anyone: another YouGov survey found that 45 per cent of those surveyed thought that ethnic minorities were over-represented on TV.[21] This is especially true of TV adverts and, increasingly, of dramas.

Various claims have been made, the latest in a children's book, published in 2023, that the Roman emperor Septimius Severus was "black" (his father was Carthaginian but neither then, nor now, were the people of North Africa "black"). Examples proliferate of black actors playing non-black roles, like that of Cleopatra, provoking adverse reaction in Egypt. Douglas Murray cites the latest Hollywood version of *Peter Pan* where "Tinkerbell was black", and the 2022 Broadway production of *Macbeth* has Banquo "inexplicably played by a black woman" while his assassin "was even more inexplicably in a wheelchair". UK Christmas TV saw black actors playing Dr Who and an Agatha Christie detective; her book *Murder is Easy* was "retrofitted to suit the BBC's obsession with racism and colonialism".[22] Much was made of this, whereas the introduction of East Asian and even South Asian actors into white roles is much less apparent.

Culture wars have impacted across various fronts. The Northern School of Contemporary Dance "dropped proficiency in ballet as an entry requirement because it was rooted in 'white European ideas'".[23] Museums and galleries appear to be in the front line. "Huge billboards" in Pitt Rivers in Oxford "tell the visitor that the museum is 'a footprint of colonialism'"; "we are repeatedly hectored about 'imperialism and colonialism'". In Tate Britain, Rex Whistler's vast mural in the basement was closed off, because of two small uncontentious details involving black children. The Tate "bowed to the chants of malevolent activists and effectively agreed that the mural was 'pro-slavery' and that Whistler held racist views"; not so, and he was killed in action in 1944.[24] There was shock when the Wellcome Collection closed its display dedicated to its founder Sir Henry Wellcome "because of its alleged racism and sexism."[25]

Rarely far from controversy, Melanie Philipps describes the Tate Modern: "I wandered through room after room featuring art works inveighing against colonialism, oppression and other presumed abuses of western capitalist power structures." After other examples, she refers to a report by Professor Eric Kaufmann for Policy Exchange which revealed that "59 per cent of school leavers said they were explicitly taught, or at least had heard from an adult at school, about 'white privilege', 'unconscious bias' or 'systemic racism'."[26]

Historians now working in Britain such as David Olusoga and Sathnam Sanghera have recently taken up the cudgels over the British Empire and the Raj.

The linkage between migration and culture wars was overtly made by Olusoga, who told the Hay Festival that the National Trust and other institutions were right to address the issues of slavery and colonialism, including the possibility of "repatriating" artefacts, as this was "essential to their long-term survival" (he presumably meant that of the institutions). He explained "By one projection, by 2050 a third of the country will be diverse or mixed." Charles Moore later criticised the Trust for its "slavery and colonialism" report on NT properties, along with the Colonial Countryside Project, which "invited schoolchildren to visit NT houses and write poems deriding their former owners".[27]

Evidence of the tensions which calls to repatriate artefacts can evoke appears in a recent article by Professor Robert Tombs, *The trouble with returning the Benin Bronzes*.[28] Seized by a British force in 1897, these were dispersed to various museums and some, like Cambridge's Museum of Archaeology and Anthropology and others in Germany, planned to send the bronzes to Nigeria. The Nigerian president wished them to go to the present Oba of Benin. As Tombs points out, "Benin itself was a violent, slave-holding and slave-raiding society", practising human sacrifice – in 1897 "some bronzes, many of them busts of royal ancestors, were covered in the blood of sacrificed slaves". In June 2023 the Restitution Study Group (RSG), representing descendants of West African slaves, as Tombs describes, "premiered a short film asserting their moral right over the disposal of these objects, made of brass the Obas gained by the sale of their ancestors". The RSG "vehemently objects to the bronzes being returned to the successors" of these slave owners – "and instead wishes them to stay in western museums where they are accessible to all".

After Dr Tony Sewell's Government-commissioned report on race and ethnic disparities was attacked by Labour, Kemi Badenoch, business and equalities minister, Conservative leadership contender in late 2022 (and again in 2024), said of those who exaggerate racism in the UK "I don't think that people who make this argument understand that they are playing with fire. They are poisoning the well of society."[29]

Professor Tombs asserted: "The orthodoxy in schools, in museums and on television is always the same: Britain was racist in the past and so it is racist today. Producing evidence that this is untrue or exaggerated is heresy." He added that "settler societies have the grave problem of dispossessed indigenous minorities which we do not. For that reason, 'history wars' in America, Canada and Australia are far more serious and potentially damaging than in Britain."[30]

13,000 British schools, including primary age pupils, were reported as receiving learning resources from the Key, a national information service. This, "largely imported from the US", related to racial divisions there including teaching critical race theory, which asserts that racism is entrenched in society. Tomiwa Owolade, author of *This is not America*, said that theories originating in the US do not "reflect the actual experiences of British children." More recently, Melanie McDonough, who reviews children's books, describes how these are "all over the inclusion and diversity agenda".[31]

Douglas Murray warns that "until recent years, being founded by [Thomas] Jefferson" whether in the case of the United States itself or the University of Virginia "was a badge of honour", whereas "today it is a mark of Cain", on account of Jefferson being "not just a slave-holder but a slave-rapist" (this latter is disputed). So statues of Jefferson were toppled. And after an earlier 2021 decision by New York to remove the Jefferson statue in City Hall, Lionel Shriver (*Topple Jefferson and no one is fit to stand*) remarked that, on this basis, the US "will be obliged to throw loads of its public statuary onto the scrapheap", as James Madison, Monroe, Benjamin Franklin, and George Washington himself all owned slaves.[32]

Richard Dawkins described how under New Zealand's former Ardern government, "spawned" by her brief successor Hipkins, science classes were to be taught that Maori "Ways of Knowing" had equal standing with "western" science. This was reinforced by a claim that "to insist that Maori children be taught to read is an act of colonisation". Douglas Murray describes how "the English countryside is about to be 'studied' by 'hate crime experts' to find out whether 'rural racism' is lurking". This will be "led by academics 'specialising in British colonialism and hate studies'". He criticises the Government's Prevent programme, directed mainly at Islamist extremism, but extended, with advice from left-wing activist groups, to include right-wing extremism. An analysis by Prevent's Research Information and Communications Unit (RICU) in 2019, referred to individuals taking information and opinions from "pro-Brexit and centre-right commentators" such as those quoted in these recent paragraphs. A "reading list of historical texts which produce red flags to RICU" included Hobbes' *Leviathan*, Burke's *Reflections on the Revolution in France*, as well as works by Thomas Carlyle, Adam Smith, C S Lewis, J R R Tolkien and Aldous Huxley.

The present author's 1970s Conservative Research Department colleague, Michael Dobbs (Lord Dobbs of Wylye) wrote how his colleague, Lord Willoughby de Broke, having refused to participate in a "mind-numbing" politically-correct Lords training scheme , was banned from many Lords facilities, including the Peers' Dining Room. Dobbs took him in as his guest: "a small act of defiance in a world losing any sense of proportion".[33]

If it all goes wrong?

The consequences of the various episodes described in this volume were usually disagreeable for the peoples let down by those with responsibility and authority. The consequences for the inhabitants of the Western Roman Empire have, despite problems with evidence, been discussed in detail, especially as far as Britain was concerned. While the resistance of the Eastern Roman Empire was admirable, the consequences of its various periods of weakness, in the 7th and 8th centuries and after the mid-11th century, were dire for its inhabitants.

Key in this present study, the Revolution in France produced the Reign of Terror, over 20 years of almost continuous European warfare, and over 80 years – at least – of regime instability. For Russia, the consequences of Revolution were (and remain) monstrous.

In addition to specific barbarities in France and Russia, much historical conflict, before the 17th century in western Europe and more generally outside western Europe has been fairly barbarous, as described in the Introduction. This also applies to various colonial wars against indigenous peoples in the Americas, in Africa, especially German and Italian excesses, and Asia, including the Russian conquest of Central Asia and the Caucasus. Since independence from European powers, both Asia and Africa have witnessed numerous episodes of barbarism, some approaching genocide.

Falling short of genocide, in Europe we have seen used the device of expulsion of those not considered to belong, most notably of Muslims and Jews from Spain under Isabella in 1492, and later of the Moriscos (ostensibly Christianised former Muslims) under Philip III. Reference has already been made to the expulsion of Greeks from Turkey in 1922 but less reported in traditional history are the forced expulsions of Muslims from the Balkans as the Ottomans were driven out of these countries. According to the US historian and demographer Justin McCarthy, in the century after 1821 5 million Muslims were driven from their homes and another five and a half million died, some killed in wars, others perishing as refugees.[34]

Understandable in the circumstances was the expulsion of Germans in and after 1945 from the various central and east European countries where they had been settled, sometimes for centuries. This involved large numbers of fatalities. And, still later, came the brutal ethnic cleansing of minorities as the former Yugoslavia fell to pieces in the 1990s.

The unhappy examples in the preceding paragraphs are intended to reinforce warnings if ethnic transition in Western Europe goes too far. This author dares not speculate what might happen in those circumstances.

The challenge

A correspondent to the *Spectator* set it out: "Currently there are simply far too many people coming to the UK and staying here, illegally or otherwise. Unless the political class grasps this issue, the public will come to the conclusion that their leaders just don't care. If this happens, political forces will arise which will bypass the existing consensus …"[35]

This last point was powerfully reinforced by Juliet Samuel in *The Times*: "The need to protect national cohesion by slowing the pace of population change is always seen as less urgent than some other more immediate problem, like the shortage of care workers. The Tories are finding it impossible to reduce migration because they think like multinational corporate managers rather than national statesmen." So they resort to the "cheapest, quickest way possible" even if this involves "a policy that, over the long run, accelerates cultural and social change at an unprecedented pace". She repeated this condemnation as tensions rose: "In immigration policy, economic models that focus on labour costs … have eclipsed qualitative arguments about social cohesion, values and cultural change."[36]

She adds: "We are being governed by a political class incapable of recognising and protecting our national interests … because too many of them don't even believe those interests are legitimate. Either they will change their view or, ultimately, the voters will change them."[37]

To hammer the lesson home, coinciding precisely with the triumph in the Netherlands of the populist Rightist PVV party led by Geert Wilders, doubling its seats and obtaining a quarter of the vote, and the revelation that UK net immigration in 2022 had risen to nearly 750,000 (139,000 more than previously thought), Iain Martin warned the Tories (and the UK generally) of the likely impact in the 2024 Election of Nigel Farage and the Reform party: *Reform and Farage give Tories sleepless nights*.[38]

One of Wilders's allies, leader of another powerful Dutch anti-immigrant party, is herself of migrant (Kurdish-Turkish) origin, Dilan Yesilgoz. A well-known, not Rightist (he was a former Labour parliamentary candidate), British columnist of Indian descent, Matthew Syed, fiercely reacted to the British Supreme Court rejecting the Sunak government's Rwanda solution to illegal immigration. This was on account of the "refoulement principle", which bans deportation to countries where immigrants might face persecution: one might query how many of such countries receive UK overseas aid or are members of the Commonwealth. Syed continues: "When it comes to asylum, most western nations feel as if they are trapped in an unbreakable snooker … Liberals fear asylum is like a ticking time bomb", with tens of millions "who qualify as refugees". In addition to identity cards, he argued that "the only tenable way out is to remove this (refoulement) principle from all treaties and domestic laws". "Indeed", he concluded, "the future of the West just might depend on it."[39]

FOOTNOTES

1 *The Times*, 30 May 2022.
2 *Spectator*, 20 May 2023, 2 December 2023.
3 *Spectator*, 1 July 2023.
4 *Spectator*, 24 September 2022.
5 *Sunday Times* report, 17 September 2023; *The Times*, 9 November 2023.
6 *Spectator*, 20 May 2023.
7 *Spectator*; 23 September 2023.
8 *The Times*, 11 July 2023, and see p xxx.
9 *The Times*, 29 September 2023.
10 *Spectator*, 6 May 2023, 20 May 2023, respectively.
11 *The Times*, 30 November 2021, *Spectator*, 28 October 2023 and 1 July 2023, respectively.
12 *Boiling Point, Spectator*, 8 July 2023.
13 Bower, *Johnson, op cit*, p519.
14 *The Times*, 9 June 2023.
15 *Spectator*, 30 September 2023.
16 *Spectator*, 15 May 2023.
17 *Spectator*, 5 August 2023.
18 *Daily Telegraph*, 21 July 2023.
19 *Spectator*, 4 February 2023.
20 *Spectator*, 7 October 2023.
21 Lionel Shriver, *The Times* 16 April 2022, 2 June 2022; also *The Times*, 1 March 2023.
22 *Spectator*, 19 August 2023; Philip Patrick, *Spectator Diary*, 29 December 2023.
23 *The Times*, 25 November 2022.
24 Details and quotes from Douglas Murray, *Spectator*, 3 December 2022.
25 *The Times*, 28 November 2022.
26 *The Times*, 6 June 2023.
27 Olusaga in *The Times*, 31 May 2023; Moore in *Spectator*, 4 November 2023.
28 *Spectator*, 10 June 2023.
29 *Sunday Times*, summer 2022.
30 *Spectator*, 5 August 2023.
31 *The Times*, 1 August 2023; *The Times*, 5 December 2023.
32 *Spectator*, 4 March 2023; *The Times*, 27 October 2021.
33 These two paragraphs from, respectively, *Spectator,* 4 March, 4 February, 8 April, 18 February, 28 January 2023, 3 December 2022.
34 Justin McCarthy, *Death and Exile: The Ethnic Cleansing of Ottoman Muslims, 1821–1922*, Darwin Press, 1996; also Berna Pekesen, "Expulsion and Emigration of the Muslims from the Balkans", in *European History Online*, the Leibniz Institute of European History, Mainz, 2012.
35 *Spectator*, 18 March 2023.
36 *The Times*, 18 May 2023 and 9 November 2023.
37 *The Times*, 18 May 2023.
38 *The Times*, 23 November 2023.
39 *Sunday Times*, 19 November 2023.

Bibliography

Adams, Max, *The First Kingdom: Britain in the Age of Arthur*, Head of Zeus, 2021

Aronson, Theo, *The Fall of the Third Napoleon*, Cassell, 1970, p47.

Bale, Tim, *The Conservative Party from Thatcher to Cameron*, Polity Press, 2010

Bell, David, *Shadows of Revolution: Reflections on France, Past and Present*, OUP, 2016

Beloff, Nora, *The General Says No*, Penguin, 1963

Bennett, Gareth, *The Tory Crisis in Church and State: The Career of Francis Atterbury Bishop of Rochester*, Clarendon Press, 1975

Biddle, Sheila, *Bolingbroke and Harley*, George Allen and Unwin, 1975

Biggar, Nigel, *Colonialism: A Moral Reckoning*, William Collins, 2023

Biggs-Davison, John, *The Walls of Europe*, Johnson, 1962

Black, Jeremy, *The British Abroad: The Grand Tour in the Eighteenth Century*, Sutton, 1992.

Black, Jeremy, *America or Europe? British Foreign Policy 1739–63*, UCL Press, 1998

Black, Jeremy, *Britain as a Military Power 1688–1815*, Routledge, 2002

Bogdanor, Vernon, *Britain and Europe in a Troubled World*, Yale UP, 2020

Bower, Tom, *Gordon Brown*, Harper Collins, 2004

Bower, Tom, *Boris Johnson: The Gambler*, W H Allen, 2021

Brenton, Tony, editor, *Historically Inevitable? Turning Points of the Russian Revolution*, Profile books, 2016

Brenton, Tony, "The Short Life and Early Death of Russian Democracy January 1918", in Brenton, ed

Broers, Michael, *Europe Under Napoleon*, I B Tauris, 2015

Brown, Peter, *The Rise of Western Christendom*, Wiley-Blackwell, 2003

Bury, J P T, *France 1814–1940*, Routledge, 1985

Catterall, Peter, editor, *The Macmillan Diaries: The Cabinet Years 1950–57*, Pan Macmillan, 2004

Churchill, W S, *Marlborough, His Life and Times*, Vol IV, George C Harrap, 1938

Clark, Sir George, *Oxford History of England: The Later Stuarts 1660–1714*, OUP, Second Edition, 1956

Clarke, Kenneth, *Kind Of Blue: A Political Memoir*, Macmillan, 2016

Clarke, Stephen, *The French Revolution and What Went Wrong*, Cornerstone, 2019

Crawford, Donald, "The Last Tsar", in Brenton, ed

Dalrymple, William, *From the Holy Mountain*, Harper Perennial, 2005

Davidson, Ian, *The French Revolution: From Enlightenment to Tyranny*, Profile Books, 2016

Dixon, Simon, "The Assassination of Stolypin", in Brenton, ed

Du Cann, Sir Edward, *Two Lives*, Images Publishing, 1995

Dutton, David, *Anthony Eden: A Life and Reputation*, Arnold, 1997

Dutton, David, "Anticipating Maastricht: The Conservative Party and Britain's First Application to Join the European Community", in Contemporary Record, Vol 7, No 3, Winter 1993

Esdaile, Charles, *The Peninsular War*, Allen Lane, 2002
Figes, Orlando, "The 'Harmless Drunk': Lenin and the October Insurrection", in Brenton, ed
Foss, Clive, *The Persians in Asia Minor*, HER, 1975
Foss, Clive, *Ephesus After Antiquity*, CUP, 1979
Foss, Clive, "Life in City and Country", in Mango, ed
Frankopan, Peter, *The First Crusade: The Call from the East*, The Bodley Head, 2011
Fuller, Maj Gen J F C, *Decisive Battles of the Western World*, Vol I, BCA by arrangement with Cassell, 2003, first published 1954
Furet, François, *Revolutionary France 1770–1880*, Blackwell Publishing, 1992
Gerrard, James, *The Ruin of Roman Britain*, CUP, 2013
Goldsworthy, Adrian, *Pax Romana: War, Peace and Conquest in the Roman World*, Weidenfeld and Nicolson, 2017
Goodhart, David, *The British Dream: Successes and Failures of Post War Immigration*, Atlantic Books, 2013
Hall, Major John *The Bourbon Restoration*, Alston Rivers, 1909
Halsall, Guy, *Barbarian Migrations and the Roman West 376–568*, CUP, 2007
Halsall, Guy *"Two Worlds Become One: A Counter-Intuitive View of the Roman Empire and Germanic Migration"*, in *German History*, Vol 32(4), OUP, 2014
Hardman, John, *Life of Louis XVI*, Yale UP, 1993
Hardman, John, *Marie Antoinette*, Yale UP, 2019
Harris, Tim, *Revolution – The Great Crisis of the British Monarchy 1685–1720*, Allen Lane, 2006
Harvey, Robert, *The War of Wars*, Constable, 2007
Heather, Peter, *The Fall of the Roman Empire*, Pan Macmillan, 2005
Heather, Peter, *Empires and Barbarians: Migration, Development and the Birth of Europe*, Macmillan, 2009
Heather, Peter, *The Restoration of Rome*, Macmillan, 2013
Heather, Peter, *Rome Resurgent: War and Empire in the Age of Justinian*, OUP, 2018
Heather, Peter, "Race, Migration and National Origins", in *History, Memory and Public Life*, Routledge, 2018
Heather, Peter, *Christendom: The Triumph of a Religion*, Allen Lane, 2022
Hennessy, Peter, *Never Again: Britain 1945–51*, Penguin edition, 2006
Hennessy, Peter, *Having It So Good: Britain in the Fifties*, Allen Lane, 2006
Hennessy, Peter, *The Prime Minister: The Office and its Holders since 1945*, Penguin, 2001
Herrin, Judith, *Byzantium: The Surprising Life of a Medieval Empire*, Allen Lane, 2007
Hickson, Kevin, *Britain's Conservative Right Since 1945: Traditional Toryism in a Cold Climate*, Palgrave Macmillan, 2020
Holmes, Geoffrey, *Politics, Religion and Society in England 1679–1742*, Hambledon Press, 1986

Howard-Johnston, James, "Al-Tabari on the last great war of Antiquity", in *East Rome, Sasanian Persia and the End of Antiquity*, Ashgate Variorum, 2006

Howard-Johnston, James, "Heraclius' Persian Campaigns and the revival of the Eastern Roman Empire 622–630", in *East Rome, Sasanian Persia and the End of Antiquity*

Howard-Johnston, James, "Pride and Fall: Khusro II and His Regime", in *East Rome, Sasanian Persia and the End of Antiquity*

Huerta, Carlos de la, *The Great Conspiracy: Britain's Secret War Against Revolutionary France 1794–1805*, Amberley, 2016

Hurd, Douglas, *Memoirs*, Little, Brown, 2003

Jackson, Peter, *The Mongols and the Islamic World: From Conquest to Conversion*, Yale UP, 2017

Jones, Colin, *The Great Nation: France from Louis XIV to Napoleon*, Penguin, 2003

Kaegi, Walter E, *Byzantium and the Early Islamic Conquests*, CUP, 1992

Karlin-Hayter, Patricia, "Iconoclasm", in Mango, ed

Keegan, William, *The Prudence of Mr Gordon Brown*, Wiley, 2003

Keay, John, *India: A History*, Harper Collins, 2000

Keay, John, *China: A History*, Harper, 2009

Kelly, Catriona, "The Bolsheviks and the Church", in Brenton, ed

Kennedy, Hugh, *The Court of the Caliphs*, Phoenix, 2005

Kennedy, Hugh, "The Last Century of Byzantine Syria: A Reinterpretation" in *The Byzantine and Early Islamic Near East*, Ashgate Variorum, 2006

Kennedy, Hugh, "The Arab-Byzantine frontier in the eighth and ninth centuries: military organisation and society in the borderlands" in *The Byzantine and Early Islamic Near East*, Ashgate Variorum, 2006

Kennedy, Hugh, "Antioch: from Byzantium to Islam and back again", in *The Byzantine and Early Islamic Near East*, Ashgate Variorum, 2006

Kennedy, Hugh, *The Great Arab Conquests*, Weidenfeld and Nicolson, 2007

Kneale, Matthew, *Rome: A History in Seven Sackings*, Atlantic Books, 2017

Lamont, Lamont, *In Office*, Warner Books, 2000

Landis, Erik, "Fate of the Soviet Countryside", in Brenton, ed

Laurent, J, *Byzance et les Turcs Seljoucides*, Berger-Levrault, 1914–19

Laws, David, *Coalition Diaries 2012–2015*, Biteback, 2017

Lawson, Nigel, *The View from No 11*, Bantam, 1992

Lefebvre, Georges, *The Great Fear of 1789: Rural Panic in Revolutionary France*, Pantheon Books, 1973.

Lewis, Bernard, *What Went Wrong: The Clash between Islam and Modernity in the Middle East*, Weidenfeld and Nicolson, 2002

Lieven, Dominic, *Nicholas II, Emperor of All the Russias*, BCA, 1994

Lieven, Dominic, *Towards the Flame: Empire, War and the End of Tsarist Russia*, Allen Lane, 2015

Lieven, Dominic, *In the Shadow of the Gods: The Emperor in World History*, Allen Lane, 2022
Lucas-Dubreton J, *The Restoration and the July Monarchy*, Heinemann, 1929
Macmillan, Harold, *Tides of Fortune 1945–55*, Macmillan, 1969
Magdalino, Paul, "The Medieval Empire 780–1204", in Mango, ed
Manco, Jean, *The Origins of the Anglo-Saxons*, Thames and Hudson, 2018
Mango, Cyril, editor, *Oxford History of Byzantium*, OUP, 2002
Mango, Cyril, "The Revival of Learning" in Mango, ed
Mansel, Philip, *Louis XVIII*, Blond and Briggs, 1981
Mawdsley, Evan, "Sea Change in the Civil War", in Brenton, ed.
McCarthy, Justin, *Death and Exile: The Ethnic Cleansing of Ottoman Muslims, 1821–1922*, Darwin Press, 1996
MoLynn, France, *1759 The Year Britain Became Master of the World*, BCA, 2004
McLynn, Frank, *Napoleon – A Biography*, Vintage, 1998
McMeekin Sean, *History's Greatest Heist – The Looting of Russia by the Bolsheviks*, Yale UP, 2009
McMeekin, Sean, *The Russian Revolution: A New History*, Profile Books, 2017
McMillan, James, *Profiles in Power: Napoleon III*, Longman, 1991
Major, John, *The Autobiography*, HarperCollins, 1999
Merridale, Catherine, *Lenin on the Train*, Penguin, 2017
Mitford, Nancy, *Madame de Pompadour*, Sphere Books, 1968
Moller, Violet, *The Map of Knowledge: How Classical Ideas were Lost and Found*, Picador, 2019
Morton, Nicholas, *The Mongol Storm: Making and Breaking Empires in the Medieval Near East*, Basic Books, 2023
Moore, Charles, *Margaret Thatcher: The Authorized Biography*, Allen Lane, Vol II, 2016; Vol III, 2019
Mosbacher, Michael and Wiseman, Oliver, *Brexit Revolt: How the UK Voted to Leave the EU*, New Culture Forum, 2016
Nicholson, David, *Crisis of the British Empire – Turning Points After 1880*, Halsgrove, 2017
Nixey, Catherine, *The Darkening Age: The Christian Destruction of the Classical World*, Macmillan, 2017
Norwich, John Julius, *Byzantium: I The Early Centuries*, Viking, 1988
Norwich, John Julius, *Byzantium: II, The Apogee*, Viking, 1993
Norwich, John Julius, *Byzantium: III, The Decline and Fall*, Viking, 1995
Oosthuizen, Susan, *The Emergence of the English*, Arc Humanities Press, 2019
O'Donnell, James, *Augustine, Sinner and Saint*, Profile Books, 2005
Parker, Geoffrey, *Global Crisis: War, Climate Change and Catastrophe in the Seventeenth Century*, Yale UP, 2013.
Payne, Sebastian, *Broken Heartlands: A Journey through Labour's Lost England*, Macmillan, 2021

Peacock, A C S, *The Great Seljuq Empire*, Edinburgh University Press, 2015
Peston, Robert, *Brown's Britain*, Short Books, 2006
Pipes, Richard, *Three Whys of the Russian Revolution*, Pimlico, 1998
Pipes, Richard, "The Kornilov Affair", in Brenton, ed
Polastron, Lucien, *Books on Fire: The Destruction of Libraries Throughout History*, English translation Inner Traditions International, Rochester, Vermont, USA, 2007
Price, Munro, *The Perilous Crown – France between Revolutions 1814–48*, Macmillan, 2007
Ramsay, William, and Bell, Gertrude, *The Thousand and One Churches*, with a new foreword by Robert G Ousterhout and Mark Jackson, University of Pennsylvania Museum of Archaeology and Anthropology, Philadelphia, 2008
Rawnsley, Andrew, *The End of the Party: The Rise and Fall of New Labour*, Penguin Books, 2010
Reinert, Stephen, "Fragmentation 1204–1453", in Mango, ed
Roberts, J M, *The Penguin History of the World*, Penguin, 1995
Russell, Miles and Laycock, Stuart, *UnRoman Britain: Exposing the Great Myth of Britannia*, The History Press, 2010
Sarris, Peter, *Empires of Faith: The Fall of Rome to the Rise of Islam*, OUP, 2011
Sarris, Peter, "The Eastern Empire from Constantine to Heraclius (306–641)", in Mango, ed
Seldon, Anthony, *Major: A Political Life*, Orion, 1999
Seldon, Anthony, *Blair*, The Free Press, 2004
Seldon, Snowdon and Collings, *Blair Unbound*, Simon and Schuster, 2007
Seldon, Anthony and Lodge, Guy, *Brown At 10*, Biteback, 2010
Seldon, Anthony and Snowdon, Peter, *Cameron At Ten*, William Collins, 2016
Service, Robert, *Trotsky: A Biography*, Pan Macmillan, 2010
Service, Robert, *Stalin: A Biography*, Pan Macmillan, 2010
Service, Robert, *Lenin: A Biography*, Pan Macmillan, 2010
Seward, Desmond, *The King over the Water: A Complete History of the Jacobites*, Birlinn, 2019
Shephard, Jonathan, "Spreading the Word: Byzantine Missions", in Mango, ed
Shipman, Tim, *All Out War: The Full Story of How Brexit Sank Britain's Political Class*, William Collins, 2016
Sixsmith, Martin, *Russia, A 1000 year Chronicle of the Wild East*, BBC Books, 2011
Sixsmith, Martin, "Fanny Kaplan's attempt to kill Lenin, August 1918", in Brenton, ed
Snowdon, Peter, *Back from the Brink: The Inside Story of the Tory Resurrection*, Harper Press, 2010
Stephens, Philip, "The Blair Government and Europe", in Political Quarterly 2001, Vol 72
Stewart, Rory, *Politics on the Edge*, Jonathan Cape, 2023
Stone, Norman, *The Eastern Front 1914–1917*, Hodder and Stoughton, 1975

Strauss-Schom, Alan, *The Shadow Emperor – A Biography of Napoleon III*, Amberley Publishing, 2018

Thorpe, D R, *Supermac: the Life of Harold Macmillan*, Chatto and Windus, 2010

Tompkins, Arthur, *Plundering Beauty-a history of art crime during war*, Lund Humphries, 2018

Treadgold, Warren, "The Struggle for Survival (641–780)", in Mango, ed

Tugendhat, Christopher, *The Worm in the Apple: A History of the Conservative Party and Europe from Churchill to Cameron*, Haus Publishing, 2022

Vallance, Edward, *The Glorious Revolution*, Little, Brown, 2006

Venning, Timothy, *If Rome Hadn't Fallen: What Might Have Happened if the Western Empire Had Survived*, Pen and Sword, 2011

Walters, Simon, *Tory Wars: Conservatives in Crisis*, Politico's, 2001

Ward Perkins, Bryan, *Cambridge Ancient History, Vol xiv, Later Antiquity: Empire and Successors 425–600*, CUP, 2000

Ward Perkins, Bryan, *The Fall of Rome and the End of Civilisation*, OUP, 2005

Western, J R, *Monarchy and Revolution, The English State in the 1680s*, Blandford Press, 1972

Williams, Basil, revised by CH Stuart, *Oxford History of England: The Whig Supremacy 1714–60*, OUP, 1961

Woolf, Stuart, *Napoleon's Integration of Europe*, Routledge, 1991

Zamoyski, Adam, *Phantom Terror: The Threat of Revolution and the Repression of Liberty 1789–1848*, William Collins, 2015

Zeldin, Theodore, *The Political System of Napoleon III*, Macmillan, 1958

Zeldin, Theodore, *France 1848–1945*, OUP, 1973

Index of Names

Some names, mentioned only once in the text, are omitted, and titles etc are only relevant to the time the individual is mentioned.

Acheson, Dean, 248
Adenauer, Dr. Konrad, 247-48
Aetius, Flavius, 38-40, 44
Alaric, 38
Alekseev, General M V, 205, 210-11, 215, 217
Alexander I, Tsar, 164-65
Alexander II, Tsar, 193-94
Alexander III, Tsar, 194
Alexis, Tsarevich, 209-12
Alexius I Comnenus, Emperor, 75, 77-78
Amery, Julian, 236, 240, 251, 255
Amery, Leo, 239-41
Anne, Queen, 95, 101-02, 104, 108, 113-17
Artois, Comte d', see Charles X
Attila, 39
Augustine, Saint, 18,

Balls, Ed, 295-97, 307
Barillon, Paul, 95, 102, 104
Basil II, Emperor, 71, 74
Beaverbrook, Lord (Max), 244, 249
Belisarius, Flavius, 49-50
Benedetti, Vincent, 185-86
Bevin, Ernest, 234
Biffen, John, 255-56, 262, 275, 281
Biggar, Professor Nigel, 19, 319
Biggs-Davison, John, 237, 253-55
Bismarck, Otto von, 184-87
Black, Conrad, 281, 288
Blair, Tony, 6, 273, 285-86, 292, 294-98, 306
Boethius, Anicius, 12, 48

Bonaparte, Napoleon, 156-61, 164-66, 176, 234
Boothby, Robert, 239-40
Bordeaux, Henri, Duc de, 166, 174, 188-89
Bouillé, François, Marquis de, 149-50
Brady, Graham, 302
Breteuil, Louis Charles de, 135, 144-45
Brienne, Loménie de, 138-41
Brown, Gordon, 284, 295-98, 300
Brusilov, General Alexei, 206, 210, 215
Butler, R A, 245, 248-49

Calonne, Charles-Alexandre, 135-40
Cameron, David, 234, 294-95, 298-307
Carswell, Douglas, 304-05,
Cash, William, 273, 277, 289
Castries, Charles, Marquis de, 135, 140
Charles, Archduke, 111-15
Charles II, King, 92-94
Charles, The Young Pretender, 122-24
Charles X, previously Comte d'Artois, 133, 139, 144-45, 152, 166, 173-74
Chateaubriand, François-René, de, 165, 168
Chernov, Victor, 198
Choiseul, Etienne, Duc de, 129, 132
Churchill, John, see Marlborough, Duke of,
Churchill, Winston, 92, 114, 117, 213, 238-45, 291, 348
Clarke, Kenneth, 22, 270, 275, 277, 279-81, 284, 288-94, 298-99
Clegg, Nick, 299-300, 302-03,

Colston, Edward, 318
Compton, Henry, Bishop, 96-98, 102
Constantine the Great, Emperor, 24-25, 34-35, 60
Constantine VII, Emperor, 70, 85
Constantine XI, Emperor, 84
Coudenhove-Kalergi, Count Richard, 239, 253

Danby, Thomas, Earl, 98, 100, 104
Danton, Georges, 153-55
Dartmouth, Admiral Lord George, 99-100, 102
De Gaulle, Charles, President, 240, 242, 247, 251-52
Decazes, Elie, Duc de, 166
Delors, Jacques, 258, 260, 267-68, 285
Denikin, General Anton, 221-23
D'Estaing, Giscard, 147, 241
Diocletian, Emperor, 25, 34-35, 60
Disraeli, Benjamin, 236
Dobbs, Lord Michael, 304, 322
Du Cann, Sir Edward, 259-60
Duncan-Smith, Iain, 22, 289, 291, 293-4, 306
Durnovo, Peter, 197-99, 201-03
Dzerzhinsky, Felix, 219, 226

Eden, Sir Anthony, 238-39, 242-46, 249
Eisenstein, Sergei, 84, 198, 219
Eugénie, Empress, 179, 182, 185, 187-88

Farage, Nigel, 8, 300, 303, 305, 319
Fraser, Sir Michael, 248, 251

Gaitskell, Hugh, 235, 249
Gambetta, Léon, 183, 189

Gardiner, George, 273, 281
Garel-Jones, Tristan, 269, 276
Geiseric, 39-40
Genghis Khan, 16-17
George I, King, 114, 118, 122.
George II, King, 118, 122, 125
George III, King, 120, 124-25
Goldsmith, Sir James, 281, 288, 290
Golitsyn, Prince N D, 207
Gove, Michael, 275, 303
Gramont, Agenor, Duc de, 186
Guchkov, Alexander, 202-3, 205, 207, 210
Guizot, François, 176-78, 186

Hague, William, 21, 281, 288, 291-94, 302-3, 316-7
Hailsham, Quintin, Viscount, 249
Halifax, George, Marquess, 96-98, 101
Hannan, Daniel, 261, 293
Harley, Robert, later Earl of Oxford, 113, 115-8
Harris, Ralph, Lord, 282
Harun, al-Raschid, Caliph, 72, 86
Hawke, Admiral Lord Edward, 123-24
Heath, Edward, 252-57, 291, 295
Heffer, Simon, 270, 276
Heraclius, Emperor, 61-66
Heseltine, Michael, 263, 267-70, 279-80, 286-87, 291
Hilton, Steve, 287, 303
Hitler, Adolf, 16, 18, 20, 266
Hobsbawm, Professor Eric, 27
Hogg, Sarah, 273, 279
Honorius, Emperor, 37-8, 44
Howard, Michael, 275, 284, 287, 289-91, 294-95, 306
Howe, Sir Geoffrey, 258, 262, 268-69
Hulagu Khan, 16, 18

Hurd, Douglas, 265-67, 269-70, 275, 286, 288

James II, King, 92-111
James, The Old Pretender, 111, 113, 115-16, 118-19
John III Ducas, Emperor, 80
John Tzimisces, Emperor, 58, 71, 73-74
Johnson, Boris, 8, 22, 28, 303, 305-6, 308, 313, 318
Julian, Emperor, 25, 35
Justinian, Emperor, 43, 49-51, 60

Kamenev, Lev, 216, 218-19, 229
Kaplan, Fanny, 225
Kerensky, Alexander, 205, 207-13, 215-20
Khusro I, King, 50, 60
Khusro II, King, 60-63
Kilmuir, Earl of, see Maxwell-Fyfe,
Kireev, Alexander, 196
Knapman, Roger, 4, 258, 292
Kohl, Helmut, Chancellor, 257, 265, 278-80
Kokovstov, Vladimir, 202
Kolchak, Admiral A V, 223
Kornilov, General Lavr, 216-17
Krivoshein, Alexander, 202
Krylenko, N V, 220
Kun, Bela, 224

La Fayette, Gilbert, Marquis de, 139, 148, 151-52, 166, 174
Lamont, Norman, 269-70, 273-75, 277-84, 286-88, 291, 306
Laws, David, 302-3
Lawson, Nigel, 261-64, 266-67, 270, 282, 304, 306
Lee, Sir Frank, 247

Lenin, V I, 195, 198, 213-16, 218-29
Louis Philippe, King, 164-65, 167, 173-79
Louis XIV, King, 92, 97, 99, 106, 109-18, 129
Louis XV, King, 129, 131-33
Louis XVI, King, 133-54
Louis XVIII, King, previously Comte de Provence, 135, 139, 144, 150, 164-67
Louis-Napoleon, Bonaparte, see Napoleon III,
Lvov, Prince Georgy, 206-12, 216
Lyttelton, Oliver, later Viscount Chandos, 242, 249

MacMahon, Patrice de, Marshal, 187-88
Macmillan, Harold, 236-51
Major, John, 8, 259, 263, 265-70, 273-91, 294
Mandelson, Peter, 296, 298, 300
Manuel Comnenus, Emperor, 78-79
Marat, Jean-Paul, 151, 153, 154
Marie Antoinette, Queen, 136-37, 141, 144-46, 148, 151-52, 155
Marlborough, John, Duke of, 98, 101, 111-14, 116, 121
Marmont, Auguste de, Marshal, 173
Marx, Karl, 27, 180
Mary II, Queen, 95, 98-104
Maudling, Reginald, 247
Maupeou, René de, 132-33
Maxwell-Fyfe, David, later Viscount Kilmuir, 242, 244, 250
McAlpine, Alistair, 281, 288
Mehmet II, Sultan, 56, 83-84
Merkel, Angela, Chancellor, 299, 301, 303, 307

Metternich, Prince Klemens von, 161, 168, 175
Meyer, Sir Anthony, 264
Michael, Grand Duke, 207, 209-12
Milyukov, Pavel, 198, 206-13, 217, 221
Mirabeau, Honoré, Comte de, 133, 138, 143, 147, 148, 153
Mitterrand, François, President, 258, 260, 265, 268, 274, 277
Modi, Narendra, 7, 315
Molé, Louis-Mathieu, Comte, 176-78
Monmouth, James, Duke of, 94-95
Monnet, Jean, 236-37, 239, 245
Morny, Charles, Duc de, 180, 182
Murad I, Sultan, 82
Murdoch, Rupert, 270, 281, 288, 298
Murray, Douglas, 315, 317, 320, 322
Mutasim, Caliph, 72-73

Napoleon I, Emperor, see Bonaparte,
Napoleon III, Emperor, 164, 176-77, 180-88, 234
Necker, Jacques, 134-35, 141-46, 148
Nelson, Fraser, 317
Nicephorus Phocas, Emperor, 58, 71, 73
Nicholas, Grand Duke, 205, 208, 210, 212
Nicholas I, Tsar, 168, 175
Nicholas II, Tsar, 194-212

Odovacar, King, 41, 49
Ollivier, Emile, 183, 186-87
Olusoga, David, 320-21
Orléans, Philippe, Duc de, Regent, 118, 129
Orléans, Philippe-Egalité, Duc de, 130, 140, 143-45
Ormonde, James, Duke of, 114, 116-19

Osborne, George, 287, 295, 302-3, 306

Patten, Chris, 264, 269-70
Persigny, Gilbert, Duc de, 180, 182, 185
Perth, James, Earl of, 96, 105
Petrovsky, G I, 226
Philip V, King, 111, 114-15
Plethon, George Gemistus, 85-87
Polignac, Jules, Prince de, 167-68, 173-74
Pompidou, Georges, President, 251
Portillo, Michael, 255, 275, 277, 283, 286-88, 291-94
Powell, Enoch, 5, 254-56, 259, 314
Putin, Vladimir, 4, 20

Rasputin, Gregory, 203, 207
Redwood, John, 283, 287-88, 291
Richelieu, Armand-Emmanuel, Duc de, 165
Ricimer, Flavius, 40-41
Ridley, Nicholas, 255, 266
Rifkind, Malcolm, 288, 290
Robespierre, Maximilien, 150, 153-56
Rodzianko, Mikhail, 205, 207-12
Romanus IV Diogenes, Emperor, 76

Salisbury, Robert, 5th Marquess, 242, 244, 248, 249
Samuel, Juliet, 6, 324
Sancroft, William, Archbishop, 97, 105
Sandys, Duncan, 240, 245, 255
Sanghera, Sathnam, 6, 26, 320
Savinkov, Boris, 216, 225
Sazonov, Sergei, 203-04
Schlesinger, Dr Helmut, 278-80
Schuman, Robert, 237, 242-43
Selwyn Lloyd, John, 247, 249

Shriver, Lionel, 6, 314-15, 317, 322
Soames, Sir Christopher, 251-52
Spaak, Paul, 239, 245-46
Spicer, Michael, 277
St John, Henry, later Viscount Bolingbroke, 113-18
Stalin, Joseph, 16, 20, 198, 219-20, 229-31
Stanhope, James, Earl of, 112, 116, 118
Stilicho, Flavius, 38
Stolypin, Peter, 193-94, 200-02
Straw, Jack, 296, 298, 300
Streeter, Gary, 302
Sukhomlinov, General Vladimir, 204
Sunak, Rishi, 7, 313
Sunderland, Robert, Earl of, 95, 97, 101
Sverdlov, Jakov, 225
Svyatopolk-Mirsky, Peter, 197
Syed, Matthew, 5, 13, 324-25

Talleyrand, Charles-Maurice de, 128, 138, 149
Tebbit, Norman, 255, 262, 269, 273, 275, 286, 288
Thatcher, Margaret, Baroness (1992), 92, 235-36, 255-70, 273, 276-77, 282, 286, 288, 291, 314
Theoderic, King, 48-49
Theodosius I, Emperor, 25, 37
Thiers, Adolphe, 173, 178-79, 186-88
Thorneycroft, Peter, 246-47
Tickell, Sir Crispin, 236
Tikhon, Patriarch, 227
Tombs, Professor Robert, 319, 321
Trotsky, Leon, 192, 195, 198, 215, 218-30
Tukhachevsky, Mikhail, 224, 229

Turgot, Anne Robert, 133-34
Tyrconnell, Richard, Earl, 96, 106

Valens, Emperor, 35, 37-38
Vergennes, Charles-Gravier, Comte de, 135, 138
Villèle, Joseph de, 165-68
Voltaire, 8, 120, 132, 133

Walters, Professor Alan, 260, 262-63
Whitelaw, William, Viscount (1983), 234, 262-63, 273
William III, King, 95, 98-111, 181
Wilson, Harold, 235
Witte, Count Sergei, 195-96, 198-99, 201
Wrangel, General Pyotr, 223
Younger, George, 264
Yudenich, General Nikolai, 206, 223
Zinoviev, Grigory, 218-19, 225-26, 229
Zubatov, Sergei, 195-96